Miracle-Gro®
Complete Guide to
Vegetables, Fruits & Herbs

WILEY

John Wiley & Sons, Inc.

This book is printed on acid-free paper.

Published by John Wiley & Sons, Inc., Hoboken, New Jersey

Published simultaneously in Canada

Library of Congress Control Number: 2007933531

ISBN: 978-0-696-23636-5

Printed in the United States of America

10

John Wiley & Sons, Inc.

Publisher: Natalie Chapman

Executive Editor: Anne Ficklen

Miracle-Gro Complete Guide to Vegetables, Fruits & Herbs
Editor: Denny Schrock
Contributing Writers: Mike MacCaskey, Charlie Nardozzi
Copy Chief: Terri Fredrickson
Copy Editor: Kevin Cox
Publishing Operations Manager: Karen Schirm
Senior Editor, Asset and Information Management: Phillip Morgan
Edit and Design Production Coordinator: Mary Lee Gavin
Art and Editorial Sourcing Coordinator: Jackie Swartz
Editorial Assistant: Susan Ferguson
Book Production Managers: Pam Kvitne, Marjorie J. Schenkelberg, Mark Weaver
Imaging Center Operator: Cari Johnson
Contributing Copy Editor: Susan Lang
Contributing Technical Proofreaders: Marcia Eames-Sheavly, B. Rosie Lerner, Dave Slaybaugh
Contributing Proofreaders: Fern Bradley, Becky Etchen, Carolyn Peterson
Contributing Map Illustrator: Jana Fothergill
Contributing Prop/Photo Stylists: Brad Ruppert, Sundie Ruppert
Contributing Indexer: Ellen Sherron
Other Contributors: Gardener's Supply Company

Additional Editorial Contributions from Art Rep Services
Director: Chip Nadeau
Illustrators: Shawn Wallace

Additional Editorial Contributions from Bittersweet Lane LLC
Editors: Mike MacCaskey, Lynn Ocone

Additional Editorial Contributions from Squarecrow Creative
Designer: Greg Nettles

Photographers
Photographers credited may retain copyright © to the listed photographs. L=Left, R=Right, C=Center, B=Bottom, T=Top

William D. Adams 57CR, 58TL, 71R, 80R, 91TR, 110TL, 119L, 119TR, 119BR, 128R, 156TL, 156BCL, 156TCR, 159, 164CL, 200BL, 201BL, 203R, 205BR, 205BR, 210BL, 210CR; Liz Ball, Positive Images 211CR; David Cavagnaro 167CR; Walter Chandoha 5TL, 24TL, 58TR, 113, 167L, 168TL, 185TL, 199TCR, 208RBC; Wally Eberhart, Positive Images 167TR; Derek Fell 60TR, 81L, 83TR, 101BR, 122BL, 124R, 125, 130LC, 140R, 152BL, 156BCR, 156BR, 162BR, 166R, 185BL, 201TL, 208BL, 208TR, 210BR; Dennis Frates, Positive Images 146R; Lynne Harrison 122BLC, 148TR, 154L; Saxon Holt 7TR, 108T, 116TC, 116TR, 158TL, 158BR, 160TR, 193L, 201BC; Jerry Howard, Positive Images 24TR, 164R; Bill Johnson 208B, 209TL, 210TL; Lee Lockwood, Positive Images 209TR; Jerry Pavia 83L, 146RC, 148L, 149, 162BL, 180R; Diane A. Pratt, Positive Images 195TR; Richard Shiell 160BL, 180TL, 198TL, 199CR; Joseph G. Strauch Jr. 47BL, 141T, 178L, 201TC

Note to the Readers: Due to differing conditions, tools, and individual skills, John Wiley & Sons, Inc. assumes no responsibility for any damages, injuries suffered, or losses incurred as a result of following the information published in this book. Before beginning any project, review the instructions carefully, and if any doubts or questions remain, consult local experts or authorities. Because codes and regulations vary greatly, you always should check with authorities to ensure that your project complies with all applicable local codes and regulations. Always read and observe all of the safety precautions provided by manufacturers of any tools, equipment, or supplies, and follow all accepted safety procedures.

Contents

Imagining your garden

▲ Colorful and tasty produce fresh from the garden is a delight to the eyes and the palate. This bounty of tomatoes, broccoli, peppers, carrots, and zucchini can turn an ordinary meal into a sumptuous gourmet feast.

There's magic in growing your own produce. If you've ever tasted just-picked tomatoes or raspberries right off the bush, then you know the glory of truly fresh food. Freshness magnifies flavor and texture. Tastes become bigger and bolder, whether sweet, hot, bitter, or spicy. Crisp vegetables are crisper and moist ones juicier.

When it comes to vegetables, fruits, and herbs, productive gardens don't have to be ordinary. They can also be beautiful. The spreading branches and rounded crowns of fruit trees cast shade as pleasing as any ornamental tree. Hot pepper plants with lush foliage and decorative red fruits accent sunny borders. Artichokes can form an architectural focal point in a flowerbed. Rhubarb, with its long red stalks and giant leaves, brings drama to any garden, while the brilliant stalks of 'Bright Lights' chard make wonderful color accents in a border.

Delight in the countless choices of vegetables, fruits, and herbs to grow. If history interests you, choose heirloom varieties grown for generations. But if the new and exciting is appealing, read about, grow, and taste a world of novel colors, shapes, flavors, and sizes of food crops.

Vegetable gardening is a wholesome hobby to share with your family. Showing children that potatoes come from the earth and not the supermarket opens their minds to an understanding of nature that will grow over their lifetimes.

Best of all, growing your own food is fun. Fruit and vegetable gardening is perfect for multitaskers. It gives you the chance to spend time in the garden on a perfect day, exercising gently and being productive at the same time. It satisfies a need deep within to touch the soil, nurture a

▲ Fresh-picked blueberries have an appealing waxy sheen that invites sampling directly from the harvest container. Enjoy them fresh from your garden and freeze some for delicious desserts throughout the winter.

▼ An arbor covered with grapevines shelters an outdoor living room. The dense canopy of foliage provides overhead protection from glaring sun, and in late summer you can harvest dangling clusters of luscious fruit.

▲ Encourage involvement of children in the garden by including child-size seating, play areas, and tools that fit their small hands. Mix flowers in with the vegetables.

▲ Food crops can be ornamental as well as edible. The fall color of this persimmon tree is eyecatching in the autumn landscape.

garden, harvest a crop, and consume what you grow.

Growing your own vegetables, fruits, and herbs doesn't have to be complicated. Instead, this book is about helping you avoid some of the errors you might make and add some excitement to your gardening adventure.

Selecting a site

Some leafy vegetables will thrive in low light, but most edible plants, including the majority of the vegetables, fruits, and herbs in this book, need eight hours or more of direct sunlight. Find a sunny location for your garden, whether it's close to your back door or farther away.

Consider other important growing conditions, including air circulation. Moderate air circulation reduces the possibility and severity of disease because breezes help dry foliage. Damp, still environments promote the spread of fungal and bacterial diseases.

Select a site that isn't prone to floods or standing water. Few plants thrive if their "feet" are always wet. In poorly drained soil plants cannot absorb nutrients easily and roots also may rot. If your only choice tends to be wet, plant in raised beds, or install drainage systems.

Avoid low-lying areas. Cold air naturally drains into low areas, so frost can settle on your crop even when

surrounding areas are frost-free. If you plant in a frost pocket, your growing season is likely to be shorter and the risk of freeze damage to crops higher.

Once you've identified places in the yard with acceptable growing conditions, consider time available for gardening, your style, and your preferences. For instance, a few ornamental peppers and a cherry tomato plant tucked into flower beds in the front yard might be enough, along with a lamppost surrounded by rosemary or lavender.

On the other hand, if you're more ambitious and space allows, you might prefer to plan and plant a traditional garden, giving your vegetables, fruits, and herbs space of their own. In this case raised beds that stay neat all year may be right for your vegetables, surrounded by espaliered apples and pears, and herbs arranged in a formal knot garden at the entrance.

▲ Most vegetables, fruits, and herbs grow best on a site with full sun and good drainage.

EATING WELL

While the latest dietary studies swirl in the headlines and health-minded readers puzzle through how much is enough or too much of one nutrient or another, the truest advice is also the simplest: Eat more plants, especially green, leafy plants such as spinach, chard, and kale, and colorful ones like blueberries, strawberries, and carrots.

Though modern, large-scale food production is a miracle of productivity, its downsides are becoming more apparent. Rising demand for organic foods proves that more people are seeking quality food. Fresh, homegrown vegetables and fruits can be the highest quality, most nutritious food there is.

Consider one more angle: flavor. Many home gardeners will explain that the reason they grow their own food is not nutrition but superior flavor. And it's true that the flavor of just-picked produce is naturally superior to its store-bought counterpart simply because it is fresher. As maturing vegetables and fruits approach the moment of best flavor, their vitamin and nutrient content also peaks. Once harvested they begin to deteriorate. Eating the harvest at the peak of maturity means enjoying optimal nutritional content. Fresher is better.

Laying out your garden

Vegetable, fruit, and herb gardens are as unique as the gardeners who create them. While no precise formula for designing your garden exists, consider the ideas described on these pages. Whatever design you choose, include your favorite garden elements in the garden plan and you are sure to enjoy the space. Place whimsical pieces of art, chairs, benches, and perhaps a bird bath in your garden, anything that expresses your personal style and preferences.

▲ Planting in rows in the traditional style is best suited to spacious gardens where quantity production is desired.

Garden styles

● **Traditional gardens** In a traditional rectangular vegetable garden, crops are laid out in orderly rows separated by broad paths. The entire plot may be surrounded with low fruiting shrubs or apple and pear trees trained to grow flat against a fence. A garden in rows allows equal access to every plant. It makes weeding, feeding, and harvesting a snap. If you have plenty of sunny ground for planting, this may be the best garden layout for you.

Hoes, rakes, and other maintenance tools are easy to use in row gardens, especially when you space vegetables equally within rows. If you're planning to cultivate with a rotary tiller, make paths wide enough to accommodate the machine.

The best traditional gardens are well structured and organized yet lush with harvestable crops at any time of the growing season.

To increase productivity of a row-type garden, grow sprawling vegetables such as cucumbers, tomatoes, certain melons, pole beans, and summer squash vertically. Besides saving space, vegetables grown vertically dry off faster after rain or watering, a plus for avoiding mildew and other fungal diseases. Use trellises, nets, strings, cages, poles, tepees, or invent just about any sort

▲ Thinning carrots is easier in raised planting beds because less stooping and kneeling is necessary.

▲ Wood frames filled with amended soil improve plant growth, save space, and ease maintenance.

of contraption that is stable and strong. For techniques on staking vegetables, see page 43.

For higher yields in the same space, plant edibles in wider rows or blocks, 3 to 4 feet across, with paths between them. Wide-row planting devotes less space to paths and more to crops. You can cheat distances between plants within each row, but remember that weeding and harvesting becomes more challenging when plants are spaced closely. Avoid overcrowding that cuts down on air circulation and invites foliage diseases.

● **Raised beds** You can grow a fine garden directly at ground level, but often it's easier to grow and maintain beautiful vegetables in raised beds. Raised beds offer many advantages, not the least of which is eliminating the need for deep digging. They also provide excellent drainage. Many vegetables and herbs will die in wet, poorly drained soil.

Raised beds are much appreciated by anyone with knee problems or lower back aches because they reduce the need for deep bending and squatting. Some raised beds, particularly tall ones made of brick or stone, go one step further with seatlike edges that allow the gardener to sit while sowing, maintaining, and harvesting the crops. At the right height, raised beds are also convenient for young children and for those using wheelchairs.

▲ Lettuce and purple basil thrive adjacent to the stone paver border of a raised bed.

▲ Prefabricated raised bed systems significantly ease design and assembly.

Raised beds benefit small gardens because they use space and resources efficiently. In addition to allowing close planting, they're resource-efficient because you concentrate all of your soil amending and improving on the soil inside the bed and don't waste materials or energy on soil that will become pathways. They are low maintenance because you weed, water, and care for only the small surface area of the raised bed. In

▼ Increase the convenience of raised bed gardening, and improve the look of the beds, by adding a seat edge. Thinning, weeding, and harvesting become much easier because you can sit, not stoop and bend.

▲ Low walls create raised bed terraces on sloping ground. Level beds allow water to soak in evenly to the benefit of plants, and erosion is prevented.

▲ Cultivating and amending native soil a spade's depth below a raised bed is the modern version of French intensive double-digging.

▲ Raised beds focus gardening activity only where crops grow. Paved or mulched paths substantially reduce weed problems.

spring, raised beds warm up early in the growing season, so you can start gardening sooner.

As long as you place them in full sun, you can site raised beds just about anywhere, including areas that are wet, sloped, or otherwise unsuitable for inground planting. Like the soil in containers, soil in raised beds dries faster than soil at ground level. Until crops sink their roots deep enough, they are likely to need more frequent watering than the same crops in the ground.

Fill raised beds with a combination of soil mix or topsoil and compost. Avoid stepping inside the bed and compacting the soil. Sow seeds or plant seedlings in rows or masses. Plant successive crops in the same bed or intermingle vegetables with different harvest times. To suppress weeds and reduce the frequency of watering, mulch the bed with weed-free straw.

Make a raised bed for vegetables or herbs 3 to 4 feet wide, a distance that allows you to reach the middle of

the bed from either side, and at least 10 inches deep. Beds can be as long as you like, depending upon your needs and the design of the garden. Just as important as bed size is the amount of space between beds. If you intend to take your wheelbarrow from bed to bed, measure its width and add a couple of inches on either side for bed clearance. For taller crops such as corn and pole beans, set the beds on an east-west axis if possible. That will ensure the plants receive the maximum amount of sunlight over the course of a day.

You can choose among a variety of materials to build raised beds. Stone or brick raised beds are long-lasting and attractive but more costly. Decorative cement block and cinder block are less expensive but equally enduring. Rot-resistant untreated woods such as cedar or black locust are also long-lasting.

● **French intensive garden beds** This method is an alternative to raised beds if

your location is without the permanent structure. Rather than being contained by built walls the rich planting soil is supported by sloping sides.

French intensive beds are cultivated deeply, or "double-dug." Double-digging beds to a depth of 2 feet ensures extensive root growth.

With deeply worked soil you can space plants more

closely. That's the "intensive" part. Space plants so their leaves just touch at maturity. The plants' close proximity helps stop moisture loss and shades out many weeds. Pull weeds by hand rather than tilling or hoeing. If a plant becomes sick or pest ridden, pull it out instead of taking drastic corrective measures.

MAXIMIZING SPACE

Whether your garden is large or small, two planting techniques, and variations on them, increase garden productivity by making the most of space.

● **Succession planting** For a continuous harvest, plant small amounts of the same plant in succession through the growing season. For example, sow a small crop of bush beans, and carrots every two weeks from spring until midsummer. After harvesting the first crop, pull the plants and put in another crop that will mature before the first frost.

As an alternative, follow your first planting of fast-growing early crops with a second planting of a different vegetable in the same space. For example, follow an early spring planting of arugula, radishes, spinach, or peas with bush beans, cucumbers, or eggplant.

For late fall to winter harvest, start planting cool-season crops such as spinach and broccoli in mid- to late summer. When planting in the middle of summer, some plants, including lettuce, cabbage and broccoli, grow best from transplants (young seedlings).

Even if you have only a few open spaces in your midsummer vegetable garden, tuck in an extra broccoli or lettuce seedling. You'll be surprised by how much more you can produce from a small garden by planting in open spaces as soon as they become available.

● **Intercropping** Sometime called interplanting, this technique pairs fast-maturing crops with those slower to grow so valuable garden space won't lie empty. As an example, sow lettuce or cilantro seed in the spaces between tomato plants. By the time the tomatoes take up their full space and are fruiting, the lettuce or cilantro is long gone. Radishes intercrop well with beans for the same reason. Or use radishes to mark rows of slower germinating carrots. When you harvest the radishes the carrots will continue to grow.

For another type of intercropping, place compact plants that tolerate a bit of shade under or near taller plants that require full sun. For example, plant arugula, beets, cress, cilantro, or leaf lettuce next to corn, pole beans, or trellised cucumbers.

▲ Stagger crop plantings so that harvest doesn't come all at once and to make maximum use of available space.

▲ Lettuce and broccoli interplanted with tomatoes grow and are harvested before the tomato plants mature.

Integrating edibles into your landscape

▲ Espaliered apple trees frame this modern version of a classic cottage garden. Raised beds and gravel paths are neat and refined, but the traditional mix of vegetables, herbs, and fruit trees flourishes in the rich soil.

▲ Tomatoes and herbs thrive on a sunny, southern exposed side yard along with climbing roses.

▲ An ornamental birdhouse and tall hollyhock add vertical elements to a cottage garden of flowers and edibles.

▲ Annual and perennial flowers grow well and look good in the same situations in which vegetables thrive.

▲ The random exuberance of self-sown dill and poppies neatly accents the orderliness of raised beds.

While a traditional row garden with primarily edibles may be productive and functional, the alternative of mixing edibles with each other and combining them in beds and borders with ornamental plants may be more your style preference. In many cases the ornamental qualities of the edible plants—rich color, texture, and form—are showcased. These qualities are valuable in creating a garden that is both productive and pleasing to the eye.

Cottage-style gardens are an example of this approach to design. Typically, they contain useful plants—fragrant flowers and herbs for cutting and eating, vegetables, and fruiting trees and shrubs. The layout is often somewhat formal with symmetrical beds and borders, but plantings tend to be loose and informal. Paths softened by herbs and flowers spilling over the edges crisscross the garden, giving it a relaxed look. The garden also owes its spontaneity to an abundance of self-sowing herbs and flowers such as fennel, cosmos, anise hyssop, and violets that pop up here and there.

● **Potager** A potager, a French word for kitchen garden, pairs food crops with ornamental plants in geometric designs. A classic potager is formal, meaning that the shape of the beds is usually geometric—circles, ovals, squares, triangles, and rectangles—and the layout of the beds is symmetrical. Manicured paths separate the beds, giving easy access to the crops. Although the plants usually look loose and informal, the formal structure of the garden orders

▼ Surrounded by nasturium and geranium flowers, a dwarf apple tree is the focal point of a small garden.

▼ Cottage garden informality is underscored by the use of pruned tree branches as a tepee trellis.

the space and helps keep the plantings under control.

Bay or citrus trees clipped like lollipops mark the corners of a traditional potager, adding height and emphasizing the garden's lines. You can also use fruit trees without such a geometric shape, such as dwarf apples or pears. Within individual beds, trees, topiaries, urns, bean tepees,

▼ Foot-high clipped hedges of boxwood create separate planting areas for herbs and provide a bright color accent.

▼ A formal urn featuring cardoon serves as an effective focal point. Surrounding it is tricolor sage.

▲ A row of lemon trees with sweet alyssum grow in terra-cotta pots that are surrounded by woolly thyme.

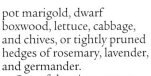

▲ Vegetable gardens can be beautiful. Here red leaf lettuce alternates with blue-green cabbage and kale.

▲ Relaxing while surrounded by the lushness of vegetables and shaded by a cherry tree is a luxury of summer.

or any sort of tall, striking plants may be focal points and add vertical interest. Grow mint in an urn on a pedestal to keep it from reaching the soil and taking over your beds. Strawberries and nasturtiums make handsome carpetlike groundcovers underneath a dominant sculptural plant.

Potagers depend upon vegetables for the bulk of the plantings. It's not unusual for a potager to have a bed devoted to lettuces. By choosing red and green varieties, you can plant the bed in a colorful pattern of stripes, squares, or triangles. In other beds, combine vegetables with annual or tender perennial flowers such as pansies and scented geraniums.

Surround each bed with low edging plants. Use different plants to edge each bed or unify the potager by using the same edger throughout. Popular choices for edging include pot marigold, dwarf boxwood, lettuce, cabbage, and chives, or tightly pruned hedges of rosemary, lavender, and germander.

One of the nicest aspects of a potager is its enduring structure. Even in winter when the growing season has passed, the harmonious outline of the beds remains. By paying careful attention to the garden's location before you plant, you can appreciate its form all year.

▶ Purple basil has plenty of basil flavor and a color that complements many other kinds of plants.

BEDS AND BORDERS

A bed is a landscape planting that stands alone, enclosed by lawn, brick, or any other short even surface. Beds can have any outline, but the most popular are kidney-shape or geometric, including oval, round, square, or rectangular. You often find small beds around trees, protecting trunks from mower damage, and around lampposts and mailboxes. Large informal beds can encompass a grove of small fruit trees or help direct movement in a landscape.

Borders, on the other hand, comprise plantings set against neutral scenery, such as boxwood or yew hedges, brick walls, or wooden fences. Lawn or a path usually determines the border's front edge. Borders about 5 feet wide can accommodate vegetables, fruiting shrubs, and dwarf fruit trees as well as flowering plants. They can be as short as a few feet or run the entire length of a property.

Incorporating vegetables, fruits, and herbs into beds and borders saves time, effort, and money. You can use existing garden space to grow your edibles. Just make certain that you plant the food crops with ornamentals that have similar growing requirements.

If you want to start a bed or border from scratch to fulfill a particular purpose in your landscape, you can include vegetables, fruits, and herbs as part of the initial design. When fitting vegetables, fruits, and herbs into your landscape, make sure you select them for their taste and beauty as well as their landscape purpose.

When designing a bed or border, arrange the plants to maximize their exposure to sunlight. In a bed, place the tallest plants in the center and the shortest ones around the edge. In borders, tall plants go in the back, midsize plants in the center, and short plants at the front.

ELEMENTS OF STYLE

In order to talk about garden styles in meaningful ways, gardeners have come up with various categories or types of gardens that share various features. Two of the broadest categories are *formal* and *informal*. These design approaches create a frame of reference that is broad enough to include all the different kinds of gardens that have worked well in the past. In practice, many gardens are a combination of both styles.

● **Formal style** Usually a formal garden has a symmetrical balance, with plantings on one side of a main axis mirroring plantings on the other side. Pruning transforms shrubs into topiaries or hedges that outline geometrically shaped beds and walkways. Knot gardens are a familiar formal garden style based on historic English patterns. Ancient knots were often planted with herbs, making them both useful and attractive.

● **Informal style** Informal gardens rely on a more naturalistic arrangement of plants and curving paths and borders that flow with the terrain. Straight lines and sharp corners are minimized.

As you envision and plan your garden keep in mind the key elements of any kind of garden: paths, focal points, and efficient use of space for the purposes that will bring you the most pleasure. Paths in particular are essential because you'll appreciate easy and sure-footed access. The easier it is to move around in your garden, the more likely it will be healthy and productive and utilized.

Focal points are important because of how our eyes and brains are wired. They are places where the eye can stop and around which our minds can organize the scene. Focal points make the space feel right. The effect is subliminal, but real.

Fitting fruit into the landscape

When you landscape with fruit, you combine beauty with practicality. Fruit can serve many functions. For example, apple trees make superb shade trees anywhere in the yard if you prune them to allow passage underneath. A large crabapple tree or a spreading cherry will also provide welcome shade.

Any fruit tree you like can be used as a focal point or accent in the yard or garden. Among the most striking trees in bloom are apples, cherries, crabapples, and some of the showier flowering peaches.

Shrub fruits can also play an important role in the landscape, either as individual accents or as hedges or shrub borders. A hedgerow of fruiting shrubs, for example serviceberry, provides privacy but also can bring lovely flowers in spring, luscious fruits in summer, and rich fall color. Try blueberries for their burgundy-orange fall leaf color or currants for their lovely flower clusters and brilliant scarlet fruit.

▲ An ornamental container and trailing flowers help turn an already showy lime tree into a dramatic focal point.

▲ Wiry stems and yellow flowers of fennel reach up and out of a pot of trailing nasturium and sage.

▲ Semidwarf apple trees in large pots flanking a brightly colored door announce the garden's entrance.

HERE'S A TIP...

Growing fruit trees in lawns

Fruit trees provide wonderful shade and striking focal points when they bloom. But they need a helping hand when planted as a lawn tree. Prevent competition from grass and weeds, which reduces yield. Remove sod and weeds from the tree trunk to the dripline, and beyond if possible. Use organic mulches to prevent grass and weeds from growing back under the tree canopy. Spread the mulch 4 to 6 inches deep under the tree, keeping it away from the trunk. Also, fertilize the tree according to what it needs, not according to lawn plant food recommendations. Fruit trees that get too much plant food from lawns are more pest-prone and they set fewer, lower-quality fruits.

▲ This pair of mature serviceberry trees screen and shade like any lawn tree. But unlike an ornamental, these produce a crop of red fruits abundant enough for you to harvest bushels and still leave enough to delight neighborhood birds.

Genetic dwarf peach trees make splendid flowering hedges, and showy-flowered dwarf or standard peaches can be trained in the same way. Espaliered apples or pears can also form attractive hedges or borders. (See page 118 for more on training fruit tree hedges.)

You can even use fruit as a groundcover. Strawberry plants are effective, especially in smaller areas, but plan to replace them every three years with new plants if you want a heavy fruit crop. Lowbush blueberries create a woody groundcover with a year-round presence and luscious summer fruit.

The edible landscape

As noted above, many food plants are easily integrated with ornamental landscape plants and do not require a separate area to grow well. Integrating edibles is a useful way to get the most from your yard, especially when space is limited. Consider the garden as an extension of the house and use the space architecturally. If you have a sunny wall, train an apple tree to grow flat against it on a trellis. Put containers of vegetables on your patio. Imagine a fall scene with dramatic purple and blue-green kale and cabbage in containers flanking your front steps, blueberries with crimson fall color in the foundation planting, and farther out front a persimmon tree, resplendent with orange and gold autumn leaves.

If your house is tall and narrow, consider a

▲ Edible fruits, such as this kiwi vine, serve many of the same functions as ornamentals.

▲ This fruit-laden apple is trained horizontally, espalier style, to create a border for the garden.

▲ In fall, the reds and yellows of blueberry plants are the equal of any ornamental shrub.

▲ Blueberries, such as these behind the geranium pots, make outstanding screening shrubs.

▲ Conveniently close to a sitting area, this informal garden screen is composed of trailing blackberries.

geometric knot garden of herbs in a pattern you can see from the upstairs windows. Even in a small yard an apple orchard is not out of reach. Take advantage of columnar apple trees and line up a few short rows in a limited space. With some creative thinking, you can grow bountiful and ornamental produce in a small raised bed that's uniquely your own. For example, combine leeks,

HERE'S A TIP...

Growing strawberries, up
Strawberry pyramids provide an excellent space-saving method for growing the fruits in a small area. A pyramid is a square or circular terraced bed with retaining walls made of plastic, wood, or aluminum. You can make one yourself or purchase an inexpensive kit in a gardening catalog. To thrive, strawberries need plenty of sunshine and well-drained soils high in organic matter. Early blossoms produce the biggest fruits, so protect your plants from spring frosts that can kill the flowers.

Maximize space and sunlight for strawberries by planting them in narrow terraces, or a "pyramid."

spinach, broccoli, and red lettuce for a striking medley of rich red and green hues and play of texture.

To create shade, a rectangular pergola or arbor covered with kiwi or grape vines can fill in one side of the patio or can extend off the eaves of a shed or garage at the back of the property.

At the side of the house or wherever there's a bed or border, you can include vegetables, fruits, and herbs in the design. Their pleasing colors and striking shapes combine with most flowering annuals, perennials, and shrubs. Ensure the edible plants will get the sunshine they need to flourish and combine them with ornamentals that have compatible requirements for soil type, water, and plant food. See more on beds and borders on page 11.

Matters of size

A garden of vegetables, fruits, and herbs can be as simple as a few pots on the patio or as extensive as a full orchard surrounded by beds of vegetables and herbs. Its size and quantities planted hinge on the available space, the amount of sunlight, how busy you are, and how much time you plan to spend in the garden. Also consider how much time you want to devote to processing and storing your produce. Growing conditions in your locale and the length of your growing season also affect what you can grow.

Bigger is not necessarily better in food gardening. Large gardens increase your workload, quickly become unkempt if you can't keep up

with them, and may yield more produce than you can use.

Small, well-kept gardens can be more enjoyable and often yield better-quality produce. With good planting and care, a 10×15-foot site is ample space for a high-yielding vegetable garden. Add to that containers of herbs, a few productive fruit trees, and some lush berry plants and you and your family will be rich with produce. For more information on individual crop yields, see plant entries in the plant chapters that follow.

Planning and action

If you're still in the planning-dreaming stage, browse the information at the beginning of the next chapter about climate regions. That's where you'll find guidance about what you can plant—and when—according to where you live. You'll likely need to refer to these pages throughout the planning and planting stages of your garden.

When you are ready to start planting, turn to the pertinent chapter: page 34 for vegetables; page 108 for fruits; and page 170 for herbs. In those sections you'll find all the information you're likely to need, whatever stage your garden or garden experience is at. Should it be 'Beefmaster' or 'Brandywine' tomato; 'Granny Smith' or 'Winter Banana' apple? When is it ripe? What pests should you be watching for? Crop descriptions identify those pests peculiar to that crop. But the most common pests are shown and described beginning on page 194.

▲ Dwarf apples trained horizontally

THINK HIGHER

Space efficiency usually means growing plants up, on a trellis or arbor, or trained flat, like an espaliered apple against a fence. If you think in such terms you'll get more plants and more variety into your garden, which will be more fun and productive.

If all of your vegetables are allowed to spread out at ground level, you'll have less room for plants and you'll be doing a lot of bending over. When plants are trained up, they allow closer planting and save your back too. Cucumbers spreading up a trellis instead of randomly over the ground, or sprawling tomatoes trained to stakes instead of being allowed to grow naturally, are common examples. Trellised grape, kiwi, or bramble vines are fruits that are trained up: Allowed to grow naturally they shortly become a tangled mass. Espaliered fruit trees are a more extreme example. A standard apple, for instance, will become a 15- to 20-foot-tall tree in just a few years. With pruning and training, train it flat against a wall, espalier style, and have a more human-scale tree. Training espaliered trees is described on page 118.

Food growing basics

Figuring out what you want to plant can be a little mind-boggling, considering the many different vegetables, fruits, and herbs that are available. There are tall ones and short ones; some live for decades while others move from seed to plate in days. For the purposes of this book, the two broadest categories of edible plants regard their life cycles: it's an *annual* if it grows from seed to flower in one season; a *perennial* if it grows for three or more years. Most vegetables are annuals, while most fruits and herbs are perennial. How long a plant lives, its size, and its ability to adapt to conditions in your garden are the key parameters to use as you decide what to plant.

Beyond all that, focus on this: What do you want to eat? Begin by making a short list of crops you'd like to grow, perhaps limiting your selection to four to six if you're new to gardening. Lettuce, carrots, tomatoes, and basil are easy-to-grow compared to cauliflower and celery. If there are children, give some thought to the kinds of vegetables they're most likely to eat and most likely to enjoy in the garden.

Another consideration is the efficient use of the space you have. Some crops, like tomatoes, produce more per square foot than most other vegetables. One more reason perhaps why tomatoes are so popular.

As a home gardener you can greatly expand upon the variety available at the market. You'll see throughout this book that most fruits and vegetables are available in many varieties. Some of those differ with regard to hardiness or disease resistance. But many more vary according to flavor, color, or some other culinary characteristic. This is the cornucopia that becomes available once you begin growing your own food.

Choosing vegetables and herbs

It's easy to get swept up and overwhelmed when you're reading vegetable and herb catalog entries or exploring the options at the local nursery. Keep yourself in

▲ Chard is easy to grow and notably tolerant of summer heat yet offers color and charm.

check by thinking first of what your household will actually eat, and limit yourself according to how much you'll use. The tables and charts on these pages can help you do just that.

Try to match the growing conditions in your garden with the needs of the particular crop you'd like to produce. Most vegetables and herbs grow best on sites that receive at least 8 to 10 hours of direct sun a day. But if you've slightly shaded areas

▲ Look around your landscape for underutilized space, such as this front yard, that can be used for food crops.

▲ Quick-growing, cool-season crops such as carrots and radishes require minimal space.

▲ Fruit trees, such as this cherry, do double duty as both an ornamental accent and food producer.

▼ While lacking impressive size, cherry tomatoes grow fast, are very productive, and offer a flavor that equals or exceeds the best full-size tomatoes.

that you'd like to use, some crops can successfully grow there. Or if your garden space is limited, aim to grow crops in containers. Many favorite vegetables grow as well in a container as in the garden as long as they are watered and fertilized regularly.

AVERAGE CROP YIELDS

Crop	Plants per 50 square feet	Pounds per 50 square feet	Pounds per plant
Artichoke	7	30–40	4–7
Asparagus	10	3–10	—
Basil	15–20	10–20	½–1
Bean, bush	10–15	50–60	4–5
Beet (roots)	260	60–75	¼
Broccoli, heading	26	50	2
Brussels sprouts	25	30–40	½–1½
Cabbage	25	75	1–4
Carrot	230	50	⅛–¼
Cauliflower	25	50	1–2
Celery (stalks)	50–60	90	1½–2
Chard, Swiss	60	50	½–1½
Chinese cabbage	40	40	1
Collards	130	50	½–1
Corn	60	30	2
Cucumber	25–50	25	1–2
Eggplant	26	50–75	1–3
Garlic	80	100	½–1½
Kale	30	50–75	1½–2
Kohlrabi	30	40	1½
Lettuce	80	25–50	½–1½
Melon, cantaloupe	20	75	3>
Okra	15	50	3–4
Onion	40–60	50	½–1
Pea	100	10	1
Pepper, bell	75	30–40	½–1
Pepper, chili	80	40	½
Potato	15–20	90	4–6
Pumpkin	20	50	3>
Radish	300	50–75	<¼
Rutabaga	130	50	¼–1½
Spinach	125	50–75	½–1
Squash, zucchini	10–15	50–75	3–9
Squash, winter	5–10	50–75	5–15
Sweet potato	20–30	20–60	1–3
Tomato	10–30	25–75	2–8
Turnip	30	50	1–2
Watermelon	5–10	50	5–10

Choosing a fruit tree

First decide how much room you have available. A full-size standard apple or cherry tree can reach 30 feet high and 20 to 30 feet wide, which is fine if you have the space. Options include dwarf and semidwarf trees. They typically reach one-half to three-fourths the height of a standard tree and will grow and fruit well in containers.

Climate is all-important when it comes to choosing a fruit tree, primarily winter minimum temperatures, spring frosts, and chilling hours. See page 18 for more about fruit climates.

Another consideration when choosing fruit trees is pollination, or rather cross-pollination. Some fruit trees are self-fruitful, meaning one plant can pollinate itself, and produce fruit. But others require pollination from a similar but separate plant. Check the pollination requirements of those you want to grow. If cross-pollination is needed, you don't necessarily have to plant another tree. You may be able to graft a pollenizer branch onto the chosen tree or even place a bouquet of flowering stems cut from another variety in a bucket of water at its base. For more about fruit tree pollination, see page 111.

CROPS FOR SHADE

If your yard is shaded, try the following. They are more tolerant of the shade cast by a building, hedge, or tree.

Arugula
Bean
Beet
Brussels sprouts
Cabbage
Cauliflower
Celery
Chard
Cress
Garlic
Kale
Kohlrabi
Leaf lettuce
Leek
Parsnip
Pea
Potato
Radish
Rhubarb
Rutabaga
Sorrel
Spinach
Turnip

CROPS FOR POTS

You can grow just about any vegetable in a container, but these are the most readily adaptable.

Carrots (baby)
Chard
Eggplant
Lettuce
Peppers
Potatoes
Snap beans
Spinach
Tomatoes

BARGAIN CROPS

Crops differ in their yield relative to the effort required. To maximize your economic payback, plant the following.

Beans (pole, bush)
Beets
Broccoli
Carrots
Chard
Cucumbers
Edible pod peas
Green bunching onions
Head lettuce
Leaf lettuce
Onion (storage bulbs)
Peppers
Summer squash
Tomatoes
Turnip (greens and roots)

KIDS' CROPS

Kids are quickly interested in just about any kind of food crop. But a few are notable hits, year after year.

Carrots
Cucumbers
Peas
Pole beans
Popcorn
Potatoes
Pumpkins
Radishes
Strawberries
Tomatoes

Get in sync with the seasons

A thick mulch of straw over a bed of carrots is sufficient to see the roots through a Zone 4 winter. Here, in early spring, the straw is removed so that the protected carrots can be harvested.

▲ Extend your garden season in both spring and fall with a cold frame. The protection they provide from wind, frost, and rain, and the slightly warmer temperatures inside, will add weeks and can lead to a greater harvest.

Relative to climate, vegetables are divided into two groups, cool- and warm-season. Cool-season vegetables grow best when temperatures range between 40° and 75°F. In most areas, cool-season crops can be planted two to four weeks before the last spring frost. Cool-season crops are most often those that develop edible roots, stems, leaves, or buds. (The warm-season sweet potato and New Zealand spinach are exceptions.) More specifically, cool-season vegetables are frost-tolerant, and in some cases hardy, and their seeds germinate in cooler soils. The root systems of cool-season crops are shallower, and plants are smaller. Cool-season crops stop producing in early summer when daytime temperatures reach 80°F and higher. In regions where nights remain cool, you can make small, successive sowings throughout summer. In hotter regions, plant cool-season vegetables as early as possible in spring and replant them for fall. There also are cold-hardy vegetables that can survive throughout winter in some regions, especially under a cover of snow. These include carrots, parsnips, and garlic.

Warm-season vegetables, such as tomatoes, peppers, corn, and okra, originated in tropical climates. These are the crops that develop edible fruits (cool-season peas and broad bean are exceptions.) They are killed by a frost, and won't germinate or perform well if temperatures fall below 50°F. You can sustain many warm-season crops into fall if you protect them from frosts and freezes with cold frames, row covers, or other season-extending devices. But they perform best during the height of summer.

● **Frost** For tender plants frost—temperatures of 32°F or below—marks the beginning and end of the season. Not only are most killed by low temperatures, they grow from seed to harvest in one summer, the time from the last frost in spring to the first frost in fall. Hence, these first and last frosts, and average number of days between frosts, are critical markers for vegetable gardeners.

In the North, spring comes later, fall sooner, and summer days are longer but relatively cool. In the South, spring comes earlier and lasts longer, and fall comes later and more gradually. Summers are longer and hotter. You can see all of these seasonal effects in the maps at right. It's the business of the gardener equipped with a calendar and guides such as these maps to be sufficiently aware of the seasons and the crops to plant at the proper time. Another task is to work around the margins, smoothing out seasonal transitions to the benefit of the crops. Three of the best ways to do that are using cold frames, hot caps, and row covers, and you can read and see more about these devices on pages 40 and 41.

▲ A typical high-summer vegetable garden harvest includes the heat lovers such as tomatoes, peppers, cucumbers, and eggplant.

▼ Ornamental kale is a dual-purpose crop, showy enough to compete with fall-blooming chrysanthemums in a flower garden, but still yielding edible and handsome leaves.

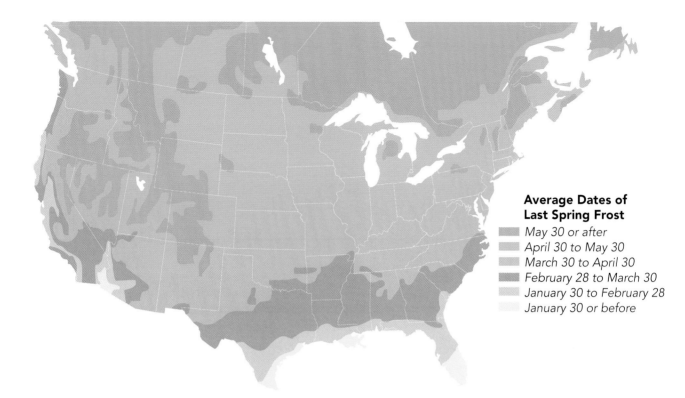

**Average Dates of
Last Spring Frost**

May 30 or after
April 30 to May 30
March 30 to April 30
February 28 to March 30
January 30 to February 28
January 30 or before

**Average Dates of
First Autumn Frost**

June 30 to July 30
July 30 to August 30
August 30 to September 30
September 30 to October 30
October 30 to November 30
November 30 to December 3

▲ These maps show the average dates of first and last frosts in North America, the key dates vegetable gardeners plan around. Many factors combine to determine the actual date in your garden, mainly the vagaries of weather combined with the contours and orientation of your land.

Climate and fruit

With fruit trees and fruiting shrubs the first consideration is whether the plant can tolerate the average winter minimum temperature where you live. The USDA Plant Hardiness Zone Map plots out these temperatures in graphic form. Developed by the United States Department of Agriculture, these zones are based on the average lowest recorded temperatures. Find your approximate location on the map below and then match the color of the area to the corresponding key to see your zone. Zone 1, where winter minimum temperatures reach –50°F, is the coldest. Zone 11, where winter minimums rarely dip below 40°F, is the warmest.

● **Too cold** Fruit trees, fruiting shrubs, and perennial herbs are rated according to the coldest zone they can endure because cold is the most common factor limiting their growth. For example, plants hardy to Zone 6 survive where winter temperatures drop to –10°F, while those hardy only to Zone 8 will be killed by temperatures below 10°F. Plants that are rated for a range of hardiness zones can usually survive winter in the coldest region as well as tolerate the summer heat of the warmest one.

All of the perennial vegetables, fruits, and herbs in this book are rated according to their USDA Hardiness Zone, but note that in many cases there is great variation among varieties of one crop. Among apricots for example, planting a 'Moorpark' north of Zone 6 is inviting failure, while a 'Harogem' is likely to thrive all the way to Zone 4.

Late spring frosts that nip the tender buds of a fruit tree won't kill the tree but will prevent the crop from developing.

● **Too hot** Most fruit trees also have both a requirement

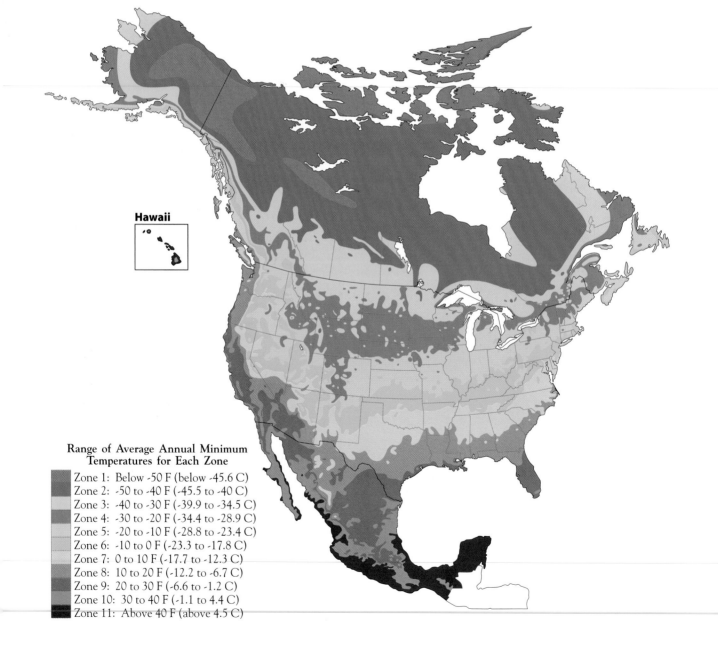

Hawaii

Range of Average Annual Minimum Temperatures for Each Zone

Zone 1: Below -50 F (below -45.6 C)
Zone 2: -50 to -40 F (-45.5 to -40 C)
Zone 3: -40 to -30 F (-39.9 to -34.5 C)
Zone 4: -30 to -20 F (-34.4 to -28.9 C)
Zone 5: -20 to -10 F (-28.8 to -23.4 C)
Zone 6: -10 to 0 F (-23.3 to -17.8 C)
Zone 7: 0 to 10 F (-17.7 to -12.3 C)
Zone 8: 10 to 20 F (-12.2 to -6.7 C)
Zone 9: 20 to 30 F (-6.6 to -1.2 C)
Zone 10: 30 to 40 F (-1.1 to 4.4 C)
Zone 11: Above 40 F (above 4.5 C)

▲ This 'Moro' blood orange is growing in a favorable microclimate. Not only is it protected by the house at left, but it also is planted on a south facing slope for extra warmth, and at the top of a slope for good cold air drainage.

▲ 'Dwarf Brazilian' bananas thrive in a Zone 10 Southern California garden where temperatures only rarely dip below freezing.

for heat accumulation and a limited tolerance to high temperatures. Peaches and nectarines generally require long hot summers to produce high quality fruit. Apricots, on the other hand, prefer cooler summers and do not reach peak flavor where the heat would be ideal for peaches. Still, most fruit trees have a wide enough adaptation to temperatures so that they produce acceptable fruit in all but extremely hot- or cold-summer areas.

In addition to winter minimum temperature and timing of spring frosts, one more significant climate element limits successful growth of some crops, namely insufficient winter chill (hours of temperatures below 45°F). Plant an apple, cherry, peach, or pear that's adapted to a northern winter in Houston and it will suffer. If you want to grow these hardy fruits where winters are mild, look for varieties that are "low-chill."

● **Just right** The cost of cheating too much on a plant's recommended zone is a dead plant, a failed crop, or higher maintenance. For reliable crops, stick with plants that are hardy in your zone. But if you want to expand your plant palette and experiment in the garden, then push the limits. Also keep in mind that new heat- or cold-tolerant cultivars and species often become available. If you see a new offering, check its hardiness rating. It might be worth trying.

Microclimates

The USDA bases its zone map on the law of averages, and it works on the premise of flat, open landscapes with uniform conditions. But few yards are completely flat and open, and that's a good thing for food gardeners. Slopes, buildings, depressions, trees, ponds, driveways, and other landscape features affect growing conditions, creating microclimates—small areas that are naturally warmer or cooler than would be expected based on your zone. A colder than typical microclimate exists, for example, in a shaded depression at the base of a slope where cool night air pools; an example of a warm microclimate is a paved patio backed by a southwest-facing masonry wall that traps and reflects heat.

▼ Bell-shape flowers of the very hardy lowbush blueberry appear reliably in spring, even after a Zone 3, northern Minnesota -40°F winter. Leaves of the 2-foot high ornamental edible turn bright red in fall, and in spring the plants are covered with blueberries.

▼ Highbush blueberries produce large, thick-skinned berries in moderate climates where they receive adequate cold through the winter to satisfy their chilling requirement and where temperatures remain mild enough to prevent cold-temperature injury to flower buds. Given the acidic soil they require, they will be productive.

Soil sense

▲ Miracle-Gro® Garden Soil for Flowers & Vegetables provides an ideal growing medium without the hassle of amending your existing soil.

The key functions of soil in relation to plants are to provide an anchor for the plant's roots, provide a medium through which plants draw nutrients and water, and act as a reservoir for the oxygen that plant roots need to live and grow.

Soil is made up of weathered rock and minerals. Weathering pulverizes the rock, which becomes the mineral portion of the soil. Different kinds of rocks, and the ways that weathering affects different types of rock, result in the wide variety of soils that we have. For example, soil that is derived from granite tends to be acidic. Because granite is a hard material, the soil particles might be relatively large, especially when compared to soils derived from limestone, which are also more alkaline. The material from which soils originate affect the kinds of plants that grow well, the frequency of irrigation, need for more or less plant food, and need to adjust the soil's pH (see page 22).

Climate also has a strong effect on soil formation. Soils that develop in warm, wet environments weather quickly. In addition, many of the minerals that act as plant nutrients are washed away. The soil becomes more acidic and contains a large percentage of iron. These red or yellow soils will need additional fertilization to produce healthy plants.

Soils in arid environments are often low in nutrients. Weathering is slow. Without water, salts accumulate, which are detrimental to plant growth. In arid environments, soils often need to be leached (washed) with large quantities of water to remove excess salts before plants can be grown successfully, and periodically thereafter to keep salts from building up. Soils in dry climates tend to be on the alkaline side.

● **Organic matter** The organic component of soil is possibly the most fascinating aspect because of its diversity. It may be living or dead, composed of plant or animal material, and be easily visible or infinitesimally small. A teaspoon of healthy soil contains an entire universe of microorganisms. Yeasts, bacteria, and fungi are invisible but vitally important to soil health because they help decompose organic matter. Earthworms, ants, and many insects tunnel through the soil, opening pathways through which air can circulate. When organic matter finally stabilizes and stops decomposing, the result is humus—a naturally rich, dark, crumbly material that increases soil fertility.

The percentage of organic matter in soil is often in direct proportion to the amount of rainfall. Where rainfall is regular and abundant, organic matter content averages 5 to 6 percent or even higher—up to 10 percent in some regions. In arid climates, organic matter can be as little as a fraction of a percent. Although a few percentage points may not seem like much, it makes a difference in the fertility and workability of soil.

Organic matter improves workability or structure of clay soils. As fine soil particles bind with micro-organisms, clay particles become stable clumps, or aggregates. Thus, instead of forming a tight mass that sheds water, soil has space between aggregates for water and air to penetrate. In a similar way, organic matter also improves sandy soil, helping it to better retain water and fertility.

● **Water and air** Pore space is the space not occupied by minerals or organic matter. These spaces are essential for air, water, and roots to move through the soil and for microbes to survive. Plants need all of these resources to be accessible at their roots to perform their life functions.

▲ With experience you can determine soil texture by simply feeling it. Start with a handful of moist soil that is free of gravel and rocks. The microscopic particles of clay soil form a dense and sticky lump when squeezed (top left). Sandy soil, composed of relatively large particles, crumbles (top right). The favorable combination of clay and sand plus organic matter called loam holds its shape when squeezed (above), and only crumbles if squeezed hard.

TESTING SOIL DRAINAGE

1 Dig a hole about 12 inches deep and 8–12 inches in diameter in soil that is moist but not soggy wet.

2 Fill the hole with water. Allow it to drain and re-fill it 12 hours later, noting the time.

3 If the soil drains well, all the water will be gone in 2 to 3 hours. But if it takes 10 or more hours to empty, most plants will grow poorly in that area.

Both the mineral and organic portions of soil influence the amount of pore space the soil contains. The larger the mineral particles, the more pore space there will be. A balance of pore sizes is important in healthy soil because large pores let water flow through, while small pores hold water for plants to use as they need it. Large pores also allow oxygen to move into the soil and to give carbon dioxide an escape route.

Soil types

Soils are classified by the relative proportions of the mineral particles they are made of. There are three basic types of particles—sand, silt, and clay. The particles vary in size from large to small. Most soils are a combination of two or more of these types.

● **Sand** Soils primarily made up of sand have the largest particles and the largest amount of pore space. You can usually see individual particles in a sandy soil. As a result of the large pores, sandy soils drain quickly. The fast drainage keeps water from accumulating in the soil and from rotting roots. Sandy soils can be worked soon after rain or irrigation. In cold climates, gardeners appreciate sandy soil because it warms faster in spring than clay soil allowing them to get their vegetable and annual flower gardens in the ground and off to an early start.

Unfortunately, water may pass through sandy soil so rapidly that roots cannot supply plants with enough moisture for optimum growth. As water passes through sandy soils, it takes nutrients with it, which is the reason sandy soils are usually low in fertility.

● **Silt** Silt particles are rounded, nearly microscopic soil particles. Because the small size results in more surface area and smaller pore spaces than sand, a silty soil will drain more slowly than a sandy soil and retain more nutrients.

● **Clay** Individual clay particles are microscopic. An ounce of soil contains millions of clay particles. All these small particles add up to a very large surface area that is, notably, negatively charged. Because most plant nutrients have a positive charge, nutrients cling to clay particles. Also because of the small pores and huge negatively charged surface area, clay soils hold a great deal more water than other soil types.

Clay soil has drawbacks, however. Individual particles are flattened so they can pack together tightly, which makes it difficult for roots to work their way through the soil. Clay is sticky when wet and can become brick-hard when dry (adobe is made from dried clay soil). Even though clay is moisture-retentive, the water is not necessarily available to plants. Soils with a high percentage of clay may be difficult to garden in. Adding organic matter will allow the soil to form aggregates, making the soil easier to work.

Soil texture

Soils are almost always a mixture of sand, silt, and clay. The ideal is a loamy soil, which scientists classify as consisting of 40 percent sand, 40 percent silt, and 20 percent clay. Loam is ideal because it retains moisture and is fertile, yet has a favorable quantity of pore space for air, water, and roots.

Nature, however, is seldom easily classified, and the percentage of each size of particle in a soil can vary widely. Your garden soil may be a sandy clay loam, a silty clay, a loamy sand, or any of myriad other potential combinations.

● **Determining your soil's texture** You can determine soil texture with a simple test, similar to the one shown in the photos on page 20. Moisten a tablespoon of soil, roll it into a small ball, and try forming it into a ribbon between your hands.

If the ball packs together and easily forms a ribbon, the soil is clay or has a high clay component. Soils with a high percentage of clay will be sticky and will probably stain your skin. If the soil ribbon feels smooth instead of sticky, it is probably a silty clay. If it is gritty, it is a sandy clay.

If the soil ribbon will hold together but is looser and tends to crumble, it contains a high amount of silt, sand, or organic matter. It is most likely a loam soil.

If the soil will not hold together, breaking apart regardless of how much water you apply, it is a sandy soil. It will be gritty and you will feel individual grains.

Soil drainage

What does the often repeated "good drainage" mean? Basically, drainage is how fast and how much water moves through the soil. Soil with good drainage has a great supply of oxygen, which is vital to root and plant health.

In addition, roots grow through the pore space in soil. If soils are soggy, the oxygen in the pore space is displaced by water. Although many plants can tolerate wet roots, this condition is more likely to rot roots. In short, clay soils drain slowly, while sandy soils drain rapidly.

The best way to determine how well your soil drains is to dig a hole about 12 inches deep. Fill the hole with water. Depending on your soil type and existing moisture, the water should drain in a few hours or at least overnight. If water remains in the hole after 8 to 10 hours, you will need to improve the drainage, unless you're willing to limit your plant choices to those that tolerate wet feet. Improving poorly drained soil is a big job. Either choose plants that are adapted to and naturally thrive in wet soil, or plant in mounds or beds raised higher than surrounding soil. See page 8 for more about raised beds.

Soil sense *(continued)*

Choose from many techniques to improve your soil and a world of products that promise to transform the most difficult soils to a crumbly, chocolate cake consistency. Make smart soil amendment decisions by first gathering facts about your garden soil.

Testing soil

A soil test can pinpoint nutrient deficiencies and excesses, as well as guide you toward materials that will help correct problems. Soil tests are a time- and money-saving tool because they point out exactly what amendments are needed, thus eliminating needless plant food applications. Find a soil-testing lab in your area for the most accurate results. Most county extension services will run soil tests or provide referrals to commercial labs.

If a comprehensive soil test is not an option, you can concentrate instead on learning one critical piece of knowledge: the pH of your soil. Technically, pH is a measure of the hydrogen ions in a soil, or how acid or alkaline it is. A pH reading in the slightly acid range, 6.0 to 6.8, is optimal for most edible plants. (Blueberries and their kin are a notable exception: they prefer acidic soil of pH 4.5 or 5.) Chances are, though, that your soil will either be acidic (less than 6.5) or alkaline (greater than 7.5).

● **Getting pH right** Chemical amendments are commonly used to modify soil pH. Acid soils are easier to correct than alkaline ones. Limestone is an effective amendment that raises soil pH. Two types are available: dolomitic limestone, which is high in both calcium magnesium, and calcitic limestone, which is high in calcium. In most cases dolomitic limestone is the best form to use.

Where annual rainfall is low, such as throughout much of the western half of the U.S. and especially the Desert Southwest, soils are commonly alkaline, not acid. Amendments to acidify soil include iron sulfate and elemental sulfur. Use iron sulfate when the pH is only slightly high, applying 5 to 10 pounds per 1,000 square feet. But if the pH is 7.5 or higher, use elemental sulfur to lower it. Do not over apply. Excessive amounts of sulfur can damage plants. Extremely high-pH soils and soils formed from limestone are almost impossible to acidify to a level where acid-loving plants will grow well.

Gypsum is sometimes recommended to improve drainage in heavy soils. However, gypsum is effective for this purpose only when the soil contains excess sodium. Use gypsum when soil test recommendations indicate a need for it.

Organic soil amendments

Organic matter makes clay soils easier to work and improves drainage. It adds valuable nutrients to sandy soil and improves its water-holding abilities. In both clay and sandy soil, organic matter contributes to a healthy soil system.

One of the best organic soil amendments is compost, which you can buy bagged or in bulk, or make yourself. (There's more about doing that on the next page.) Similarly, you can grow your own organic matter by utilizing various green manure or cover crops, about which you can read more on page 24. But in addition to compost and green manures, here are descriptions of some of the best organic soil amendments to use.

● **Manures** Years ago, suburban neighborhoods often smelled like steer manure as thousands of homeowners spread it on their gardens in springtime. Manure, which can be high in salts, is an inexpensive source of nitrogen and it can increase microorganism activity. If mixed into soil annually, manure will gradually improve soil structure as it decomposes. Use only aged manure near growing plants or prior to planting; fresh manure can burn plants but is fine to apply in the fall or whenever it will have time to partially break down before plant roots reach it. Poultry manure is also used as an amendment, sometimes combined with steer manure.

Specialty manures, such as bat guano and worm castings, are effective. Because worm castings and specialty manures are usually expensive, you may decide to reserve them for your most prized plants. Processed sewage sludge is a popular amendment. It contains nitrogen and can also be used as a soil amendment.

● **Wood products** The most prevalent commercial organic amendments for soil are wood products, such as ground bark and composted wood chips. These organic amendments are sold in bags and in bulk. They are especially good for opening up heavy soil. Wood products work well as long as they are thoroughly composted. Wood byproducts such as sawdust and shavings that are not composted can consume the nitrogen in the soil to the detriment of plants. If you use them, add some nitrogen plant food at the same time. Sometimes suppliers combine manures and wood products. Again, be sure that these are thoroughly composted. A reputable supplier should be able to provide you with certification and proof that the compost you purchase is not contaminated with excessive weed seeds or weed control products.

▲ Most edible plants prefer a soil pH of about 6.5. Adjust your soil down with soil sulfur, or up with lime.

▲ Laboratory testing a sample of the soil from your garden is a shortcut to a beautiful and bountiful harvest.

HERE'S A TIP...

Applying organic amendments

Organic amendments are simple to apply. Spread a layer of material at least 2 inches deep on the soil surface. Six cubic yards of material will cover 1,000 square feet with a 2-inch layer. Incorporate material into the top 6 to 8 inches of soil. Use a spade in small areas and a rotary tiller for large patches.

If you are planting permanent specimens such as fruiting shrubs or trees, you get only one chance to amend properly. Don't skimp on materials. If you are planting annual crops such as vegetables, incorporate organic matter every season.

Making compost

◀ Composters with lockable lids are safe for kitchen scraps as well as garden refuse.

Ready-made compost is available at many nurseries and garden centers. But if you have an existing landscape and some free space, you can make compost that is just as good as or better than any brand of prepackaged compost. Once you have made your own black gold, you'll learn to treasure potato peels and autumn leaves.

Compost is simply organic matter that is converted to humus, the brown crumbly substance that makes your garden plants healthy and beautiful. Conversion of organic matter to humus requires oxygen, nitrogen, water, and microorganisms.

Organic matter includes a wide range of material, from leaves to grass to kitchen scraps to manure. Some organic matter is high in carbon. These materials are dry and brown, such as fallen leaves, dried grass, small wood chips, twigs, and shredded newspapers. Organic matter that is moist and green is lower in carbon and higher in nitrogen. Fresh grass clippings, kitchen scraps, and garden waste are examples.

Compost is created by combining brown matter that is high in carbon with green matter that is high in nitrogen. Use equal amounts by weight of brown and green material. If you have mostly carbon material, you can add just a handful of high-nitrogen plant food to make up for the deficit. Mix the brown and green substances together and keep the pile moist. Soon bacteria will grow and decomposition will begin. When it's complete, you have humus.

A properly managed compost pile or bin smells sweet and earthy. Foul-smelling compost results from adding too much green material, such as clippings or food scraps, overwatering the pile, or not turning it.

Compost is an entirely natural process and there's no best way to do it. Choose the method that makes the most sense for you and that you're most likely to use. Here are descriptions of some favorite composting systems that gardeners have invented.

● **Sheet composting** If you have annual vegetable or flower beds and live in a cold climate where the garden is dormant during winter, you can sheet compost. Lay organic matter on top of the soil in the fall, and then incorporate it into the soil. By the next spring, it should be decomposed.

● **Trench composting** Dig a trench 6 to 8 inches deep and fill it with organic matter. Cover it with about 2 inches of soil. Water the materials occasionally to keep them moist, not soggy. The organic matter will decompose, adding valuable nutrients and structure to the soil. Depending on heat and moisture, you can plant in the trench six months to two years later. This method is especially good for vegetable gardens that are arranged in rows. You can alternate a planting row and a composting row.

● **Pile composting** This traditional composting method involves layering brown and green material. For example, begin the pile with a 6-inch-deep layer of brown material, such as dried leaves or twigs. Top the brown layer with a 2-inch green layer, such as fresh grass clippings or fruit and vegetable kitchen waste.

If you don't have green material to add, use a handful of nitrogen-rich plant food on the pile. Continue layering the brown and green material until the pile is about 3 feet tall and wide. Add a few shovelfuls of garden soil as you build the pile. Water the pile generously until it is like a damp sponge. Too much water will make it soggy and smelly. Continue watering the pile as needed to keep it damp.

After a few weeks, turn the compost with a shovel or garden fork. If the mixture is warm and steamy inside, the microorganisms are actively breaking down the material. If the pile is not warm, add more green ingredients. Aerobic composting occurs when organisms, called

▲ A barrel-type composter on an axle makes turning compost particularly easy.

thermophiles, become active. Once they are active the temperature of the pile can rise to temperatures as high as 140°F or more.

At these high temperatures, weed seeds, insect eggs, and many disease organisms are destroyed. Continue watering and turning the pile until humus is formed. The process of decomposition usually takes from four months to two years, depending on the components and the maintenance of the pile.

● **Bin composting** Similar to pile composting, bin composting involves layering brown and green material. This neat and tidy method of composting holds all of the ingredients within a homemade or prefabricated bin. Wooden bins eventually deteriorate unless you use rot-resistant wood. Tend compost in a bin as you would a freestanding pile.

▼ Use your compost to amend soil around new plants and as a light mulch around established plants.

▼ Fresh refuse starts in the right bin, is turned into the middle bin, then turned once more into the left bin to finish.

Cover crops

▲ Buckwheat grows fast enough to outcompete weeds, and its stems are easy to work into the soil. In the North sow buckwheat seeds in spring or late summer; in the South sow seeds in fall. Mow or till plants into the soil before seeds set.

▲ Sow seeds of winter rye in fall to prevent erosion and reduce weeds. Mow prior to working into the soil.

▲ Cover seeds of all cover crops by lightly raking and then firming soil over them. Keep soil moist by frequent watering until a week after germination.

▲ The benefits of a permanent cover crop for an orchard include some nitrogen contribution (if the cover crop includes legumes) and the enhancement of beneficial insect and spider populations.

Does your garden need more compost than you can manufacture in one season? Consider cultivating "green manure" cover crops as a way to improve soil texture and fertility while the garden rests during the winter. Or, if you are a four-season gardener, consider dividing your plot into two or more sections, so you can grow cover crops in one or more of them while the others produce food crops.

Growing cover crops and tilling them in as green manure—meaning not yet decomposed—adds organic matter and nutrients to the soil. While the crops grow they keep the soil aerated and protected from erosion, and also help discourage weed growth. Cover crops grown between rows of fruit trees help to prevent soil erosion and protect the tree roots. Some cover crops produce flowers that attract honeybees, which benefit the whole garden.

Choose cover crops based on where you live and the type of soil you want to improve. Cereal grains such as winter rye and buckwheat are commonly grown as cover crops in northern zones, as are annual ryegrass and legumes such as soybeans. In warmer climates, fall-seeded legumes such as hairy vetch, bigflower vetch, crimson clover, and alfalfa are popular choices; rye and oats are good nonlegume choices. Legumes are the preferred choice for soil enrichment. Bacteria in nodules that form on the roots of legumes convert nitrogen in the atmosphere into nitrogen in the soil, where it remains available to the succeeding crops. To speed up the nitrogen fixing process, dust your cover crop seeds with rhizobia, a bacterial inoculant. For smaller gardens where growing space is limited, quick-growing rye, hull-less oats, millet, or wheat may be a better choice than legumes. Oilseed radish, a type of

HERE'S A TIP...

No-till gardening

Frequent turning and tilling of soil causes compaction, erosion, and the oxidation of organic matter. Farmers in many parts of the United States have adapted no-till row crop farming as a means of conserving and improving soils. No-till practitioners plant their crop seeds directly into the remains or stubble of the previous crop without turning the soil. More vegetable gardeners are experimenting with this technique as a way of saving time and eliminating the need for tilling. One technique is to sow a fall cover crop (for example, oats or hairy vetch) that can be cut down at soil level in spring. Seeds and transplants can then be planted directly into the decaying cover crop.

▲ A variety of specialized tools are available to facilitate planting, but the basic of shovel, spade, fork, and rake remain most useful. Left: The basic round point shovel, D-handled spade, and spading fork can handle most any digging operation. Right: Use a bow-head rake to level and smooth planting beds.

mustard, grows quickly in cool weather and is a good choice for use in compacted soil or dry conditions.

● **When to work a cover crop into soil** In northern climates plant a non-legume cover crop in autumn when the harvest is over, and it will have time to sprout and grow before dying in winter. Till it under in early spring; wait a few weeks to be sure it has decomposed, and then begin planting your vegetable crops. In warm-winter areas, sow cover crops in summer and till them under in fall a few weeks before planting.

Turn a cover crop into the soil anytime. But to be a green manure it needs to be tilled when it is still green, which is usually just as the flower buds are about to open. Moreover, tilling in before seeds set is important in some cases to prevent the cover crop from reseeding

and becoming a weed. In the South you may be able to plant again in the same year after tilling. If you need to till under a mature crop but also need to plant again soon, just cut the crop low with a regular lawn mower and compost the clippings, then till the rest under. You can plant again in a few weeks.

Turning soil and making new beds

Digging by hand is practical for preparing small beds. Remove weeds and rocks with a heavy-duty, short-handled combination pick and hoe called a mattock. Loosen the soil with a garden fork. Strip sod by sliding a spade or shovel just under the surface of the soil and prying it up. Or, to remove a lot of sod, rent a mechanical sod cutter, or call a professional. When the soil is clear, distribute amendments over it. Using a shovel with a pointed blade, dig up and turn amendments into the soil. Digging to the depth of a shovel blade is called single digging. Digging

◀ Use stepping-stones or a board to distribute weight and protect prepared soil from compaction.

CONVERTING LAWN TO GARDEN

Some type of lawn covers the land around most American homes. Often, the challenge is to find the easiest way to kill or remove it so you can create a new garden bed or planting site for vegetables, fruits, or herbs.

Remove sod with a shovel or spade to prevent grass from becoming a weed in your new vegetable garden.

Here are several common techniques for eliminating sod to make room for vegetables, fruits, and herbs.

● **Strip sod** Cut through sod with a garden spade along the outline for the bed. Then use your spade to strip off the sod, leaving the soil in place. Incorporate organic matter into the top 6 to 8 inches of soil.

● **Use a spray** Apply a nonselective weed control product (glyphosate or glufosinate-ammonium, for example) to the area that you have clearly outlined with string and short stakes. The area should be ready to plant within two weeks, but check the product label just to be sure. You can use a garden spade to slice through and remove the dead mat of lawn, or simply incorporate it the soil by cultivating or tilling.

● **Smother the sod** Cover the area in fall with multiple layers of newspaper, and then pile 8 to 12 inches of compost on top of the newspaper. The sod beneath it will die and begin decomposing by spring. At that point you can remove the sod or cultivate it into the soil.

● **Raised beds** Raised beds are planting areas that are higher than the existing soil grade. You can create raised beds by mounding soil on top of lawn you have killed using one of the methods described above. The beds can be any shape or size and may be enclosed by lumber, stones, or other structural materials, or simply left open.

two blades deep is called double digging and is usually reserved for poor soils or beds that will not be renovated for a long time. See page 9 for more on double digging.

Work when the soil is moist, but not wet, to avoid damaging soil structure and to minimize the effort of cutting into the earth and the weight of the soil. Scoop only small amounts of soil at a time. Don't load your spade as full as possible each time. Grip the spade far down the handle (close to the blade) to give yourself better control.

Getting ready to plant

With the soil prepared you're ready to plant. For detailed guidance about how to plant vegetable seeds and seedlings, see pages 36 to 39. For more on planting herbs, see pages 174 and 175. And for tips and instructions for planting fruit trees, either bare-root or from containers, see page 110.

see pages 36 to 39. see pages 174 and 175. see page 110.

> **HERE'S A TIP...**
>
> **Tools for digging and leveling**
> Spreading organic matter and working it into the soil requires what are probably among the earliest kinds of tools ever invented, albeit more modern versions. You'll need a shovel or spade to dig into the soil, and a rake to spread and smooth soil. Shovels are more all-round tools, and with their longer handle provide greater lifting leverage. But the strong, straight blade of a spade is preferred for slicing into sod and similar tasks. Spading forks are more useful at times, especially when turning heavy or dense soil—it's easier to push the individual tines into such soil then an entire blade. If you have large beds to clear and cultivate, or are creating new beds, a powered tiller will probably prove useful.

Water and watering

Supplying water to root systems when it's needed is the single most important thing gardeners do for plants. Vegetables and many herbs are short-lived and have relatively shallow root systems. Any setback in their growth for lack of water will have consequences, whether in the total harvest, its quality, or both. The combined influence of the soil, weather, and the plant determine how much to water, and when.

Even if you live in a high rainfall region, keep in mind that natural rainfall alone will probably not give your new plants adequate water, or at the right time. New plants especially require frequent watering to promote root growth. Here are some guidelines to follow when determining when and how much to water.

● **Soil texture** How much and how fast a soil can absorb water depends upon its texture, namely the relative amounts of sand, silt, and clay it contains. Clay soils hold the most water for the longest time but absorb it slowly. Rain and irrigation may wash off and not soak into clay soil. Sandy soils are the opposite. They absorb water quickly, but retain little of it. Most plants in sandy soils need more frequent watering. Adding organic matter to either clay or sandy soils helps compensate for the weaknesses of both.

● **Growth rate** Annual plants, such as most vegetables and many herbs, grow fast and need soil that is consistently moist. Young perennial herbs and young fruiting shrubs and trees also need water frequently, compared to the same plant once its roots are established.

Standard fruit trees need a lot of water. If this isn't supplied by rain, deep irrigation is necessary. Dwarf trees may not need as much water, but they do require a constant supply. A newly planted tree would have a root spread of up to 2 square feet and needs roughly 2 to 4 gallons of water a week minimum. Make appropriate adjustments for rainfall, high temperatures, and soil type.

● **Weather** Weather always figures prominently and unpredictably in the watering calculation. Clear, sunny days that are windy will pull much more water from plants and the soil, for instance, than the same sunny day when the air is calm. Similarly, an 80°F day when humidity is low will place much more water demand on plants than if humidity is high.

● **Drought tolerance** Once perennial edible plants are established, the differences between plants' water needs becomes more apparent. Some herbs, such as lavender, have small, waxy, whitish leaves that resist water loss even on hot days. Others, such as mint or lemon balm, have relatively thin leaves through which water passes readily, meaning their roots will need more frequent replenishment, all other things being equal.

Because water is pulled up through soil and into the air by evaporation, the depth of the plant's roots also determines the frequency and the amount of water needed. Tomato roots at the end of the season in good soil might reach 24 inches deep or so.

▲ Small amounts of water gently delivered is ideal for newly planted vegetables.

▲ Where summer irrigation is a necessity, low-volume sprays are ideal for fruit trees and shrubs.

Roots of lettuce plants are maybe half that. Most roots of perennial herbs and small fruits are about 12 inches deep, though they may spread outward 3 or more feet. Roots of tree fruits may extend 2 or more feet deep, but are mostly less than that and are wide spreading. Plants with roots that can reach deeper and wider potentially have access to more moisture, allowing more time between watering.

Supplying just the right amount of water, and working with and around natural rainfall, is a balancing act. Roots need moisture, but they also need air, which is why plants die in soils that are flooded or just too soggy. Similarly, in the water-short West, soaking soil to depths beyond which roots can reach is wasteful.

There are two ways to know if your watering is meeting the plants' needs. First, observe the plants themselves. If you watch closely you'll learn to tell when water is needed, and long before the obvious signal—wilting. The other way is to check the soil. Use a trowel, shovel, or a soil sampling tube. This last tool extracts a core of soil about an inch in diameter from the top several inches. You can see the depth of the moist soil easily.

▲ One of the simplest ways to check soil moisture is to probe with a screwdriver. If it penetrates easily, the soil is moist.

▲ Newly planted trees and shrubs will likely need regular supplemental water until their second or third season.

◀ Furrow irrigation of snap beans

▶ Trickle irrigation is a convenient method to water vegetables, fruits, and herbs in containers. This drip emitter keeps a pot of lemon verbena moist.

HERE'S A TIP...

Winter hose care
Get a long and useful life from your garden hose by storing it in winter. First disconnect and drain it. This prevents bursting and cracking caused by swelling ice. Coil hoses once they're drained, and connect the two ends to keep the coil neat. Store hoses flat, not hanging, ideally in a garage or basement where they won't freeze.

Ways to water

There are nearly as many ways to apply water as there are gardeners. Here are brief summaries of the most common techniques. If your garden is like most, you'll likely use some combination of these methods regularly.

Some methods, including hand-watering and some sprinklers, deliver water fast and make water puddle or run off long before the soil receives as much water as it needs. Even though water is running off you may be wetting only the top few inches of the soil. Because the rate of water absorption into the soil may be slow, it may take several hours to several days to wet some types of soil deeply. To water deeply and prevent runoff, apply water at the same rate at which it enters the soil. If your irrigation system cannot be adjusted to apply water that slowly, use another system, or water until runoff begins, stop watering for an hour, then water again, until the soil has been wetted as deeply as necessary.

● **Hand-watering** This method involves watering the garden with a handheld hose, usually with a spray head on the end. Hand-watering is a simple watering method. It involves no previous soil preparation or equipment installation. But it is time-consuming and leads to under-watering because most gardeners do not have the patience to water for as long as needed.

● **Furrow irrigation** Furrow irrigation works best when you are watering rows of plants; it is often used in vegetable gardens. Furrows beside plant rows are filled with water and left to soak in. Plant foliage stays dry when furrow irrigation is used, which helps minimize disease development.

● **Basin irrigation** Watering basins are used mainly around fruit trees and shrubs. A ridge of soil is built to contain the water, and then the basin formed by this ridge is filled with water, either from a handheld hose or a bubbler head on a permanent sprinkler system. A few basins can be filled quickly with water, but if many plants are irrigated by hand in this manner, watering may be time-consuming. Plant foliage stays dry when water basins are used.

● **Sprinklers** Both hose-end sprinklers and underground installed sprinklers irrigate a large area at once. They are most effective when used to water heavily planted areas. Sprinklers are wasteful if they are used to irrigate sparsely planted areas. They are also hard to control in windy areas, and they wet plant leaves, which may lead to disease problems. But they are effective for delivering water evenly over a large area and require less time than most other systems.

● **Drip irrigation** Drip irrigation systems apply water slowly, allowing it to seep into the soil. They are left on for many hours at a time, often for 4 to 16 hours per day. Many types of delivery systems are available. If they are properly operated, drip systems do the best watering job because they keep the soil at a relatively constant state of moisture, without the wet-to-dry fluctuations of other methods. Drip systems work best in light soils and are a perfect solution to watering plants on steep slopes. They do not wet the leaves.

▲ A soaker hose snaking around these red lettuce plants delivers water with ease and no waste.

◀ A battery-powered digital water timer offers the convenience of permanent, hard-wired timers at a fraction of the expense.

WATERING GUIDELINES

● **Water after planting.** The amount will depend on the type of soil, the size of the planting area, and the weather conditions at planting time.

● **Water plants in sandy soils more frequently.** Soils high in clay absorb, release, and drain water slowly. Adding large amounts of organic matter to soils helps them hold more water for plant growth and drain away excess water.

● **Water before leaves wilt.** Plants may require watering two to three times per week or more often in spring if rainfall is lacking.

● **Water deeply.** Dig down 4 to 6 inches with a screwdriver or other soil probe to test for moisture.

● **Water in the morning.** Avoid wetting foliage if watering late in the day. Plants need time to dry off before nightfall to avoid disease.

● **Water all season.** Roots actively grow in cool fall weather even though leaf growth has ceased.

● **Water established fruit trees and shrubs deeply and less frequently.** This practice encourages a more extensive root system and improved plant growth.

● **Water carefully where soil drainage is inadequate.** Roots die off when the soil's pore spaces are filled with water instead of air for more than 24 hours.

What about plant foods?

▶ Vegetables growing in containers, such as these tomatoes, need regular feeding, either diluted in irrigation water or from a constant-feed granular product applied to the soil.

▲ Highest-quality harvests of any type of crop always begin with optimum soil health and fertility.

Use the illustration to the right as a guide (1 tablespoon per plant). Work into the top 1-3" of soil or mulch, then water thoroughly to start the feeding process.

3. Reapply every 3 months for a beautiful garden all season long.

Miracle-Gro® Shake 'n Feed®
Continuous Release All Purpose Plant Food

10-10-10 Guaranteed Analysis		F1198
Total Nitrogen (N)*		10%
10.0% Ammoniacal Nitrogen		
Available Phosphate (P₂O₅)*		10%
Soluble Potash (K₂0)*		10%
Sulfur (S) (Total)		20%
4.0% Combined Sulfur (S)		
16.0% Free Sulfur (S)		

▲ The language of plant food products labels is very specific and regulated making comparisons possible.

▲ Miracle-Gro® Organic Choice Plant Food provides a nonsynthetic option for feeding your vegetables.

Fertilizer is often called plant food, but strictly speaking that term is misleading. Plants make their own food through photosynthesis, using air and water with sunlight. The plant foods we give them are more like food supplements than food. The soil they grow in is a reservoir of mineral nutrients. The gardener's job is not to feed the plant, but to keep the reservoir from becoming depleted. "Feed the soil, not the plant" is the old gardener's adage. In practical terms, when selecting a fertilizer, the two primary considerations are the nutrients it contains and its convenience.

● **Nutrients** The nutrients that plants use in large quantities and that might be deficient are nitrogen (chemical symbol N), phosphorus (P), and potassium (K). Plants also need sulfur, calcium, and magnesium in large quantities, but these are seldom deficient, or they are added as lime. Plants need another group of minerals in minute amounts. Of these, iron and manganese are the most commonly deficient. Plants require regular addition of nitrogen in just about all situations. In areas with lots of summer rainfall,

plants also usually need phosphorus and potassium.

● **Convenience** Plant foods come in many forms, each of which reacts in its own way. The right form for you depends on how you prefer to manage your soil. The most commonly available are water-soluble plant foods. They may be applied as a granule and dissolved with irrigation water, or they may be dissolved in water and applied as a liquid. This type persists in the soil for the least amount of time. It is easy to apply and inexpensive, but it must be applied more frequently than other types. Controlled-release plant foods are chemically constituted to release their nutrients slowly, sometimes over a period of years.

● **Formulations** Many plant foods are formulated for a specific crop, such as tomatoes or citrus trees. These plant foods contain the correct balance of nutrients for one crop and often adjust other factors, such as the soil acidity.

Organic plant foods

Not too long ago, it was difficult to find organic plant foods at nurseries or garden centers. Now so many choices are available that it can be difficult to decide which to use. The difference between inorganic and organic plant foods is the source of the material. Inorganic plant foods are manufactured; organic plant foods were once a living material. Although plants respond the same to both plant foods, the source difference affects your garden soil. Organic matter is an important component of healthy soil, and organic plant food improves the soil.

Because decomposition takes some time, the

nutrients in organic plant foods are released over a long period of time and mostly during warm weather. When the non-mineral portion of organic plant foods decomposes, it forms humus, an excellent soil amendment. Organic plant foods are more expensive and bulky than soluble plant foods but need to be added infrequently.

Organic plant food, which is concentrated organic matter, keeps soil bacteria and microorganisms in good condition. The table on page 29 shows some of the common kinds of organic plant foods available and the nutrients they contain.

● **New organic options** Another material that's relatively new to the market is humic acids. Often they are combined with dried kelp, yucca extracts, and other substances to make an organic plant food. Humic acids are derived from decayed organic matter, called humates. These materials naturally form as organic matter breaks down. The products promise outstanding results, including stimulating seed germination and viability, and aiding root respiration, formation, and growth. But whether they really work is still in question.

Although not technically a plant food, packaged mycorrhizal inoculants promise enhanced soil health and plant growth. It is generally recommended to incorporate inoculants into the soil before planting because the mycorrhizae will not work their way into the soil if simply placed on the soil surface and watered in.

KINDS AND CONTENT OF SOME ORGANIC PLANT FOODS

Material	Nutrients
Alfalfa pellets	3-0.5-3
Bat guano	10-4-2
Blood meal	13-0-0
Bone meal, steamed	1-22-0
Compost, municipal	1.5-1-1
Corn gluten	9-0-0
Cottonseed meal	6-2-2
Fish emulsion	5-1-1
Fish meal	9-7-0
Kelp	1-0.25-2
Manure, dairy	0.5-0.25-0.75
Manure, horse	0.75-0.25-0.75
Sewage sludge, activated	6-2-0
Soybean meal	7-1.5-2

KINDS AND ANALYSIS OF SOME MANUFACTURED PLANT FOODS

Ammonium sulfate	21-0-0
Calcium nitrate	15-0-0
Potassium nitrate	13-0-44
Sodium nitrate*	16-0-0
Superphosphate, concentrated	0-45-0
Urea	46-0-0
Urea formaldehyde	38-0-0

Mined, not manufactured

In neighborhoods where construction has stripped off topsoil, or in soils with a very low organic percentage, injected mycorrhizae may improve plant performance. However, research results are mixed.

▶ Packaged fertilizers that release their nutrients gradually are well suited to the delicate roots of fast-growing vegetables.

Applying plant food

Base the initial plant food dose for your garden on soil test results, mixing it into the soil before planting the garden. Never exceed recommended rates on the package. Applying too much plant food is a waste of time and money and may harm both your crops—by burning leaves and roots—and the environment—by polluting the water supply.

Spread dry plant foods over the garden and till them into the top 6 to 10 inches of soil, or irrigate to dissolve them. You can also feed as you plant by mixing a controlled-release plant food with the backfill.

Depending on the kind of plant food you use, the type of soil in the garden, and the crops you grow, you may need to feed several times a season. Most fast-release plant foods are available to plants for only two to six

weeks. Sandy soil requires frequent feeding. And some crops are heavy feeders, while others may need a boost during certain stages of growth, such as when sweet corn forms ears. A controlled-release plant food, which can provide nutrients for eight weeks to nine months depending on the type, eliminates the need to feed more than once.

If you don't use controlled-release plant food, sidedress plants with a midseason application of quick-release plant food. Scratch the plant food into the soil around plants and then water it in. You can also spray plants with liquid and water-soluble plant foods, or pour them over the root zone. Time the applications for early morning, early evening, or a cloudy day. Water evaporates more slowly at these times, so

◀ Water-soluble plant foods, such as Miracle-Gro® LiquaFeed, are easy to apply through a hose-end sprayer, and the nutrients are immediately available.

HERE'S A TIP...

Brewing tea
One of the newest products on the organic plant food market is compost tea. The tea itself is being sold as are brewing systems for making your own tea. The concept behind compost tea is simple; people have been brewing it at home for years without fancy equipment. Place compost in some type of permeable bag—burlap is often used—then soak the bag in water to extract the nutrients. The resulting tea is a fine liquid plant food.

If you make your own compost, making the tea is simple and inexpensive. There are several techniques. One is to use a 5-gallon bucket or a clean trash can. Loosely fill the bucket with finished compost and add water to within a few inches of the rim of the bucket. Leave it for a week, stirring every day. Strain the liquid (window screening makes a good strainer). Mix 1 part tea with 10 parts water.

Or combine 1 part manure or compost with 3 parts water. Place the manure in a cloth bag in the bottom of a 30-gallon garbage can. Add the water, let steep for 24 hours.

Some gardeners simply put a few shovelfuls of compost in a burlap bag, submerge it in water for about 30 minutes, and then apply it.

There are as many variations on this technique as there are gardeners. If you are using the long-term brewing techniques, add air pumps to the bucket to keep the material circulating.

Generally, compost tea should be used shortly after it is brewed. It is full of living microorganisms that will decompose, causing the tea to rapidly lose its potency.

the crop absorbs more of the applied nutrients.

Another quick boost for plants is to make compost tea as described above and apply it around plants.

Mulch magic

◀ Roots of cabbages, peppers, and basil thrive under a mulch of weed-free straw, and weed seeds are smothered before they can germinate.

Mulch is defined as any material applied as a top layer on the soil. Mulch is a garden workhorse that improves soil and shelters plants. Its benefits to the garden are many.

● **Conserves water** A cover of mulch on bare soil slows evaporation. Because a thick mulch layer shelters soil from the sun, it reduces soil temperature and, thus, helps slow water loss.

● **Insulates soil** A thick layer of mulch protects plant roots from temperature swings, preventing roots from freezing in the winter or baking in the summer.

● **Promotes porous soil** If soil has a tendency to crust, mulch keeps the surface porous and open, allowing water to penetrate to the roots instead of running off.

● **Reduces weeds** Mulch keeps weeds at bay by depriving weed seed of light. Plants that manage to germinate will have to struggle up to the surface through an inhospitable layer that slows their growth and saps their vitality.

● **Keeps gardens neat** Mulches make the garden a clean, pleasant place to work. They keep dirt-laden water from splashing on leaves and house siding during a rainstorm or when you are watering. After a rain, you can work in mulched beds or walk on mulch-covered paths without getting muddy. The mulch layer also protects the soil, preventing the wet soil from compacting as you walk on it.

● **Adds a finishing touch** Mulches are aesthetically pleasing. Even a newly planted plot takes on a polished look after it's mulched. At the garden center, you'll find mulch materials to match or complement any garden theme or design.

Types of mulch

Mulches can be organic or inorganic. Organic mulches are derived from plants, while inorganic mulches are created from rocks and plastics.

● **Organic mulch** Bark is one of the most popular organic mulches, and it is available in many forms. Nurseries and garden centers stock bark mulch in bags that range from 1½ to 3 cubic feet, or in bulk by the cubic yard. Some suppliers deliver bark mulch by the truckload.

Shredded bark is a popular mulch choice. It neatly mats together and blends into a planting area. Bark chips are

▲ Weeds that do manage to grow through a mulch into the sunlight are much easier to completely remove.

▼ Extend your use of mulch throughout the garden, spreading it under shrubs and perennials as well as around vegetables and herbs.

▲ Ornamental mulches such as pebbles and bark convert a plain utility path into an ornamental feature.

another option and are available in a range of sizes, from about ¼ inch to 3 inches in diameter. Although long-lasting, chips have a tendency to float away when it rains.

Many other materials work well as organic mulches. Some gardeners pile freshly pulled weeds in their gardens. This, however, can create problems. If the weeds have gone to seed, you're simply planting a new crop. Other homegrown mulches include leaves, pine needles, grass clippings, and straw.

Depending on where you live, you may be able to obtain food processing waste, such as nut husks, mushroom compost, and peanut shells. Although not attractive, newspapers can be spread out in layers as mulch, too. Cover newspapers with another mulch material to hold them in place. If you apply lawn clippings as mulch, be sure to spread the clippings in thin layers; deep layers of fresh clippings will mat and perhaps become slimy and smelly. And of course, if you apply weed control chemicals to your lawn, do not use the mower clippings in your vegetable or food garden.

Another good source of organic mulch is tree or shrub chippings. In many cities and counties, municipal landfills offer truckloads of chipped wood for minimal cost. A full truckload, however, can be a massive amount that is suitable only for large gardens or neighborhood efforts. When using tree chippings, or any wood byproduct that has not been composted, scatter some additional nitrogen plant food over the mulch to ensure it doesn't consume all the available nutrients in the process of breaking down.

Although all organic mulches decompose after time and need to be replenished, this is an advantage. The materials turn into compost as they decompose, nourishing and conditioning the soil.

● **Inorganic mulch** Black plastic sheeting, used in the spring to quickly warm soil, is a favorite of vegetable gardeners; however, plastic mulches are short-lived and they prevent the movement of air and water into the soil. A better alternative to black plastic is one of the new, colored plastic mulches (discussed below), or a nonwoven geotextile garden fabric or weed barrier. The fabric allows both air and water to pass through while reducing or eliminating weeds, which can't penetrate through the fabric.

Applying mulch

Mulch material dictates its installation depth. Spread gravel to 2 inches deep, and apply organic mulches at a depth between 1 to 4 inches. Doing so will conserve soil moisture, suppress weeds, and buffer temperature swings. Overly thick mulch layers can cause problems. Layers deeper than 3 or 4 inches can indirectly contribute to disease problems and provide insect hiding places.

When mulching, avoid smothering the base of plants. Do not pile mulch at the base of trees; maintain a mulch-free circle around plant stems and trunks. Also keep organic mulches from resting against the walls of houses or other structures.

You may need to adjust your watering techniques after mulching. The frequency or rate of application may be too much for mulched soil. The mulch will absorb some water, so you may need to water longer to meet plant needs; but you probably won't need to water as often after mulching.

Be aware that organic mulches sometimes provide hiding places for pests such as slugs.

▲ If you live around pine trees you're lucky—the needles that regularly drop make an excellent mulch and are free for the raking.

HERE'S A TIP...

How much mulch?
If you plan to mulch at the recommended rate of 2 inches deep, 2 cubic feet will cover 12 square feet; 3 cubic feet will cover 18 square feet; and 1 cubic yard will cover 162 square feet. When mulching at a depth of 3 inches deep, 2 cubic feet will cover 8 square feet; 3 cubic feet will cover 12 square feet; and 1 cubic yard will cover 108 square feet.

▼ Cover soil around fruit trees with a 3- to 4-inch layer of mulch that begins just beyond the trunk and reaches out as far as outermost branches. Periodically refresh mulch and move away any that is covering the lower trunk.

HERE'S A TIP...

When tomatoes see red

Plastic mulch is the food gardener's secret weapon. And colored mulches produce even more surprising results. It used to be a choice of clear or black; the former warmed soil more, the latter stopped weeds. Now consider: Red plastic mulch bumps up tomato yields by 20 percent, and dark green mulch spikes melon yields 35 percent. Dark blue mulch punches up cucumber yields by 30 percent, and silver mulch increases pepper yields by 20 percent. All warm the soil, so continue to use cooling organic mulches, such as straw, around cool-loving plants such as lettuce and broccoli, but apply them only after the soil has already warmed to 60° F. For the heat-lovers, however, use plastic mulches and see dramatic results.

Edibles in containers

Many vegetable plants are well suited for containers, including small carrots, bush tomatoes, peppers, bush beans, herbs, salad greens, and bush cucumbers. Dwarf citrus, fig, or kumquat trees can be grown in containers indoors in winter and moved outside during the summer months. Strawberries can thrive in pots outside the back door or even in a hanging basket.

Choose roomy containers, such as tubs, buckets, or half barrels. They retain more soil moisture than smaller ones. Pots at least 10 inches in diameter can hold herbs, green onions, lettuces, and other small crops. Containers holding 5 to 15 gallons or more work best for larger plants and small trees. Grow three pepper plants in a half barrel, or one tomato plant with a few basil plants.

Make sure all containers have drainage holes in the bottom. Cover the holes with fine-mesh screen to prevent soil from washing out. Use a high-quality potting soil or make your own. Position plants' root balls on enough potting mixture so their crowns are slightly below the rim of the container. Fill in around the plants with more potting mix to about an inch below the pot rim. Water thoroughly. For nursery-grown fruits, remove the commercial container and

▲ Grape tomatoes along with basil combine in a single hanging basket as a living salad bowl.

loosen the roots with your fingers or a garden fork. Use a clean knife or scissors to cut away any long roots that have circled the pot. Set the plant in your own container at the same depth as it was in the nursery pot, fill the container with potting mix to about an inch below the rim, and water the soil thoroughly.

Soil dries out more quickly in containers than in the garden. Water frequently; water every day in hot weather and whenever the soil just beneath the surface feels dry.

Potted plants are not as cold-tolerant as those in the ground, so protect them from severe cold or move them indoors when temperatures dip below freezing.

Use the growth of the plant and its general appearance as your main guides to feeding. Plants should leaf out and grow vigorously in the spring and early summer, and leaves

▲ A fruiting lemon tree in an ornamental pot is as attractive as it is useful. The bright yellow and green of Irish moss prevents soil from splashing, and it looks good.

▲ A pot of fresh herbs can be moved in a moment from a patio step to table centerpiece. Give each diner scissors to make sampling easy.

▼ Recycled half whisky barrels with a small trellis attached make a home for lettuce interplanted with cucumber.

should be a healthy medium green. Yellowed leaves suggest a lack of nitrogen, while very dark leaves may mean you're feeding too much.

One method is to give each plant half the recommended quantity of complete plant food (containing nitrogen, phosphorus, and potassium or potash) twice as often. If the container says 1 tablespoon per gallon of water, use 1½ teaspoons instead. A liquid plant food is easy to handle and less likely to burn delicate roots when diluted properly.

Another good method is to use one of the pelleted controlled-release plant foods. These dissolve slowly over a period of time, so you won't wash them away in the first week or so.

Feed as long as the plant is growing. Stop feeding about mid-July if the plant needs to become dormant in fall. That will give new growth time to harden prior to winter cold.

● **Fruit trees** Because fruit trees are larger and longer-lived, growing them in containers takes more commitment and effort. But the results are well worth it. Even tender plants far from their natural climate zone will grow well, since you can move them to shelter when cold weather comes (or wheel them to a shady spot if desert heat is your problem). In a container, it's possible to have 'Meyer' lemons in Michigan or peaches in North Dakota.

Many favorite deciduous fruit tree varieties are available as grafted dwarfs. These grow on a rootstock that keeps the plant small but doesn't affect fruit quality. On the other hand, genetic dwarfs remain small on their own roots. Although both types can succeed in containers, genetic dwarfs resist temperature changes better, are less prone to wind damage, and often bear more fruit. Crops available as genetic dwarfs include apple, apricot, citrus, nectarine, peach, and cherry.

Other subtropical fruits that are suitable for growing in containers include banana,

▲ A window box of herbes de Provence includes rosemary, marjoram, basil, thyme, parsley, and other herbs as well as marigold and viola flowers.

fig, guava, passion fruit, and pineapple guava.

Start with a container that is 2 or 3 inches wider than the roots of your plants. If you start with a bareroot apple or pear, or one of the genetic dwarf fruits, your first container will be about the size of a 5-gallon can. In fact, since it will be in use for only one growing season, you might use any available container and place it inside a basket or box to dress it up. Let the young tree grow for a season and fill the container with roots, then repot it the following spring.

The best container for fruit trees is about half-barrel size. Anything bigger will be too bulky to move and work with unless it's on wheels. The minimum size is about 18 inches on a side and 18 inches deep. The smaller the container, the more work is involved in feeding, watering, and root pruning.

Every two to three years potted fruit trees need to be root-pruned. Without root pruning, all the feeder roots bunch at the walls of the container and the plant languishes. To root-prune, remove the plant from its container while it is dormant, and shave off an inch of soil and roots at the sides and bottom of the root ball.

▶ Remove and replenish the outer 1 or 2 inches of soil on the top, bottom and sides of root ball in early spring to revitalize long-lived container plants.

Prune the top slightly at the same time to compensate for the loss of roots. Return the plant to the same container, adding fresh potting mix to replace the soil you have removed, and water the root zone thoroughly.

Large containers are more practical if they can be taken apart. It makes root pruning and repotting much simpler.

Feed deciduous trees weekly when they begin to leaf out and grow, then taper off in midsummer. Provide full sun when the trees are in leaf. Where they are not hardy, deciduous fruit trees can be stored in a cool but protected place or wrapped in insulating material for the winter. Where winters are mild, be sure to select a low-chill variety that is adapted to your area.

▲ Use pot feet to raise containers slightly, ease water drainage, improve air circulation, and minimize water stains.

HERE'S A TIP...

Pollination
Deciduous fruit trees and citrus depend on bees for pollination, which can be a problem if your container plant is indoors. If citrus is blooming indoors, use a small brush to transfer pollen from the stamens of some flowers to the pistils of others. In addition, some kinds of fruit trees need cross-pollination by flowers of another variety to produce well or at all. (For more, see descriptions of the individual fruits beginning on page 120.)

Growing vegetables

▲ The satisfaction of harvesting your own tomatoes, combined with the distinctive, often superior flavors that are available only to home gardeners, is all the motivation necessary to have a vegetable garden.

Before you begin growing your own vegetables you'll find it helps to know a little bit about the different kinds of vegetables and how they grow. Like other plants, vegetables can be categorized by their life cycle: annual, biennial, or perennial. Although some vegetables, such as asparagus and rhubarb, are perennial and can grow for many years in the garden, most are annuals. Even vegetables that technically are perennial in a frost-free climate, such as tomatoes and peppers, are usually grown for only one season. Cold weather, diseases, or insect pests too often thwart these heat lovers, so even if you live in a climate where the plants can survive winter you're always better off starting anew each spring. Some vegetables, such as cabbage and carrot, technically are biennial because they flower and set seeds in their second year of growth. However, the part that we eat—roots, leaves, or stems—is produced in the first year. Thus, unless you're saving the seeds, there's no need to grow biennials for more than one year.

Another and perhaps more practical way to group vegetables is by their optimum temperature needs. As explained on page 16, vegetables are also categorized as either warm or cool season. Cool-season plants grow, mature, and taste best in the mild temperatures common in spring and fall. (In mild coastal areas such cool temperatures may prevail in summer and winter as well.) Therefore, planting cool-season vegetables is normally synchronized to peak primarily in spring and fall. On the other hand, warm-season vegetables need heat to produce to their full potential and so are timed to mature mostly in summer. The lists at right and on the the next page show which vegetables are which.

each vegetable and some unusual terms, most of which are explained on the next page. However, the terms "hybrid," "open-pollinated (OP)," and "heirloom" are so important they are elaborated upon here. Once you understand these terms and the concepts behind them, you'll know a great deal more about a particular vegetable

Choosing a vegetable variety

As you peruse mail order catalogs and seed racks you will notice many varieties of

◀ If you purchase tomato transplants, look for plants that are not too tall and not flowering. Roots should be white and not packed into a dense mass.

COOL-SEASON VEGETABLES

Artichoke
Arugula
Asian greens
Asparagus
Beet*
Broad bean
Broccoli
Brussels sprouts
Cabbage
Carrot*
Cauliflower*
Celeriac
Celery*
Chard*
Chicory*
Chinese cabbage*
Collards
Endive*
Florence fennel
Garlic
Kale
Kohlrabi
Leek
Lettuce*
Mâche
Mesclun
Onion
Parsnip*
Pea
Potato*
Radish
Rhubarb
Spinach
Turnip

* *Somewhat more sensitive to freezes*

WARM-SEASON VEGETABLES

Amaranth
Cowpea
Cucumber*
Eggplant*
Jerusalem artichoke
Lima bean*
Malabar spinach
Muskmelon*
New Zealand spinach
Okra*
Peanut
Pepper*
Pumpkin*
Snap bean
Soybean
Squash*
Sweet corn
Sweet potato*
Tomatillo
Tomato
Watermelon*
Especially sensitive to frost

DECODING A SEED PACKET

With a seed packet in hand you already have much of the information you'll need to grow the plant successfully, though it might take a little decoding to figure out. Here's a description of some of the particulars you are likely to find on a seed packet.

● **Hybrid/heirloom** Whether a variety is a hybrid, open pollinated, or an heirloom may influence your decision to buy it.

● **Days to maturity** This number tells you how many days the vegetable needs to mature either from seed or transplant. For vegetables normally grown from seeds sown directly in the soil, such as beans, peas, lettuce, and squash, the days to maturity refers to the typical number of days required from seeding until harvest. For vegetables normally transplanted into the garden as seedlings, such as tomatoes, peppers, broccoli, cabbage, and eggplant, the days to maturity refers to days from transplant to harvest. If you live in a cold climate and have a short growing season, it's important to select varieties that mature quickly.

You'll probably notice variations in the days to maturity listed for even the same variety by different seed companies. This variability is due to several factors: where the seed was grown, local weather conditions, and the season in which the variety was grown. For example, cool-season vegetables grown in fall tend to mature more slowly than those grown in spring because of lower temperatures and light. Warm-season vegetables cultivated in southern climes mature faster than the same varieties grown in northern areas. Try to select seeds from companies in your region: They are more likely to be adapted to your local climate, and the

days to maturity will be closer to what occurs in your garden.

● **Growing description** The narrative variety description may not provide much useful information. However, many packets offer important information about plant growth, spacing, and how and when to plant that vegetable.

● **Disease resistance** Letters such as V, F, and N are often listed after the variety name to indicate specific diseases the variety can tolerate or resist. If you have had problems with diseases in your garden in the past, select varieties with specific disease resistance. See the tomato disease abbreviation key on page 106 for a definition of these letters.

● **Packet dates** Check the packet date to be sure you're buying this year's seeds. Sometimes garden centers sell last year's leftover seeds at a deep discount. Refer to the chart of seed longevity on page 36.

● **Treated, untreated, organic** The seeds of many vegetables, such as sweet corn, squash, pumpkins, and melons, are often treated with a fungicide or pesticide to prevent rotting or insect attack while the seed is germinating. This protection may be particularly important if you live in a cool-season area where the soil warms slowly in spring, or if you have had problems with soil-dwelling insects attacking your seeds. Wash your hands after handling treated seed and keep young kids away from the seeds. Teach older ones how to use them safely. Certified organic seeds are collected from plants grown organically, and the seed has not been treated with any chemicals. Certified organic gardeners and farmers must use certified organic seeds to grow their crops.

The front of a seed packet shows the variety photo or illustration, name, and may include a detailed description.

The back of a packet usually includes specific, useful planting and growing information.

variety even before setting foot in the garden.

● **Hybrid** Also known as an F_1 variety, a hybrid results from the intentional cross of a selected group of plants. To produce a hybrid, breeders cross promising plants by hand and check the offspring for specific characteristics, such as earliness, disease resistance, and uniformity in the seeds that develop. The time and careful work invested explain why hybrid seeds are expensive—and why the seeds of hybrids aren't worth saving. The resulting offspring will display a mix of the characteristics of all the different parents used to create the variety. Hybrid seed production has blossomed in the last half century, and these seeds are the primary type available for many of our favorite vegetables such as sweet corn and tomatoes.

● **Open-pollinated** These varieties are natural or chance seedlings that gardeners discover. Breeders grow them and save the seeds from the best plants. In general, open-pollinated varieties don't have the wide adaptability, vigor, uniformity, and disease resistance of modern hybrids, and the plants often show variability. However, these seeds can be saved and will

produce the same variety. Some common vegetables such as peas and beans are primarily open-pollinated.

● **Heirloom** Open-pollinated varieties that were popular before the 1940s are called heirlooms. As with open-pollinated varieties, heirloom

seeds can be saved from year to year, but the plants are unlikely to have the vigor, disease resistance, uniformity, and adaptability of hybrids. However, many gardeners choose to grow heirlooms for their unique fruit shapes, sizes, colors, and flavors.

Tomatoes are perhaps the most familiar heirloom vegetable, but squashes, peppers, and lettuces also have many popular and widely grown heirloom selections.

Seeds or transplants

▲ Starting your own vegetable seeds requires some basic supplies, namely some kind of container to hold the soil, a labeling system, and trays to make watering easier. Add some warmth and light, and nature will do the rest.

Once you have drawn up a list of the vegetables you want to grow, you must decide which ones to start from seed and which to buy as transplants. Growing from seed takes longer and may require additional skill to ensure success. However, some vegetables grow better when direct-seeded than transplanted. And you'll have a wider selection of varieties to choose from when starting plants from seed.

Growing from seeds

There is something magical about a seed, a tiny package loaded with all the genetic codes needed to grow your favorite vegetable. Although many vegetables can now be bought as transplants at local garden centers, at home improvement centers, or through the mail, it's still fascinating to experience this particular metamorphosis.

Seeds have some practical advantages as well. They offer the greatest selection at negligible cost, and they're available everywhere in spring: at grocery stores, hardware stores, and garden centers as well as online and from seed catalogs. Especially in the catalogs, you'll see the incredible diversity that's offered, far beyond what is available as transplants.

Note that some seeds are best sown directly in the soil while others need planting indoors for transplanting into the garden later on. Mostly it's a question of timing because some plants need to start growing before it's safe to plant them outdoors. Large seeds that germinate quickly are easier to sow outdoors. Small seeds that germinate slowly or germinate best at a specific soil temperature are often easier to manage indoors. Beans, peas, carrots, and radishes are some of the vegetables sown directly in the garden. Artichokes, celery, tomatoes, peppers, and eggplants should be started indoors before transplanting into the garden, or purchased as transplants. Some vegetables—onions, broccoli, lettuce, squash, cucumbers, and cabbage—go either way. You can sow seeds in the garden or start them from transplants, whichever better suits your season and temperament. Just follow the planting directions on the packet for the best results.

Growing from transplants

Some seeds can be tricky and time-consuming to start indoors or to sow directly in the garden. If you prefer to have a garden center do the work, you can buy many vegetables in four-packs, six-packs, or 4-inch pots. Buying transplants takes the guesswork out of starting seeds and is great for someone growing only a few vegetables in a bed or in containers. These small plants are still relatively inexpensive, give you immediate satisfaction, and are easy to pop into the ground or into a planter.

When shopping for transplants use these guidelines to purchase the healthiest seedlings.

● **Check for healthy roots** They should fill the pot but not crowd it. Avoid transplants with roots growing out the bottom or circling inside the pot. Such plants are slower to recover after planting.

● **Look for insect damage** Two common indications of insect activity are holes in the leaves and chewed leaf margins. Examine the stems, the soil, and the tops and bottoms of the leaves for any signs of crawling or flying insects.

● **Check for signs of disease** Reject any plants with foliage marked by spots, streaks, sickly yellowing, or brown crispy edges. The leaves should be green, even on the underside (unless that

SEED LONGEVITY

Vegetable	Years
Asparagus	3
Beans	3
Beets	4
Broccoli	3
Brussels sprouts	4
Cabbage	4
Carrot	3
Cauliflower	4
Celeriac	3
Celery	3
Chard	4
Chicory	4
Cucumber	5
Chinese cabbage	3
Eggplant	4
Endive	5
Kale	4
Kohlrabi	3
Leek	2
Lettuce	1
Muskmelon	5
New Zealand spinach	3
Okra	2
Onion	1
Parsnip	1
Pea	3
Pepper	2
Pumpkin	4
Radish	4
Rutabaga	4
Spinach	3
Squash	4
Sweet corn	2
Tomato	4
Turnip	4
Watermelon	5

Adapted from Colorado State University Extension

particular variety is supposed to be variegated or have foliage of a different color).
● **Stems should be dense and sturdy** Put back plants with straggly or leggy stems.

Saving leftover seeds

Buying fresh packets of seeds each year from a reputable source is a great way to start vegetable gardening. But in subsequent years what about all those opened, half-filled seed packets from previous years?

How long seeds last in storage depends on several factors. Most seeds are ideally stored at 50°F and 25 percent humidity. Under these ideal conditions the longevity listed in the chart on the facing page is typical. Seeds are alive, though in a dormant state, which is why storage conditions make such a big difference. In practice the best way to store opened seed packets is sealed inside a resealable bag with all the air removed. Then double-seal the seeds in another bag and store them in the refrigerator crisper.

Testing seeds

To check older seeds before planting them, test their viability.
● Place 10 seeds on top of a damp, folded paper towel.
● Put the towel and seeds into a plastic sandwich bag and seal it.
● Label the bag with the date and seed variety being tested.
● Leave most seeds at room temperature in a location out of direct sunlight for a

◀ For many home gardeners fluorescent lights are the easiest way to ensure seedlings get enough light. Adjust the distance as seedlings grow; keep tubes about 3 inches from leaves.

week or so. (Leave carrot and celery longer; they're slow to germinate.)

Germination above 80 percent—8 of the 10 seeds—is considered good enough for planting in the garden. If your seeds test at 70 percent germination isn't necessarily reason to throw them away. You can still plant them in the garden, but sow the seeds thicker than recommended. But if only 6 or fewer of 10 seeds germinate, Germmination in the garden will almost certainly be poorer than under the controlled conditions of the test.

Sowing seeds indoors

Vegetables such as beans, peas, and sweet corn are best grown from seeds sown directly in the garden in spring. Most root crop vegetables, such as carrots, beets, parsnips, and radishes, don't transplant well and need to be directly sown. Certain other vegetables are better started indoors or purchased as transplants. If vegetables that need a long season to mature, such as tomatoes, peppers, and eggplant, are directly sown, they won't be able to fruit before a fall frost in many locations. In fact, the tender seedlings may not survive uneven spring weather. If you

▲ Starting seeds indoors begins by watching the calendar and sowing at the right time. Assemble materials (top left) and fill containers with seed-starting mix (top right). Firm the soil gently and make small depressions to receive seeds. Sow seeds, using a tool for small seeds if needed (above left), water, and label (above right).

want to experiment, sow some tomato seeds in your garden this spring and also put out some tomato transplants, then compare how many fruits they produce before the first frost.

Start lettuce, onions, cucumbers, squash, broccoli, cabbage, cauliflower, and chard indoors to get a jump on the season. Later, sow seeds of the same vegetables in the garden. Doing a little of each extends the harvest.

Although starting seeds indoors to be transplanted outdoors is not as popular as it once was, many gardeners find it satisfying to start seeds indoors while snow and cold

winds blow outdoors. With modern methods and products, starting seed indoors is a lot easier and more likely to be a success.

First you have to begin with the right materials and the right conditions.

Containers

Many types of containers are appropriate for starting seedlings indoors. Look for ones that drain well and are large enough to hold the proper amount of soil for the varieties you're growing.
● **Plastic trays** When starting a large number of plants, try using plastic trays, which are usually 10 inches wide, 20 inches long, and 2 inches deep with no individual cells. Fill the tray with soilless seed-starting mix, and sprinkle seeds in rows. Once the true leaves (the second set of leaves) form, transplant seedlings into individual pots. Plastic trays are great if you're planting a large garden with many seedlings of the same vegetable, such as a large crop of tomatoes.

◀ Once you can distinguish the more from the less vigorous, snip off weaker, competing seedlings.

▲ Separate a mass of seedlings by tilting the container and gently loosening and separating the roots. Often a tool, such as a pencil or chopstick, is handy. Stems are delicate so hold them gingerly if at all.

● **Plastic pots** This type of container is the most commonly used for starting seeds. The pots are sold in multiple cell trays called cell packs, which usually have six cells, each 2 inches wide and deep. Recently, because gardens are smaller and fewer plants are needed, four-packs have become popular. The cells are large enough to grow some vegetables, such as lettuce and broccoli, to a size large enough to transplant directly into the garden. Other vegetables, such as eggplant and tomato, will need to be moved into larger pots (4- or 6-inch-diameter pots) to grow a few weeks longer indoors and then transplanted into the garden. Plastic pots can be reused each year if they are cleaned out with a 10 percent solution of household bleach and water (1 part bleach to 9 parts water). Soak pots in the bleach solution for 10 minutes to kill disease spores and wash away fertilizer salts.

● **Peat pots** Made of compressed peat moss, coir (coconut husks), or compost, these pots are sold individually or in multi-packs. Their advantage is you plant the entire pot without disturbing the roots within, and the pot gradually disintegrates into the soil. They are especially good for cucumber or squash, which have sensitive roots. Soil in peat pots dry out faster than soil in plastic and thus need more frequent watering.

● **Peat pellets** These disks are made of compressed peat. Simply place the disk in water and watch it expand into a cylinder 2 inches tall and wide. Plant the seed in the expanded disk, which you then treat the same as a peat pot.

● **Found containers** Materials around the home, such as egg cartons, yogurt containers, and waxed paper cups, can be used as containers for starting seeds. All that's needed are drainage holes. You can even make seed starting containers from newspaper using a paper pot maker (available at some garden centers and through mail order catalogs). Newspaper pots are planted in the soil like peat pots. Seedlings started in household containers that aren't biodegradable need to be removed from the container before planting in the garden.

Soil for seeds

Never use garden soil for seed starting because it compacts, preventing tender roots from expanding, and it may contain weed seeds, diseases, and insects. Choose a commercial soilless seed-starting mix made of peat moss, perlite, and starter fertilizer. These mixes are sterilized and especially formulated for seedlings.

Each component in a seed-starting soilless mix has a role to play: Perlite is a volcanic material that helps with aeration; peat moss provides the bulk needed for roots to grow; and starter fertilizer pellets help seeds grow strongly.

Light

Most vegetable seeds don't need direct light to germinate, but once growing they do need adequate light so they don't become tall and leggy. Leggy seedlings are weak and won't transplant as successfully as short, stocky seedlings. Even though a lot of light may seem to pour through your windows in winter, it usually isn't enough for seedlings. The light may alternate between too much and too little, or a cold snap may slow the growth of seedlings near the window. An indoor lighting setup that includes fluorescent lights is more dependable. A combination of cool white and warm or natural daylight tubes is best. The light quality and intensity is just right for seedlings, even though you won't be able to grow tomatoes or other fruiting plants to maturity under these fluorescents.

Planting

Create a schedule for all the seeds you want to start indoors, based on the right time to start seeds in your area (see the individual plant entries in the encyclopedia). Here's how to plant in the containers you have chosen.

● Moisten the soilless mix in a pail so it's damp but not soaked.

● Place the pots or trays on a watertight tray. Fill the plastic or peat pots to within ½ inch of the top of the container or flat.

● Use a pencil or chopstick to poke a hole in the soil. Plant one or two seeds per individual container. With trays, make a furrow and plant in rows. (You'll have to transplant seedlings from trays into individual containers following germination.)

● Sow seeds twice as deep as the seed's diameter.

● Label the container with the variety name and date using a pencil or water-proof marker.

Germination

Seeds tend to need warmer temperatures to germinate than to grow. Most vegetables germinate best with soil

▲ Holding the leaves, gently lower a seedling's roots into the hole prepared in the transplant container.

temperatures between 70° and 90°F. Even cool-season vegetables, such as broccoli and leeks, germinate fastest with soil temperatures around 80°F. The faster that seeds germinate, the less likely they are to rot or be damaged by insects. Under ideal soil temperatures most seeds will germinate within one week. However, some vegetables, such as leeks, may take longer.

Setting your trays or pots over a warming mat speeds germination greatly. Commercial temperature-controlled, waterproof heating mats are available to ease the process. Or you can place the seedling trays on the top of the refrigerator or anyplace that provides a little extra warmth. Check the trays daily to ensure the soil stays moist; gently water with a hand mister or bottom-water as needed. To water a tray from the bottom—and avoid displacing tiny seeds—pour a small amount of water into the watertight tray holding the cell packs or open trays. Water will naturally travel into the dry soil. Move the trays under lights as soon as the first seeds begin to germinate.

Place the fluorescent tubes 2 or 3 inches from the top of the seedlings. Move the fixtures every few days to keep them at the proper distance from the seedlings. Set the lights on a timer so that they are on 14 to 16 hours a day. Keep the air temperatures between 60° and 70°F, with temperatures at night 10 degrees cooler.

Transplanting seedlings

Once seedlings form a second set of leaves, called true leaves, transplant them into individual four- or six-packs or peat pots. For plantings sown initially into peat pots or cell packs, thin the seedlings to one per pot or cell; use scissors to snip off the weaker seedlings at the soil line. Don't pull out the weaker seedlings by hand or you will disturb the root system of the one you want to keep. When transplanting seedlings grown in an open tray, gently hold the young leaves and lift them out of the soil using a pencil or spoon to reach into the soil at the same time. Don't hold them by the stem, which is fragile and may break and kill the seedling. Place the seedling in the cell pack or peat pot, firming the soil around the roots, and gently water. Place the transplants back under the lights.

For large plants, such as tomatoes, peppers, and eggplants, you might need to transplant a second time into larger pots before planting them outdoors. Figure that once a seedling's height is three times the diameter of the pot, it's time to move it into a slightly larger container.

Seedling care

Keep seedlings watered and fertilized with one-quarter strength liquid fertilizer applied every time you water. Maintain the room temperature at 60° to 70°F, and keep the humidity between 50 and 70 percent by misting the plants periodically. A small fan lightly moving air over the seedlings can help avoid disease development.

▲ A cold frame is a convenient way to harden or acclimate seedlings to the outdoors because it's so easy to adjust exposure by opening and closing the top. The sloping shape, if oriented to the south or west, maximizes sunlight.

Hardening off

One week before you're ready to transplant your seedlings into the garden, start hardening them—acclimating them to outdoor conditions before planting them in the garden.

Find an outdoor location that's protected from wind and receives morning sun. Place the seedlings outside, ideally on a cloudy, windless day that's above 50°F, for a few hours, then bring them indoors. Gradually extend the amount of time they are outdoors over a one-week period. By the end of the week, you can leave them outdoors overnight. If the weather isn't right for transplanting, you can hold seedlings in a cold frame or under cloches (see page 41 for more about cold frames and cloches) until you're ready to plant.

DAMPING OFF

The biggest hazard in starting seeds indoors is damping off disease. This fungus literally attacks overnight and can wipe out a whole tray of seedlings by morning. The telltale sign of damping off disease is seedlings that have rotted at the soil line. The disease thrives under damp conditions with little air circulation. To prevent damping off fungus from attacking, don't overwater seedlings, don't overcrowd seedlings in a small area, and have a fan gently blow across them as they are germinating. For more about damping off, see page 202.

▶ In lieu of a cold frame, any partially shaded, protected location—such as under this staircase— can serve for hardening seedlings.

Protecting seedlings in the garden

▲ A pepper seedling like this one is ready to plant after the soil is warm, the threat of frost has passed, and the plant is hardened. A planting guide, such as a string, helps keep rows straight but is not necessary.

▲ Remove the bottoms of gallon plastic jugs to create miniature greenhouses to protect transplants from frost.

Even after acclimating them to the elements, your seedlings may need some protection from strong sunlight, cold temperatures, high winds, or heavy rain. If hot, dry conditions are predicted soon after transplanting, consider placing a shade cloth over the transplants to protect them from the sun. If the threat is cold, wind, or rain, lay a floating row cover over them, or grow them in a plastic row cover tunnel.

Floating row covers

Made from a spunbonded fabric resembling fine-mesh cheesecloth, floating row covers are lightweight, easy to use, and effective for many tasks in the garden. They let in sunlight, water, and air, but block insects and keep the transplants slightly warmer. Some types are extremely lightweight and meant only for insect protection in summer. Others made of heavier fabric provide more cold protection.

To use a row cover, simply drape the fabric over the young seedlings and anchor the sides. Floating row covers are so lightweight that vegetables will lift them as

they grow. Some vegetables, such as lettuce, Asian greens, and broccoli, can be grown to maturity under them. However, if warm temperatures are expected, it's best to open the row covers to cool the plants. Vegetables that need added warmth, such as tomatoes and melons, can be grown under the row covers until they are too tall or start to trail. Vegetables that are flowering likely need to be uncovered and available to bees for pollination.

Plastic row covers perform the same duty as floating row

◄ Protect seedlings from hot sun or wind by placing a shingle or piece of plywood on the sunny or windy side.

▲ An ornamental glass cloche adds charm to the garden as it protects seedlings. Prop a side up on sunny days so the seedling doesn't overheat.

▲ If frost threatens, or to give seedlings a jump on the season, use a water-containing cloche. The water absorbs heat during the day and releases it at night.

covers, but they are made from clear plastic supported over the rows of vegetables by wire or plastic hoops. You can buy ready-made tunnels or spread 2-mil clear plastic over hoops of 10-gauge wire or ½-inch PVC pipe to form 14- to 18-inch tall arches over beds and garden rows. Space the hoops 2 feet apart, and push the ends 2 inches into the ground. Secure the edges of the plastic with bricks or heavy pieces of wood. Remove the tunnel when outdoor air temperatures stay between 60° and 70°F.

Protect individual plants with mini greenhouses called cloches. You can buy classic attractive glass cloches, or fashion your own by cutting the bottom off gallon-size clear plastic jugs. After removing the bottom, make a V-shape slit in the handle's top and set the jug over a plant. Insert a long stick through the handle and deep enough into the ground to keep the jug in place. Don't use the cap unless you expect frost. Take the cloche off the plant on days over 50°F to keep excess heat from building up inside, but put it back in the evening if you expect cold temperatures. During sunny spring weather you may need to cover and uncover plants under cloches several times each day.

Cold frames

A cold frame is simply a walled bottomless box with a plastic or glass top. You can buy a commercial product or construct your own from straw bales, scrap wood, window sashes, and clear plastic. Make your cold frame no larger than 3 feet wide and 6 feet long so it's easy to work with. The back should be at least 4 to 6 inches higher than the front to take advantage of the sun's natural angle once the frame is placed in a protected, south-facing location. Loosen the existing soil and add compost and topsoil to the box. As with cloches and floating row covers, vent the top on sunny days so the plants don't overheat. Some commercially available cold frames have automatic venting lids that open when temperatures reach a certain level.

You'll find that a cold frame is very handy. Use it to protect young seedlings or to grow warm-season crops that need a jump on the season. You can temporarily place

▲ Floating row covers, supported here with light wire hoops over new transplants, are lightweight, air- and water-permeable fabrics. They efficiently cover whole rows of crops, often providing a slight but essential margin of extra warmth.

seedlings in the cold frame to help harden them, or plant an early crop of cold-tolerant greens such as mâche or spinach in early spring, or plant a late crop in fall to extend the season by several weeks. In some climates you can grow salad greens through the winter in a cold frame.

In northern areas warm-season crops such as melons and cucumbers can be started earlier than usual in a cold frame and grown to maturity with vines extending beyond the frame in summer. The cold frame will give your plants a head start on the season and allow you to harvest more fruits sooner than if those plants were grown directly in a garden.

Sowing seeds

▲ These seven squash seeds have just emerged from a mound or hill of soil, a practical way to plant melons and pumpkins as well as squashes. Once seedlings have a second set of leaves, choose the most vigorous two or three and cut off the others at the soil surface.

▲ Planting seeds in narrow rows begins by marking out the location, usually with stakes and string, and then creating the furrow or depression in the soil for the seeds. Here a tool handle is pressed into the cultivated soil to make the seed furrow. Place the seeds into the furrow at the correct spacing, press them into the soil to ensure good contact between seed and soil, cover lightly, gently firm the soil again, and water.

▲ Use the back side of a bow-head rake to cover and lightly tamp soil over seeds. First drag loose soil over the open furrow and seeds. Then, with the rake in a vertical position, lightly tamp and firm the soil over the seeds.

The time to begin planting in the garden is spring, after snow has melted, the soil has thawed and drained, and another hard freeze is unlikely. For most North Americans, this means sometime between late February and late May (see page 17 for more). Plant either seeds or transplants of cool-season crops before the last frost date for your area. They'll thrive once the soil reaches about 40°F and is fairly dry.

Wait until the soil reaches 65°–70°F before planting any warm-season crops. In practice, this might be a week or two after the last frost date.

Climate often provides exceptions to these general rules. For instance, if you live in South Florida, you can plant warm-season tomatoes in fall for harvest the following spring. Similarly, if you live on the San Francisco Peninsula, you can plant cool-season spinach in fall. The point is to match the needs of the particular crop to the natural climate and weather cycles where you live.

Before planting seeds in the garden, loosen the soil

by tilling or turning it with a long-handled garden fork. The topsoil should be finely textured and free of large clods so that sprouts can push through the soil surface and water and fertilizer can seep into the root zone. After tilling, shape the soil into rows or beds. Here are some descriptions of the options you can use.

● **Narrow rows** The most common way to plant seeds is in straight narrow rows. Dig a shallow furrow in the middle of the row by pressing a board or tool handle into the soft soil (as shown at left). To construct a straight row, run a plumb line from a stake at either end of each row as a guide. In general, cover small seeds such as lettuce and carrots with a scant ¼ inch of soil; cover larger seeds such as corn and beans with an inch. Check the seed packet recommendation or the individual encyclopedia entries in this book for specific planting depths.

● **Wide rows** Another way of planting seeds is in wide rows, which offer several advantages over narrow rows. You can plant more seeds in less space and have greater yields. When building wide rows you devote less space to pathways and more to the beds where the plants grow. Mark out the wide rows, making them no wider than 4 feet across but as long as you like. A 3- to 4-foot width allows you to comfortably reach the center of the bed from either side to work. Use string to lay out the beds so

▲ Use sturdy fencing or reinforcing wire to encircle a young tomato plant. Use one or two stakes tied to the cage to support it. As the tomato plant grows, its fruit-laden branches will grow out through wire, and so is supported by it.

▲ The delicate tendrils of peas readily take hold of the strings strung between these stakes. Even though the plants have grown well above the trellis, they still benefit from the support provided.

it's clear where the rows and paths are located. Loosen the soil and sprinkle seeds on the top of the wide row bed. Keep small seeds ½ to 1 inch apart and large seeds 1 to 2 inches apart. Use soil from outside the bed to lightly cover the seeds to the proper depth. Once most of the seeds have germinated, thin any crowded seedlings to the proper spacing.

You aren't limited to just planting seeds in wide rows. You can transplant tomatoes, peppers, squash, and other space-hogging crops in wide rows. Instead of creating straight rows on the wide row bed, try staggering the planting scheme to accommodate more plants.

● **Hills** Some vining vegetables, among them winter squash, melons, and pumpkins, are traditionally grown on mounds of soil, called *hills*. Create a 3-foot-diameter, flat-top mound on heavy soil or just a circle on the ground on sandy soil. Plant five to six evenly spaced seeds per hill, and space the hills based on the individual vegetable you're growing. Thin out all but the strongest two or three seedlings to the proper spacing. Hills give these vining vegetables lots

of room to spread and fill in a garden area.

● **Sunken beds** While raised beds work great, especially in areas with a great deal of natural rainfall, in dry areas conserving moisture is more the issue, which is why the Native American technique of sunken beds is more appropriate. Make a sunken bed by creating 6-inch-high berms around a wide bed. Loosen the soil in the bed and move it to the edges to create the berm. The ridges retain rainfall or irrigation water in the beds, protect young seedlings from drying winds, and keep the bed a little warmer to counter late-season chills in high deserts.

Cages and trellises

Trellis structures can be as simple as a wooden stake or as intricate as interwoven lattice. Plants are trained on a trellis to conserve space, increase light penetration into the plant, display the plant and fruits in an interesting way, improve air circulation, reduce disease, and ease harvesting. Set a stake at the same time that the plant goes into the ground and loosely tether the plant to the stake with

a soft tie to keep it from toppling or being damaged by strong wind.

Tomato plants are usually trained to grow in cages. Wire mesh cages keep the foliage and fruit from coming into contact with the soil, thus avoiding rotting. Sometimes, tomato plants require heavy stakes and flexible ties to help them remain upright. Tomatoes and other plants can be trained to a two-dimensional trellis that is mounted on a wall or a place where a normally bushy plant would not grow.

Peas, pole beans, and other vining or climbing vegetables can be trained on a fence, wire trellis, wall, or arbor. When trained on an A-frame or tepee-type structure, the fruit of peas or beans can be picked from inside as well as outside the support. Some vines have tendrils that cling to a support and help the plants climb and remain upright; others require ties to keep heavy plants from falling over or being whipped by the wind.

▶ Commonly used for beans, a trellis tepee also serves for cucumbers. One benefit: Hanging cukes grow straight.

HERE'S A TIP...

Square foot gardening
Square foot gardening is a raised bed technique that divides a 4×4-foot-square permanent raised bed into 16 squares, each 1×1 foot. In each square you plant 1, 4, 9, or 16 seeds or plants, depending on the type of vegetable and the amount of space it takes to grow. Build as many of these raised beds as you like to create your garden. It's easy and efficient. See squarefootgardening.com for more information.

Amaranth (*Amaranthus*)

Type: Warm-season annual
Edible part: Leaves, seeds
Typical yield: 4–6 pounds leaves per 10-foot row; ¼ pound seeds per 10-foot row
Typical size: 12–18"H×12"W (greens); 4–7'H×2'W (mature, for seeds)

This Native American vegetable is valued for its tasty, coleuslike, oval to heart-shape red, green, or bicolor leaves when young and its small abundant seeds when mature. A favorite in Asian cooking, amaranth leaves can be eaten in salads, soups, and stir-fries. The leaves have a sweet, nutty, yet tangy flavor and so are best mixed

'Red Calaloo' vegetable amaranth

with milder greens. They contain more vitamins than either spinach or beet greens. Amaranth plants that are allowed to mature produce highly nutritious little seeds that can be gathered and used in cereals and breads.

When: Direct-sow seeds or transplant seedlings when the soil temperature reaches 70°F, about two weeks after the last frost date. Amaranth plants are quite frost-sensitive and grow best when the soil and air are warm.

Planting: Sow the seeds in rows 12 inches apart, and cover with only ¼ inch of soil. Thin seedlings to 6 inches apart once true leaves appear. You can also start seeds indoors four weeks before the last frost date and transplant seedlings into the garden once the soil has warmed.

Growing: Fertilize with a high-nitrogen plant food monthly to encourage leaf growth. To promote bushiness and more leaf production, remove the stem tips a few weeks after seeding or transplanting. Keep the soil moderately moist, hand weed, and after the soil has warmed apply an organic mulch to conserve moisture and prevent weed growth.

'Wario' grain amaranth

Harvesting: Leaves can be harvested 30 to 50 days after seeding. Seeds can be harvested 100 to 110 days after seeding. To harvest foliage, remove individual leaves as needed or cut back the

Vegetable amaranth may have nearly solid red leaves.

whole plant to 8 inches from the ground. Cutting back the plant will encourage additional leaf growth and production. To harvest the many tiny seeds, bend the mature seed-heads over a bowl and shake them to catch the ripe seeds.

Pests and diseases: Japanese beetles and flea beetles may attack the foliage, causing holes in the leaves. Plants also may be susceptible to root rot during periods of wet weather.

Varieties: **'Hopi Red Dye'** (105 days) is a dramatic 4- to 6-foot-tall amaranth featuring red leaves and flowers. The mature plant is highly decorative. Not only are the young leaves edible, but also the flowers can be used as a natural dye and the black seeds ground into gluten-free flour. **'Red Calaloo'** (50 days) vegetable amaranth produces flavorful leaves of green overlaid with burgundy.

Artichoke (*Cynara scolymus*)

Type: Cool-season perennial, Zones 8–10
Edible part: Flower buds
Typical yield: 6–20 buds per plant
Typical size: 4–5'H×5–6'W

Artichokes ready to harvest

This thistle-family member produces large attractive plants. The edible flower bud is the familiar artichoke of commerce. Once steamed or boiled the bracts (fleshy green "leaves" enclosing the bud) can be pulled from the bud and dipped in melted butter or sauces. The highly desired artichoke heart is at the base of the bracts below the hairy center. This Italian delicacy is a meal in itself or can be added to pasta dishes or green salads.

Artichokes grow best where winters are mild and summers cool. The plant is a short-lived perennial and usually survives three to four years. Newer varieties are adapted to growing in northern regions as an annual.

When: Where winters are mild (Zones 8 to 10), set out transplants in fall directly into the garden. In all other zones, sow seeds indoors six to eight weeks before your last frost date in spring. Plant after all danger of frost has passed.

Planting: When planting indoors, thin to one seedling per

Cardoon is ornamental as well as edible.

4-inch flower buds by midsummer. **'Violetto'** bears slightly elongated violet or green flower buds, which are smaller than those of **'Green Globe Improved'**.

Cardoon (*Cynara cardunculus*) is similar to artichoke, but it's the fleshy leaf stems and leaves that are cooked and eaten, not the flower buds. Cardoon is a leafy 3- to 4-foot-tall plant with a similar spread. You can eat the leaf stems green or blanch the leaves by wrapping the bottom of the plant with newspaper and tying it with string. Cardoon is root-hardy to Zone 7. In colder areas treat it as an annual.

Arugula, roquette, rocket salad

(Eruca vesicaria sativa)
Type: Cool-season annual
Edible part: Leaves
Typical yield: 3–5 pounds per 10-foot row
Typical size: 8–10"H×8"W

Arugula, ready to harvest as baby greens

This easy-to-grow green is known for the spicy, nutty taste of its dark green lobed leaves. It grows best during cool weather, full heads maturing in 40 days and baby greens in only 20 days. Once the weather turns hot, the flavor becomes more peppery and bitter. Often used in mesclun mixes, arugula adds zip to salads, pesto, and sautes.

When: Direct-sow seeds two to four weeks before your last frost date and again in late summer for a fall harvest. Arugula can withstand a light frost. In cool-summer areas you can sow seeds every three weeks through the summer for a continuous supply of greens.

Planting: Sow seeds ¼ inch deep and 1 inch apart in rows 1 foot apart. Or scatter seeds over wide rows or raised beds, and cover them with ¼ inch of soil. Thin plants to 6 to 8 inches apart.

Growing: Mix in a 1-inch layer of compost before planting. For tender flavorful leaves, keep the soil around these shallow-rooted plants well watered. Since the plants mature so quickly, they rarely need additional nitrogen fertilizer.

Harvesting: Cut off young leaves once they're 2 to 3 inches in diameter. Either handpick individual leaves, cutting them at the base, or pull up the whole plant. By removing the whole plant you make room for other nearby plants to grow. Arugula is highly perishable and is best eaten within a few days of harvest.

Pests and diseases: Flea beetles can attack arugula leaves as the weather warms, causing holes in leaves.

Varieties: **'Astro'** (38 days) is a heat-tolerant variety with straplike leaves and a mild taste. **'Sputnik'** (40 days) has variable leaf shapes—from smooth, straplike leaves to finely cut and lobed leaves. **Sylvetta** (*Diplotaxis tenuifolia*), often called wild arugula, is a 3- to 5-inch-tall plant that is slow growing (50 days) and produces leaves with a sharper taste.

4-inch container. Set transplants or seedlings 6 feet apart in rows 8 feet apart.

If you're growing artichoke as an annual, space plants 2 to 3 feet apart in rows 3 to 4 feet apart. Move the plants outdoors early enough for exposure to at least 10 days of temperatures between 32° and 50°F to induce budding.

Artichokes need constant moisture while growing but can rot if grown in standing water. Plants grow best in sandy, very well-drained soil. If your soil doesn't fit that description, try planting on mounds or in raised beds.

Growing: Amend the soil prior to planting by mixing in a 2-inch layer of compost and organic matter. Fertilize existing plants monthly with a high-nitrogen fertilizer. Keep the soil consistently moist by watering and mulching with an organic material such as straw. Dry conditions can result in poor-quality, loose flower buds.

When growing artichoke as a perennial, amend the soil around the plants each spring with a 1- to 2-inch layer of compost. In Zones 7 and 8, where artichoke is marginally hardy, cut back the plant in fall and mulch the roots with a 6-inch layer of straw to protect them in winter.

Harvesting: The edible part of the artichoke is the immature flower bud, which needs to be harvested before opening. Where the crop is grown as a perennial, the main harvest is in spring. Plants will continue producing throughout the growing season with a secondary peak in production in fall. Where artichoke is grown as an annual, a spring planting is harvested from midsummer through fall.

Harvest the buds with a sharp knife, cutting 1 to 2 inches below the bud base. Handle the artichoke carefully so as not to bruise the bracts. Some blackening of the outer leaves may occur if the buds are exposed to a late spring or early fall frost. Perennial plants may produce up to 20 buds per plant, while annual plants typically produce 6 to 8 buds per plant. After removing all the buds on a stalk, cut the stalk back to the ground. Artichokes can be stored in the refrigerator for up to two weeks.

Pests and diseases: Slugs and snails feed on perennial artichokes in winter, causing holes in leaves and deforming flower buds. Fungal diseases, such as gray mold and botrytis, are most prevalent during rainy weather, resulting in damage to flower buds. Grow artichoke in raised beds and rotate crops to avoid these diseases.

Varieties: **'Green Globe Improved'** (88 days) is a widely grown, standard variety that produces globe-shape, thick buds with a purple tinge on the leaf bracts. **'Imperial Star'** (85 days) was specifically bred for annual production. Spring-planted artichokes will produce up to eight 3- to

Asian greens (*Brassica rapa, B. juncea, Chrysanthemum*)

Type: Cool-season annual
Edible part: Leaves
Typical yield: 3–5 pounds per 10-foot row
Typical size: 6–24"H×6–24"W

'Green Spray' mibuna

'Red Giant' mustard

Asian greens produce edible leaves that range from mild to spicy. Plants come in a variety of shapes and growth habits. Some have curled or rounded leaves while others produce flat, broad leaves. Leaf colors range from deep red to light green, making Asian greens extremely ornamental. Young greens have the mildest flavor and are best in salads. Often these greens are part of mesclun mixes. Older plants have a stronger flavor and are better stir-fried, steamed, or sautéed.

'Kyoto' mizuna

When: These greens produce the best flavor when planted in early spring, two weeks before the average last frost, or in late summer or fall to mature while temperatures remain below 70°F. Sowing too early in spring can cause some greens to bolt (develop a seed stalk) prematurely. Plant successive crops in spring, sowing seeds every two weeks. Plant again in late summer for a late fall harvest. In mild-winter areas sow seeds in fall for a winter harvest.

Planting: Sow seeds 1 inch apart and ¼ inch deep in rows 1 foot apart. Another method is to broadcast seeds on wide rows and raised beds. Thin and eat young plants, leaving other plants to mature 6 to 12 inches apart.

Growing: Amend the soil with a 1-inch layer of compost in spring. Asian greens like a moist, rich soil. Keep plants well watered, weed free, and mulched with an organic material such as straw. The mulch will conserve moisture, keep the soil cool, and prevent weed growth. When true leaves form, fertilize each plant with a high-nitrogen fertilizer.

Harvesting: Asian greens grow quickly, maturing 40 days after seeding. Young leaves can be harvested as soon as 20 days after seeding; snip individual leaves as needed or remove entire young plants when you're thinning the crop. Allow some greens, such as tatsoi and mibuna, to form into larger plants, and pull up the whole plant or cut to the base for use in cooking. Some greens will regrow after cutting.

Pests and diseases: Flea beetles can attack the leaves, causing shotgunlike holes. Grow Asian greens under a floating row cover to prevent these assaults.

Varieties: 'Kyoto' (35–50 days) **mizuna** has pencil-thin white stalks and deeply fringed leaves with a mild flavor. **Mibuna** plants grow 12 inches tall producing smooth, elongated leaves; **'Red Komatsuna'** (21–35 days) is an upright plant that bears dark maroon leaves with a green underside. **Shungiku**, or edible chrysanthemum, produces 4- to 8-inch-tall finely cut leaves for salads, sushi, and pickles. **Tatsoi** plants form a compact, thick rosette of leaves; thin to 6 to 8 inches apart to for a full-size rosette.

Tatsoi

Komatsuna

'Osaka Purple' (70–80 days) and **'Red Giant'** (50–70 days) **mustard** produce 1- to 2-foot-tall plants with colorful large leaves. Mild-tasting young leaves are best for salads, while older leaves have a stronger flavor and are best for cooking. **'Tendergreen'** (35–40 days) **spinach mustard** produces long smooth dark green leaves that are tasty when cooked as steamed greens.

Asparagus *(Asparagus officinalis)*

Type: Perennial, Zones 4–9
Edible part: Young shoots
Typical yield: 3 pounds per 10-foot row
Typical size: Edible spears; 7–9"H; 6'H×4'W (mature)

Planting asparagus

Cultivated for thousands of years, asparagus is thought to have originated on the sandy coasts along the Mediterranean Sea, which could explain its tolerance to salty soil. It is one of the first vegetables to harvest in spring. The spears (new shoots), which emerge from the soil and can be harvested for up to eight weeks, are delicious in salads and casseroles or sautéed in melted butter. Spears that are not harvested grow into tall fern-like stems that rejuvenate the roots for next year's production.

When: In spring buy crowns or dormant one-year-old roots.

Planting: Moist sandy soil is ideal; asparagus won't thrive in heavy clay soils or on sites that periodically flood. Take care in preparing your asparagus bed because the plant is long-lived and can produce for decades. The plant thrives in a rich, well-drained spot, so generously amend the ground with compost or composted manure before planting. If necessary, add lime to adjust your soil pH to around neutral. Asparagus can grow in slightly acidic soil but is more susceptible to diseases there.

Dig trenches 6 inches deep in clay soil or 8 to 10 inches deep in sandy soil, and space root crowns 4 to 5 feet apart. Young asparagus plants benefit from phosphorus, so add a phosphate fertilizer to the planting trench according to package directions and a soil test. Avoid application of high-nitrogen fertilizers.

A month before the last frost in early spring, set crowns 12 inches apart in the trenches. Cover the crowns loosely with about 3 inches of soil. After the new plants grow for six weeks, and add another 3 inches of compost-enriched soil. Finish filling the trench in fall.

Growing: Each spring layer the rows with 2 inches of compost or composted manure. In general, asparagus consumes much potassium so be alert to your plants' need for it, but don't add it unless a soil test indicates it is in short supply. If needed, add a 5-10-10 fertilizer in spring.

Weeding is critical to keep an asparagus bed productive. Hand weeding is the best option for home gardeners. Be careful not to damage the young roots. Avoid the outdated practice of applying salt to kill weeds, since this will eventually harm the crowns. Even though older asparagus plants are drought-tolerant, keep young beds well watered until established. Allow shoots to develop after spring

Asparagus beetles feed on new shoots.

harvest, but cut them back to the ground in fall after a hard freeze.

Harvesting: Leave asparagus unharvested the year of planting. Harvesting can weaken the plant and decrease yields the following year. In the second year after planting crowns, harvest for only two weeks. In the third year harvest for the usual five to eight weeks. Start harvesting when spears are ½ inch in diameter. In the morning while it's still cool, cut or break off 7- to 9-inch long spears with tightly closed tips. Harvest every day during warm weather and every three to four days during cool weather. Asparagus is highly perishable. Store it for a few days wrapped in a damp paper towel in a plastic bag in the refrigerator.

Harvesting asparagus

Pests and diseases: Fusarium root rot fungal disease can attack crowns and eventually destroy them. Rust disease can disfigure and kill the ferny stalks and branches. To avoid these problems, select disease-resistant varieties and grow them where asparagus hasn't been grown before.

The small elongated black and red asparagus beetle feeds on spears and ferns. A beetle population that is high enough can decrease fern production and eventually the yields of spears. The sluglike black larvae are often found on ferns in summer. Clean up and destroy old ferns in fall, and spray the adult beetles with neem oil. Knock the larvae off the ferns with a broom. Since they can't climb back up, they will die on the ground.

Varieties: The older **'Mary Washington'** and **'Martha Washington'** varieties have been replaced by the more productive and disease-resistant varieties such as those of the Jersey all-male hybrid series. These New Jersey varieties feature plants with few female ferns, so less energy goes into berry production and more into producing spears. **'Jersey Giant'** is the most widely grown and features green spears with purple bracts. **'Jersey Knight'** grows well in heavier soils. **'Jersey Supreme'** has higher yields than others in the Jersey series with good resistance to fusarium wilt and rust diseases.

For warm-weather gardens, try the male variety **'UC 157'** from California. It's better suited to hot and dry conditions. For a colorful alternative, grow **'Purple Passion'.** Purple spears are sweeter than green ones, but the yield is less and the spears turn green when cooked.

> ### HERE'S A TIP…
>
> **Growing white asparagus**
> Try blanching asparagus to make it more tender. White asparagus isn't a unique variety, just spears that have been grown in the dark. Mound soil around emerging spears or cover them with plastic pots to omit light and create these delicate white shoots.
>
>

Asparagus bean *(see Bean)*
Balsam pear *(see Squash)*

TOP GARDEN BEANS*

Name	Days to mature	Seedpod	Key features
BUSH SNAP BEAN			
'Provider'	50	5" green	Early. Widely adapted
'Maxibel Filet'	50	7" green	Slender. Firm texture
'Roc d'Or'	52	6" yellow	Firm texture. Deep yellow color
'Roc d'Or Yellow Wax'	52	6" yellow	Thin pods. Very productive
'Nickel Filet'	53	4" green	Heat- and cold-tolerant
'Jumbo'	55	7" flat green	Italian type. Stringless even when large
'Royal Burgundy'	55	5" dark purple	Pods turn green when cooked
'Venture'	55	5–6" green	High yielding 'Blue Lake' type
'Derby'	57	7" green	Tender. Easy to harvest. Good disease resistance
'Blue Lake 274'	58	6" green	Reliable. Widely adapted
POLE SNAP BEAN			
'Gold Marie'	55	6–7" flat yellow	Vigorous vine. Holds tenderness even when overmature
'Fortex'	60	11" dark green	Early. Productive. Stringless even when overmature
'Kentucky Wonder'	67	8" green	Old-fashioned. Vigorous, disease-resistant. Also comes in bush form.
'Romano'	70	6" flat green	Stringless even when large
SOUTHERN PEA (COWPEA)			
'Pink-Eyed Purple Hull'	64	Ivory seeds with maroon eyes	Vining. Drought- and disease-resistant
'Mississippi Silver Crowder'	64	Silver seeds streaked with red	Semivining. Humidity- and heat-tolerant. Good for the Southeast
'California Black Eyed'	65	White seeds with dark eyes	Vining. High yielding. Meaty texture
'Zipper Cream'	66	Creamy white seeds	High yields. Bush habit
SOYBEAN			
'Envy'	75	2–3 beans per pod	Very early maturing

Bean (*Glycine, Phaseolus, Vicia, Vigna*)

Type: Warm-season annual
Edible part: Pods, seeds
Typical yield: 12–15 pounds pods per 10-foot row;
   3–5 pounds seeds per 10-foot row
Typical size: 30"H×30"W (bush); 8–12'H×2'W (pole)

Yellow wax beans

Beans, many of them North American natives, are among the easiest vegetables to cultivate and great as a first plant to grow with kids. The bean comes in a variety of shapes, colors, and sizes, and some plants produce colorful flowers, pods, and seeds. Snap bush beans, soybeans (*Glycine max*), and dried bush beans grow on shrubby plants 2 feet tall (or more). Pole beans and asparagus beans (*Vigna unguiculata*) climb 8 to 12 feet tall and need support. Fava beans (*Vicia faba*) grow into majestic 5-foot-tall plants. Southern peas or cowpeas (*Vigna unguiculata*) and lima beans (*Phaseolus lunatus*) come in bush

HERE'S A TIP…

Inoculate beans to fix nitrogen

As members of the legume family, beans have the ability to fix atmospheric nitrogen through a symbiotic relationship with rhizobia bacteria. The bacteria live on the roots of legumes and are evident as tiny nodules. In exchange for having a host site to live, the bacteria fix nitrogen for the bean plant to use. Rhizobia are normally widespread in soils, but to ensure their presence, inoculate your beans seeds before planting with a commercial rhizobial product for your particular bean type. Done once, this will insure the rhizobia are in your garden soil for years to come.

Name	Days to mature	Seedpod	Key features
'Sayamusume'	85	3–4 beans per pod	High yields. Pacific Northwest favorite
'Butterbeans'	90	3 beans per pod	High yielding
SHELLING BEAN AND DRIED BEAN			
'Tongue of Fire'	70 shelled	6–7" large round	Red-streaked pods and seeds. Bush habit
'Vermont Cranberry'	75 shelled; 95 dried	Red pods and pink-streaked seeds	Large beans. Mild taste. Available in bush or pole types
French horticultural	68 shelled; 90 dried	Oval, cream-colored seeds with dark red speckles	Heirloom. Pods mature to bright red and yellow color. Bush habit
Scarlet runner	70 shelled; 115 dried	8" flat green. Red seeds with black blotches	Lima bean shape. Attractive red flowers. Multiple-use bean. Pole habit
Cannellini	80 shelled; 100 dried	Large white seeds	Kidney shape. Mild flavor. Great for soups. Bush habit
Blue speckled tepary	90 dried	Brown seeds with red speckles	Good for Southwest deserts
Pinto	90 dried	Buff colored seeds speckled with brown	Thin skin. Cook up firm and tender. Bush habit
Yin yang	100 dried	White-and-black seeds	Seeds lose coloring when cooked. Bush habit
LIMA BEAN			
'Jackson Wonder'	75	3–4 light brown seeds	Baby lima. Good for cool-summer areas. Bush habit
'Fordhook 242'	85	3–5 white seeds	Adapted to cold, heat, and drought. Bush habit
'Florida Speckled Butter'	85	3–5 light brown seeds splashed with maroon	Heat- and drought-tolerant. Good southern variety. Bush habit
'King of the Garden'	88	4–6 large cream-colored seeds	Large seeds. High yield. Pole habit
NOVELTY BEAN			
'Windsor' fava bean	75	3–5 green seeds	Grow best in cool, mild conditions
'Red Noodle' asparagus bean	85	20" long, thin red	Color doesn't fade when cooked. Pole habit

*Listed in order of maturity

Scarlet runner beans and flowers

'Romano' pole bean

and vining varieties.

Beans harvested at different stages are called different names. A bean harvested when young, before the seeds form, is called a snap bean. Once the seeds form but the pods are still green, it's called a shelling bean. Finally, once the pod is dried and seeds mature, it's called a dried bean. While some beans can be harvested at various stages for eating, most varieties are best eaten as a snap bean, shelling bean, or dried bean.

When: Direct-sow seeds after danger of frost has passed in spring and the soil is at least 60°F. Beans do best where daytime temperatures are 70° to 80°F. At temperatures in excess of 85°F most are likely to drop their blossoms (exceptions are noted). Temperatures below 35°F kill the flowers and pods.

Planting: Amend the soil with a 1-inch layer of compost before planting. Sow bush bean seeds 1 inch deep and 2 to 3 inches apart in rows 2 feet apart. Thin the seedlings to 4 to 6 inches apart after they form true leaves. Plant pole beans and asparagus beans so they can

Bean

climb 6- to 8-foot-tall poles arranged in a tepee. Plant three to five seeds 2 to 3 inches apart around each pole. Plant southern peas 6 to 12 inches apart in rows that are 2 to 3 feet apart.

Plant or sow successive crops of snap bush beans every two to three weeks until mid-summer to ensure a continuous supply of beans into fall.

HERE'S A TIP...

Interplant pole beans

Pole beans are perfect for interplanting to save space in the garden. Once you set up a pole bean tepee and plant the seeds, plant some quick-maturing vegetables under the structure. Crops such as lettuce, radish, and Asian greens will grow and mature while the pole beans are climbing. The beans will provide shade and cooling temperatures for the tender greens. By the time the teepee is full of bean foliage, you will have finished harvesting the low-growing plants.

'Sayamusume' green soybean, or *edamame*

Fava beans are the exception in the heat-loving bean family: They require cool to grow and produce their best. Staking or trellising is also recommended. Plant favas when you plant peas in early spring, about two to four weeks before the last frost. In warm areas, plant in fall for a winter harvest. Fava bean plants are hardy and can survive temperatures of 15° F. Space the seeds 4 to 6 inches apart in rows 2 to 3 feet apart. Thin seedlings to 12 inches apart.

Filet beans

Growing: Shallowly weed around the rows and poles being careful not to disturb the tender bean roots. When the beans are 3 to 4 inches tall and after making sure the planting is free of weeds, mulch the area with a 2- to 3-inch layer of organic material such as straw, pine needles, chopped leaves, or grass clippings.

Keep beans evenly watered especially during flowering and fruiting. Extra fertilizer is not needed unless the soil is poor, in which case feed monthly with a balanced product such as 5-5-5.

Harvesting: Most snap bush beans are ready to harvest 40 to 55 days

Purple beans

after planting, when the pods are full and 6 to 8 inches long. Even though modern varieties are considered stringless, pick before the seeds reach full size or the pods will become tough and chewy. Specialty bush beans called filet beans should be harvested when very slender (¼ inch in diameter). Snap bush beans tend to produce all at once, making them perfect for processing. After two or three pickings, the bush bean is mostly finished producing and can be pulled out.

Shelling fava bean

Plant another bean crop or, if late in the season, a cool-season vegetable such as spinach. To avoid a glut of bush beans, stagger your plantings, sowing short rows every two weeks.

Snap pole beans and asparagus beans begin producing around 60 to 80 days after planting and produce handfuls of 7- to 12-inch-long beans until frost. Fresh pole beans and bush beans can be stored unwashed in plastic bags in the refrigerator for several days.

Harvest shelling beans once seeds have reached full size, about 80 days from seeding but before the pods dry.

Harvest dried beans around 100 to 120 days after planting, when the pods have changed color and are fully mature. Since pods split and can drop the beans when dry, set a wide pan beneath the plants when picking. In very humid climates, pull out the plants when the pods have changed their hue and suspend them

Lima beans

upside down to dry in a shady, dry room with good air circulation. Store dried beans in an airtight jar in a cool, dry cupboard.

Harvest lima beans and fava beans 70 to 80 days after sowing the crop, when the seeds have reached full size in the pods and the pods are plump. Store the same as bush beans.

'Red Noodle' asparagus bean

Pests and diseases: The Mexican bean beetle is the main insect pest attacking beans. This brown beetle has black spots and sometimes can be confused with the beneficial ladybug beetle. The soft-bodied yellow Mexican bean beetle larvae skeletonize bean leaves, reducing the bean harvest. To control this pest, crush eggs and larvae by hand and spray adults with a pest control product. Cutworms can attack germinating bean seedlings, and Japanese beetles can also feed on bean foliage.

'California Blackeye 46' southern pea

Rust is a serious disease of beans. This fungus causes orange spots on leaves and bean pods. To avoid spreading the disease, don't weed after a rain or early in the morning when foliage is still wet from dew. Also, grow disease-resistant bean varieties.

Animals such as woodchucks and rabbits, which love tender young bean shoots, can quickly decimate a crop. Fence or use animal repellants to keep these pests at bay.

Mexican bean beetle

Beet *(Beta vulgaris)*

Type: Cool-season annual
Edible part: Leaves, roots
Typical yield: 3–5 pounds leaves per 10-foot row; 15 pounds roots per 10-foot row
Typical size: 4–6"H×4"W (leaves); 1–2"W (roots)

This native Mediterranean crop is best known for its bright, colorful roots and flavorful greens. The roots come in striped, yellow, pink, and red, and the greens sometimes have red stems. Since beets mature quickly, it's possible to have

'Red Ace' beet

multiple crops a year. Beets can be used fresh in salads, soups, and casseroles. The roots also are good steamed, pickled, or canned. The greens are great steamed or sautéed.

When: Sow seeds in spring two weeks before the last frost. The ideal temperature for growing beets is 60° to 65°F. In cool-summer areas sow every three weeks into the summer for a continual harvest. In warm-summer areas sow in spring and again in fall so that the roots mature during cool periods.

Planting: Amend the soil with a 1- to 2-inch layer of compost before planting. Beets grow best in soil with a neutral pH. If necessary, amend your soil with lime (to raise the pH) or sulfur (to lower the pH) as indicated by a soil test. Beets also need a loose, friable soil high in organic matter. Unless your soil is sandy, create a raised bed and remove any stones and debris.

> **HERE'S A TIP...**
>
> **Beet seeds?**
> Beet seeds aren't actually seeds at all but rather the dried fruit of the beet plant. Because there are multiple seeds per fruit, you'll often see two to three seedlings emerging from a spot where you expected to see only one. With proper thinning, your beets will grow fine.

Improve germination by mixing some potting soil into the seedbed so that the soil is less likely to form a crust that the sprouting seedlings can't penetrate.

Sow seeds ½ inch deep and 1 inch apart in rows 15 inches apart. Keep the seedbed well watered to increase germination.

Growing: Thin beet seedlings to 4 inches apart once true leaves form, and save the tender green thinnings for salads. Hand weed carefully until the beets

'Bull's Blood' beet

A collection of colorful beets

are established in the bed. Mulch the soil surface with a 1- to 2-inch layer of organic material to deter weeds and conserve soil moisture.

Beets need fertile soil; apply a balanced fertilizer such as 5-5-5 once beet leaves are 3 to 4 inches tall. Keep the beds well watered so that sweet, blemish-free roots develop.

Harvesting: Collect beet greens when they're 4 to 6 inches tall. Beet roots can be eaten at any time during their development, but they are best harvested around 40 to 50 days after seeding or when they are 1 to 2 inches in diameter. For most varieties, as the roots get larger they become more fibrous and woody. When harvesting, leave 1 inch of foliage on the root to keep it from bleeding during cooking.

Beets can be stored for three to four months if kept in conditions similar to a root cellar—temperatures near freezing with high humidity. Otherwise, store the roots in a refrigerator crisper at 40°F.

Pests and diseases: Aphids, leaf miners, and flea beetles can attack beet leaves, causing holes. Cover plantings with floating row covers to prevent this damage. Nematodes can attack the roots, deforming them. Rotate crops to avoid nematodes.

Varieties: **'Bull's Blood'** (58 days) features deep burgundy leaves and roots with a candy-stripe interior. **'Chioggia'** (55 days) is an Italian heirloom with green leaves, pink stems, and candy-stripe roots. **'Cylindrica'** (60 days) features dark red cylindrical roots. **'Golden'** (55 days) has green leaves with yellow stems and sweet golden roots. **'Lutz Green Leaf'**, also known as **'Winterkeeper'**, (80 days) features green leaves, pink stems, and purplish red roots; its roots stay tender even when allowed to grow large. **'Red Ace'** (50 days) roots are round, smooth, and deep red, and its leaves have red veins.

Bitter gourd *(see Squash)*
Bok choy *(see Mesclun mix)*

Broccoli *(Brassica oleracea Italica group)*

Type: Cool-season annual
Edible part: Flower buds
Typical yield: 10 pounds per 10-foot row
Typical size: 2'H×2'W

'Green Goliath' broccoli

This Italian delicacy has become widely popular in the last 10 to 20 years and is now a staple at salad bars and restaurants. Broccoli is loaded with health-

Chartreuse, green, and purple broccoli

promoting nutrients: It is high in vitamins A and C as well as calcium, and it contains the cancer-fighting substance sulforaphane.

Whether you're steaming, sautéing, baking, or eating it raw, broccoli adds a tasty nutritional boost to your meal.

When: A planting needs to mature during cool weather. Direct-sow seeds in spring two weeks before your last frost date or start transplants indoors four weeks before setting them in the garden. Plant a fall crop in late summer or early fall. Where winters are mild, such as along the Pacific and Gulf coasts, grow overwintering varieties in fall to mature the following spring.

Planting: Broccoli requires rich soil with plenty of nitrogen, phosphorus, and calcium. Work into the soil a 2-inch layer of well-rotted manure or compost before planting. Plant three seeds together ½ inch deep every 18 inches in rows 36 inches apart, thinning seedlings to the most vigorous one in each group. For a quicker harvest, transplant seedlings 8 to 18 inches apart in the same row spacing.

Growing: Hand weed established plants being careful to not disturb the roots. Keep the soil evenly moist by applying 1 inch of water per week. Mulch the broccoli bed with a 2- to 4-inch layer of organic material such as straw, pine straw, or grass clippings to prevent weed growth, conserve soil moisture, and keep the soil cool.

Three weeks after transplanting feed with a 5-10-10 plant food. Every three weeks afterward sidedress with a high-nitrogen fertilizer. Small heads, called buttons, are due to cold weather or a lack of water or fertilizer. If your seedling stems are less than 1 inch in diameter and temperatures are between 35° and 50°F for several weeks, broccoli transplants will flower prematurely. Protect transplants with floating row covers during periods of cool weather. Purple leaves are a sign of phosphorus deficiency, but if it occurs early in the season wait until the soil warms before adding fertilizer. Phosphorus may not be readily available when the soil is cool.

Harvesting: Most broccoli varieties produce one main head and then smaller side heads after the main head is cut. Sever heads with a sharp knife when they're tight and firm, keeping a 6-inch stem; slice at an angle to reduce the likelihood of the stem rotting. Heads with buds beginning to separate into yellow flowers indicate the broccoli is past its peak, although it is still edible. Continue

Harvesting broccoli side shoots

'Spring' broccoli raab

to harvest smaller side heads as they mature. The flavor is best right after harvest, but broccoli heads can be stored unwashed in open plastic bags in the refrigerator's crisper drawer for up to one week.

Pests and diseases: The cabbageworm and the cabbage looper are the two primary insect pests of broccoli. The small green caterpillars eat holes in the leaves and are often found hiding but dead in harvested heads when cooked. Aphids and cutworms also attack broccoli seedlings. Woodchucks and rabbits have been known to munch on young seedlings as well. For more about these and other pests, see pages 212 and 213.

Varieties: '**Arcadia**' (69 days) is a good disease-resistant variety for foggy and wet areas such as the Pacific Northwest. Its 8-inch-diameter main head is tightly clustered, causing water to shed and preventing rot. '**DeCicco**' (48 days) is an heirloom producing a small main head but a steady supply of side shoots all season long. The widely adapted '**Green Goliath**' hybrid (55 days) produces a tight, 8-inch-diameter main head that is good for freezing. '**Packman**' (52 days), which bears a 9-inch-diameter main head, is ideal in the South because it produces early and tolerates heat. '**Purple Sprouting**' (125 days) is an Italian heirloom that forms a 3-inch-diameter purple main head that turns green when cooked. In mild-winter areas, such as the Pacific Northwest, it can be sown in fall and overwintered for an early spring harvest. '**Small Miracle Hybrid**' (55 days) grows only 1 foot tall and thus needs to be spaced only 8 inches apart. It makes a small main head and numerous side shoots.

Broccoli raab (*Brassica rapa*), an Italian delicacy related to broccoli, has edible leaves, stems, and heads. '**Spring**' (40 days) is a versatile selection that can be grown as a spring, fall, or overwintering crop.

Brussels sprouts *(Brassica oleracea Gemmifera group)*

Type: Cool-season biennial grown as an annual
Edible part: Sprouts
Typical yield: 8 pounds per 10-foot row
Typical size: 2–3'H×1–2'W

Brussels sprouts look like baby cabbages clustered on a stalk. A single stalk may produce 50 to 100 tiny 1- to 2-inch-wide

'Red Rubine' Brussels sprouts

heads at the union of the leaves and stalk. This rather slow-growing vegetable prefers cool, humid climates and can withstand some frost. Sprouts

taste milder and sweeter when picked after a few frosts and eaten within two days. They're great in casseroles or just sautéed with olive oil or melted butter.

When: Brussels sprouts need a long cool season to mature. Start transplants indoors four to six weeks before your last frost date. Transplant three weeks later.

Brussels sprouts, mature plant

Planting: Amend the soil with a 2- to 3-inch layer of compost or composted manure before planting. Space transplants 18 inches apart in rows 24 inches apart.

Growing: When the plants are 12 inches tall apply a balanced fertilizer such as 5-5-5. Water to keep the crop growing vigorously, especially during the heat of summer. Hand weed the shallow-rooted plants to avoid damaging delicate surface roots, then mulch the bed with a 2- to 4-inch layer of an organic material such as straw, pine straw, or grass clippings. Organic mulches prevent weed growth and conserve soil moisture, and they keep the soil cool so the plants can grow strongly. Stake mature plants to prevent them from blowing over in a storm.

Harvesting: Once sprouts are 1 to 1½ inches in diameter, harvest them with a sharp knife beginning at the bottom of the stalk. First remove the leaf under the sprout, then the sprout. To hasten maturity, remove the growing tip of the plant when the bottom sprouts measure ½ inch in diameter; sprouts should be ready about two weeks later.

Pests and diseases: Cabbageworm and cabbage looper are the two primary insects pests of Brussels sprouts. The small green caterpillars eat holes in the leaves and are often found hiding in harvested sprouts when cooked. Aphids and cutworms also attack seedlings. Woodchucks and rabbits have been known to munch on young seedlings as well. For

Harvesting Brussels sprouts

more about these and other pests, see pages 212 and 213.

Varieties: '**Diablo Hybrid**' (110 days) is a late-maturing variety with sprouts that keep well on the plant once they've matured. '**Jade E Cross Hybrid**' (90 days) produces uniform sprouts all the way up the stalk. '**Oliver Hybrid**' (90 days) is an early variety that's widely adapted. '**Red Rubine**' (95 days) is an heirloom with purplish red sprouts that hold their color even after cooking.

Bulb fennel *(see Florence fennel)*
Bush bean *(see Bean)*

TOP GARDEN CABBAGES*

Name	Size (pounds)	Days to mature	Key features
ROUND HEAD			
'Stonehead Hybrid'	3–4	50	Early with a solid, dense head. Good for storing. Disease-resistant
'Golden Acre'	3–4	58	Early. Disease-resistant
'Dynamo Hybrid'	2	60	Small blue-green head. Great for single serving
'Gonzales Hybrid'	2–3	60	Compact, dense, aqua-green head. Holds well in garden
'Early Jersey Wakefield'	2–3	64	Heirloom, compact, conical head. Good salad variety
'Super Red 80 Hybrid'	2–3	73	Medium-size dark red head. Peppery flavor. Good for storing
'Ruby Ball Hybrid'	3–4	78	Mild, sweet flavor. Holds well in garden. Good for processing
'Danish Ball Head'	5–6	100	Dependable heirloom. Holds well into winter
FLAT HEAD			
'Late Flat Dutch'	3–4	95	Sweet, juicy, flavorful heirloom. Holds well in fall and winter
SAVOY HEAD			
'Savoy Express Hybrid'	1	55	Early mini cabbage. Great for slaw and kraut
'Savoy Ace Hybrid'	3–5	78	Firm, deep green head. Holds well in garden
'Savoy King Hybrid'	5	80	Large head with creamy interior color

*Listed in order of maturity

Cabbage (*Brassica oleracea* Capitata group)

Type: Cool-season biennial grown as an annual
Edible part: Leaves
Typical yield: 15 pounds per 10-foot row
Typical size: 6–12"H×10–30"W

Cabbage is a classic vegetable that's been a staple of European diets for hundreds of years. It's used raw in fresh coleslaw and cooked with corned beef. Early-maturing cabbage tends to be smaller than later types and thus is easier to grow in small gardens. Early-maturing cabbage produces 1- to 3-pound heads, and later cabbages 4- to 8-pound heads.

The variety of cabbage available to home gardeners can be overwhelming. There are early, midseason, and late varieties; round or flat-headed types; varieties with smooth leaves or savoyed (crinkled); and cabbages with red or varying shades of green leaves. It's best to grow a few diverse varieties to extend the growing season and provide for different uses. Round and savoy types are best for salads and sautéing, and flat heads are best for stuffing. Late varieties are considered superior for processing into kraut.

When: For spring crops, sow seeds indoors five to seven weeks before the last frost date, and transplant seedlings into the garden three to five weeks after that date. Direct-sow seeds in summer for fall cabbage. Cabbages grow and mature best when temperatures don't exceed 80°F. The plants can withstand temperatures down to 25°F. In warm areas transplant cabbage in fall for overwintering and harvest in spring.

Planting: Work in a 2-inch layer of well-rotted manure or compost before planting. Sow seeds ½ inch deep and 12 to 24 inches apart in rows about 32 inches apart. Small-head varieties can be planted closer together. In general, closer spacing results in smaller heads.

Growing: Keep seedlings well watered and weeded. Gently weed around cabbage transplants, and put down a 2- to 4-inch layer of organic mulch such as straw, pine straw, or grass clippings. The mulch not only maintains soil moisture and prevents weed growth but also keeps the soil cool.

Apply a high-nitrogen fertilizer about four weeks after transplanting to encourage leaf growth. Avoid fertilizing during head formation;

Red cabbage with flowers

Red cabbage has a purple cast.

'Savoy Ace Hybrid' cabbage

feeding plants at that time results in fast growth that causes the developing head to crack or split.

Harvesting: Once a head is full size and firm when you squeeze it, cut it off at ground level with a sharp knife. Discard the outer leaves and inspect the head for insects before storing it. When a head is mature, a sudden heavy rain may cause it to crack or split, leaving it susceptible to disease.

'Early Jersey Wakefield' cabbage

After the main head is harvested, small cabbage heads, or sprouts, may form at the plant base. You can allow them to grow and form 2- to 4-inch-diameter baby cabbages later in the season.

Unwashed smooth-leaf cabbage heads can be stored for up to two weeks in the refrigerator. Savoy-leaf varieties store for only a few days. Storage varieties can last for months in a root cellar or similar environment (35°F and high humidity).

Pests and diseases: The cabbageworm and the cabbage looper are the two primary insect pests of cabbage. The small green caterpillars eat holes in the leaves and are often found hiding in harvested heads when cooked. Aphids and cutworms also attack seedlings. Woodchucks and rabbits have been known to munch on young seedlings as well.

Diseases such as fusarium wilt (called cabbage yellows), and black rot stunt cabbage and cause them to rot in the garden. Choose resistant varieties and rotate crops by not planting cabbage-family crops in the same ground for three years. For more about these and other pests, see page 194.

> **HERE'S A TIP...**
>
> **Preventing cabbage splitting**
>
>
>
> Mature cabbage heads split when they take up water too quickly. If your heads are ready for picking, but you're not ready to harvest them, you can slow their water uptake by driving a spade into the soil on one side of the plant. This will sever some of the roots, slow the plant's growth, and allow you to wait a few days to harvest.

Cantaloupe (see Melon)
Cardoon (see Artichoke)

Carrot (Daucus carota sativus)

Type: Cool-season biennial grown as an annual
Edible part: Roots
Typical yield: 10 pounds per 10-foot row
Typical size: 6–12"H×6–12"W

This major root crop has undergone a colorful revival. In their native Afganistan, red, white, yellow, and purple carrots are more common than our traditional orange roots. Modern breeders have rediscovered those roots and now there are varieties available in a rainbow of colors.

The sweet roots are loaded with vitamin A and beta-carotene, both known antioxidants and cancer fighters.

Bunches of harvested carrots

Carrots are used raw in salads and juices, cooked in soups and stews, and glazed or curried as side dishes. Cooking carrots makes the calcium more available, another nutritional bonus.

An array of raw purple, orange, yellow, and white carrots on a platter makes an appealing hors d'oeuvre served with dip.

When: Sow carrot seeds two to four weeks before the last frost date or, in warm climates, in late summer and autumn for winter and spring crops. Carrots taste best when grown at temperatures between 60° and 70°F.

Planting: To extend their roots into the soil and grow their best, carrots need a fertile sandy loam that has been worked deeply and raked free of any rocks. If you don't have the right kind of soil, grow carrots in a raised bed, which allow

'Thumbelina' carrot

roots room to grow without being impeded as they would be in more compacted soil For the same reason, carrots grow well in containers filled with soil mix.

Direct-sow seeds, spacing them four per inch in rows 18 inches apart. Carrot seeds are tiny so cover them with only ¼ inch of sifted compost or fine potting soil. Moisten the soil to prevent the seeds from blowing away. Watering

'Purple Haze' carrot

gently, keep the soil moist so it doesn't crust over before the seedlings emerge. Carrot seeds can take up to three weeks to germinate at soil temperatures between 60° and 70°F. In windy, dry areas try placing a floating row cover or shade cloth over the bed to conserve soil moisture until the seeds germinate.

Growing: Amend the soil with a 1- to 2-inch-thick layer of compost before planting. Avoid adding a high-nitrogen fertilizer or fresh manure, either of which will cause excessive top growth and forked roots. Carrots need phosphorus and potassium to grow properly; if a soil test indicates they are needed, apply a complete fertilizer that is high in those nutrients, such as 5-10-10.

Because of their small seed size carrots usually need to be thinned at least twice during the growing season. Once the true leaves

> **HERE'S A TIP...**
>
> **Pelleted seeds**
>
> Since carrot seeds are so small, it's hard to space them correctly. One way to sow properly without having to thin extensively later is to buy pelleted seeds, which are coated with a biodegradable material making each individual seed larger and easier to pick up. The coating protects the seeds from drying out and doesn't affect germination. Sow pelleted seed ½ inch deep.

TOP GARDEN CARROTS*

Name	Length (inches)	Days to mature	Key features
BABY			**Short. Quick to mature. Better than other types in heavy soils and containers**
'Parmex'	1–2	50	Early. Small tops. Round roots
'Thumbelina'	2	65	Silver-dollar size. Good for baking
'Little Fingers'	3–4	65	Sweet. Smooth skin. Small core
CHANTENAY			**Wide shoulders tapered to a point**
'Short 'n Sweet'	4–5	68	Bright orange core. Better than most for heavy soils
'Royal Chantenay'	5–6	70	Strong tops. Good juicing and storage variety
'Red Cored Chantenay'	5–6	70	Heirloom with deep orange color from skin to core
'Kuroda'	6	70	Large yields. Good for juicing and storage
DANVERS			**Tapered and thin**
'Danvers 126'	7–8	70	Heat-resistant. Widely adapted
'Danvers Half Long'	6–8	78	Dark orange. Good in all soils
'Healthmaster Hybrid'	10	130	Grows slowly. One-third more Vitamin A than most carrots
IMPERATOR			**Longer than Danvers**
'Purple Haze Hybrid'	10–12	70	Sweet flavor. Purple skin. Orange core. Color fades when cooked
'Yellowstone Hybrid'	12–14	72	Long yellow roots. Widely adapted
'Imperator 58'	8–9	75	Sweet, tender roots. Grows best in loose soils
'Rainbow Hybrid'	8	75	Roots orange, yellow, or white
NANTES			**Cylindrical shape with blunt end**
'Ithaca Hybrid'	7–8	65	Large roots. Great for juicing
'Sweetness III Hybrid'	6–8	66	Extrasweet flavor. Uniform, deep orange roots
'Scarlet Nantes'	6	70	Crisp, tender, almost coreless roots
'Bolero Hybrid'	7–8	75	Disease-resistant. Good fall and storage variety
'Lunar White'	8	75	Mild flavor. Harvest before frost
'Merida'	7–8	240	For fall planting and overwintering in northern climates

*Listed in order of maturity

form, thin seedlings to 1 to 2 inches apart. Thin again three to four weeks later so that plants are 3 to 4 inches apart.

Carrots are not drought-tolerant. The seeds need constant moisture while germinating. Once the seedlings appear, water deeply every few days as needed, applying 1 inch a week. Carrots don't compete well with weeds so hand weed, especially early in the season, to give the roots room to expand. After weeding, apply an organic mulch such as straw around rows to conserve soil moisture and prevent more weed growth. As the carrots mature cut back on watering or the roots may crack.

If the tops of carrot roots show above ground, cover them with mulch or soil. Exposed carrot roots will turn green and will be off-flavored.

HERE'S A TIP...
Carrots love radishes
Because carrots are so slow to germinate and have a difficult time pushing through crusty soil, try planting radishes with your carrot seeds. Radishes germinate more quickly and are stronger. They break up the soil, easing germination for the carrot seeds. In addition, radishes are ready to harvest much sooner than carrots. As you harvest you'll be creating more space for the carrots.

Harvesting: Begin pulling carrots as soon as they're at full color. This is also a good way to thin rows to give the remaining carrots a chance to grow larger. Small roots tend to be juicier and more tender. If the tops break off when you pull them, use a garden fork to gently pry the roots loose. In northern areas wait until after a heavy frost before digging the rest of the carrots; the cold will increase their sweetness.

Carrots can also be overwintered in the ground. In fall cut off the green tops to about 1 inch tall and mulch the plants with a 6- to 8-inch

Nematodes cause forking

layer of straw. Harvest them in early spring before new growth starts.

Carrot roots will keep for several months in the refrigerator in perforated plastic bags. The roots store better when the leaves are removed. Although usually composted, the leaves are edible and can be used in soups and stews.

Pests and diseases: Carrot roots can be damaged due to several causes. Too much nitrogen in the soil causes hairy roots. Forked or deformed roots can be caused by overwatering, rocks or debris in the soil, or insect damage. Nematodes cause roots to fork, and carrot rust fly larvae can cause holes in and rotting of roots. Cover carrots with a floating row cover to prevent the rust fly from laying eggs. Rabbits and woodchucks love to eat the tender tops. Viral diseases such as aster yellows can cause poor color and bitter taste. Choose disease-resistant varieties and rotate crops.

Cauliflower (Brassica oleracea, Botrytis group)

Type: Cool-season biennial, grown as an annual
Edible part: Pre-flower "curds"
Typical yield: 10 pounds per 10-foot row
Typical size: 8–24"H×18–36"W

Cauliflower is more finicky to grow than its cousin broccoli. Both originate from southern Europe and require similar growing conditions. However, cauliflower produces only one head per plant. If you grow a crop under the proper conditions and give it consistent moisture, your reward will be beautiful heads.

Even though cauliflower may have its challenges, the effort of growing them is worth it. The crisp heads are delicious eaten raw with dips or steamed, boiled, or sautéed in a variety of dishes. Heads come in a

Cauliflower ready to harvest

variety of colors beside the traditional white, such as purple, gold, and green.

When: The crop grows best when it matures during cool weather no hotter than 70°F. In most regions it's best grown as a fall crop. Sow seeds or transplant seedlings 90 days before your first fall frost date. In cool-summer areas, you can also transplant seedlings in spring two to three weeks before your last frost. In mild-winter areas, such as the Pacific Northwest and the Gulf Coast, plant in fall for overwintering and maturing in early spring.

Planting: Work in a 2-inch layer of well-rotted manure or compost before planting. Sow seeds ½ inch deep and 24 inches apart in rows 3 feet apart. Start seedlings indoors four to six weeks before transplanting into the garden. Transplant seedlings once they have five leaves.

Growing: Cauliflower needs a consistent supply of fertilizer and water to grow uninterrupted to maturity. Apply a complete fertilizer such as 5-5-5 when transplanting and a high-nitrogen one month later. Keep the soil moist by watering as needed, providing at least 1 inch of water per week. Avoid damaging the shallow roots by hand weeding carefully. Mulch with an organic material such as straw or grass clippings to conserve soil moisture and prevent weed growth.

Some new varieties are self-blanching, meaning the outer or wrapper leaves naturally cover the white head. If growing

an older variety, blanch the white heads once they are 2 inches in diameter and start showing through the leaves. Blanching ensures a bright white head and a mild flavor. To blanch, wrap the long outer leaves

Wrap and tie leaves to blanch developing heads.

over the head and hold them together with twine, clothespins, or rubber bands. Varieties with colored heads don't require blanching.

Harvesting: Pick a head when it is 6 to 8 inches in diameter, about 10 days after blanching. When curds, start separating and have a coarse, ricelike appearance, the head is past its peak. Use a sharp knife to harvest mature heads, cutting below the inner leaves. Harvested cauliflower will keep for a few weeks in high humidity at 35°F. If you plan to store the entire head, cut the cauliflower below the outer leaves and keep them wrapped around the head for protection.

Pests and diseases: Cabbageworm and cabbage looper are the two primary insects pests of cauliflower. The small green caterpillars damage plants by eating holes in the leaves; you might find them hiding in harvested heads. Aphids and cutworms also attack seedlings. Woodchucks and rabbits have been known to munch on young seedlings as well.

Diseases such as fusarium wilt (called cabbage yellows), and black rot infect cauliflower, stunting them or causing them to rot. Choose resistant varieties and rotate crops by not planting cabbage-family crops in the same ground for three years. For more about these diseases and other pests, see page 194.

Varieties: **'Cheddar Hybrid'** (68 days) produces orange

'Graffiti Hybrid' cauliflower

heads with 25 times the beta-carotene of white cauliflower. The color holds during cooking. **'Graffiti Hybrid'** (80 days) produces medium-size bright purple heads that hold their color when cooked with 1 teaspoon of vinegar added to the water.

'Fremont Hybrid' (70 days) is a reliable self-blanching white variety that can grow under adverse conditions. **'Snow Crown Hybrid'** (60 days) is a standard white variety that's early maturing, widely adapted, and easy to grow. **'Veronica Hybrid'** (78 days), a romanesco-type cauliflower, produces unusual spiky lime green heads with a mild, nutty flavor.

'Veronica Hybrid' cauliflower

Celery (Apium graveolens dulce)

Type: Cool-season biennial grown as an annual
Edible part: Leafstalks, leaves
Typical yield: 18 stalks per 10-foot row
Typical size: 24"H×12"W

Celery, red variety

Celery is a long-season vegetable (four months to mature) that grows best in areas with moderate summer and winter temperatures. Although not a common home garden vegetable, freshly grown celery stalks are delicious raw in salads and appetizers or cooked in sauces, soups, and stews. Consisting mostly of water, celery is a crunchy, low-calorie treat.

When: Sow seeds indoors 10 to 12 weeks before your last spring frost date. Transplant the seedlings after your last frost date.

Planting: Soak the seeds overnight to hasten germination, and sow indoors in a flat or pots. When the plants are 2 inches tall, transplant them into individual pots or in flats, spacing the seedlings at least 2 inches apart. Amend the soil with a 1- to 2-inch layer of compost. Transplant 4- to 6-inch-tall seedlings into the garden, setting them 12 inches apart in rows 18 inches apart. The temperature must be above 55°F because seedlings exposed to lower temperatures for a week or more will bolt. Celery grows best with temperatures between 55° and 70°F.

Growing: Fertilize new transplants with a balanced fertilizer such as 5-5-5; sidedress monthly. Keep the soil evenly moist by applying an inch or more of water each week. Dry soil causes celery stalks to crack. Mulch with an organic material such as straw or grass clippings to conserve soil moisture and prevent weed growth.

Harvesting: Start harvesting individual stalks when they reach about 10 inches tall, cutting them to the base of the plant with a sharp knife. You can also harvest the entire plant at one time.

Blanching the stalks gives them a milder flavor. Wrap the nearly mature stems with any convenient light blocking cylinder. Then mound 6 inches of soil around the base of the plant. Harvest two to three weeks later.

Store celery in a refrigerator for up to two weeks.

Blanching celery stalks

Pests and diseases: Aphids and slugs may feed on young transplants and stunt their growth. Leaf blights and root rot can attack plants especially during wet periods.

Varieties: **'Conquistador'** (80 days) is an early-maturing variety that grows well under drought and heat stress. **'Cutting Celery'** (80 days) is grown for its flavorful leaves, not stems. **'Giant Red Reselection'** (120 days) offers improved color and hardiness. **'Golden Self-Blanching'** (110 days) is a unique pale yellow variety with a mild flavor. **'Utah 52-70 Improved'** (90 days) is a popular dark green celery with a compact habit. **'Ventura'** (100 days) is a widely grown variety that's disease-resistant and adaptable.

Celery root, celeriac (Apium graveolens rapaceum)

Type: Cool-season biennial grown as an annual
Edible part: Roots
Typical yield: 10 pounds per 10-foot row
Typical size: 12"H×12"W

Harvesting celeriac

This celery relative is grown for its tasty roots. Celeriac, also called celery root, is actually the enlarged knob of a stem that grows belowground. Buff to brownish on the outside, it is firm, white, crunchy, and delicious on the inside. Peel the root first and eat it raw or blanched in celery remoulade or cooked in soups and stews.

When: In cool-summer areas, sow seeds indoors 8 to 12 weeks before your last frost date. Transplant to the garden two weeks before the last frost. In mild-winter areas, sow indoors in summer and transplant in early fall.

Planting: Amend the soil with a 2- to 3-inch layer of compost. The plants need moist, fertile, well-drained soil. Seeding information is the same as that for celery. When the soil temperature is above 55°F, set the transplants 4 to 6 inches apart in rows 18 to 24 inches apart. Celeriac needs a long, cool growing season to form roots.

Growing: Keep the soil evenly moist with regular watering. Mulch with an organic material such as straw or grass clippings to conserve soil moisture, keep the soil cool, and prevent weed growth. Fertilize monthly with a balanced product such as 5-5-5.

Harvesting: Start harvesting roots when they are 2 to 3 inches in diameter. The best flavor develops after a frost. Pull the whole plant and discard the leafy tops. Peel the knobby exterior and use the firm white flesh.

Celeriac

Celeriac keeps well for up to four months in conditions similar to a root cellar—35°F and high humidity. It can also be frozen in the ground but in that case must be cooked soon after harvest.

Pests and diseases: Slugs can attack the leafy greens, slowing plant growth. Carrot rust fly larvae can cause holes in the roots. Cover plants with floating row covers to prevent the rust fly from laying eggs.

Varieties: 'Brilliant' (110 days) produces baseball-sized roots with a nutty flavor. **'Diamant'** (110 days) produces dense large roots that resist diseases.

Chard, Swiss chard (Beta vulgaris cicla)

Type: Cool-season biennial grown as an annual
Edible part: Leaves, leafstalks
Typical yield: 8–12 pounds leaves and stalks per 10-foot row
Typical size: 6–20"H×10–30"W

'Bright Lights' chard

Chard has come of age. Not only is it a versatile green eaten raw in salads and cooked in a variety of dishes, but also newer selections with colorful leafstalks and veins are beautiful additions to a flower, vegetable, or container garden.

Similar to its relative the beet, chard hails from southern Europe. The only real difference between the two is that chard doesn't form an edible root. You can use chard much as you do spinach, but unlike spinach chard doesn't bolt in the heat. This feature alone makes it an excellent summer green.

When: Plants tolerate summer heat and light frost. Sow seeds after danger of spring frost has passed.

Planting: Amend the soil with a 1- to 2-inch layer of compost. Chard grows best in soil that is rich, well drained, and slightly alkaline. Soak seeds overnight to hasten germination. Sow seeds ½ inch deep and 2 inches apart in rows 2 feet apart. Like beets, Swiss chard seeds are actually a dried fruit that produces multiple seedlings. Thin plants to 12 inches apart, using the seedlings for soups and salads.

Growing: When the plants are 6 inches tall, fertilize them with a liquid high-nitrogen fertilizer; apply it when watering. Sidedress plants every six weeks. Keep the soil evenly moist and weed free, mulching with an organic material such as straw or grass

Harvesting outer shoots of chard

clippings to conserve soil moisture, keep the soil cool, and prevent weed growth.

Harvesting: Chard can be harvested throughout the summer. Start picking outer leaves when plants are about 5 inches tall. Removing the outer leaves encourages the development of new tender inner leaves. Cut the whole plant at ground level before a hard freeze.

Pests and diseases: Aphids, flea beetles, and leaf miners attack young chard leaves, causing holes and lowering yields. Remove and destroy damaged leaves. See page 208 for more about these pests.

'Fordhook Giant' chard

Varieties: 'Bright Lights' (55 days) produces stems and leaf veins of many colors, including gold, pink, orange, purple, red, and white, with slightly ruffled mild-tasting leaves. It's slightly less frost-tolerant than other chards. **'Bright Yellow'** (57 days) produces yellow stems and veins on deep green leaves. **'Fordhook Giant'** (50 days) bears large ruffled leaves with white ribs. **'Rhubarb'** (59 days) produces dark green, red-veined leaves on deep red stems.

Chayote (see Squash)

Chicory, endive, escarole, radicchio
(Cichorium endivia and C. intybus)

Type: Cool-season annual and perennial
Edible part: Leaves
Typical yield: 5 pounds per 10-foot row
Typical size: 3–9"H×6–18"W

'Chioggia Red' radicchio (left) and Belgian endive

These European gourmet salad greens have a fuller, more distinct flavor than lettuce. The unique crunchy texture and slightly bitter flavor of these greens make them the perfect complement to other milder salad greens.

Endive and escarole are annuals, while radicchio and chicory are considered perennials. The difference between endive and escarole is in the leaves: Endive produces deeply cut, curled leaves; escarole has broad, thin, smooth ones. Endive has a mild flavor and is often found in mesclun mixes. Escarole has a reputation for being slightly bitter, but grown under cool conditions the flavor is milder, adding a

'Neos' endive

'Early Treviso' radicchio

distinctive flavor to salads. Young greens of either can be eaten raw in salads. Allow the plant to mature and blanch the loose heads to create a milder flavor. They are also delicious in soups. Radicchio forms a head and can be eaten like leaf lettuce or allowed to mature into a tight, cabbagelike head of red leaves with white veins.

When: These cool-season greens grow best planted in spring, 3 to 4 weeks before the last frost date, or in midsummer, 15 weeks before the first fall frost. In warm areas you can plant an overwintering crop in fall to be harvested in early spring.

Planting: Amend the soil with a 1- to 2-inch layer of compost. In spring direct-sow seeds ¼ inch deep in rows 18 inches apart. For a quicker start, sow seeds indoors four to six weeks before the last frost date to transplant into the garden two to three weeks later. Chicory grows best with temperatures between 60° and 70°F. In cool-summer areas with nighttime temperatures that dip below 60°F, sow seeds every few weeks for a continuous harvest all summer and fall. Thin to 7 to 8 inches between plants.

Growing: Give chicory the same sort of care you give lettuce. Keep plants well watered for continuous growth. Hand weed and mulch with an organic material such as straw or grass clippings to conserve soil moisture, keep the soil cool, and prevent further weed growth. Apply a liquid high-nitrogen fertilizer four weeks after transplanting.

Escarole

For summer-maturing plants blanch the leaves to avoid bitterness. Set an upside-down pot over each plant, blocking the drainage holes with pebbles, for two weeks before harvest. Another option is to pull the outside leaves over the smaller inner leaves and hold them in place with a loose rubber band.

Harvesting: Pick young endive and escarole leaves for use in salads and mesclun mixes. Harvest heads about 45 days after planting for direct-sown baby varieties and 60 to 100 days for mature heads. Collect leaves from the outside inward or harvest the whole head by cutting at the base. You can store unwashed endive and escarole in the refrigerator for a week.

Harvest radicchio about 80 to 85 days after planting when heads are firm, similar to iceberg lettuce. Harvest mature heads promptly or they will develop a tough texture and bitter flavor. You can keep radicchio in a perforated plastic bag in the refrigerator for two to three weeks.

Pests and diseases: Chicory, endive, escarole, and radicchio are occasionally troubled by aphids and slugs. Rabbits and woodchucks love the tender lettucelike greens.

Damping off fungal disease affects young seedlings, causing them to wilt and die. To prevent the disease, grow them in raised beds and don't overwater. Keep plants adequately thinned to prevent other rot diseases such as botrytis and mildew. Grow disease-resistant varieties to avoid tip or leaf burn.

Varieties: Endive and escarole: 'Batavian Full-Heart' escarole (85 days) has broad, smooth outer leaves with a closely bunched creamy yellow center. 'Bianca Ricci' endive (35 days) is widely adapted to heat and cold; the light green head is made up of leaves with a pink base. 'Neos' endive (45 days) is a Frisee type with an extrafrilly self-blanching compact head and a mild bittersweet flavor.

Radicchio: 'Chioggia Red Preco No. 1' (60 days), an early radicchio with large round purple-red heads, is bolt-tolerant. 'Early Treviso' (85 days) is a good overwintering variety with a long compact head that turns deep red with cool weather. 'Palla Rossa' (85 days) forms a medium-size round head that is good for summer and fall harvests. 'Indigo' hybrid (65 days) produces a medium-size round burgundy head; it is adapted to heat and cold, making it good for spring, summer, and fall production.

Endive

Chihli cabbage (see Chinese cabbage)

Chinese cabbage (*Brassica rapa* Chinensis group, and *B. r.* Pekinensis group)

Type: Cool-season biennial grown as an annual
Edible part: Leaves
Typical yield: 10 pounds per 10-foot row
Typical size: 9–18"H×4–9"W

'Minuet Hybrid' Chinese cabbage

Chinese cabbage is a delicious peppery Asian alternative to traditional cabbage. It's more closely related to turnips than to cabbage. It forms a head with wide green leaves and white stems. Use its thin, crunchy lettucelike leaves shredded fresh in salads or stir-fried or steamed for greens. There are two types of Chinese cabbage, napa and chihli. Napa types are stubby and barrel shaped with tightly packed heads. Chihli types form tall narrow heads with thick white stalks and dark green leaves. Chinese cabbage thrives in a cool (60°F to 70°F), humid climate.

When: For a spring crop, sow seeds indoors four weeks before the last frost date. Transplant into the garden after your last frost date. For a fall crop, direct-sow seeds in summer to mature during the cooler autumn weather.

Planting: Work in a 2-inch layer of well-rotted manure or compost before planting. Sow indoors in 1-inch pots and transplant into the garden once seedlings produce about 10 leaves. Protect young seedlings from cold since transplants bolt when exposed to frost or several consecutive days of temperatures below 50°F. If direct seeding, plant three seeds per hole, every 12 to 18 inches in rows that are about

Chinese cabbage 'Joi Choi Hybrid'

18 inches apart for chihli types and 24 inches apart for napa types. Thin each trio of seedlings, keeping the single most vigorous one in each group. Space transplants a similar distance apart.

Growing: Provide 1 inch of water each week and fertilize with a high-nitrogen liquid plant food one month after transplanting. Weed and mulch as you would for cabbage and broccoli. Hot, dry weather causes Chinese cabbage to bolt and send up a flower stalk, making the head inedible.

Harvesting: With a sharp knife, cut mature heads when they are compact and firm. For fall crops harvest before a frost. Chinese cabbage stores in the refrigerator for up to two weeks.

Pests and diseases: Aphids and flea beetles are the primary insect pests of Chinese cabbage, causing holes in the seedlings and stunting plants.

Varieties: Napa types: 'Lettucy Hybrid' (45 days) produces a 3-pound ruffled head with a sweet-tangy flavor. This popular salad variety is often used in place of romaine lettuce. **'Minuet Hybrid'** (48 days) is an early, slow-to-bolt, disease-resistant variety that has dark green leaves, a pale yellow interior, and a sweet taste.

Chihli types: 'Jade Pagoda Hybrid' (72 days) grows 16 inches tall and produces slow-bolting, creamy yellow hearts. **'Joi Choi Hybrid'** (50 days) is a 1-foot-tall, thick white-stalk variety that's slow to bolt and tolerates heat and cold. **'Mei Qing Choy Hybrid'** (45 days) has flat thick, light green stems that, even when mature, are only 6 inches tall.

Chocho (*see Squash*)

Collards (*Brassica oleracea* Acephala group)

Type: Cool-season biennial grown as an annual
Edible part: Leaves
Typical yield: 8–10 pounds per 10-foot row
Typical size: 24–36"H×18–36"W

This cabbage-family crop is a stalwart in many southern gardens, although it adapts well to most climates. Collards are cabbages that don't form heads. Unlike other more tender greens, collards stalks and leaves are tough and best eaten cooked. Tear the leaves off the stems and shred them by hand before sautéing them or adding them to soups and stews. They are a favorite mixed with southern peas and bacon. The leaves are highly nutritious, loaded with vitamins A and C as well as potassium, iron, and calcium.

When: For a summer crop sow seeds four weeks before the last frost date. For a fall crop sow three months before the first fall frost.

Planting: Amend the soil with a 1- to 2-inch layer of compost. Sow seeds ½ inch deep and 1 inch apart or transplant 3-inch-tall seedlings 6 to 8 inches apart. Grow collards in rows 2 to 3 feet apart.

Growing: Apply a liquid high-nitrogen fertilizer when plants are 4 to 6 inches tall. Although collards can tolerate drought, they grow best in moist soil, so water at least 1 inch per week or as needed. Mulch with an organic material such as straw or grass clippings to conserve soil moisture, keep the soil cool, and prevent weed growth.

Harvesting: Pick leaves as needed, taking outer leaves of the plant first. The top bud is a delicacy, but leave it if you want the plant to continue making leaves. You can also harvest the whole plant at once, 50 to 70 days after seeding, and store it in the crisper drawer of your refrigerator for up to a week.

Pests and diseases: Aphids as well as the cabbageworm and the cabbage looper—the same pests that attack cabbage—feed on the leaves, making holes in them. For more about these pests, see page 208.

Varieties: 'Champion' (60 days) is a popular, compact Vates-type variety that's slow to bolt. **'Flash Hybrid'** (78 days) is known for high yields of smooth leaves and is also slow to bolt. **'Georgia'** (60 days) produces sweet ruffled leaves.

Collards

Corn *(Zea mays)*

Type: Warm-season annual
Edible part: Seeds
Typical yield: 12 pounds per 10-foot row
Typical size: 3–8'H×1–3'W

'Silver Queen' corn

Fresh corn on the cob is as American as apple pie and baseball. Eating this Native American crop freshly picked from your backyard garden transforms a good flavor into greatness. For years the key to great corn on the cob was cooking the ears immediately after harvesting while they were still sweet. You would wait until the last possible moment to harvest and then steam the ears to perfection. With the advent of new supersweet varieties that hold their sweetness longer after harvest, the pressure is off.

Newer varieties are productive and shorter, so they're perfect for small gardens. If you choose early, midseason, and late varieties, you can harvest sweet corn from midsummer until frost.

Harvesting bicolor corn

'Bonus' baby corn

Although steamed corn on the cob is most common, corn can also be roasted, made into soup, sautéed, and baked in breads. You can also make creamed corn or use kernels in fritters, corn pudding, salads, salsas, casseroles, and succotash. Grind dried kernels into cornmeal, grits, and flour. It's the quintessential versatile vegetable.

Ornamental corn, baby corn, and popcorn are grown the same as sweet corn. The big difference among them is in harvesting and storage.

When: Direct-sow seeds two weeks after the last frost date once the soil has warmed to at least 60°F; 90° to 95°F soil temperatures are optimum.

Planting: Grow corn in well-drained, loose, slightly acidic soil. Corn is in the grass family and needs high amounts of nitrogen to grow best, which is why it's ideal to plant in an area where nitrogen-fixing legumes such as beans were grown the year before.

Sow seeds ½ inch deep in moist soil or 1 to 1½ inches deep in dry soil. Space seeds 8 inches apart when planting early varieties, which are smaller, and in small gardens, where you should fudge on the ideal spacing. Otherwise thin seeds to 12 inches apart. If growing corn in heavy, cool soils, consider buying seeds that were treated with a disease control product to prevent them from rotting before they germinate.

Although the traditional method of planting corn is in hills or mounds of three to five plants, farmers usually plant corn in rows. One reason is that corn is wind-pollinated. Each corn kernel in the ear needs to be pollinated by pollen from tassels. Wind blows the pollen onto the ear's silk to pollinate each kernel. If the rows are too far apart, not all the kernels get pollinated and your corn ears look as if they're missing some teeth.

To ensure proper pollination so that the ears are full of kernels, grow corn in short rows or blocks. A block consists of at least four rows, each 10 to 20 feet long. Space the rows 2 feet apart with walkways between blocks that are 3 to 4 feet apart so you can easily harvest.

Block planting also helps prevent shallow-rooted corn from falling over in high winds. If a few seeds in a block fail to germinate, don't reseed: The older plants will shade the

---

HERE'S A TIP...

Presprout seeds for an early crop

If you're growing corn in heavy clay soil in a cool area, presprout seeds to hasten germination. Soak them overnight in warm water, drain, and place them in a partially open clear plastic bag in a warm location. Rinse the seeds daily. In four to five days the corn will start to sprout. Carefully plant the sprouted seeds in a 4- to 6-inch-deep furrow; cover them with an inch of soil.

Various varieties of popcorn

Squeezing a kernel to test ripeness

younger ones, and pollination won't occur at the same time.

Blocks of varieties maturing at the same time should be separated from each other to avoid cross-pollination. Separation is particularly important for supersweet varieties that can cross with standard varieties and become starchy and less sweet. Either plant varieties that mature at different times or plant supersweet varieties at least 250 feet away from the main corn planting. If yellow varieties are crossed with white ones, the kernels will turn yellow.

Growing: Corn grows quickly during periods of hot, humid weather. It needs a rich, fertile soil, so work in a 3- to 4-inch-thick layer of compost or composted manure before planting. When the plants are knee-high and again when the silks form, use a high-nitrogen fertilizer, applying about 1 pound per 100 square feet. A sign of nitrogen deficiency is yellowing corn leaves. However, too much nitrogen fertilizer can cause dark green leaves and plants more likely to lodge, or fall over in the wind.

Keep corn blocks weeded by hilling the soil around the base of each plant when it is 8 inches tall. Hilling not only kills weeds, but also it helps hold the tall corn plants upright during wind storms.

Keep the soil evenly moist by applying 1 to 2 inches of water a week as needed. To prevent diseases water in the morning so the leaves dry before evening. Water to a depth of at least 6 inches; light sprinklings only encourage shallow-rooted plants that are more likely to blow over. Thin and curled corn leaves are signs of water stress. The most critical periods for watering are during pollination and ear filling. High temperatures or lack of water during pollination can result in small ears with missing kernels and poor development of the ear tips. After weeding mulch with a 3- to 5-inch layer of straw to conserve moisture and prevent further weed growth.

If suckers or sprouts form at the base of a plant, leave them. Removing suckers won't increase ear size or quality.

Harvesting: Most corn varieties yield one or two good-size ears per stalk, and some heirlooms produce two or three per stalk. Sweet corn is ready to harvest roughly 20 days after the first silks appear, about 60 to 95 days after planting, when ears are in the milk stage—when a squeezed kernel squirts a milky liquid. Pick frequently because this stage lasts less than a week. The kernels will be formed but not mature, the ears will feel firm, and the silks will start to dry and turn brown. At this point, peel back the husk to see if the kernels are plump and the juice in them milky. Immature kernels are watery, and overmature ones are tough and doughy. With a sharp downward twisting movement, break the shank or stem below the ear without breaking the parent stalk.

Harvest in the morning while it's still cool. Either cook and eat the ears immediately or prepare them for storage by cooling the ears quickly to as close to 32°F as possible. Even supersweet varieties will become starchy if stored at higher temperatures.

Baby corn, popular in many Asian dishes, can be cultivated in a home garden. It's grown much like regular sweet corn, except that the ears should be harvested one or two days after the silks emerge, when the cobs are only 2 to 4 inches long.

Harvest popcorn and ornamental corn once the stalks and husks are brown and dry. In rainy regions cut the stalks when the corn is mature, and hang them to dry in a well-ventilated place away from rain and animals. Remove the husks once they are dry, and cure the popcorn cobs either in the sun or in the oven at the lowest setting. Store the dried popcorn cobs whole or strip the kernels off; keep them in airtight containers in cool storage.

Pests and diseases: Corn is attacked by many insect

Mound soil around seedlings to increase wind resistance.

HERE'S A TIP...

Growing corn in a small space

Although corn grows best in a large space, you can harvest a crop from a small raised bed or a large container. Select early dwarf varieties such as 'Earlivee'. Fill the bed or container with compost amended with potting soil. Plant seeds 4 inches apart and 1 inch deep. Thin the seedlings to 8 inches apart. Plan on at least 12 cornstalks to ensure pollination.

Keep the raised bed or container well watered, and apply a liquid fertilizer once a week. When the tassels form, gently shake them to be sure the pollen lands on the developing ears.

TOP GARDEN CORN*

Name	Ear size (inches)	Days to mature	Key features
STANDARD HYBRIDS AND HEIRLOOMS (SU)			
Yellow			
'Earlivee Hybrid'	6–7	60	Early and vigorous. 5' tall. Great for small gardens
'Early Sunglow Hybrid'	7	63	Early. 4' tall. Great for small gardens
'Golden Bantam'	5–7	85	Heirloom, small-space variety
White			
'Stowell's Evergreen'	8–9	90	Heirloom. Produces 2–3 ears per stalk
'Country Gentleman'	7	90	Heirloom. 8' tall. Creamy texture
'Silver Queen Hybrid'	7–8	92	Considered one of the best-tasting corns ever
Bicolor			
'Sugar and Gold Hybrid'	8	75	Good for canning and freezing as well as fresh eating
'Honey 'n Cream Hybrid'	7–8	78	Fat ears on a 6' stalk
Black/Blue			
'Black Aztec'	8	80	Heirloom Southwest variety. Drought-tolerant. Kernels turn black when mature
SUGAR-ENHANCED (SE)			
Yellow			
'Sugar Buns Hybrid'	5–7	72	Sweet flavor and creamy texture
'Bodacious Hybrid'	8	75	Dependable. Disease-resistant. Good for canning
'Kandy Korn Hybrid'	8	81	Red-hued leaves. Creamy, juicy ears
White			
'Sugar Pearl Hybrid'	7–8	72	Tapered ears with good tip cover. Germinates well in cool soils
'Silver King Hybrid'	7–8	82	Good disease tolerance. Good Southeast variety
Bicolor			
'Quickie Hybrid'	7	68	Early maturing. Tolerant of cool soil
'Peaches 'n Cream Hybrid'	8–9	70	Small, tender kernels
'Serendipity Hybrid'	8	82	Triplesweet variety with good balance of sweet flavor and traditional flavor

Opened corn husk reveals corn earworm feeding

and animal pests. Corn earworm adults lay eggs on corn silks; the eggs hatch and the young caterpillars tunnel into the ears, producing wormy, rotted tips. Corn borer larvae tunnel into cornstalks, causing them to snap. Japanese beetles feed on corn foliage and the pollen on the tassels, resulting in a weakened plants and poor pollination. Corn rootworm larvae feed on the roots of corn plants, weakening and stunting them; rotate crops to avoid this pest.

Birds and raccoons are the two most notorious animal pests of corn. Birds will pull up young corn sprouts to eat the seeds. They will also sit on the maturing ears and peck away at the tender kernels. Cover young seedlings with a floating row cover to prevent bird damage. Cover a small block planting with bird netting to prevent birds from eating the ears.

Raccoons have an uncanny ability to know just when the corn is ready to pick. Invariably they attack your garden the night before you're going to harvest your first crop. Raccoons are messy eaters, often taking small bites from many ears of corn, ruining them all. An electric fence can keep them away. In small plantings consider covering individual ears with a paper bag after pollination to thwart this animal.

Name	Ear size (inches)	Days to mature	Key features
Red			
'Ruby Queen Hybrid'	8	75	Holds ruby red kernel color when cooked
SUPERSWEET (SH2)			
Yellow			
'Northern X-tra Sweet Hybrid'	8–9	71	Early yet productive
'Illini X-tra Sweet'	8	85	8' plant. Ears freeze well
White			
'X-tra Tender Hybrid'	7–8	76	Tender kernels. Sturdy 5–6' plant
'How Sweet It Is Hybrid'	8–9	87	Very sweet, tender kernels
Bicolor			
'Mirai Hybrid'	7–8	71	Sweet but not too sugary. 7' tall. Stores up to 6 weeks in refrigerator. Form with all-yellow kernels available
'Honey 'n Pearl Hybrid'	9	76	Early. Tender kernels. Tight husks resist earworms
Baby corn			
'Bonus Hybrid'	2–4	32	Produces 3–5 ears per 5' stalk
Popcorn			
'Tom Thumb'	3–4	85	Heirloom. 3' tall. Good ornamental
'Japanese Hulless'	4	95	Heirloom. Hulls almost disappear when popped
'Strawberry'	2	100	Attractive, small red ears. Kernels turn white when popped
'Robust 128YH Hybrid'	7–8	112	8' tall. Large, tender ears
Ornamental corn			
'Painted Mountain'	6–7	85	Multicolor ears for fall decorations, for easy grinding, and for eating fresh, parched (roasted), or in hominy grits
'Wampum'	7–8	107	Small kernels in variety of colors. Maroon and white husks
'Red Stalker'	7–8	107	Purple, burgundy, cream, and gold kernels. Burgundy stalks

Listed according to days to maturity

Diseases such as bacterial wilt, leaf blight, and mosaic virus can infect corn plantings as well. The best control is to select disease-resistant varieties and reduce attacks by insects such as aphids, which can transmit diseases. See page 208 for more about controlling aphids.

Varieties: Home gardeners can choose from many varieties of corn, including ones with white, yellow, bicolor, red, and even blue kernels. Modern sweet corn is grouped as standard (su), sugar-enhanced (se), or supersweet (sh2). Standard and heirloom varieties are typically strong-growing plants with a robust corn flavor but a variable sweetness that diminishes quickly after harvest. Sugar-enhanced varieties are sweeter, creamier, and more tender than standard varieties, but they still have the strong growth habit. Supersweet varieties are sweet and tender and hold their sweetness after harvest. However, they require warmer (65°F) and moister soils to germinate well. If different varieties of supersweet corn cross-pollinate, the quality of the corn is affected, and if they cross-pollinate with a non-supersweet, supersweet varieties lose their sweetness and become starchy and tough.

Triplesweet is a new class of supersweet corn that is 75 percent sugar-enhanced (se) and 25 percent supersweet (sh2). This class combines the strong growth of a sugar-enhanced variety with the extra sweetness of the supersweets.

Popcorn varieties have small white, yellow, or red kernels. Ornamental corn produces ears in a rainbow of colors depending on the variety.

Ornamental corn used decoratively

Cornsalad *(see Mâche, Mesclun mix)*
Cowpea *(see Bean)*

Cucumber *(Cucumis sativus)*

Type: Warm-season annual
Edible part: Fruits
Typical yield: 12 pounds per 10-foot row
Typical size: 12–72"H×12–18"W

This native of India has been in cultivation for more than 3,000 years for good reason: It produces quickly and abundantly in the garden and in containers, providing bushels of crunchy, refreshing fruits. The many types of cucumbers are grouped as slicers or picklers. A new group of slicers is especially adapted to greenhouse or plastic-tunnel growing. All slicers are long and thin and are best eaten fresh in salads and cold soups. Picklers, which are short with more pronounced spines or bumps on their skin, are most often used preserved but can be eaten fresh too.

When: Direct-sow seeds after spring frosts are past and the soil has warmed to 70°F. In warm climates sow two or three successive crops until midsummer for an early fall harvest. The optimum soil temperature range for cucumber germination is 65°F to 95°F.

Planting: Cucumbers grow best in highly fertile soils; before planting, amend the bed with a 2- to 3-inch layer of compost or composted manure. The plants do poorly in heavy clay and wet soils. If your soil is heavy clay, grow the crop in a raised bed. Sow seeds ½ inch deep and 2 inches apart in rows 4 feet apart. Or sow four to six seeds per hill and thin to three plants per hill after the true leaves emerge. In cool-summer areas cover cucumber beds with black plastic mulch two weeks before planting to warm the soil. Start seedlings indoors four weeks before the last frost date. Transplant the seedlings into rows, poking holes in the plastic according to the spacing needs. Bush varieties such as 'Salad Bush' and 'Bush Pickle' produce vines only a few feet long and are well suited to container growing.

Growing: Young cucumber plants are susceptible to cold winds. In cool areas consider protecting seedlings with a floating row cover until the weather has warmed. Row covers not only shield the tender plants from low temperatures, but also they provide some defense against insects. Remove the row covers before the cucumbers flower so that bees can reach and pollinate the blossoms.

If you haven't laid black plastic mulch to warm the soil, try mulching the cucumber beds with plastic or straw to

'Bush Pickle' cucumber

conserve soil moisture and keep weeds at bay. Weed the beds while the plants are still young, being careful not to disturb the shallow root system.

Trailing cucumber types can vine up to 5 feet. In a small-space garden, grow bush varieties or perhaps build a trellis for the vines to climb. Not only will a trellis reduce the space required for growing a vine, but the fruits will less likely be blemished or curled as they hang down from the support.

Like most vegetables, cucumbers grow fast and thus need a steady supply of water and fertilizer to produce the best crops. Bitterness is most often caused by water stress. Watering is most critical during blossoming and fruiting. In general, cucumbers need 1 inch of water a week, but during periods of heat or drought they may need double that amount. If using overhead sprinklers, run them early in the day to reduce water evaporation, reduce disease by letting the leaves dry before evening, and allow for bees to pollinate the flowers. One week after blossoming starts and again three weeks later, apply a balanced fertilizer such as 5-5-5 as a sidedressing. However, do not overfertilize since too much food can encourage excessive vine growth and delay fruiting.

Harvesting: Once cucumber fruits set they can grow quickly, especially during periods of warm, humid weather. You'll need to check the plants every few days to keep up with the harvest. The more you harvest, the more the plants will produce. Oversize fruits tend to be seedy and bitter.

Use scissors or pruning shears to cut the stems ¼ inch from the fruits. Start harvesting slicing cucumbers when the fruits are between 6 and 9 inches long. Harvest pickling cucumbers when the fruits are less than 2 inches in diameter and about 2 to 4 inches long. Some Asian and greenhouse varieties can be harvested when they are up to 1 foot long. Cucumbers can be stored for up to two weeks in the refrigerator.

Pests and diseases: The most troublesome insect pest of cucumbers is the striped or spotted cucumber

Cucumber, pickling variety

HERE'S A TIP...

Training cucumbers to a trellis
For a top-notch crop of cucumbers, train the vine to a trellis. Place posts 5 to 10 feet apart and string wires tightly between them. Fruits supported on a trellis are less susceptible to pests and diseases and have fewer blemishes. Since a cucumber plant cannot easily climb a trellis on its own, you'll need to train it on the support. Attach the main stem loosely to the trellis and guide it until it reaches over the top. For higher yields cut off the first four to six side runners near the bottom of the plant. Let higher runners stay on the plant. Harvesting is easier because the fruit is visible instead of hidden on the ground by leaves.

TOP GARDEN CUCUMBERS*

Name	Size (inches)	Days to mature	Key features
PICKLERS			**Short fruits with thin skins**
'Bush Pickle'	5	45	Best container variety
'County Fair Hybrid'	3	50	Bacterial wilt-resistant
'Homemade Pickles'	6	55	Heavy yields. Long productive season
'Little Leaf'	3–4	55	Self-fruitful. Small leaves make harvest easy
'Lemon'	2–3	65	Round heirloom with yellow skin
SLICERS			**Long fruits with dark green, thick skin**
'Marketmore 97 Hybrid'	8–9	51	Productive. Disease-resistant
'Salad Bush Hybrid'	8	57	Good container variety
'Diva Hybrid'	4–5	58	Parthenocarpic. Thin no-peel skin
'Fanfare Hybrid'	8–9	63	Semibush. Highly productive
ASIAN AND BURPLESS			**Long thin fruits. Don't need pollination**
'Sweeter Yet Hybrid'	10	45	Early. Disease-resistant. Burpless
'Sweet Success Hybrid'	14	54	Disease-resistant slicer. Burpless
'Tasty Jade' Hybrid	12	54	Vigorous, high yielding. Must be trellised. Asian
'Suyo Long'	12–15	61	Tolerates heat. Must be trellised. Asian
'Orient Express Hybrid'	14	64	Thin-skinned slicer. Productive. Burpless

Listed in order of days to maturity

beetle. Not only will the beetles attack and kill young plants, but they can transmit diseases such as bacterial wilt from plant to plant, ruining an entire crop. Look for these black-and-yellow beetles feeding on cucumber leaves and flowers; they leave holes and brown areas. Aphids and flea beetles can be problems early in the season as the seedlings emerge, and they transmit cucumber mosaic virus. Inspect new growth for the tiny aphids, and also check for any shotgunlike holes on the leaves caused by flea beetles feeding. For more help dealing with these pests, see page 208.

Cucumbers can also succumb to diseases such as anthracnose, cucumber mosaic virus, bacterial wilt, and powdery mildew. Anthracnose fungal disease is responsible for browning leaf margins and eventually rotting and oozing fruits. Bacterial wilt causes the mature cucumber plant to suddenly wilt; it can be identified by stringy sap in the vines. Cucumber mosaic virus curls the leaves, stunts the plant, and reduces fruiting. Powdery mildew fungus is a particular problem in warm, humid areas; the foliage turns whitish and eventually browns and dies. Select disease-resistant varieties and control insect pests to avoid these problems.

Varieties: Cucumbers have two different flowering habits. Traditional varieties are monoecious, meaning each vine has separate male and female flowers. Newer varieties are gynoecious, meaning they have only female flowers, the ones that produce fruit. Gynoecious vines are more efficient because of the absence of nonproducing male flowers. The seed packets of all-female varieties usually include seeds of a male pollinator that should be planted nearby. Some varieties are called burpless because of their thin skin and mild, unbitter flavor.

Fruiting on both monoecious and gynoecious vines is dependent on bees and other pollinators being present and active to carry the pollen from the male to the female flowers. Pollinators that are inactive due to cloudy or rainy weather often are responsible for lack of fruiting.

The most recent breeding achievement helps solve this pollination problem: parthenocarpic varieties, which produce seedless fruits without pollination. While many parthenocarpic cucumbers are grown in greenhouses to optimize production, new varieties adapted to growing outdoors are available for home gardeners. However, they should be isolated from other cucumber varieties or they will be pollinated and form seeds. The parthenocarpic types produce vigorous plants with long, thin, smooth-skinned, seedless fruits, the type you see individually wrapped in grocery stores.

In areas with a short-growing season select quick-maturing varieties or grow cucumbers in a greenhouse or under a plastic tunnel.

Cucumber, Asian type

Edible chrysanthemum *(see Asian greens)*

Eggplant (Solanum melongena)

Type: Warm-season perennial grown as an annual
Edible part: Fruits
Typical yield: 10 pounds per 10-foot row
Typical size: 1–3'H×1–2'W

'Purple Rain' eggplant

Eggplant is the consummate international food. This tomato and pepper relative hails originally from India, but today you can grow varieties from Japan, Turkey, and Italy too. Variously called the apple of love, garden egg, aubergine, and poor man's caviar, eggplant is a smooth-skinned vegetable that absorbs the flavor of foods cooked with it. The colors and shapes of the fruits are almost as varied as their common names. The skins come in white, green, purple, pink, striped, and even orange. The fruits range in form from round and small as a grape to huge oval teardrops. The thin, elongated Asian and Italian varieties have become popular for their productiveness and ease of growing.

Eggplant is always eaten cooked. Stick with the international theme when cooking, and try eggplant mashed in Indian bengan bartha, sliced in Greek moussaka, or chunked in French ratatouille.

The eggplant also is a beautiful plant. Its appealing shape and star-shape pink flowers make an attractive addition to any flower garden.

When: In most areas sow seeds indoors six to eight weeks before the last frost date. Plant outdoors two weeks after all danger of frost has passed and soil temperatures are at least 60°F. In warm areas with a long growing season seeds can be direct-sown once the soil has warmed.

Planting: Amend the soil with a 2- to 3-inch layer of compost. In cool areas lay black plastic over the beds two weeks before transplanting to warm the soil. Transplant the seedlings in holes poked in the plastic. Thin or space plants 18 to 24 inches apart in rows 30 inches apart. Eggplant likes humidity and heat and grows best when air temperatures are above 80°F during the day and 70°F at night.

Growing: In cool areas protect young transplants with floating row covers in

Harvesting 'Rosa Bianca' eggplant

spring until the weather has warmed. An eggplant won't set fruit when the temperature is consistently below 65°F.

Eggplants draw many nutrients from the soil. Sidedress monthly with a balanced fertilizer such as 5-5-5. Avoid high-nitrogen fertilizers, which are likely to promote excess leaf growth at the expense of fruit. Keep the area around plants weed free, and apply plastic mulch in cool regions or organic mulch in warm-summer areas. Keep plants well watered, giving them 1 to 2 inches per week or as needed.

The plants can be pruned and staked like tomatoes, but they are usually more productive if they retain all their leaves, especially in cool-summer areas. These shoots will eventually grow, flower, and fruit, but because the season is so short, chances are they will not mature before frost. Even though pruning will decrease the overall yields, the fruits remaining will mature sooner and be larger.

Stake individual plants or use small tomato cages to keep the plants upright and long fruits straight and off the ground.

Harvesting: Pick ripe fruits 60 to 90 days after transplanting by cutting them with a sharp knife so the cap and a short piece of stem are left on the fruit. Handle the fruits with care because they're more subject to bruising than they look. You might want to wear gloves if the eggplant

Grow eggplant in containers
One of the best ways to grow eggplant, especially where the growing season is short, is in containers. The plants love the heat generated in containers. You can move the pots around the garden or patio to ensure the plants are growing in full sun and are protected from cold weather. Also, if your soil is infected with verticillium wilt, cultivating eggplant in containers filled with potting soil is a way to avoid this disease. Put just one plant in a pot that is at least 12 inches in diameter, and water and fertilize regularly.

Checking eggplant skin to gauge maturity

Eggplant, cylindrical type

TOP GARDEN EGGPLANTS*

Name	Fruit Size (inches)	Days to mature	Key features
LARGE, OVAL			**Plants grow 3–4' with 8–10 fruits**
'Dusky Hybrid'	6–7	63	Early fruiting. Compact. Disease-resistant
'Purple Rain Hybrid'	6–7	66	Wine purple skin streaked with creamy white. Mild flavor
'Rosita'	8–9	70	Pink-lavender skin. Very white flesh
'Black Beauty'	6–7	80	Purple-black skin. Ideal for eggplant parmigiana
'Ghostbuster Hybrid'	6–7	80	White skin. Slightly sweeter than purple-skinned varieties
'Florida High Bush'	10	85	Heirloom Florida variety. Large. Purple-black skins. Good in heat
CYLINDRICAL			**Plants grow 2–3' with 12–15 thin fruits**
'Fairy Tale Hybrid'	2–4	50	Purple and white-stripe skin. Fruits in clusters. Not bitter
'Tango Hybrid'	7	60	Slender. White skin
'Vittoria Hybrid'	10	61	Purple-black skin. Tall, upright plant
'Ping Tung Long'	12	65	Taiwanese variety. Violet-purple skin. Thrives in heat and humidity
'Bride Hybrid'	8	65	Slender. White skin with faint stripes of pale lavender
'Green Goddess Hybrid'	8	68	Lime green skin. Very productive
'Little Fingers'	6–8	68	Dark purple skin. Fruits in clusters
SMALL AND ROUND			**Plants grow 1–2' with 20–25 fruits**
'Easter Egg'	2	52	Egg size. Shape and color of fruits very ornamental
'Kermit Hybrid'	2	60	Green and white skin. Thai specialty variety
'Calliope Hybrid'	2–3	64	White skin with purple streaks. Spineless plant
'Rosa Bianca'	4–5	73	Italian heirloom. White and violet-streaked skin. Creamy white flesh
'Sweet African Orange'	4	90	Skin starts white, matures to orange. Sweet flavor

Listed in order of days to maturity

White eggplant developing on plant

Some of the various shapes and colors of eggplant

variety has sharp spines on the plant. Ripe eggplants are shiny and firm to the touch. Dull skin and brown seeds when you cut the eggplant open mean the fruit is overripe; the flesh will be bitter. Another way to tell when to harvest an eggplant is to press the skin with your finger. If the skin bounces back without cracking, then the fruit is ready to harvest. If your finger indents the skin, the fruit is overripe. Pick and discard overmature fruits. The more you pick, the more fruits will continue to develop.

The fruits can be stored for up to one week in high humidity and temperatures between 40° and 50°F.

Pests and diseases: Eggplant suffers from many of the same pests that attack potatoes and tomatoes, and Colorado potato beetles prefer eggplant over potatoes. The orange-red larvae can quickly defoliate a plant. Check the underside of leaves for the orange eggs and crush them to reduce the population. Flea beetles attack young eggplant seedlings creating the classic "shotgun" holes in the leaves.

Verticillium wilt is perhaps the main disease of eggplant. It causes stunting and wilting of plants. To keep plants from succumbing to wilt, rotate crops and do not plant eggplant or any other eggplant-family crops (tomatoes, peppers, potatoes, and tomatillos) in the same ground for three years. Also, plant eggplants in containers filled with fresh potting soil (see page 32).

Endive (see Chicory, Mesclun mix)
Escarole (see Chicory)
Fava bean (see Bean)
Filet bean (see Bean)

Florence fennel, bulb fennel
(Foeniculum vulgare azoricum)

Type: Cool-season perennial grown as an annual
Edible part: Leaves, bulbs (swollen leaf base)
Typical yield: 15–20 pounds per 10-foot row
Typical size: 24"H×12"W

Florence fennel ready to harvest

This fragrant Mediterranean vegetable is a mainstay in many Italian dishes. Although the leaves and leaf stalks are also edible, the most desirable part of fennel is the blanched white, swollen leaf base that develops near the ground 75 to 90 days from seeding. It differs from the perennial herb (*F. vulgare dulce*) of the same name in that fennel herbs are grown for their foliage and seeds. Fennel herbs self-sow readily and can become invasive in warm climates.

Florence fennel has a light licorice flavor. It's delicious raw in salads, grilled, stir-fried with meat, steamed as a side dish, or roasted until caramelized with sweet potatoes and onions.
When: In cold climates start seeds indoors three weeks before the last frost date. In warm regions direct-sow from midspring through late summer for a fall harvest.
Planting: Amend the soil with a 2- to 3-inch layer of compost. Like its relative carrot, fennel grows well in raised beds. Sow seeds ¼ inch deep and 4 inches apart in rows 18 inches apart. Thin seedlings to 8 inches apart once plants are 3 to 4 inches tall.
Growing: Fennel is frost-sensitive, but will bolt if grown during hot weather. The crop needs rich soil; sidedress twice monthly with a liquid fertilizer. To prevent bolting in hot weather, keep the soil cool, weed free, and moist by mulching with a 2- to 4-inch layer of an organic material such as straw. When the bulb reaches 2 inches in diameter, mound mulch around it to blanch it; leave the top uncovered. Cut off any flower stalks that form to divert more energy into forming the bulb.
Harvesting: Pull up bulbs when they reach 3 inches in diameter. Store fennel in the refrigerator for up to one week.
Pests and diseases: Florence fennel is relatively pest free. Occasionally the larvae of butterflies such as the black swallowtail feed on the leaves. Handpick any caterpillars.
Varieties: **'Orion'** (80 days) produces larger, thicker bulbs than older varieties. **'Zefa Fino'** (75 days) is an early-maturing, bolt-resistant variety. **'Perfection'** (75 days) is a new European variety that is larger and more uniform than 'Zefa Fino'.

Garlic *(Allium sativum)*

Type: Cool-season perennial grown as an annual
Edible part: Bulbs, flower stalks
Typical yield: 20 pounds bulbs per 10-foot row
Typical size: 8–24"H×4–6"W

Braiding elephant garlic with statice

This onion-family relative has been grown for thousands of years for its medicinal and culinary uses. Native to central Asia, it's most associated with southern European and Asian cooking. Raw garlic brings power to salsa, and cooked garlic is a key ingredient in many Mediterranean and Asian cuisines. While the bulb is the main attraction, flower stalks, or scapes, can be used to flavor salads and stir-fries.

Mulching new fall garlic planting

Among the different types of garlic you can grow are hardneck garlic (*Allium sativum ophioscorodon*), softneck garlic (*A. s. sativum*) and elephant garlic (*A. ampeloprasum*).
Hardneck garlic, which is very cold hardy, forms 5 to 10 cloves of variable flavor around a woody stem. It sends up curly scapes that are ornamental as well as edible. Softneck garlic has spicy flavor. Its bulbs consist of 6 to 18 cloves in layers around a soft neck or stem, which braids with ease. The plant generally doesn't form scapes. Elephant garlic is a giant form of softneck garlic producing 4- to 5-foot-tall plants and 4 large cloves per bulb.
When: Plant garlic in fall, around the first frost date, to mature the following summer

Garlic plants growing in garden

Harvesting garlic

around the solstice. Fall planting gives the plant time to develop roots but not enough time to make leaf growth that can be killed by cold. In warm-winters areas you can plant until January. Garlic grows best during cool weather and stops growing in temperatures above 90°F.

Spring plantings made as soon as the ground can be worked are possible in cool climates, but the plants will yield smaller bulbs.

Planting: Amend the soil with a 1- to 2-inch layer of compost. Garlic tends to rot in poorly drained soils, so plant in raised beds when possible. Set individual cloves, pointy side up, 6 inches apart and 2 to 3 inches deep in rows 1 to 2 feet apart. Plant elephant garlic 8 inches apart and 6 inches deep.

Growing: Keep garlic well watered in fall. In cold-winter areas, mulch with a 4- to 6-inch layer of straw after a few hard freezes to prevent the bulbs from heaving out of the ground due to freeze-thaw cycles.

In spring apply a high-nitrogen fertilizer once three leaves have formed; repeat monthly until bulbs begin to form. Garlic competes poorly with weeds, so the bed needs to be hand weeded regularly for the plant to produce large bulbs. Mulch bulbs with a 1- to 2-inch layer of straw to keep the soil evenly moist, cool, and weed free.

Harvesting: When about half of the garlic leaves begin to yellow and wilt, stop watering and knock over the tops. Let the garlic cure for one week in the garden. Harvest the bulbs, knock off any extra soil, and hang them to dry in a cool, shady location with good air circulation. Once the tops are dry (10 to 14 days), trim them off to ½ inch above the bulb (except for softneck types that you want to braid) and trim the roots at the base of the bulbs. Store them in mesh bags in a cool (40°F to 50°F) room.

Most hardneck garlic varieties keep for up to to six months. Softneck garlic varieties store for up to nine months.

Pests and diseases: The same troublemakers that attack onions can cause similar damage to garlic. Onion thrips are small insects that infest garlic tops, feeding on the leaves. Onion maggots sometimes damage the bulbs. Rotating crops and keeping the beds weed free are the two best ways to reduce the insect populations.

Varieties: Hardneck: 'Persian Star', which produces 8 to 10 purple-skinned cloves per bulb, is a good warm-climate variety. **'Russian Red'** has purple stripes, 6 to 9 cloves per bulb, and good winter

Garlic just after harvest

hardiness. **'Spanish Roja'** has a medium-hot flavor, peels easily, has 7 to 10 reddish brown skinned cloves per bulb, and is great for roasting.

Softneck: 'Inchelium Red' produces hard-to-peel cloves that are white with purple skin. However, it's one of the best softneck varieties for cold climates. **'New York White',** also called **'Polish White',** is a hardy disease-resistant variety good for northern growing, producing up to 10 cloves per bulb. **'Silver White'** silverskin is best suited to warm climates with mild winters. It produces easy-to-peel white bulbs.

Gourd (see Squash)
Groundnut, ground pea (see Peanut)

Jerusalem artichoke, sunchoke
(Helianthus tuberosus)

Type: Warm-season perennial, Zones 3–9
Edible part: Tubers
Typical yield: 30–50 pounds per 10-foot row
Typical size: 2–8'H×1–4'W

'French Mammoth White' Jerusalem artichoke

Jerusalem artichoke didn't originate in Jerusalem and is not related to the artichoke. It is a North American native in the sunflower family. The tall, spreading plant produces small sunflowers at the end of the season.

The species is mostly known for the nutty, sweet, knobby, edible tubers that form in summer and are harvested in fall. They're tasty raw or cooked. Use raw slices, similar in taste and crunch to water chestnuts, in salads. The tubers can also be steamed, sautéed, or used like potatoes in soups and stews. Since Jerusalem artichoke produces tubers in abundance, once established in an area it can become weedy.

When: Plant tubers two to four weeks before the last frost date. In warm-winter climates the crop can be planted in fall for a spring harvest.

Planting: Jerusalem artichoke will grow in almost any soil. Plant whole tubers (or tuber chunks with at least two buds, or eyes) 4 inches deep and 18 inches apart.

Growing: Keep the soil consistently moist until the tubers are established. Jerusalem artichoke can tolerate drought and wet soils once established. Each tuber will send up multiple stalks. The plants grow vigorously. Hand weed at the beginning of the season until plants are established; at that point, the stalks will crowd and shade out any weeds. Remove flowers the first year to direct more energy into tuber production. Mulch with a 3- to 5-inch layer of straw to conserve moisture.

Harvesting: Dig up the 4- to 6-inch tubers anytime in early fall after the soil has cooled. In cold climates, for the sweetest flavor, wait until the leaves have browned and the ground begins to chill before digging.

Dig up the whole plant, removing the largest tubers to eat. Leave other tubers in the ground to form next year's plants.

Pests and diseases: Jerusalem artichoke has no major pests.
Varieties: 'French Mammoth White' produces large ½-pound white tubers that are very cold hardy. **'Fuseau'** makes smooth red-skinned tubers with a smoky taste.

Kale (*Brassica oleracea* Acephala group)

Type: Cool-season biennial grown as an annual
Edible part: Leaves
Typical yield: 10–15 pounds per 10-foot row
Typical size: 12–18"H×12–36"W

Kale is among the most nutritious vegetables you can grow and eat, and it can be one of the most colorful greens. Instead of forming a head, this cabbage produces attractive curly, ruffled, or flat leaves of blue-green, green, or burgundy. Although all forms are edible, some varieties are grown just for their vibrant leaves in fall. Kale color and flavor

'Laciniata' kale with gourds and squash

improve with cool weather, and the plants are hardy to below zero if protected. The mild-flavor greens are a good addition to salads, stir-fries, and steamed side dishes. Kale is a frequent ingredient in fall and winter soups and stews.

When: Plant four weeks before your last frost date in spring for a summer harvest and again six weeks before your first frost date in fall for an autumn and early winter harvest. In warm climates kale is also planted in winter for an early spring harvest.

Planting: Amend the soil with a 1- to 2-inch layer of compost. Sow seeds ½ inch deep and 1 inch apart or transplant seedlings 6 inches apart, making rows 2 to 3 feet apart. Thin seedlings to 1 foot apart.

Growing: When seedlings are 4 inches tall, fertilize with a liquid high-nitrogen plant food. Mulch with a 2- to 3-inch layer of organic material such as straw to conserve moisture, keep the soil cool, and prevent weed growth.

'Toscano' kale

Harvesting: Pick baby greens 20 to 30 days after seeding, and mature leaves 50 to 75 days after seeding. Wait until frost or cold weather has turned the leaves sweeter tasting. To keep a plant producing, pick the big outer leaves and let the center continue to grow. The

'Dwarf Blue Curled Vates' kale

tender young center leaves are fine in salads. The chewier larger older leaves are best steamed, sautéed, or cooked like cabbage. Fresh greens can be stored for up to one week in the refrigerator.

Pests and diseases: Kale has similar pest problems as cabbage and broccoli. Check leaves regularly for aphids, flea beetles, cabbageworms, and cabbage loopers. See page 208 for more details about these pests.

Varieties: '**Improved Dwarf Siberian**' (50 days) produces frilly dark green leaves that are very cold tolerant. '**Red Russian**' (50 days) has purple stems and purple-veined flat leaves that are more tender than those of other frilly kale varieties. '**Redbor**' hybrid (55 days) features highly attractive frilly burgundy red leaves that get darker in cold weather. '**Toscano**' (65 days) is a dinosaur, or laciniata-type, kale with long thin puckered dark green leaves that tolerate heat and cold. '**Nagoya**' hybrid is primarily an ornamental kale with frilly green outer leaves and rose to white center leaves.

Kohlrabi (*Brassica oleracea* Gongylodes group)

Type: Cool-season biennial grown as an annual
Edible part: Leaves, stem
Typical yield: 5–10 pounds per 10-foot row
Typical size: 9–12"H×9–12"W

'Early White Vienna' Kohlrabi

This odd-looking member of the cabbage family is often compared to a spaceship or a satellite. It is grown for the swollen edible stem that develops just above the soil line. Crisp and sweet with a flavor similar to turnip but milder, the stem makes an excellent addition to salads, soups, and stews.

When: Direct-sow seeds four to six weeks before your last frost date. Indoors, start seedlings anytime from four weeks before to two weeks after the last frost date. Sow again for a fall crop 10 weeks before your first frost date.

Planting: Amend the soil with a 2-inch-thick layer of compost before planting. Direct-sow seeds ½ inch deep and 1 inch apart in rows 18 inches apart. Transplant seedlings and thin direct-sown seeds to 8 inches apart.

Growing: Kohlrabi is the least hardy of the cabbage-family crops, and temperatures below 45°F will force the plant to

Kohlrabi, purple variety

bolt. Conversely, hot weather causes the stems to become tough and woody. Sidedress plants three weeks after transplanting with a balanced fertilizer such as 5-5-5. Keep the soil moist by watering as needed, providing at least 1 inch per week. Hand weed carefully to avoid disturbing the shallow roots. Mulch with an organic material such as straw or grass clippings to conserve soil moisture, keep the soil cool, and prevent weed growth.

Harvesting: For the best-quality stems, begin harvesting 45 to 65 days after transplanting, when the stems are 1 inch in diameter. Continue to harvest until stems reach 3 inches in diameter. On most varieties any stems larger than 3 inches will be tough and woody. However, some varieties will grow large and maintain their tenderness.

Kohlrabi lasts for three weeks or longer in a refrigerator crisper drawer. The stems also freeze well when peeled, diced, and blanched. Young leaves may be steamed and eaten like other greens.

Pests and diseases: Kohlrabi is vulnerable to the same insect pests and diseases as cabbage and broccoli. Check the leaves regularly for aphids, flea beetles, cabbageworms, and cabbage loopers. To avoid diseases, rotate crops, do not plant a cabbage-family crop in the same ground for three years, and clean up crop debris in fall.

Varieties: 'Early White Vienna' (55 days) has smooth light green skin and mild-flavored, tender white flesh. **'Gigante'** (130 days) is a Czech heirloom that grows 10 inches in diameter and weighs up to 25 pounds. Amazingly, the white flesh stays tender and mild. **'Kolibri'** (45 days) is a purple-skinned variety with fiberless white flesh. **'Kossack Hybrid'** (85 days) produces an 8- to 10-inch-diameter stem with green skin and white flesh; it isn't woody despite its size.

Leek *(Allium porrum)*

Type: Cool-season biennial grown as an annual
Edible part: Leaves, leafstalks
Typical yield: 12 pounds per 10-foot row
Typical size: 8–24"H×½–2"W

A common delicacy, this frost-hardy, long-season onion-family crop can provide fresh, sweet onion flavor from midsummer into the following spring in areas with mild winters. Leeks are beautiful too. The white shanks are topped with dark green or blue-green leaves. Eat leeks raw in salads, broiled, or in stews, soups, and stir-fries.

When: Leeks can be direct sown in the garden four weeks before your last frost. Since they take such a long time to mature, they grow to a larger size if started as seedlings indoors. Start transplants eight weeks before the last frost date in your area. For hefty transplants keep seedling tops cut to 3 inches tall. Set out transplants on or just after the last frost date.

Transplanting leek seedlings

Planting: Amend the soil with a 2-inch-thick layer of compost before planting. In clay or heavy soils plant in raised beds. Direct-sow seeds ½ inch deep and 1 inch apart in rows 18 inches apart. Thin seedlings to 6 inches apart with 1 to 2 feet between rows. Set transplants about 6 inches apart and 4 inches deep in 8-inch-deep and -wide trenches spaced 18 inches apart.

Growing: To blanch the stems, slowly fill in the trenches as the plants grow or mound soil around the stems. Keep the soil evenly moist by applying 1 inch of water weekly or as needed. Hand weed frequently to keep the soil around the growing leeks free of weeds, which otherwise will reduce the quality of the leeks. Fertilize monthly with a balanced product such as 5-5-5.

Harvesting: Leeks take 70 to 120 days to mature, and they taste sweetest after a frost. Harvest when the stem is at least ½ inch in diameter. The best leeks will have a white stem or shank at least 3 inches long. Although leek leaves are edible, trim the tops to a manageable size for cooking.

In mild climates, overwinter leeks and harvest in early spring. In cold areas mulch with a 4- to 6-inch thick layer of straw to protect the plants when overwintering them in the garden. Keep leeks in a refrigerator for up to one week.

Pests and diseases: Leeks have no significant pest problems.

Varieties: 'Giant Musselburgh' (105 days), a Scottish heirloom that produces 2- to 3-inch-thick stems, is very cold tolerant. **'King Richard'** (75 days) is a tall, thin variety with medium-size green leaves. **'Lancelot Hybrid'** (100 days) is a cold-tolerant variety.

'King Richard' leek

Lettuce *(Lactuca sativa)*

Type: Cool-season annual
Edible part: Leaves
Typical yield: 5–10 pounds per 10-foot row
Typical size: 2–10"H×2–8"W

'Outredgeous' lettuce

Despite a plethora of new greens available to home gardeners, good old-fashioned lettuce is still the most popular. It comes in a variety of shapes, textures, and colors. The four basic types are crisphead, butterhead, looseleaf, and romaine. Crisphead, or batavian, lettuce forms tight, firm heads of crisp leaves. This true head, or iceberg, lettuce requires a long and cool growing season. Butterhead lettuce

produces a smaller, softer head of loosely folded medium green leaves. Looseleaf lettuce has an open growth pattern and doesn't form a head. Available in a wide range of leaf colors and textures, looseleaf varieties mature quickly and are easy to grow. Romaine, or cos, lettuce forms upright, cylindrical heads of tightly folded leaves.

Romaine lettuce

Romaine lettuce is considered the sweetest of the lettuce types and is often used in Caesar salads.

Extend your harvest by planting a combination of lettuce types. In cool-summer areas you can grow them all summer and into fall. In areas where winters are mild you can grow

lettuce into the fall and winter, and where both summers and winters are mild you can grow lettuce year-round.

Use lettuce fresh or wilted in salads or as a garnish. Mix it with other raw greens such as bok choy, tatsoi, and red- and green-leaf mustards to make a delicious peppery mesclun. Lettuce adds crunch and lightness to any meal. Mild to nutty, buttery to bland, it's the ideal base for a spicy dressing.

When: Lettuce grows best at temperatures between

Butterhead lettuce

'Summertime' crisphead lettuce

45° and 65°F. Seeds will germinate at temperatures as low as 40°F. Direct-sow butterhead, looseleaf, and romaine types in early spring as soon as you can work the soil. Sow small beds every three weeks until late spring. Start sowing again in late summer for a fall and winter harvest. Lettuce can become bitter and bolt in summer heat. Start crisphead lettuce varieties indoors four to six weeks before the last frost date in your area to transplant three to four weeks later.

Planting: Amend the soil with a 2-inch-thick layer of compost before planting. The ideal medium for growing lettuce is a sandy loam soil free of dirt clods and rocks. Sow seeds ¼ inch deep and 1 inch apart in rows about 18 inches apart. Once three or four leaves form, thin looseleaf varieties to 4 to 6 inches apart, butterhead and romaine types to 6 to 10 inches apart, and crisphead to 10 to 12 inches apart in the row.

Growing: Because lettuce has a shallow root system, pull weeds by hand or hoe lightly to avoid disturbing the plant. Keep the soil consistently moist but not waterlogged. Mulch the rows with a 2- to 3-inch layer of straw or grass clippings to keep the soil cool, weed free, and moist. Sidedress plants with a liquid high-nitrogen fertilizer every three to four weeks.

Harvesting: Pick the outer leaves of butterhead, looseleaf, and romaine varieties when the leaves are 2 inches long, about 50 to 60 days after seeding. When the leaves reach 4 to 6 inches long, cut the whole plant to within 1 inch of the ground with a sharp knife. If harvesting in spring, new leaves will emerge to be harvested later before the hot weather.

> **HERE'S A TIP...**
>
> **Interplant looseleaf lettuce**
> Since lettuce grows well in part shade and enjoys cool soil and air, try interplanting looseleaf lettuce with other longer-maturing crops such as tomatoes, eggplant, and sweet corn. Set lettuce transplants around these taller plants, and harvest the young greens before the bigger plants shade them out completely.

'Royal Oak Leaf' lettuce

Looseleaf lettuce

TOP GARDEN LETTUCES*

Name	Leaf color	Days to mature	Key features
LOOSELEAF			**Open growth with no heads**
'Green Ice'	Light green	45	Extra-crisp, savoyed leaves. Slow to bolt
'Salad Bowl'	Green or red	45	A mix of green- or red-leaf varieties. Good in hot areas
'Black Seeded Simpson'	Light green	46	Large, crinkly leaves. Widely adapted
'Royal Oak Leaf'	Dark green	50	Tolerates heat. Unique leaf shape. Also comes in red-leaf version
'Red Sails'	Burgundy red	55	Red-fringed leaves. Stays mild without bitterness. Slow to bolt
'New Red Fire'	Dark red	55	Slow growing. Striking red leaves
CRISPHEAD/BATAVIAN			**Tight, firm head of crisp leaves**
'Little Gem'	Green	55	Very early. Small 4" heads
'Rouge de Grenoblouse'	Green and red	60	Large heads with red-fringed leaves. Frost- and heat-tolerant
'Sun Devil'	Light green	60	Good Southwest variety. Heat tolerant, tipburn resistant
'Ithaca'	Light green	65	Firm heads. Good disease resistance
'Nevada'	Lime green	68	Thick, bright leaves. Nutty flavor. Disease-resistant
'Summertime'	Green	68	Tender, crisp, juicy heads. Heat-tolerant. Slow to bolt
ROMAINE			**Upright, cylindrical heads of tightly folded leaves**
'Winter Density'	Green	54	Tightly folded leaves, like a tall 'Buttercrunch'. Frost-tolerant. Good overwintering variety
'Flashy Trout Back'	Dark green with red speckles	55	Highly attractive Austrian heirloom. Buttery flavor
'Outredgeous'	Bright red	57	Loose, thick, glossy leaves. Develops full red color even in part shade
'Rouge D'Hiver'	Green with red tint	58	French variety. Tolerates cold but not heat
'Parris Island Cos'	Green leaves	68	Old-time favorite. White blanched heart. Disease-resistant. Slow to bolt
BUTTERHEAD			**Small soft heads of loosely folded leaves**
'Deer Tongue'	Green	46	Heirloom with triangular leaves. Also comes in red-leaf version
'Buttercrunch'	Dark green	46	Tightly bunched leaves form compact, yellow blanched heart. Crisp and sweet flavor
'Esmeralda'	Light green	48	Large, dense, tender heads. Disease-resistant. Slow to bolt
'Speckles'	Olive green with red speckles	50	Amish heirloom. Bibb-like head with yellow-green blanched heart
'Four Seasons' ('Merveille des Quatre Saisons')	Burgundy	54	Compact, sweet, tender head with light green blanched heart
'Tom Thumb'	Dark green	55	Compact, 3–5" head
'Bibb' ('Limestone')	Dark green	55	Soft, rounded outer leaves with creamy white heart

Listed in order of days to maturity

'Salad Bowl' lettuce, green and red forms

If harvesting in late spring or fall, pull up the whole plant. Pick crisphead lettuce when the center is firm, about 60 to 80 days after seeding.

To store lettuce, wash, pat dry, and place it in a plastic bag in the refrigerator. Lettuce keeps for about one week if stored at 35°F in high humidity.

Pests and diseases: Aphids and slugs are two of the main pests of lettuce. Rabbits and woodchucks love the tender lettuce greens.

Damping off fungal disease affects young seedlings, causing them to wilt and die overnight. To prevent this disease grow lettuce in raised beds and don't overwater. Keep plants adequately thinned to prevent other rot diseases such as botrytis and mildew. Grow disease-resistant varieties to avoid tip or leaf burn.

Luffa (see Squash)

Mâche, cornsalad *(Valerianella locusta)*

Type: Cool-season annual
Edible part: Leaves
Typical yield: 2–4 pounds leaves per 10-foot row
Typical size: 2–4"H×4–8"W

'Vit' mâche

This cool-season green is also called lamb's lettuce because sheep graze it in Europe. Mâche has small spoon-shape leaves with a mild, nutty taste. While often eaten raw in salads and mesclun mixes, it is also tasty steamed or boiled. Use mâche as you would kale or collards. Wilt or stir-fry it with a touch of olive oil and garlic, or add it to soups and stews just before serving them.

When: For the best flavor grow mâche in cool weather. Direct-sow seeds in early spring as soon as the ground can be worked for a late spring crop and in late summer after the weather has cooled to below 80°F for a fall crop. Make successive plantings every three weeks while the weather is still cool. In mild-winter areas sow in fall for a winter crop. In cool areas sow seeds in a cold frame for an early spring harvest. Mâche leaves can freeze and still be edible. The plants are hardy to 5°F.

Planting: Amend the soil with a 1-inch-thick layer of compost before planting. Since young mâche leaves look similar to many broadleaf weeds, plant them in blocks for easier identification. Create a wide row or raised bed, and broadcast seeds in weed-free 1- to 2-foot squares 6 inches apart. Cover the seeds with ¼ inch of sand or potting soil, and water lightly. When the leaves are 3 inches tall, thin the seedlings to 2 inches apart, saving the tender thinned plants to eat in salads.

Growing: Keep the soil evenly moist and hand weeded. Since this green grows quickly, it rarely needs additional fertilizer.

Harvesting: Young leaves can be harvested as soon as they are an edible size. Mature plants are ready to harvest about 50 days after seeding. With a sharp knife, cut individual leaves, or pull up the whole plant when it is 3 to 4 inches tall. Mâche loses its nutty taste as it ages. Remove a plant once it sends up a flower stalk and bolts in hot weather. Keep unwashed greens in the crisper drawer of the refrigerator for up to two weeks.

Pests and diseases: Mâche has no serious problems.

Varieties: 'Jade' (50 days) has semi-elongated leaves that are resistant to mildew, yellows, and fusarium wilt disease. **'Vit'** (50 days) is a versatile, widely adapted variety with long oval mint-flavored leaves.

Malabar spinach *(see Spinach)*

Melon, watermelon
(Cucumis melo and *Citrullus lanatus)*

Type: Warm-season annual
Edible part: Fruits
Typical yield: 4–5 fruits per 10-foot row
Typical size: 1'H×3–20'W

'Ambrosia Hybrid' muskmelon

Classic midsummer treats, melons and watermelons come in a variety of shapes, sizes, and textures. The one thing they have in common is sweet, juicy flesh.

Muskmelons *(Cucumis melo)* are the most widely grown. They produce 2- to 5-pound fruits with a netted tan rind and sweet pink to orange flesh. Charentais melons are a French novelty. They look like muskmelons but have a smooth gray-green rind and honey-flavored orange flesh. Specialty melons are now becoming more popular and common in markets. Mediterranean melons, such as galia, have yellow rind when mature and sweet aromatic pale green or white flesh.

Winter melons *(C. melo* Inodorus group) grow best in areas with hot, dry climates and a long season. Honeydew melons typically weigh 5 to 6 pounds and have a smooth creamy white rind and sweet light green or orange flesh. Casaba melons, which are 7 to 8 pounds, feature a grooved yellow to greenish yellow rind and spicy-sweet white flesh. Shaped like a long acorn, crenshaw melons weigh 7 to 10 pounds and have a rough rind and sweet pinkish-orange flesh.

Watermelons *(Citrullus lanatus)* can be oval or round with red, pink, yellow, or orange flesh. They range from a few pounds to more than 100 pounds depending on the variety. Newer varieties are seedless.

Melons and watermelons are delicious in their own right, but they also combine well in fruit salads, cold soups, salsas, and shakes. The rind from some watermelon varieties can be used for preserves and pickles.

When: Melons and watermelons need heat to germinate and

Charentais specialty melon

TOP GARDEN MELONS AND WATERMELONS*

Name	Fruit size (pounds)	Days to mature	Key features
MUSKMELONS (CANTALOUPES)			**Orange to salmon flesh**
'Earligold Hybrid'	4	72	Early. Sweet orange flesh. Good for cool areas. Powdery mildew–resistant
'EarliQueen Hybrid'	3–4	74	Thick, sweet orange flesh. Resists cracking
'Athena Hybrid'	5–6	79	Sweet salmon-color flesh. Good disease and crack resistance
'Hale's Best Jumbo'	3–4	80	Heirloom. Aromatic, deep salmon–color flesh. Very productive
'Ambrosia Hybrid'	5	86	Salmon-color flesh. Powdery mildew–resistant
'Superstar Hybrid'	6–8	86	Large fruits. Orange flesh
WINTER MELONS			**Honeydew, casaba and crenshaw**
'Honey Orange Hybrid' (honeydew)	3	74	Salmon-orange flesh and ivory rind. Tolerates cool conditions
'Earlidew Hybrid' (honeydew)	2–3	80	Sweet yellow-green flesh. Ripe fruits slip off vine like muskmelons. Early. Good for North
'Super Dew Hybrid' (honeydew)	6	80	Fragrant white flesh with green edges. Early. Productive
'Early Crenshaw Hybrid'	14	90	Large, oblong fruits. Pink, creamy flesh
'Tam-Dew' (honeydew)	4–5	100	Southern variety. Jade green flesh and ivory rind. Mildew-resistant
'Golden Beauty'(casaba)	7–8	110	Heirloom. White flesh and golden rind. Good keeper. Good for Southwest and California
SPECIALTY MELONS			**Unique shapes, flesh color, and flavor**
'Passport' (galia)	5–6	73	Early. Widely adapted tropical melon. Mint green flesh with tropical fruit flavor and bananalike aroma
'Sugar Nut' (canary)	2	77	Sweet white flesh with smooth texture. Small fruits great for snacking
'Savor' (charentais)	2	78	Deep orange flesh and gray-green rind. Disease-resistant
'San Juan' (ananas)	4–5	78	Sweet and spicy ivory flesh. Disease-resistant
'Ogen'	7–8	85–95	Israeli heirloom. Sweet, creamy white flesh and pale yellow rind
'Banana'	4–5	80–100	Heirloom. Unique banana shape. Sweet and juicy orange flesh
WATERMELON			**Round and oval. Seeded and seedless**
'Yellow Doll Hybrid'	5–8	76	Round. Yellow flesh. Short vines
'Sugar Baby'	8–10	76	Round "icebox" type. Red flesh. Tough rinds resist cracking. Comes in bush form with 3–4' vines
'Sweet Beauty Hybrid'	5–7	80	Oval. Red seedless flesh
'Orange Sweet'	4–6	80	Round. Bright orange seedless flesh
'Crimson Sweet'	15–25	85	Oval. Sweet red flesh
'Orange Sunshine Hybrid'	10–15	85	Oval. Seedless orange flesh. Extrasweet
'Desert King'	20–30	90	Oval. Yellow flesh. Drought- and sunburn-tolerant. Good for Southwest
'Jubilee II Hybrid'	30	90	Elongated oval. Red flesh. Disease-resistant. Good for Southeast
'Carolina Cross #183'	Up to 200	100	Mammoth oval fruits that stay smooth even when large. Red flesh
'Moon and Stars'	25	100	Oval. Heirloom. Red flesh and dark green skin with yellow stars

Ranked according to season length

grow best. Wait until two weeks after your last frost date and sow seeds when the soil temperature is at least 70°F. Start seedlings indoors four weeks before your last frost date. Plant seedlings when the soil temperature is at least 60°F.
Planting: Amend the soil with a 2- to 3-inch-thick layer of compost or composted manure. Direct-sow seeds in hills 4 to 6 feet apart, with six seeds per hill. Set transplants 12 to 18 inches apart in rows 3 feet apart.

The plants grow well in warm areas where temperatures are consistently above 70°F. In cool-summer areas preheat the soil by laying black or dark green plastic over the beds two weeks before planting. Poke holes in the plastic to plant

'Crenshaw' melon

seeds or seedlings. For the best growth and pollination, plant in areas away from high winds. If you plan on saving seeds, separate the different varieties from each other.

Growing: Melons and watermelons need space, food, and water to grow best. Thin direct-sown plants to three seedlings per hill after the first set of true leaves appears. When watermelon vines are 1 to 2 feet long, thin again and keep only one or two of the most vigorous vines per hill.

Like cucumbers, melons have male and female flowers on each plant and need insects such as bees to pollinate the flowers if the plant is to produce fruit. Encourage pollinating insects by planting in an open, full-sun location and growing flowers that will attract pollinators nearby. Seedless watermelons need a separate pollinator variety planted nearby in order to set fruit. Seeds of the pollinator are included in the pack.

Keep plants well watered, applying at least 1 inch per week—more during hot, dry, windy periods. The most critical watering periods are when the vines are flowering and fruiting. Hand weed until the leaves are big enough to shade out weeds. In cool-summer areas mulch with black plastic to prevent weed growth, keep the soil warm, and conserve soil moisture. Cover young seedlings with floating row covers to keep the air temperatures warm and

'Sugar Nut' canary melon

Do Seedless Watermelons Have *Any* Seeds?

Although spitting watermelon seeds is part of the fun of eating this delicious fruit, many gardeners prefer the newer seedless varieties. But the question is, how do you get seeds if the watermelon doesn't produce any?

Seedless watermelons are also called triploid watermelons because they have three sets of chromosomes. Breeders treat a seeded diploid variety, which has two sets of chromosomes, with a plant growth hormone to produce a tetraploid watermelon, which has four sets of chromosomes. Then they cross the tetraploid with a diploid to get watermelons with triploid seeds. The seeds from these crosses are sterile. So when you plant the triploid watermelon seeds the fruits never develop any viable seeds, hence a seedless watermelon.

Developing melon rests on a reflector.

watermelons. Support developing fruits with a sling made from strong netting or mesh fabric.

Apply a complete fertilizer, such as a 5-10-10, that also contains magnesium and boron three times: when transplanting, when vines begin to run, and at first fruit set. Keep ripening fruits off the ground by setting them on cardboard, upside-down pots, or pieces of wood. You can hasten

'Moon and Stars' heirloom watermelon

ripening of fruits by removing vine tips and new flowers when nights grow cool. Also, to help existing fruits ripen before frost, set fruits on aluminum-covered cardboard to intensify the heat of the day.

Harvesting: Maturity rates vary. Muskmelons, or cantaloupes, should be harvested about 35 to

prevent insects from attacking young plants. Remove the row covers once flowering starts.

In warm-summer areas apply an organic mulch such as straw after the soil temperature reaches 70°F. To save space and protect the fruits, trellis the vines of melons and small-fruited

Seedless red and 'Yellow Doll' watermelon

The Magic of Green Mulch

Green plastic mulch, that is. No longer are the choices only white, clear, or black. Researchers have developed various colored mulches that specifically increase the yields of targeted crops. It turns out the best color for melons and watermelons is green. Sold as IRT, for infrared transmitting, this dark green mulch warms the soil like clear plastic but suppresses weed growth like black plastic. It increases yields by 20 to 40 percent over those produced by plants grown in black plastic mulch.

Watermelon

WHEN ARE WATERMELONS RIPE?

Watermelons need to be harvested when fully ripe because they will not ripen off the vine. Here are four ways to know when to pick ripe fruits.

● **Look at the curly tendril near the top of the melon.** When the watermelon is ripe, it will turn brown and die.

● **Gently lift the watermelon.** It should feel heavy for its size.

● **Tip the melon and check the underside.** The spot where it sits on the ground usually turns from white to creamy yellow as it ripens.

● **Thump the melon with your knuckle.** It's ripe when you hear a dull thump instead of a tinny sound.

55 days after fruit set. Look at the fruit. The ribbing will darken to a tan or yellow and the fruit will "slip" (separate easily) off the vine when gently lifted. Muskmelons will also give off a sweet melon scent when ripe.

Harvest honeydew, casaba, and crenshaw melons when the green rind turns pale yellow and the blossom end is slightly soft. They can be harvested a few days before fully mature to continue ripening off the vine at room temperature. Store muskmelons for up to a week in the warmest spot in the refrigerator, and honeydew, casaba, and crenshaw melons for up to a month in the coldest part.

Pests and diseases: The main insect pests of melons and watermelons are cucumber beetles, squash bugs, and aphids. As they do with cucumbers, the aphids and cucumber beetles not only damage young seedlings, flowers, and fruits, but also they transmit devastating mosaic virus and bacterial wilt diseases to melon plants. See pages 208 and 209 for ways to control cucumber beetles and aphids. Crush the red eggs of squash bugs found on the underside of melon and watermelon leaves and handpick adults.

Melons and watermelons are affected by diseases such as anthracnose, bacterial wilt, stem blight, viruses, and powdery mildew. Select disease-resistant varieties, rotate crops, clean up plant debris well in fall, and control insects, such as cucumber beetles and aphids, that transmit diseases to avoid problems.

Animals such as mice and racoons love ripe melons, and so do insects like wasps. A sure sign your fruits are ripe is damage from one of these pests. Harvest fruits on time, and protect individual melons with a wire cage or by trellising the fruits off the ground.

Mesclun mix

Type: Cool-season annual
Edible part: Leaves
Typical yield: 3–5 pounds per 10-foot row
Typical size: 8"H×10"W

Mesclun salad mixes have reinvented the American salad. This mixture of baby greens was invented in Europe, where gardeners would gather wild greens in spring and mix them together for a salad. By combining various greens, you can create a salad with its own unique flavor, texture, color, and personality. Try adding piquant chicories for a bolder flavor

Harvesting 'Tangy Mesclun Mix'

or just use colorful lettuce greens for a mild taste.

When: Direct-sow seeds two to four weeks before your last frost date. Sow successive crops every two to three weeks in spring until early summer. Start sowing again in late summer for a fall harvest. In mild climates sow in fall for a winter harvest.

Planting: Amend the soil with a 1- to 2-inch-thick layer of compost before planting. Sow seeds ¼ inch deep and ½ inch apart in 2- to 3-foot-wide raised beds or wide rows. Cover the seeds with potting soil or sand. Keep the planting well watered until the seeds germinate. In cool areas cover the bed with a floating row cover to warm the soil in spring, prevent insects from attacking, and keep the bed moist.

Growing: Keep the bed well watered. Hand weed as needed, though a thickly sown planting rarely requires weeding. Since the plants mature so quickly, they don't need a fertilizer sidedressing.

Harvesting: Begin harvesting baby greens 14 to 30 days after sowing, when the leaves reach 4 to 6 inches long. Handpick individual leaves or cut whole plants to 1 inch above the ground. If cut in spring the plant can regrow for a second harvest. After cutting, water well and fertilize with a liquid plant food high in nitrogen.

Mesclun mix leaves are highly perishable and should be eaten soon after harvest. Gently wash and dry the leaves and store them in the refrigerator crisper for a few days.

Pests and diseases: The primary pests of mesclun mixes are aphids and flea beetles. Control these pests with a jet spray of water, or by applying insecticidal soap.

Varieties: Each of the mesclun mixes is specially blended by growers so the actual ingredients may vary. Here are a few samples mixes that are available. **'Mild Mesclun Mix'** (21 days) is a blend of mild-tasting greens such as lettuce, mizuna, tatsoi, kale, and mâche. **'Tangy Mesclun Mix'** (30 days) is a blend of sharper greens such as arugula, endive, pak choi (bok choy), and mustards. **'French Niçoise Blend'** (28 days) features a tart and tangy flavor

'Provençal Winter Mix' mesclun

from a blend of arugula, endive, radicchio, and cress. **'Micro Greens Mix'** (14–21 days) has the mild flavor of chard, beets, kale, pea shoots, and spinach harvested only a few days after germination.

Mibuna (see Asian greens)
Mirliton (see Squash)
Mizuna (see Asian greens, Mesclun mix)
Multiplier onion (see Onion)

Mustard (see Asian greens)
Napa cabbage (see Chinese cabbage)
New Zealand spinach (see Spinach)

Okra *(Abelmoschus esculentus)*

Type: Warm-season perennial grown as an annual
Edible part: Seedpods
Typical yield: 10 pounds per 10-foot row
Typical size: 2–8'H×1–2'W

'Clemson Spineless' okra

This member of the mallow family, related to hibiscus and hollyhock, is a tall plant that produces beautiful pale yellow flowers. Newer varieties have colorful leaves as well and are small enough to grow in containers. The flowers are followed by edible fruits, or seedpods, that range in color from green to rich deep maroon, complementing the large, broad, coarsely lobed leaves.

Africans brought okra to America, and the word "gumbo" is Swahili for okra. A staple in Southern cooking, okra thrives in hot weather and warm soil and is a key ingredient in Cajun gumbos, soups, and stews. It can also be steamed, boiled, baked, fried, grilled, or pickled.

When: Plant transplants, or direct-sow seeds two weeks after all danger of frost has passed and the soil temperature has reached to at least 60°F. In cool-summer areas start seedlings indoors six to eight weeks before your last frost date.

Planting: Amend the soil with a 2- to 3-inch-thick layer of compost or composted manure. Okra is somewhat drought tolerant but can't stand consistently wet conditions. In cool-summer areas, preheat the soil by laying black plastic mulch over the okra beds two weeks before planting. Prior to sowing the seeds, soak them in warm water for one hour to soften the seedcoat. Direct-sow the seeds ½ inch deep several inches apart in the row. As an alternative, place transplants 1 to 2 feet apart in rows 2 feet apart. Okra seedlings don't like to be disturbed, so use peat pots when growing seedlings indoors so as not to damage the roots. Thin to one seedling per pot by snipping out the weaker seedlings with a scissors. In warm areas make successive sowings every two to three weeks into August.

Growing: Thin direct-sown seedlings to 1 to 2 feet apart. Water deeply every 7 to 10 days, allowing the soil to dry out between waterings. Irrigation is particularly important during flowering and pod development. Apply a complete plant food such as 5-5-5 monthly.

'Burgundy' okra flower and pod

Harvesting: Some okra varieties have spines on the leaves and stems, so use gloves when harvesting. Okra pods are ready to pick when they are 2 to 4 inches long, about five or six days after flowering. Harvest frequently, especially during hot weather, because pods become tough quickly. On most varieties pick and compost pods longer than 5 inches since they will be too tough to eat. However, you can let overmature pods dry on the plant for use in flower arrangements. Pods can be stored for 7 to 10 days at a temperature of 45° to 50°F and at high humidity, or they can be frozen or pickled.

Pests and diseases: Okra plants are attacked by aphids, stinkbugs, and cabbageworms. Aphids and stinkbugs stunt a plant's growth, while cabbageworms eat holes in the leaves reducing yields. During periods of wet weather verticillium and fusarium wilts can become a problem, causing the plants to die prematurely. Rotate crops or grow okra in well-drained soil, raised beds, or containers to prevent these diseases.

Varieties: **'Annie Oakley II'** (48 days) is a good northern variety that produces spineless pods on 3- to 4-foot-tall plants. **'Burgundy'** (55 days) has colorful red stems and pods on 7-foot-tall plants; the pods turn deep purple when cooked. **'Cajun Delight'** (50 days) is a highly branched, 4-foot-tall, spineless, productive variety that grows well in the North. **'Clemson Spineless'** (56 days) is a classic Southern variety producing pods up to 9 inches long pods that stay tender; the pods grow on 5-foot-tall spineless plants. **'Little Lucy'** has the same red coloring as 'Burgundy', but it grows only 2 feet tall and produces 4-inch-long pods.

Onion *(Allium cepa)*

Type: Cool-season perennial grown as an annual
Edible part: Bulbs, stems
Typical yield: 10 pounds per 10-foot row
Typical size: 4–24"H×1–5"W

'Candy' onion

Like other members of the *Allium* family, onions are known for their culinary and medicinal properties. They have been grown for more than 5,000 years and were favored by the ancient cultures of India, Egypt, and Italy. Onions are basic to many recipes and so are basic to vegetable gardens too. Their strong flavor adds sharpness to salsas, but they

TOP GARDEN ONIONS*

Name	Skin color	Days to mature	Key features
LONG DAY			**Plant north of 35° latitude**
'Copra Hybrid'	Yellow	104	Firm, early-maturing storage onion. Sweeter than other storage types
'First Edition Hybrid'	Yellow	105	Pale gold flesh. Good storage. Disease-resistant
'Ailsa Craig Exhibition'	Yellow	105	2-pound, sweet Spanish–type bulb. Tolerates cool weather
'Redwing Hybrid'	Red	110	Pungent red flesh. Stores very well
'Sweet Sandwich Hybrid'	White or yellow	110	Classic variety. Gets sweeter in storage
'Walla Walla'	Yellow	125	Sweet, juicy Northwest favorite. In mild-winter areas, plant in fall
SHORT DAY			**Plant south of 35° latitude**
'Giant Red Hamburger'	Dark red	95	Sweet white flesh. Early
'Texas Supersweet'	Yellow	175	Large sweet bulb. Popular in Texas and Southwest
'Granex 33 Hybrid' (Vidalia)	Yellow	180	Known for very sweet bulb. Popular in Southeast
INTERMEDIATE DAY			**Plant anywhere**
'Superstar Hybrid'	White	109	1-pound bulbs with mild, sweet taste. Disease-resistant. Stores well
'Candy Hybrid'	Yellow	110	Mild flavored. Gets large if grown in South. Fair for storage
OTHER ONIONS			**Plant anywhere**
'Red Beard' (scallion)	White and red	45	White stalks tinted red. Mildly pungent
'Purplette' (mini onion)	Purple-red	60	Mild and sweet. Grown as a green onion. Burgundy flesh. Good for pickling
'Evergreen Hardy White' (scallion)	White	65	Hardy. Plant spring or fall and grow as a perennial. Divide clumps in spring
'White Spear' (scallion)	White	65	Blue-green leaves. Heat-resistant. Good for South
'Pikant' (shallot)	Yellow	80	Large bulbs with reddish flesh. Stores well. Grow from sets
'Ambition' (shallot)	Red	100	Reddish copper skin and white flesh. Grow from seed
'Egyptian Top Set' (multiplier)	White	Perennial	Harvest green onions in spring and bulbs in summer

Ranked according to season length

sweeten when cooked, giving depth to soups, stews, and sauces. You can eat the tops as scallions, immature bulbs as green onions, or mature bulbs as regular onions.

Grow onions from seeds, sets, or plants. Which you choose will depend on the varieties you're growing. Variety selection is also a matter of taste. Regular sweet onions are flavorful, mild tasting, and great raw in salads or cooked, but they don't last long stored. Regular storage onions have a more pungent taste and are best cooked.

'Red Beard' scallion

'Ambition' shallot

Shallots, an onion relative, are known for their small bulbs and mild flavor.

Multiplier onions are old-fashioned bulbs that reproduce like shallots. They are fall planted for a spring harvest and are perennial. One of the most popular is the Egyptian topset onion, which is known for bulbs that form on the top

'Copra' onion

of the flower stalk. It is hardy and often one of the first greens to sprout in spring.

One of the keys to success with onions is choosing the right variety for your region, or rather your latitude. The reason is day length. Some onion varieties grow best and mature during the short days of spring while others need the long days of summer to grow and develop large bulbs. That's why onions are categorized in part according to their optimum day length. There's more about onions and day length in the sidebar at right.

Yellow onions drying for storage

When: Sow seeds indoors six to eight weeks before your last frost date in spring. Keep plants stocky by trimming the tops to 3 inches tall. Plant sets or transplants in the garden three weeks before your last frost date for a summer harvest. In mild-winter regions sow seeds indoors eight weeks before your first frost date or plant transplants in early winter for an early summer harvest.

Planting: Amend the soil with a 1- to 2-inch-thick layer of compost before planting. Onions don't grow well in soil that floods or stays waterlogged. Because they need loose soil free of rocks and debris to grow best, grown them in raised beds on all but sandy

Green onions ready to harvest

soils. Raised beds provide better drainage.

Sow seeds ½ inch deep and 3 inches apart. If you plan on harvesting the tops for scallions, space the seeds 2 inches apart and thin the seedlings to the proper spacing. Plant sets or transplants 4 to 6 inches apart in rows spaced 1 foot apart (or 6 inches apart for shallots). Place the onion sets about 2 inches deep in the soil so the pointed end is just showing above ground.

Growing: Thin seedlings to 4 inches apart using the thinnings as scallions. Apply a plant food that's high in phosphorus, such as 5-10-5, at planting time. Follow up with a sidedressing of 5-5-5 every three weeks during the growing season. Onions don't compete well with weeds, so keep the bed weeded as well as watered. The latter is particularly important as the bulbs begin to size up. To keep onion plants moist and weed free, mulch between the onion beds with a 1- to 2-inch-thick layer of organic material such as straw. Remove flower stems if they form.

Harvesting: Pick scallions when they are 6 to 8 inches tall, usually eight weeks after planting. Harvest green onions anytime after the bulb has formed. Storage onions usually take three to five months to mature in the North. In mild climates fall-planted onions mature in early summer. Once the tops start yellowing, stop watering. When half of the stems have collapsed, bend the rest down. After one more week you can pull up the bulbs. Lay them in a warm dry place. When the skin is dry and papery, cut off the foliage, leaving a 1-inch stub above the bulb. Store the onions in mesh bags in a cool (35°F to 55°F), dark location.

Sweet onion varieties can be stored for only a few weeks, while more pungent storage varieties will last as long as four months.

Harvest shallots about 90 days after planting, once the side bulbs have formed and the tops have begun to dry. Remove the entire plant, separate the side bulbs, and store them as you would onions. Bulbs left in the ground will regrow the next year.

Pests and diseases: Because of their pungency, onions are relatively pest-free plants. Onion thrips and onion maggots can attack the leaves and bulbs. Cover the transplants with a floating row cover to prevent thrips damage, or spray insecticidal soap. Spread diatomaceous earth around the plants to control onion maggots. Rotate crops and grow onions in well-drained soils to avoid diseases.

ONIONS AND DAY LENGTH

Onion varieties can be confusing because they are grouped as short day, intermediate day (same as day neutral), and long day. Short-day onions form bulbs when they receive 11 to 12 hours of daylight, while intermediate-day onions need 12 to 14 hours of daylight, and long-day onions 14 to 16 hours.

If you live north of 35 degrees latitude (north of Santa Maria, California; Winslow, Arizona; Amarillo, Texas; Memphis, Tennessee; and Fayetteville, North Carolina), grow long-day onions transplanted in spring. They will begin to form bulbs after the summer solstice in late June. South of that same imaginary line, plant short-day varieties in the fall or winter. They will begin to form bulbs in spring around the vernal equinox in late March.

Intermediate-day (or day-neutral) onions will form bulbs north to south, assuming they're given enough time in the garden.

Pak choi (*see Mesclun mix*)

Parsnip *(Pastinaca sativa)*

Type: Cool-season biennial grown as an annual
Edible part: Roots
Typical yield: 10 pounds per 10-foot row
Typical size: 6–12"H×6–12"W

Parsnips

Parsnip is a popular English and continental European crop that deserves a space in North American gardens as well. The plant takes up to four months to produce cream-color, carrotlike roots with a white core. The roots have a sweet, nutty flavor when allowed to mature in cool weather and a soft texture when cooked. They are mashed like potatoes, chopped in soups and stews, or sliced as a side dish glazed with butter and brown sugar.

When: Sow seeds two weeks before your last frost date until early summer.

Planting: Amend the soil with a 1- to 2-inch-thick layer of compost or composted manure. Work the soil deeply removing any rocks and debris. Direct-sow seeds ½ inch deep and ½ inch apart in rows 18 inches apart. Germination takes about three weeks with consistent moisture.

Growing: Thin seedlings to 4 inches apart once true leaves emerge. Weed consistently because parsnips don't compete well with other plants, and do it by hand to protect their roots. Once the plants are established, mulch between rows with a 2- to 3-inch-thick layer of organic material such as straw to keep the soil cool and moist and to prevent further weed growth. Water deeply when the soil is dry, and sidedress monthly with a plant food higher in potassium than nitrogen, such as 5-10-10.

Harvesting: Parsnips taste best when exposed to two to four weeks of low temperatures during which the starch in the roots is converted into sugars. In warm areas you can harvest roots all winter. In northern areas mulch the parsnip bed with a 2- to 4-inch-thick layer of straw in late fall to protect the plants from freezing weather. In early spring remove the mulch and harvest the sweet roots before they start to grow again. Parsnips can be stored in the refrigerator for up to two months.

Pests and diseases: Parsnips are relatively pest free. To avoid diseases rotate crops every three years. Young parsnip seedlings may be attacked by leafhoppers. A severe attack may reduce the size of the roots. Cover the beds with floating row covers to stop leafhoppers from reaching the plants. A row cover will also keep carrot rust flies, which may attack parsnip roots, from laying eggs on the plants.

Varieties: **'Cobham Improved Marrow'** (120 days) is a disease-resistant variety that stays smooth when grown in heavy soils. **'Gladiator Hybrid'** (105 days) is a fast-maturing variety with silky smooth white skin and good disease resistance. **'Harris' Model'** (120 days) is a smooth, bright white variety that holds its color well after harvest. **'Lancer'** (120 days) has long, slender disease-resistant roots.

Peanut, groundnut, ground pea
(Arachis hypogaea)

Type: Warm-season annual
Edible part: Seeds
Typical yield: 5–10 pounds per 10-foot row
Typical size: 1–2'H×1–3'W

'Virginia Jumbo' peanut

Peanuts are actually seeds that grow in pods underground, hence their alternative names groundnut and ground pea. A traditional Southern crop, peanuts grow well throughout warm-summer regions. The plant is a legume that looks like clover but produces yellow flowers. Depending on variety, a peanut plant will either vine or bunch. After the flowers fade, short stems called pegs form; in about 10 days the pegs push their way underground, where shells and nuts form. The whole process from planting to harvest can take up to 120 days.

Peanuts are eaten raw, roasted, made into peanut butter, and used in cooking. They're high in protein and vitamins B and E.

When: Sow seeds or set out transplants two weeks after your last frost date. Peanuts require warm (65°F) soil for proper germination. In cold-winter areas start seedlings indoors four weeks before your last frost date.

Planting: Amend the soil with a 1- to 2-inch-thick layer of compost or composted manure. Peanuts don't grow well in heavy, wet soil, and they need good drainage. Till or mix the soil to a depth of 8 inches. Plant seeds 2 inches deep and 4 inches apart in rows 24 inches apart for bunching types and 36 inches apart for vining types.

Growing: Thin bush seedlings to 6 to 8 inches apart and vining seedlings to 12 to 15 inches apart once true leaves form. Shallowly hoe around peanut plants, mounding the soil to remove weeds and to allow the pegs to easily make their way underground. Once the pegs enter the soil, stop weeding; that's also the time to mulch with a 1- to 2-inch-

'Early Spanish' peanut plant flowers and shoots

thick layer of organic material such as straw. After the flowers fade sidedress the peanuts with a low-nitrogen plant food. Keep the beds well watered, especially when the pegs are forming; deliver at least 1 inch of water per week, or more during dry periods.

Harvesting: Harvest peanut plants once the leaves have yellowed and the plants have begun to dry, usually three to four months after seeding. Pull or carefully dig up individual plants with a spading fork and shake off the loose soil. Mature peanuts will have ridged shells and filled pods. Dry the plants and pods for one week indoors in a warm, well-ventilated location. Separate the pods from the plants and continue to dry the shells for another week. Peanuts stored in the shell in a cool, well-ventilated location can last for months. Shell and roast the peanuts as needed. Roast at 325°F for 20 minutes in the oven.

Pests and diseases: Wireworms, nematodes, and animals such as mice and voles can attack developing peanuts underground. Aphids and leafhoppers may feed on the leaves, reducing yields. Fence out rabbits and other animals, and rotate crops to control wireworms and nematodes.

Peanuts grown in heavy, wet soils are susceptible to rot diseases. Leaf spot can cause leaves to yellow and drop prematurely, especially in hot humid areas. Grow peanuts in well-drained soil or raised beds to prevent these diseases.

Varieties: 'Early Spanish' (100 days) is a bush type that matures quickly, producing two or three papery red-skin nuts per shell. 'Tennessee Red Valencia' (110 days) is a bush type that makes two to five red-skin nuts per shell. 'Virginia Jumbo' (120 days) is a vining type that bears two or three large nuts per shell and up to 50 shells per plant.

Pea *(Pisum sativum)*

Type: Cool-season annual
Edible part: Seeds, pods, young shoots
Typical yield: 2 pounds per 10-foot row
Typical size: 12–84"H×6–12"W

Fresh peas harvested straight from the garden are the ultimate spring treat. Like beans, peas are legumes and are able to succeed in less than ideal soils. However, they need cool weather to grow and mature, making them ideal spring and fall crops.

Peas are one of the most ancient crops. Found in Stone Age villages and Egyptian tombs, they have been cultivated

Harvesting peas

and eaten for thousands of years. It's no wonder. Peas are tasty eaten raw right from the garden, used in dips, sautéed, steamed, or made into soup. You can even clip the tender pea shoots and add them to salads and stir-fries.

When: Sow seeds in early spring as soon as the soil has warmed to at least 45°F and can be worked. Once growing, peas thrive in cool weather and are hardy down to 25°F. Temperatures above 80°F, on the other hand, will cause flowers to drop.

Pea seeds rot if they sit too long in cold, damp soil. In early spring they'll usually do better in raised beds. In cool-summer areas plant in midsummer for a fall crop. In areas with warm summers and mild winters, plant peas in late summer for a late fall or winter crop.

Planting: Amend the soil with a 1-inch-thick layer of compost or composted manure before planting. To fix nitrogen in the soil, dust dampened pea seeds with a rhizobial inoculant appropriate for that variety before planting the seeds. (See page 48 for more about inoculants). Sow the inoculated seeds 1 inch deep and 2 inches apart in rows 8 to 12 inches apart for dwarf pea plants and 3 feet apart if growing peas on a vertical support. In hot, dry areas dig a trench 2 inches wide and 4 inches deep, moisten the soil, and plant the seeds, covering them with 2 inches of soil. Rainwater will collect in the trench, aiding pea germination and early growth. Slowly fill in the trench as the peas grow.

To hasten germination in cool soils, presprout pea seeds indoors by wrapping them in a moist paper towel four or five days before planting.

Growing: Because peas are legumes and can fix their own nitrogen, they don't require additional nitrogen plant food other than compost before planting.

'Oregon Giant' snow pea

'Sugar Ann' snap pea

Snap peas

Weeds will outcompete peas, so keep the beds weed free, especially for the first six weeks that peas are growing. Keep the soil evenly moist, applying 1 inch of water per week. Mulch established plants with a 2-inch-thick layer of organic material such as straw to keep the soil cool, prevent weed growth, and conserve soil moisture.

All pea varieties except the shortest dwarfs require fencing, staking, or a trellis to climb on. Install a 4- to 7-foot-tall (depending on the pea variety) support before planting to avoid disturbing the emerging seedlings.

Harvesting: Pick English (pod or shell) peas when the pods are full and rounded. The peas lower on the vine mature first; pick them daily or they'll become tough and starchy. Pea plants usually finish producing one to two weeks after the first pea is picked. Peas left longer on the vine become dried peas. You can store shelled English peas in the refrigerator for up to one week.

Harvest snap peas when the pods first start to fatten but aren't completely full. Don't shell them; instead, eat the whole pod. Overmature pods become stringy. Snap pea vines continue to grow and produce pods as long as the weather is cool and the plants healthy.

Harvest snow peas when the pods are still flat and the seeds inside small and undeveloped, usually five to seven days after flowering. If you miss a few pods, let the peas inside mature and harvest them like English peas. Keep the pods picked every few days and snow peas will continue to produce. Store snap peas and snow peas in the pod in the refrigerator for up to two weeks. Blanched and frozen peas of all types can last up to one year in the freezer.

Pests and diseases: Peas are susceptible to a variety of diseases such as blight, root rot, fusarium wilt, powdery mildew, botrytis, damping off, and enation virus. Plant in well-drained soil, choose varieties bred for resistance to bacteria and fungi common in your area, and rotate crops each year to avoid these diseases.

The pests most prevalent on peas include slugs, aphids, and leafhoppers when the plants are young, and pea weevils when the plants form pods. Use barriers or baits to control slugs. Spray insecticidal soap to control aphids, and use a floating row cover to prevent leafhopper damage. Control pea weevils by placing a floating row cover over the crop before the pods form and by picking and destroying any damaged pods.

Rabbits and woodchucks love young pea plants. Use fencing to protect the plants.

Varieties: The three types of peas you can grow are based on pod type. English (pod or shell) peas produce full, rounded, tough pods that must be shelled to be eaten. Snap peas bear plump, tender pods that are eaten pod and all. Snow peas (*Pisum sativum macrocarpon*) also produce tender edible pods, but they are flat. Select varieties with different maturity times to extend the harvest season.

English peas: '**Alderman Tall Telephone**' (74 days) is an heirloom that produces 6-foot-tall vines and large pods. '**Eclipse**' (63 days) is noted for 3-foot-tall vines bearing peas that stay sweet longer after harvest than other shell pea varieties. '**Maestro**' (60 days) makes 2-foot-tall plants that produce thin, high-yielding pods; the plant is resistant to powdery mildew and enation virus. '**Premium**' (51 days) is an early variety with very sweet peas on a 30-inch-tall plant. '**Wando**' (68 days) is a 3-foot-tall heirloom that has good heat tolerance.

Snap peas: '**Cascadia**' (60 days) produces 3-foot-tall vines resistant to enation virus and powdery mildew. '**Sugar Ann**' (52 days) puts up 2-foot-tall plants that don't need staking and that bear 2- to 3-inch pods. '**Sugar Lace II**' (68 days) is a 30-inch-tall, self-supporting, disease-resistant plant with few leaves, making it easier to see the pods when harvesting. '**Sugar Snap**' (65 days) produces 6-foot-tall vines and extrasweet pods and peas. '**Super Sugar Snap**' (64 days) is more resistant to powdery mildew and a bit shorter. '**Sugar Sprint**' (58 days) is similar to 'Sugar Ann' in size and growth, but it produces pods that don't get stringy when mature.

Snow peas: '**Dwarf Gray Sugar**' (66 days) features 3-foot-tall vines with pink flowers and sweet pea pods; it is excellent for pea shoots. '**Mammoth Melting**' (68 days) is a 4- to 5-foot-tall heirloom with 5-inch-long pods that stay sweet longer than other snow pea varieties. '**Oregon Giant**' (60 days) is a 3-foot-tall snow pea with good disease resistance. '**Oregon Sugar Pod II**' (68 days) is a 2- to 3-foot-tall, disease-resistant vine with large sweet pods.

Pepper *(Capsicum annuum)*

Type: Warm-season perennial grown as an annual
Edible part: Fruits
Typical yield: 6 pounds per 10-foot row
Typical size: 6–36"H×6–24"W

This widely grown, heat-loving American native crop is a favorite in many gardens. From sweet bells to fiery hot habañeros, peppers add flavor and zip to any dish. Sweet peppers are delicious in salads, stir-fries, soups, and stews, and roasted as hors d'oeuvres. Whether grilled to accompany hamburgers or as components of Asian stir-fries or Mexican salsas—the number one condiment in North America— peppers are a culinary essential. Peppers are high in fiber and vitamins A and C. In fact, a red bell pepper contains more vitamin C than an orange.

Sweet bell pepper, gold variety

TOP GARDEN PEPPERS*

Name	Fruit length (in inches)	Days to mature	Key features
SWEET BELLS			**Usually produces 6–8 fruits per plant**
'Ace Hybrid'	3–4	50	Early. Grows well in cool climates. Abundant producer
'Islander Hybrid'	3	56	Fruits ripen violet with yellow and orange streaks, eventually dark red
'Jingle Bells Hybrid'	1–2	60	Compact plant. High yields of small fruits
'Golden Bell Hybrid'	4	62	Sweet fruit turn deep golden at maturity
'California Wonder'	4	65	Thick-walled. Good for stuffing. Leafy plant protects fruits from sunburn
'Valencia Hybrid'	4	70	Large, thick-walled, orange fruits
'Bell Boy Hybrid'	4	70	Early yields of large fruits. Good for stuffing
'Chocolate Bell Hybrid'	3–4	70	Unique chocolate skin and red flesh. Smoky-sweet flavor. Disease-resistant
'Blushing Beauty Hybrid'	4	72	Large, thick-walled, light red mature color
'Chinese Giant'	6	75	Huge 6" fruits. Good for stuffing.
'Purple Beauty'	4	75	Heirloom. Short, bushy plant. Purple fruits mature to red
SWEET NONBELLS			**Either elongated or round types**
'Gypsy Hybrid'	3–5	65	Early. Very productive. Produces well in both cool and hot regions
'Biscayne Hybrid'	6–7	65	Cubanelle type. High-quality fruit. Very productive
'Sweet Banana'	4	68	Sweet, mild tasting. Starts yellow and matures to red. Widely adapted
'Corno di Toro'	8–10	68	Italian heirloom with curved fruits. Productive
'Giant Marconi Hybrid'	8	72	Improved Italian bull's horn type. Heavy yields of large fruits
'Carmen Hybrid'	6	75	Improved Italian bull's horn type. Quick to turn red
'Sweet Pickle'	2	75	Compact, ornamental plant. Upright-facing fruits in red, orange, yellow, or purple. Good container plant
'Red Sweet Cherry'	1–2	78	Round, sweet, slightly tapered fruits. Great in salads

'Ancho 211' pepper

Peppers are tasty and healthful as well as beautiful. Bell pepper fruits come in many colors including white, yellow, orange, red, and chocolate brown. Some hot pepper plants have multicolor fruits that complement their purple or variegated leaves. Many peppers are compact growers, making them excellent container plants and welcome additions to the flower garden.

When: Peppers require a long season to mature and in most climates should be started indoors six to eight weeks before the last frost date. Transplant seedlings into the garden when soil temperatures are at least 60°F, about two weeks after the last frost date. Peppers grow best with air temperatures between 70°F and 80°F.

Planting: Amend the soil with a 2- to 3-inch-thick layer of compost. In cool areas lay black plastic over the pepper beds to preheat the soil two weeks before transplanting. Set the transplants in holes poked in the plastic, spacing them 12 to 24 inches apart in rows 24 to 36 inches apart.

Growing: Temperatures below 60°F and above 90°F cause pepper flowers to drop. Protect the plants either under floating row cover to keep them warm or under shade cloth to cool them. Amend the soil with plant food based on your soil test, being aware that peppers particularly like magnesium. Fertilize monthly with a 5-5-5 plant food. Avoid high-nitrogen plant foods that cause lush foliage growth but few flowers and fruits.

Mulching pepper plants with aluminum foil

Keep plants well weeded and watered. Unless you're growing the peppers in plastic or foil mulch, apply a 2- to 3-inch-thick layer of organic mulch such as straw after the soil has warmed to

Name	Fruit length (in inches)	Days to mature	Key features
HOT PEPPERS			**Small and hot to _very_ hot**
'Black Pearl Hybrid'	¾	60	Dwarf with black leaves, stems, and immature fruits. Holds color well in heat. Round fruits turn red at maturity. Good container plant
'Early Jalapeño'	2	60	Early yielding fruits have thick walls. Full jalapeño flavor. Good for pickling and Tex/Mex dishes
'Pretty in Purple'	1	60	Attractive purple fruits, stems, and leaves. Round fruits turn red and are hot at maturity. Good container plant
'NuMex Joe E. Parker'	6–7	65	Very productive version of 'NuMex Anaheim' pepper. Mild to medium hot. Good for grilling and roasting. Good Southwest variety
'Tam Jalapeño'	2–3	65	Semicompact plant. Milder than other jalapenos, but same flavor
'Cherry Bomb Hybrid'	2	65	Early. Productive. Round fruits good for pickling or fresh
'Riot'	2–3	70	Multicolor, narrow, medium-hot fruits stand upright. Compact, bushy plants are good in containers
'Super Cayenne III Hybrid'	5–6	70	Vigorous plants. Large fruits. Good disease resistance
'Super Chili Hybrid'	2–3	75	Thin, hot fruits. High yielding. Ornamental. Good for drying
'Serrano'	2	77	Vigorous yields. Good fresh, in sauces, and in salsas
'Hungarian Hot Wax'	6–8	78	Yellow turning to red. Medium-hot pepper. Good for pickling
'Big Chili II Hybrid'	6–7	78	Anaheim type with mild heat. Good for grilling. Grows best in Southwest
'Ancho 211'	4	80	Mildly hot heart-shape fruits. Good for stuffing, chili rellenos, drying, wreaths
'Tabasco'	3–5	80	Tall plants. Fiery hot fruits. Good for sauce. Best in Southeast
'Paprika Supreme'	6–8	80	Grown for drying and grinding into powder. Mildly pungent. Widely adapted
'Thai Hot'	½–1	90	Bright red, extremely hot, thin-fleshed fruits
'Habañero'	1–2	100	Golden-orange wrinkled fruits are blistering hot at maturity
'Caribbean Red Habañero'	1–2	110	Considered one of the hottest peppers available. Bright red wrinkled fruits at maturity

Ranked according to season length

Pepper growing in small tomato cage

prevent further weed growth and conserve soil moisture. Apply at least 1 inch of water per week. Watering is especially important at bloom time or blossoms may drop without setting fruit. Wet leaves at night will foster diseases so water early in the day.

In windy areas and if you're growing tall pepper varieties, stake or cage your plants to prevent them from blowing over.

Harvesting: Use a sharp knife or pruning shears to cut off the fruits when they are either full size or later when they are fully colored. Take care not to break the brittle branches. Not all immature fruits are green: Some varieties develop fruits that are light yellow, lilac, or purple when immature. You may harvest them before they develop their mature color. If kept harvested, peppers will continue to produce fruit until frost. Let some fruits ripen to their full color (usually red), which usually occurs two to four weeks after the mature green stage. The fully colored fruits will be

A sampling of pepper colors and shapes

COUNTING SCOVILLES

In 1912 the American chemist Wilbur Scoville invented a scale to rank the hotness of peppers (the amount of capsaicin in the fruits). The scale starts with bell pepper at 0 and goes up from there to hot peppers, such as habañero, rated at more than 500,000 at its hottest. Some are so hot that handling them can burn your hands.

The measurement is imprecise due to differences in varieties and individual tastes. However, the rating is useful for knowing which types of peppers are hotter than others.

SCOVILLE HEAT SCALE TABLE

Pepper type	Scoville rating
Bell	0
Hot cherry	100–500
Anaheim	500–1,000
Ancho/poblano	1,000–1,500
Jalapeño	2,500–8,000
Serrano	10,000–23,000
Hot wax	10,000–40,000
Tabasco	30,000–50,000
Cayenne	30,000–50,000
Habañero	100,000–577,000

'Sweet Banana' pepper

sweeter and higher in vitamins. However, mature fruits send a signal to the plants to stop producing new fruits, so the more fruits you let mature, the fewer fruits you'll get overall.

Harvest hot peppers in the green or red stage. They are quicker to turn red than sweet peppers. Hot peppers vary in hotness depending on weather and stress. Plants suffering from water or nutrient stress produce fewer but hotter peppers. Cool, cloudy weather makes peppers less hot. Wear gloves when harvesting and handling hot peppers to protect your hands and face from capsaicin, the chemical compound that makes peppers hot.

Store peppers in the refrigerator for up to a week. Ripening continues after harvest. Dry hot peppers by stringing them together with a needle and thread inserted near their caps. Hang them in a dry room with good air circulation until they are thoroughly dry.

Pests and diseases: Aphids, cutworms, corn earworms, and occasionally the pepper maggot attack pepper plants and fruits. Remove aphids with a strong spray of water, or by applying insecticidal soap. Protect young seedlings from cutworms by placing a paper collar around the seedling, setting it 1 inch below the soil and at least 2 inches aboveground. Protect your fruits from maggots by covering the plants with a floating row cover when the fruits are forming.

To avoid soilborne diseases rotate your crops and do not plant a pepper-family crop (tomato, tomatillo, potato, or eggplant) in the same place for three years. Blossom end rot is a physiological condition that causes the base of pepper fruits to rot. Mulch and keep plants evenly watered and fertilized to prevent it.

Pole bean (see Bean)

Potato (*Solanum tuberosum*)

Type: Cool-season annual
Edible part: Tubers
Typical yield: 15–20 pounds per 10-foot row
Typical size: 1–2'H×1–2'W

The potato most people are familiar with is the white-flesh Irish potato, a staple crop around the world. The part of the potato we eat is a fleshy underground stem—a tuber—that the plant uses for food storage and reproduction. Although the standard potato has a reputation for being common, inexpensive, and plain, reasons to grow it are numerous. Homegrown potatoes freshly dug from your garden taste much better than store-bought spuds that have been sitting in a bag for weeks. And potatoes have become much more exciting lately, as many new varieties expand the color and texture range of

'Red Cloud' potato

'Habañero' (red), 'Ancho' (black), and 'Anaheim' peppers

POTATO SEEDS OR SEED POTATOES?

Unlike most other vegetables, potatoes can be grown from seed or from pieces of the tuber itself. Most varieties are sold as seed potatoes, which are simply pieces of a tuber that include at least two buds, or eyes, from which sprouts grow. You can also start potatoes from bona fide seeds, although they are hard to find. Also, potatoes grown from actual seeds take longer to produce and need to be started indoors before transplanting in the garden. However, if you're growing a large plot of potatoes, seeds are more economical than seed potatoes. Some heirloom potato varieties will flower and set seeds, but don't save and grow these seeds because doing so may lead to a buildup of viruses and diseases in the soil.

'All Blue' potato compared to white variety

this South American native plant. Skin colors now include red, white, blue, tan, and brown, and flesh colors go beyond the usual white to include red, blue, yellow, and bicolors. You can grow several types of potatoes: small tender round new potatoes, buttery little fingerlings, and large blocky oval potatoes.

Cutting seed potato

From french-fried to baked, mashed, and scalloped, potatoes are a popular side dish at restaurants and on the dinner table. Many cooks use them in stews or with strong-flavored meats like pot roast and pork to soak up the tasty juices released in cooking.

When: Plant seed potatoes (pieces of tubers) two to four weeks before your last frost date. In warm regions plant potatoes in fall or winter. Potatoes form tubers best when the soil temperature is between 60° and 70°F, and plants stop making tubers when it rises above 80°F.

Planting: Potatoes need rich soil. Ideally, sow a fall green manure crop where your potatoes will grow and turn it under before spring planting. In preparation for planting the potatoes spread a plant food that's relatively high in phosphorus and potassium compared with nitrogen, such as 5-10-10. Avoid adding high-nitrogen plant food in spring because high nitrogen levels reduce plant vigor and can lead to disease.

Select certified disease-free seed potatoes to plant. Avoid using grocery store potatoes, which are often sprayed with a sprout inhibitor to prevent growth in storage.

Presprouted seed potatoes develop faster than those without sprouts. To form sprouts, set uncut seed potatoes in a sunny place for one to three days before planting. The smaller seed potatoes—those less than 2 inches across—can be planted directly in the ground, but you'll need to cut the larger ones into pieces. Use a sharp knife to cut 1-inch fleshy chunks, each with two eyes. Dry the pieces overnight to form a callus layer on the cut ends and to help protect them from rot. Plant the pieces as well as the whole small seed potatoes eyes up in trenches dug 4 inches deep in heavy soil and 6 inches deep in light soil. Space the tubers 12 to 15 inches apart in rows 20 to 24 inches apart, depending on the mature size of the variety. Cover seed potatoes with 2 to 4 inches of soil.

Growing: Keep the soil evenly moist until sprouts emerge, usually in about one week after planting. One week after the sprouts emerge, or once they are about 6 to 8 inches tall, hill the soil around them creating a mounded ridge. Hill the potato rows again two to three weeks later. Hilling not only creates a loose soil area where tubers can easily form, but

Planting seed potatoes "eyes up"

Potatoes still attached to parent plant

GROW A POTATO TOWER

If you don't have room to cultivate potatoes the usual way in the ground, try growing them vertically in a tower or container. To construct a potato tower, place a 3-foot-diameter chicken wire cage in the garden. Add a 2- to 3-inch-thick layer of soil on the bottom of the enclosure and line the inside with straw.

Plant four seed potatoes in the bottom and cover them with soil. As the potatoes grow, continue adding soil over them and straw around the inside of the enclosure until you reach the top. Keep the soil and straw moist. Once the potato plants start to die back, remove the cage and harvest the potato tubers that have developed inside.

Potatoes growing in half barrel

Pulling soil up around growing potato plants

also it shades potato tubers from the sun, preventing the skins from turning green, and helps kill weeds. Misshapen potatoes develop in hard, compact soil. Green potato skins are off-flavor and mildly toxic when eaten. However, you'd have to eat many pounds of green potatoes to actually get sick. You can peel the skin and still eat the rest of the potato.

Once the plants reach their full size, lay a 2- to 4-inch-thick layer of organic mulch such as straw on the hills. Mulch conserves soil moisture, prevents further weed growth, and helps shade any exposed tubers from the sun.

Harvesting: Harvest small 1- to 2-inch-diameter new potatoes six to eight weeks after planting, usually when the plants are flowering. Without unsettling any plants, excavate lightly next to them with a small digging fork and lift the small tubers by hand, then replace the soil. Select a few potatoes from each plant so as not to significantly decrease the later harvest. Once the potato plant tops start dying back, dig and lift the entire plant with a garden fork and harvest the tubers. In warm-summer areas let the vines die back completely so the potatoes will cure in the ground before harvest. In colder areas, frost may kill the plants before the potatoes have a chance to cure.

Sort tubers after harvest. Cull out any damaged tubers and eat those first. Pest- or disease-damaged tubers are still edible once the bad spots are removed, but they won't store well. Gently remove loose soil from the tubers. Cure them unwashed in a dark, humid place at 65° to 70°F for two weeks. Move the potatoes to a cool, dark, humid cellar, shed, or garage to store at 40° to 50°F for up to nine months, depending on the potato variety.

Pests and diseases: Rotate crops so that you plant potatoes or potato-family members including tomatoes, tomatillos, peppers, and eggplant in the same ground only once every three years. Grow certified disease-free tubers, clean up all the plant debris in fall, and keep the soil acidic (a pH of 5.3 to 6 is ideal) to prevent potato scab, blight, and other

Harvesting fingerling potatoes

A sampler of potato varieties

potato diseases. Alkaline soils are more conducive to disease organisms.

Kill flea beetles with insecticidal soap, and use floating row covers to shield young plants from leafhoppers. Where voles, mice, and gophers are a problem, harvest potatoes as soon as they are mature or grow them in containers.

Control the Colorado potato beetle by crushing the orange eggs on the underside of leaves and by spraying the larvae with *Bacillus thuringiensis* (Bt). Note that only Bt strains known as *B. t. tenebrionis* or 'San Diego' are effective. Handpicking the adults, which are striped light tan and brown, can be effective in a small garden. Mulching between the potato rows helps slow the beetle's spread.

Varieties: Potato varieties are classified as early (65 days), midseason (75 to 80 days) and late (90-plus days). Plant an assortment to extend your harvest.

Early: **'Caribe'**, with blue-purple skin and pure white flesh, is good harvested as a new potato. **'Cranberry Red'** has red skin and rose flesh that hold their color during cooking. **'Dark Red Norland'** produces oblong tubers with red skin and white flesh; they are tasty harvested as new potatoes, and are also resistant to scab and foliar diseases. **'King Harry'** produces tubers with gold skin and white flesh; the plant has hairy leaves that discourage the Colorado potato beetle, leafhoppers, and flea beetles. **'Superior'**, with tubers featuring buff-color skin and white flesh, is scab-resistant and stores a long time; the plant grows under a wide range of conditions. **'Yukon Gold'** has yellow skin and moist yellow flesh; the plant is drought-tolerant and very productive.

Midseason: **'Gold Rush'** is a scab-free, disease-resistant, russet-skin potato with dry white flesh. **'Red Cloud'**, a long keeper, has crimson skin and dry white flesh. **'Viking Purple'** has purple skin and white flesh; the plant can tolerate drought.

Late: **'All Blue'**, an heirloom with unique blue skin and moist purple flesh, is excellent for purple mashed potatoes. **'Butte'**, a classic Idaho baking potato with russet skin and white flesh, has 20 percent more protein and 58 percent more vitamin C than other varieties. **'Catalina'**, a variety grown from seed, has brown skin and white flesh. **'Kennebec'** is a disease-resistant (but not to scab) potato with buff-color skin and dry white flesh; it can be planted closer together than other varieties, making it ideal for small-space gardens. **'Rose Finn Apple'** is a fingerling type with pink skin and creamy-textured yellow flesh. **'Russian Banana'**, a fingerling type with a banana shape, has yellow skin and flesh; the tuber's waxy texture makes it good boiled. **'Swedish Peanut Fingerling'**, another variety with yellow skin and flesh, is an heirloom that's good roasted or panfried.

Pumpkin (see Squash)
Radicchio (see Chicory, mesclun mix)

Radish (Raphanus sativus)

Type: Cool-season annual
Edible part: Roots
Typical yield: 10 bunches per 10-foot row
Typical size: 2–6"H×2–6"W

Grown for crisp and spicy roots, radishes are one of the fastest-maturing crops in the garden. Some varieties can be harvested in less than one month. Although the small round red spring radishes with the crunchy, moist texture and hot, spicy taste are familiar to most gardeners, several other kinds of radishes are available too. French radishes, cylindrical

'Easter Egg II' radish

types that mature earlier than round radishes, come with white skin or red skin tipped in white. Winter radishes grow into large round or elongated roots. Slower to develop than spring radishes, they remain crisp longer, are more pungent, and can hold in the ground or store longer than spring varieties. A good example of a winter radish is the daikon, which has long white tapered roots.

Eat fresh round and long French radishes sliced in salads, where their crunch and peppery flavor seasons milder-tasting vegetables. Daikon varieties are popular ingredients in Japanese cuisine, and winter radishes generally are good for pickles, salads, and cooking.

When: Plant seeds three to four weeks before the last frost in spring and six weeks before the first frost in fall. Make successive sowings every week or two in spring to extend the summer harvest. Many winter radishes are best sown in midsummer for a fall harvest.

Planting: Amend the soil with a 1- to 2-inch-thick layer of compost before planting. Like carrots and beets, radishes need a loose soil raked free of rocks and debris if they are to extend their roots and grow properly. Unless your soil is sandy, build a raised bed and remove any rocks, sticks, and other debris. Direct-sow seeds ½ inch deep and 1 inch apart in rows 10 inches apart. Interplant with carrots, beans, and cucumbers. By interspersing slower-growing crops with radishes, you can shade the latter and use radishes as a trap crop (see page 92).

Growing: Thin small-rooted regular spring radishes to 2 inches apart when they are 1 inch tall. Thin daikons and larger-rooted winter radishes to 3 to 4 inches apart. Since radishes are such quick growers, they rarely need supplemental plant food.

Too much nitrogen plant

Sampler of radish varieties

Radishes ready to harvest

'D'Avignon' French radish

food (including compost), debris such as rocks, improper thinning, and water or heat stress can prevent roots from forming or cause them to be deformed, woody, and hot tasting. Grow spring radishes quickly to maturity by maintaining a weed-free bed, hand pulling any weeds that emerge, and keeping the soil consistently moist. Soil that alternates from wet to dry can cause radish roots to crack. Winter radishes grow more slowly than spring radishes and can take up to one month longer to mature.

Harvesting: Harvest spring radishes as soon as the roots are large enough to eat. Radishes left in the ground too long can crack, become woody, develop a seed stalk, and have a hot flavor. Harvest winter radishes when they reach full size.

Cut off the greens and taproots, and scrub the radishes with a vegetable brush under running water. Store spring radishes for up to a week in the refrigerator. Winter radishes can be stored for up to two weeks in the refrigerator.

Pests and diseases: Avoid radish diseases such as club root by rotating radish crops every five to seven years. Flea beetles, aphids, and root maggots attack radish plants. Spray insecticidal soap to control aphids and flea beetles. Spread diatomaceous earth around the bed to control root maggots.

Varieties: Spring (or French): '**Cherriette**' (26 days) has smooth round bright red roots; it is good for spring or fall growing. '**D'Avignon**' (21 days) produces a 3- to 4-inch-long tapered red root with a white tip. '**Easter Egg II**' (30 days) is a mix of red, purple, and white round radishes that mature over an extended period of time. '**French Breakfast**' (23 days) develops an oblong red root with a white tip. '**White Icicle**' (27 days) has a 4- to 5-inch-long tapered all-white root.

Winter: '**April Cross**' (55 days) is a 12- to 16-inch-long daikon that is best planted in fall for a spring to early summer harvest. '**Minowase Summer Cross No. 3**' (55 days), best grown as a fall crop, produces 8- to 10-inch-long, tapered daikon roots. '**Nero Tondo**' (50 days) is a black Spanish winter radish that features 2- to 4-inch-diameter round roots with black skin and spicy white flesh. '**Red Meat**' (50 days) develops a 2- to 4-inch-diameter round radish with green skin and sweet pink flesh.

Winter radish 'Nero Tondo'

HERE'S A TIP...

Radish as pest trap
A trap crop is grown to attract certain insects away from more highly desired main crops. Radishes are such fast growers that they attract insect pests, which you can then destroy before they reach other, slower-growing plants. Plant radishes near cabbage-family crops or eggplant to lure flea beetles and root maggot flies. Allow the pests to feed for a while, then sacrifice the radish crop by pulling it up or by spraying it with a pest control product. This process will destroy a majority of the insects.

Rhubarb *(Rheum rhabarbarum)*

Type: Cool-season perennial, Zones 2–9
Edible part: Leafstalks
Typical yield: 7 pounds per 10-foot row
Typical size: 1–3'H×2–4'W

Rhubarb is an easy-to-grow perennial that's valued for its flavorful and colorful leafstalks. It was prized by the ancient Chinese as a vegetable and medical plant. Because rhubarb is ready to harvest in spring, it is often used in pies and cobblers mixed with strawberries. You can also make rhubarb jam, bread, bars, muffins, pickles, wine, and soup.

When: Rhubarb grows best when the air temperature is below 80°F. Plant in early spring as soon as the ground can be worked or in fall once the soil and air temperatures cool.

Planting: Amend the soil with a 2- to 3-inch-thick layer of composted manure. Plant crowns 2 inches deep in holes 6 feet apart, setting each crown so the central bud is 2 inches below the soil line.

Growing: Add a 2-inch-thick layer of compost around the new plants when the air temperature rises above 80°F. Keep

Harvest rhubarb by breaking stalks off by hand.

the soil evenly moist and weed free. Cut off any flower stalks that develop down to the base of the plant. Apply a complete plant food annually in spring. After the harvest put down a layer of compost around the plants.

When the leafstalks become thin (usually after six to eight years), dig and divide the plant in spring or fall. Divide the crown so the new plant has some buds and a generous amount of roots, then replant. Keep divided plants well watered the first year.

Harvesting: Rhubarb leafstalks develop the best color and flavor when harvested while the weather is still cool. Leave first-year plants unharvested. The second year harvest by using either a sharp knife or by breaking stalks off by holding them close to the base and pulling down and to one side. Remove the leaves. Harvest for one week. In the third year harvest all stalks larger than 1 inch wide for eight weeks. Compost the leaves; although the leafstalks are completely edible, rhubarb leaves contain oxalic acid and are poisonous.

Store unwashed leafstalks in a plastic bag in the refrigerator for up to two weeks. Blanch, chop, and freeze rhubarb to be used later in pies.

Pests and diseases: Few pests and diseases seriously affect rhubarb. Remove any Japanese beetles, rhubarb curculio beetles, or caterpillars by hand. Avoid verticillium wilt by planting rhubarb in well-drained soil.

Varieties: '**MacDonald**' is a high-yielding variety with green stems that have red overtones; it grows well in heavy clay soils. '**Chipman's Canada Red**' has plump crimson stalks with a sweet-tart flavor. '**Valentine**' has deep red stalks; it grows faster than other red varieties and can be harvested sooner.

Rocket salad (see Arugula)
Roquette (see Arugula)

Rutabaga, Swede turnip (Brassica napus)

Type: Cool-season biennial grown as an annual
Edible part: Roots
Typical yield: 8–10 pounds per 10-foot row
Typical size: 12–18"H×8–12"W

A cross between a cabbage and a turnip, rutabaga produces large roots and bitter leaves. The roots, which are yellow fleshed, have a sweet, nutty flavor. Although the crop is commonly grown in northern areas, it can perform well anywhere there is an extended period of cool weather in autumn or early winter.

Rutabagas are used much like potatoes in cooking. Dice the roots and add them to soups and stews; mash or steam them for a side dish. Young roots make good raw dipping vegetables, or you can grate them into salads.

When: Sow seeds four weeks before the last frost date in spring for an early summer crop or 90 to 100 days before the first fall frost for a fall crop. In warm-summer areas, rutabaga produces better and tastes sweeter when sown as a fall crop.

'Marian' rutabaga

Planting: Amend the soil with a 2- to 3-inch-thick layer of composted manure. Plant in well-drained soil raked free of rocks and debris. Sow seeds ½ inch deep and 2 inches apart in rows about 24 inches apart.

Growing: Thin seedlings to 8 inches apart once true leaves form. Hand weed the bed. Mulch with a 2- to 3-inch-thick layer of organic material such as straw after weeding to maintain soil moisture and keep the soil cool. To keep the soil evenly moist, water 1 to 2 inches per week, especially during periods of hot, dry weather. Based on a soil test, at planting apply a complete plant food higher in potassium and lower in nitrogen such as 5-10-10.

Harvesting: Pull rutabaga roots when they are 3 to 5 inches in diameter, about 90 days after seeding. Fall-grown roots taste sweeter if exposed to a few frosts before harvest. Since rutabaga can withstand frost, only pick what you need that day and leave the rest in the garden.

To store rutabaga, trim off the foliage with a sharp knife to within 1 inch of the crown. The roots can be stored for two to four months at 35°F and high humidity. You can also store rutabagas in the garden during winter by mulching the bed with a 6- to 8-inch-thick layer of straw mulch in the fall.

Pests and diseases: Aphids and flea beetles attack the greens, and root maggots can damage the roots. Keep aphids and flea beetles in check with jet sprays of water or sprays of insecticidal soap. Control root maggots with a floating row cover or diatomaceous earth. To avoid diseases such as club root, rotate crops and do not plant rutabaga or another cabbage-family crop in the same ground for three years.

Varieties: '**Laurentian**' (95 days) roots have dark purple shoulders with pale yellow skin and sweet, mild flesh. '**Marian**' (90 days), which has pale purple shoulders, keeps well, and is club root–resistant. '**Purple Top**' (90 days) features huge yellow roots with fine-grained flesh that turns orange when cooked

Scallion (see Onion)
Shallot (see Onion)
Shungiku (see Asian greens)

Snap bean (see Bean)
Southern pea (see Bean)
Soybean (see Bean)

Spinach *(Spinacia oleracea)*

Type: Cool-season annual
Edible part: Leaves
Typical yield: 4–5 pounds per 10-foot row
Typical size: 3–8"H×2–8"W

'Tyee' spinach with peas

One of the first crops harvested in spring, spinach tastes delicious fresh in salads and steamed or sautéed in olive oil and garlic for a side dish. Its smooth or crinkled dark green leaves are full of iron, calcium, protein, and vitamin A.

Spinach grows best in cool weather. In warm-weather areas or during midsummer try growing the heat-tolerant spinach substitutes, Malabar spinach and New Zealand spinach.

When: Begin planting four to six weeks before your last frost date. Spinach seeds can germinate in soils as cool as 35°F. Continue planting every two weeks until late spring. Also plant in late summer for a fall harvest. In cold climates sow seeds in fall in a cold frame to overwinter for an early spring harvest. In warm areas plant seeds in fall to harvest in winter and early spring.

Planting: Amend the soil with a 2- to 3-inch-thick layer of compost before planting. Soak seeds overnight in warm water. Sow them ¼ inch deep and 1 inch apart in rows 12 inches apart or broadcast seeds in raised beds.

Growing: Thin seedlings to 6 inches apart when they're 3 inches tall. Maintain cool, moist soil by watering regularly and mulching with a 2- to 3-inch-thick layer of an organic material such as straw. It's best to water in the morning so the leaves can dry before evening. Proper watering and adequate spacing help prevent rust disease. If young leaves turn light green, apply a quick-acting foliar nitrogen fertilizer.

Harvesting: Begin harvesting individual leaves 20 to 30 days after sowing, when there are five or six leaves on the plant. The thinnings can be used for salads. Harvest whole plants in 35 to 50 days. Pull or cut individual plants at the soil line. Continue harvesting leaves until hot weather forces seed stalks to form, then pull and compost the plants. To store spinach leaves, wash, pat dry, and place them in a plastic bag in the refrigerator, where they will keep for about one week.

Harvesting spinach

'Malabar Red Stem' spinach growing on obelisk

Pests and diseases: Use floating row covers to protect young plants from leaf miners. Spray insecticidal soap to control flea beetles. Dislodge aphids with a spray of water from a garden hose. Choose disease-resistant varieties for blight and virus control, especially when growing spinach in humid, wet areas. Grow plants in raised beds and keep the crop properly thinned to promote good air circulation; this helps prevent diseases such as mildew and rust.

Varieties: Spinach varieties are either smooth or crinkled (savoy). Types with crinkled varieties have a good texture, but the creases can catch soil that splashes onto them during a rain, making the leaves harder to clean.

Smooth-leaf: 'Olympia' (45 days) is slow to bolt, disease-resistant, and productive. 'Oriental Giant' (40 days) produces large 12- to 15-inch-long leaves and yields up to three times more foliage than other varieties. 'Space' (39 days) is another slow-to-bolt variety that's heat-tolerant and grows equally well in spring, summer, and fall.

Crinkle-leaf: 'Bloomsdale Long Standing' (42 days) is a classic variety that's quick growing and slow to bolt. 'Melody' (42 days) produces quick-growing, 10-inch leaves. 'Tyee' (40 days) is one of the crinkle-leaf varieties most resistant to bolting and disease.

Summer spinach: 'Malabar Red Stem' *(Basella rubra),* which can be harvested 55 days after sowing, has thick red stems and dark green leaves with a mild flavor. The vigorous vines can grow 6 feet or more in the heat of summer and need trellising.

New Zealand Spinach *(Tetragonia tetragonioides),* a perennial in mild climates, produces small fleshy green leaves 70 days after sowing and keeps going until frost.

New Zealand spinach

Squash, pumpkin, gourd *(Cucurbita* spp.)

Type: Warm-season annual
Edible part: Fruits
Typical yield: 10–15 pounds per 10-foot row
Typical size: 1–2'H×10–20'W

Comparison of zucchini varieties

Perhaps no other vegetable comes in as many shapes, sizes, and colors as those in the squash family. Pumpkin, summer squash, winter squash, and gourd all belong to the same family. These Native American vegetables are famous for their part in the traditional "three sisters" garden, namely the combination of squash, beans, and corn. While the family members all grow in a similar way, the results can be very different. Pumpkins can range from a few ounces to over a thousand pounds. Summer squashes can be long and thin, crookneck, round like a baseball, or even shaped like a flying saucer. The skin of winter squashes can be almost any color of the rainbow including blue. Gourds span the range of colors, shapes, and uses. Some gourds are purely decorative, but others are used to make baskets, birdhouses, sponges, and even musical instruments.

Although pumpkins are traditionally thought of for making pies, summer and winter squashes can be used in a variety of dishes including soups, cakes, casseroles, curries, salads, and cookies. Summer

HAND POLLINATING SQUASH

Like cucumbers, squash plants produce separate male and female flowers on each plant. In order to get fruit, bees need to cross-pollinate the flowers. If bee populations are low in your area or if the weather is cloudy and cool, bees won't fly and your squash flowers won't get pollinated.

You can pollinate the flowers yourself. In midmorning go into the squash or pumpkin patch. Identify a male flower (long thin stems behind the flower and no small fruits), pick it off the plant, and remove all the yellow petals to expose the pollen-bearing stamen. Then find an open female flower (small fruit behind the flower) and swish the yellow pollen-laden stamen inside it and any other open female flowers.

GROWING GIANTS

So you want to grow one of those blue ribbon–winning giant pumpkins? Just follow these steps.
● **Sow seeds of 'Dill's Atlantic Giant'.** This is the variety that can grow big quickly.
● **Start seeds indoors** in peat pots four weeks before your last frost date. Keep the potting soil moist and warm.
● **Amend soil** generously with compost.
● **Cover seedlings** with a clear plastic tent after transplanting and for six weeks to keep them warm and growing fast. Remove the tent once they outgrow it.
● **Hand pollinate** the flowers (see below left).
● **Move fruits** once they set so the pumpkins are at right angles to the stem. This position will give them the room they need to expand and not crack the stem.
● **Be ruthless.** Select the best one or two pumpkins per plant and remove all the others. Reducing the number of fruits will send energy into the remaining fruits.
● **Prune the vine** 10 feet beyond where the pumpkin has set.
● **Feed weekly** when the plants are young with a fertilizer high in phosphorus, such as 15-30-15. Later, after the fruits set, switch to a fertilizer higher in potassium, such as 15-11-30.

squashes are picked young and eaten fresh, whereas winter squashes, pumpkins, and gourds can be stored for months for use all winter.
When: Direct-sow seeds when the air temperature reaches 70°F in spring. In cool-summer areas start seeds indoors four weeks before your last frost date and transplant the seedlings after the danger of frost has passed.
Planting: All types need rich, fertile soil and

'Sunburst' summer squash

TOP GARDEN SQUASHES*

Name	Skin color	Days to mature	Key features
SUMMER SQUASHES (*C. pepo*, unless noted)			**Eat immature, soft-skinned fruits**
'Papaya Pear Hybrid'	Yellow	42	Harvest pear-shape fruits when 3–4" in diameter. Compact. Very productive
'Magda Hybrid'	Light green	48	Zucchini type with sweet, nutty flavor. Middle eastern Cousa style, blocky fruit
'Raven Hybrid'	Dark green	48	Zucchini type high in antioxidants. Compact plant
'Peter Pan Hybrid'	Light green	50	Pattypan type. Relatively dense flesh
'Eight Ball Hybrid'	Dark green	50	Round, shiny fruits. Harvest when 2–3" in diameter
'Gold Rush Hybrid'	Deep yellow	50	Zucchini type. Uniform, smooth, straight fruits
'Sunburst' Hybrid	Deep yellow	52	Pattypan type, tender. Vigorous plant
'Early Summer Crookneck'	Yellow	53	Heirloom crookneck. Bumpy skin
'Black Beauty'	Dark green	60	Zucchini type. Smooth, straight fruits. Open plant
'Italiano Largo'	Dark green, light green stripes	60	Zucchini type. Italian heirloom with dense texture and nutty flavor. Slender, straight fruits
'Palee Hybrid' (*Momordica charantia*)	Dark green with spines	68	Bitter gourd or balsam pear. Indian vegetable with bumpy skin. Large seeds. Harvest at 7–8" long. Use bitter white flesh in soups, stir-fries
Chayote (chocho, mirliton, vegetable pear) (*Sechium edule*)	Light green	90	Tropical, pear-shape fruit with bland, zucchini-like white flesh. Roots, stems, and leaves also edible. Twelve- to 15-foot-long vine. Perennial where frost free
WINTER SQUASHES (*C. maxima*, unless noted)			**Eat fully mature, hard-skinned fruits. Store for weeks to months**
'Early Butternut Hybrid'	Tan	85	4–5 fruits, each 10–12" long
'Table Queen' (*C. pepo*)	Dark green	85	Heirloom acorn type with golden flesh. 4–6 fruits, each 2–3 pounds. Vigorous vine
'Table Ace Hybrid' (*C. pepo*)	Black-green	85	Acorn type with sweet, nutty flavor. 5–7 fruits, each 2–3 pounds. Semibush
'Spaghetti' (*C. pepo*)	Ivory maturing to yellow	88	Flesh separates into noodlelike strings after baking. 4–5 fruits, each 4 pounds
'Red Kuri' (hubbard)	Scarlet	92	Teardrop shape with smooth red flesh. 2–3 fruits, each 4–7 pounds. Good for pies
'Burgess Buttercup' (buttercup)	Dark green, gray button on bottom	95	Blocky fruits with deep orange fiberless flesh. 3–4 fruits, each 3–5 pounds
'Blue Ballet' (hubbard)	Blue-green	95	Smooth skin and sweet orange flesh. 2 fruits, each 4–6 pounds
'Sunshine Hybrid' (kabocha)	Bright scarlet	95	Slightly flat and round. Sweet, smooth bright orange flesh. 3–4 fruits, each 3–5 pounds. Short vine
'Turk's Turban' (buttercup)	Orange, green, and tan stripes	95	Edible ornamental with gold flesh. Turban shape. 3–4 fruits, each 3–5 pounds
'Bonbon Hybrid' (buttercup)	Dark green skin, gray button on bottom	95	Uniform, large buttercup type. Sweet orange flesh. 4 fruits, each 4–5 pounds
'Sweet Dumpling' (delicata) (*C. pepo*)	Ivory with dark green stripes	100	Teacup-shape fruits with sweet orange flesh. 8–10 fruits, each 4" wide. Good for stuffing

adequate heat and water to produce their best. Amend the soil with a 2- to 3-inch-thick layer of compost before planting. In cool-summer areas lay black plastic mulch over the beds two weeks before planting to preheat the soil; then poke holes in the plastic and sow seeds or set transplants into the holes. In all regions plant seeds of bush varieties of summer and winter squashes 1 to 2 inches deep and 2 to 3 feet apart in rows spaced 3 to 5 feet apart. For vining summer squashes, winter squashes, pumpkins, and gourds sow seeds 2 to 4 feet apart in rows 5 to 8 feet apart. Or plant five to seven seeds in hills spaced 4 feet apart, thinning to three plants per hill after true leaves form.

Growing: Squashes and especially large pumpkins require a constant supply of moisture to grow and size up properly.

Name	Skin color	Days to mature	Key features
'Cornell's Bush Delicata'	Ivory with dark green stripes	100	Oblong fruits each 1–2 pounds. Sweet flesh. Semibush. Powdery–mildew resistant
'Waltham' (butternut) (C. moschata)	Tan	105	Cylindrical, 9" diameter. Thick skin with sweet orange flesh. 4–5 fruits, each 4–5 pounds
'Banana Pink Jumbo'	Pink-orange	105	Cylindrical. Firm, dry, sweet, nonfibrous yellow-orange flesh. 2–3 fruits, each 50 pounds
'Green Striped Cushaw' (C. mixta)	Light green with mottled green stripes	110	Bulb-shape heirloom. Fibrous, slightly sweet yellow flesh. 2–3 fruits, each 10–12 pounds. Resistant to squash vine borer. Good for Southeast
PUMPKINS (C. pepo, unless noted)			**Harvest when skin turns mature color. Some edible, all ornamental**
'Lumina'	White	85	Unique color. Smooth skin and orange flesh. 3–4 fruits, each 10 pounds. Good for painting and carving
'Baby Boo'	White	90	Decorative mini pumpkin. 2–3" diameter. 8–10 fruits. Yellow flesh. Harvest before skin turns pale yellow
'Orange Smoothie Hybrid'	Bright orange	95	Smooth skin. Unribbed. 3–4 fruits, each 6–9 pounds. Great for painting.
'Queensland Blue'	Bluish green	100	Australian heirloom. Deeply ribbed. 2–3 fruits, each 6–10 pounds
'Small Sugar'	Orange	100	Heirloom. 3–4 fruits, each 5–8 pounds. Good for pies and canning
'Marina Di Chioggia'	Blue-green	100	Italian heirloom with bumpy turban shape. Yellow-orange flesh. 2 fruits, each 10 pounds. Good for pies and baking
'Baby Bear'	Deep orange	105	Mini pumpkin with flesh good enough for pies. Semihulless seeds good for roasting. 8 fruits, each 1–2 pounds
'Long Island Cheese'	Tan	108	Flattened, ribbed, resembles cheese wheel. Deep orange flesh. 2 fruits, each 6–10 pounds. Good for pies
'Connecticut Field'	Light orange	110	Large, slightly ribbed. 2–3 fruits, each 15–30 pounds. Good for carving
'Howden'	Deep orange	115	Classic big pumpkin with defined ribs. Strong stem handle. 2–3 fruits, each 20–30 pounds. Good for carving
'Rouge Vif d'Etamps' (C. maxima)	Scarlet	115	Flattened, ornamental, French heirloom. Mild, sweet orange flesh. 2 fruits, each 10–15 pounds
'Big Max' (C. maxima)	Pink-orange	120	Large. 2–3 fruits, each up to 100 pounds. Good for carving and pies
'Dill's Atlantic Giant' (C. maxima)	Pink-orange	120	Produces largest pumpkins, some over 1,000 pounds. 1–2 fruits per plant. Needs fertile soil and much space
GOURDS			**Hard shelled, small, ornamental, and utensils**
Luffa (Luffa cylindrica)	Dark green	70 edible; 120 sponge	Harvest at 7" for eating, at 2' when dried for sponge. Vigorous. Needs sturdy trellis and long, warm season to produce mature gourds
'Shenot Crown of Thorns Mix' (C. pepo)	Various	95	Globe shape. 4–5" fruits have up to 10 points or fingers
'Small Decorative Mix' (C. pepo)	Various	95	Small inedible decorative gourds including spoon, warted, apple, flat, striped
Bottle (Lagenaria siceracia)	Green; tan when dried	125	Large 10–12" gourds with narrow neck and smaller round section on top. For bottles and birdhouses when dried, cured, and hollowed out
Dipper (Lagenaria siceracia)	Green	125	Bulbous end is a 4" oval attached to 12" handle. Good for ladles

*Ranked according to season length

Apply 1 to 2 inches of water per week, increasing frequency during dry periods. Keep beds weeded by lightly cultivating around plants with a hoe. To maintain soil moisture and warmth in cool regions, mulch with black plastic before planting. In warm-summer areas mulch with straw after the soil has warmed.

Fertilize at planting time, using a balanced product such a 5-5-5. Once pumpkin and winter squash vines start running, sidedress the plants with a high-nitrogen fertilizer. In cool-summer areas pinch off winter squash and pumpkin blossoms and small fruits that form late in the season. These won't have time to mature before frost and will take energy away from maturing the existing fruits.

Let winter squashes and pumpkins run across a lawn,

Harvesting yellow straightneck squash

or trellis smaller-fruited varieties on a fence or other structure and use mesh bags or netting to support the fruits.

Harvesting: Summer squashes—crooknecks, zucchinis, and straightnecks—taste best when picked small, about 6 inches long. Pattypan, or scallop, squashes are best harvested when they're 3 inches across.

Cover young plants to exclude cucumber beetles.

Check plants daily because they can reach edible size literally overnight. Use a clean, sharp knife to cut the stems of summer squashes about 1 inch above the fruits. Store the squashes for up to two weeks in the refrigerator.

If a few fruits escape your detection, harvest them immediately. The more you pick, the more fruits will be produced. A young summer squash is used sliced, chopped, or grated into salads; or steamed or stir-fried. A large-fruited summer squash can be cut lengthwise, hollowed out, stuffed, and baked.

Leave winter squashes, pumpkins, and gourds on the vine until they size up and turn the appropriate skin color for that variety. The rind will feel hard when you press it with your thumbnail. Harvest before a hard frost. Use a clean, sharp knife to cut the stems 2 inches above the fruits. Carefully remove the fruits without bruising or nicking the skin: Bruised fruits won't last as long in storage. Wipe the skins clean with a mild bleach solution to kill any disease spores. Place winter squashes and pumpkins in

HERE'S A TIP...

Eat those flowers
Squash and pumpkin flowers are tasty in many dishes. Try them lightly sautéed as an appetizer. Pick mostly male blossoms for cooking and leave the female flowers to produce fruit.

'Black Beauty' zucchini

Winter squash 'Cornell's Bush Delicata'

DRYING AND CURING GOURDS

Harvest small decorative gourds before the first frost. Hard-shell gourds such as dipper gourds can tolerate a light frost. Cut gourds when the skins are hard and the stems brown and dried. Wipe the skin clean with a mild bleach solution. Don't save any that have cracked or broken shells.

Cure hard-shell gourds in a 50° to 60°F well-ventilated room. Depending on their size and shape, hard-shell gourds can take up to six months to dry. If any mold forms on the skin, you can let it dry or remove it with a mild bleach solution. When the seeds rattle, the gourd is dry and ready for crafting.

'Burgess Buttercup' winter squash

an 80° to 85°F, humid room for two weeks to cure. Store them in a dark location at 50° to 55°F. Most winter squashes and pumpkins can be stored for two to three months under proper conditions. Some, such as hubbard squash, can last up to six months.

Pests and diseases: Squashes, particularly the winter types, are vulnerable to squash bugs, which gather under the leaves. They feed on the foliage and flowers, reducing the vigor of the plant.

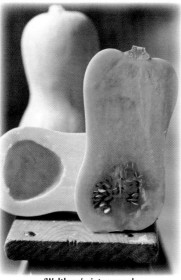

'Waltham' winter squash

A sampler of winter squash variety

'Small Sugar' pumpkin

When you see the first brown nymphs, kill them with a spray of neem oil before they can reach adulthood. Set a sheet of cardboard under the plants, and collect and destroy squash bugs hiding underneath. Rotate crops and clean up crop debris in fall to eliminate squash bug overwintering spots and fend off diseases.

Cucumber beetles harm squashes and pumpkins, feeding on young plants and flowers.

A sampling of pumpkin varieties

They also spread diseases. (See page 209 for more about controlling this pest.) Remove aphids that are feeding on young plants in spring with forceful sprays of water or insecticidal soap.

Squash vine borers especially attack buttercup winter squash varieties. Larvae tunnel into the vines, opening them to disease and rotting. Before young plants flower cover them with a floating row cover to prevent the adult flies from laying eggs in spring. Make a vertical cut with a sharp knife in the stems of wilted stems and remove larvae,

Bottle gourds mature on a fence rail

Cuttings of 'Beauregard' sweet potato ready for planting

or inject *Bacillus thuringiensis* (Bt) with a syringe into the stems to kill the larvae.

Provide proper spacing, keep the squash and pumpkin patch weed free, and select disease-resistant varieties to control fusarium wilt and powdery mildew diseases.

Varieties: Although squashes, pumpkins, and gourds all belong to the same family, there are some differences. Mostly the distinctions don't matter, but they do if you plan to save seeds for replanting the next season. Squashes and pumpkins of the same species will cross-pollinate each other, meaning the seeds you save from them won't produce fruit like the fruit they came from. On the other hand, squashes and pumpkins of different species do not readily cross-pollinate and can be planted in close proximity. This is why botanical names are listed in the chart on pages 96 and 97.

Sunchoke *(see Jerusalem artichoke)*
Swede turnip *(see Rutabaga)*

Sweet potato *(Ipomoea batatas)*

Type: Perennial grown as a warm-season annual
Edible part: Roots
Typical yield: 10 pounds per 10-foot row
Typical size: 12–30"H×12–48"W

The fleshy roots of this vine in the morning glory family are a standard in many Southern gardens and a staple at holiday tables across North America. Although native to tropical America and commercially grown mostly in the South, with specific varieties and proper growing techniques sweet potatoes can be grown in cool climates as well. Sweet potatoes are often mistakenly called yams. However, yam *(Dioscorea)* is a different tropical root crop in a different plant family and is rarely grown commercially on this continent. Yam flesh is dry and starchy compared with that of most sweet potatoes.

Sweet potatoes require at least a four-month growing season with warm days and nights. The plant's thick storage roots, which grow from nodes on the trailing stems, are high in vitamin A. The roots can be stored into the winter.

New ornamental varieties of sweet potatoes are available for flower gardens. Although these types produce edible roots, they are best grown for their vigorous vines bearing colorful foliage.

When: Plant two weeks after your last frost, when the air temperature is above 65°F. Sweet potatoes grow best with an air temperature around 80°F.

Planting: Sweet potatoes normally are started from small plants called slips. Create a 6- to 12-inch-high raised bed, and amend the soil with a 2- to 3-inch-thick layer of compost. Keep the soil slightly acidic. Plant certified disease-free sweet potato slips 12 to 18 inches apart in rows 4 feet apart for vining plants, and 2½ feet apart for bush types.

In cool-summer areas lay black plastic over the raised bed two weeks before planting time to warm the soil, and plant the slips into holes poked in the plastic at the appropriate spacing.

Growing: Plants grown through plastic mulch need little weeding. If you're not using plastic, keep the area around the plants weed free until the vines begin to run and can crowd out competing plants. When vines begin to run mulch around plants with a 2- to 3-inch-thick layer of organic material such as straw to maintain soil moisture levels. Sweet potatoes can endure dry periods once their growth is well established. Keep the slips well watered for the first few weeks and consistently moist until the last month of growth. Reduce watering three to four weeks before harvesting to avoid root rot.

When planting apply a complete fertilizer lower in nitrogen than phosphorus and potassium, such as 5-10-10. If you're growing sweet potato in a sandy soil, sidedress with a high-nitrogen fertilizer when the vines begin to run.

Harvesting: Most sweet potato varieties can be harvested starting 90 days after planting. Harvest after the vines are lightly frosted and the leaves show a little yellowing. Plants left in the ground too long will either rot from the cold soil temperatures or, in

HERE'S A TIP...

Grow your own slips
Although it's best to buy certified disease-free slips to plant, you can start your own slips indoors at home. About eight weeks before your last frost date, select healthy 2-inch-diameter sweet potato roots from those you stored from last year's crop and bury them under 2 inches of moistened potting soil in a flat; they should be close together but not touching. Cover the flat with clear plastic until shoots appear. Place the flat in bright light, water, fertilize with a soluble plant food, and keep the temperatures above 70°F. When the slips are 6 to 8 inches tall, harden them, dig them from the flat, and plant them in the garden. One sweet potato can produce 10 to 20 slips.

Planting sweet potato cuttings on raised beds

warmer areas, continue to grow larger roots. However, the longer a root stays in the ground, the more susceptible it is to insect and disease attacks. With a garden fork carefully dig up the vines and separate the sweet potato roots.

Cure sweet potatoes for one to two weeks in a room with high humidity and a warm temperature of 80° to 90°F. Store cured roots wrapped in newspaper in a dry location at 55° to 60°F. Then allow the roots to sit for a few weeks before you begin eating them. Starches begin converting to sugar in storage, but it takes six to eight weeks of storage for sweet potatoes to develop their full characteristic sweetness. The roots can be stored for up to six months.

Pests and diseases: Avoid root rot diseases by not planting sweet potatoes in the same ground more than once every three years, cleaning up crop debris well in fall, growing certified disease-free slips, growing in raised beds, and keeping the soil slightly acidic.

Sweet potato 'Jewel'

'Vardaman' is small enough to grow in a confined space.

Root weevils, wireworms, and white grubs can attack sweet potatoes. To avoid wireworm and grub attacks, don't plant in areas that were recently part of a lawn. To control root weevils, clean up all sweet potato debris in fall, remove any wild morning glory weeds (a sweet potato relative), and spray beneficial nematodes on the soil.

Varieties: Sweet potato varieties are grouped as vining or bush. The bush varieties take up less space and are better for small-space gardens. The flesh of most sweet potato varieties is moist unless otherwise stated.**'Georgia Jet'** (100 days), a productive vining variety, has red skin and orange flesh. **'Beauregard'** (90 days), with red skin and orange flesh, is a fast-maturing vining type good for Northern gardens; it

A sampler of sweet potato varieties

resists white grubs, root rot, and cracking. **'Vardaman'** (95 days) is a bush variety with golden skin and deep orange flesh. **'Bush Porto Rico'** (100 days) is a bush variety with light red flesh that pales to yellow when ripe. **'White Yam'** (110 days), a vining sweet potato, bears small tan roots with sweet, dry white flesh. **'Centennial'** (100 days) is a vining type that produces high yields of long, smooth-skinned orange roots with bright orange, tender, savory flesh. **'Jewel'** (100 days), a disease-resistant variety, has rosy red skin and deep orange flesh on high-yielding vines; the roots resist shriveling in storage.

Swiss chard (*see Chard*)
Sylvetta (*see Arugula*)
Tatsoi (*see Asian greens, Mesclun mix*)

Tomatillo, husk tomato (Physalis ixocarpa)

Type: Warm-season annual
Edible part: Fruits
Typical yield: 5–10 pounds per 10-foot row
Typical size: 2–6'H×2–6'W

Also known as husk tomato, tomatillo is a bushy tomato relative that bears 2- to 3-inch-diameter round fruits inside papery husks. This Central American native has been used in cooking for thousands of years. The sweet, tart, and somewhat citrusy flavor of the fruits is often used to counteract the hottest of chile peppers in various dishes. Tomatillos are key ingredients in salsa verde, chili verde, and other Mexican specialties.

When: Sow seeds indoors four to six weeks before your last frost date. In warm climates direct-sow seeds ½ inch deep and 2 feet apart after the last frost date. Tomatillos grow best in slightly acidic soil with soil temperatures above 60°F and air temperatures above 80°F.

Planting: Amend the soil with a 2- to 3-inch-thick layer of composted manure. Tomatillos are grown much like tomatoes. Pinch off the lowest leaves and bury the stem of the transplant so only the top leaves are aboveground. Just like tomatoes, tomatillos will develop new roots along their stem.

In cool-summer areas lay black plastic over the planting bed two weeks before planting to heat the soil. Plant seedlings into holes poked in the plastic at the appropriate spacing.

Growing: Space young transplants or thin direct-sown seedlings to 3 feet apart. Keep the soil well weeded and moist. Mulch with plastic in cool-summer areas, or a 2- to 4-inch-thick layer of straw in warm-summer areas, to supress weeds and maintain soil moisture. Mature plants are drought-tolerant.

Fertilize plants with a complete low-nitrogen fertilizer such as 5-10-10 at planting. Use the same fertilizer to sidedress once fruits form and then monthly after that.

Tomatillo plants benefit from trellising. Use a tomato cage or stake to keep the branches and fruits off the ground.

Harvesting: Use a sharp knife to harvest fruits 60 to 75 days after planting, when the green or purple husks turn light brown and split and the fruits inside are firm. Collect them daily because tomatillos can drop to the ground and rot when ripe. In cool-summer areas, remove the whole plant if frost is forecast, suspending it upside down in a sheltered place to mature the remaining fruits. Like tomatoes, tomatillos will continue to ripen after harvest. Store harvested tomatillos in their husks for up to two weeks in the refrigerator.

Pests and diseases: Tomatillos are vulnerable to the same pests as tomatoes. Protect young transplants from cutworms with paper collars. Handpick Japanese beetles, leafrollers, and hornworms.

Do the following to avoid disease problems such as verticillium wilt and mosaic virus: Remove self-sown volunteer seedlings from previous tomatillo crops, avoid planting in the same ground that tomato-family crops (eggplant, peppers, potatoes, and tomatoes) were grown in the previous three years, and clean up crop debris in fall.

Varieties: 'De Milpa' (70 days) is an heirloom with small green fruits blushed with purple. 'Purple' (65 days), which stores well, features purple skins and very sweet purple-tinged flesh that makes uniquely colored salsa. 'Toma Verde' (60 days) is an early variety with green fruits that turn yellow at maturity.

'Purple' tomatillo

GROUND CHERRY

A tomatillo relative that's easy and fun to grow is ground cherry (Physalis pruinosa), also known as Cape gooseberry. Grow the 1- to 2-foot-tall plants just like tomatoes. They produce cherry-size fruits in husks similar to tomatillo. The sweet yellow fruits drop to the ground when ripe. They can be eaten raw (kids love them) or used in pies and desserts. 'Goldie' (75 days) is a ground cherry variety that features cherry-size sweet golden fruits in husks that hang like Japanese lanterns.

Tomato (Lycopersicon esculentum)

Type: Warm-season perennial
Edible part: Fruits
Typical yield: 10 pounds per 10-foot row
Typical size: 8–72"H×12–36"W

'Celebrity' tomatoes are a popular and widely adapted variety.

Tomatoes are the most popular vegetable grown by North American gardeners—and for good reason. Tomatoes taste so much better when homegrown. There is nothing like munching on a juicy, sun-warmed, vine-ripe tomato picked fresh from the garden. Whether you like them fresh, canned, dried, grilled, stewed, juiced, or frozen, fresh-picked tomatoes are always tangier and sweeter than their supermarket counterparts.

It hasn't always been this way. Centuries ago the tomato was considered poisonous because it's in the nightshade family, a group of plants that includes many that are toxic. The plant was mostly grown as an ornamental, not the edible crop known and loved today.

This Central American native thrives in heat and produces an abundance of fruits all summer long. Tomato varieties come in most colors of the rainbow, and plants range in size from less than 1 foot tall to 10 feet tall. They can be grown trellised or in a container on a deck. The fruits are flavorful and healthful. Tomatoes are loaded with vitamins A, C, and K and contain the

A ring of concrete reinforcing wire and plastic protect this tomato plant from cold winds.

'Patio' tomato is suited to containers.

cancer-fighting antioxidant lycopene. Make salsas and salads with fresh tomatoes; use them in soups, stews, and side dishes; or make tomato sauce, tomato paste, and ketchup.

When: Although seeds can be directly sown in the garden and plants grown to maturity in warmer areas, most gardeners buy transplants or start seedlings indoors. Sow seeds indoors six to eight weeks before your last frost date. Transplant seedlings outdoors after the last frost date, when the soil temperature has warmed to above 60°F.

Planting: Tomatoes need heat, water, and fertile soil to grow their best. Before planting amend the soil with a 2- to 3-inch-thick layer of compost or composted manure. In all but the hottest regions cover the tomato beds with red plastic mulch two weeks before planting. Red plastic mulch preheats the soil for faster root growth, maintains soil moisture, and prevents weed growth, and it increases tomato yields up to 20 percent over black plastic. (Learn more about using red plastic mulch on page 31.) Set plants in holes poked in the plastic mulch and spaced 2 feet apart for small bush varieties and 3 to 4 feet apart for sprawling indeterminate varieties that are unstaked.

> **HERE'S A TIP...**
>
> **Tomato planting depth**
>
>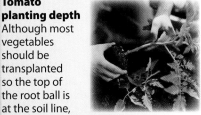
>
> Although most vegetables should be transplanted so the top of the root ball is at the soil line, tomatoes (and tomatillos) are unique. They have the ability to form roots along their stem. The extra roots help anchor the plant and provide more opportunity for water and nutrient uptake, which is especially helpful when starting with tall, leggy transplants. If the plants are very leggy, try laying the stem horizontally along a 4- to 6-inch-deep trench in the soil. Prune off the bottom leaves and turn the uppermost portion of the stem vertically so the top cluster of leaves pokes out of the soil. Alternatively, pinch off the lowest leaves and set the root ball deep enough so that only the top cluster of leaves are showing above ground.

Wire supports on sturdy posts make a good trellis for indeterminate tomatoes.

Growing: Use floating row covers to protect young transplants from cold winds in northern climates or the hot sun in southern regions. At planting fertilize with a balanced plant food such as 5-5-5. Give the plants the same fertilizer monthly starting when the first tomatoes are golf ball size.

If you are not growing the tomatoes in plastic mulch,

Feed tomatoes monthly during the summer.

apply a 2- to 3-inch-thick layer of organic material such as straw after the soil has warmed. Keep the soil evenly moist for healthy growth and to prevent blossom end rot. Run drip irrigation or soaker hoses under the plastic mulch or hand water, applying at least 1 inch of water a week—more during windy, dry periods.

Stake or cage indeterminate varieties or large determinate varieties at planting time. Installing stakes or cages after the plants are growing can injure their roots. Keeping tomato plants off the ground helps prevent fruit rot and makes the plants more disease-resistant and productive. For indeterminate plants use heavy-gauge wire cages that stand 5 to 6 feet tall. Firmly anchor the cages to the ground with stakes to keep the plants from blowing over and uprooting themselves during storms. Cages should have openings wide enough for your hand to reach inside to harvest. Stakes need to be at least 8 feet high and 1 inch wide.

> **HERE'S A TIP...**
>
> **How to pinch a sucker**
>
>
>
> Indeterminate tomatoes—but not determinate or dwarf kinds—need pruning. Both kinds produce suckers, side branches that form in the joints where the leaves meet the stems. These suckers will eventually grow, flower, and fruit. If you have a small-space garden or live in a northern climate, indeterminate plants may become too large or they may not mature the fruits before fall frost. To concentrate more energy into the rest of the fruits and plant, pinch out the suckers just beyond the first two leaves.

Pound the stake at least 1 foot into the ground and 4 inches from the plant. Attach the stem to the stake with garden twine, self-adhesive fabric, or strips of cloth.

'Sun Gold' tomatoes develop in clusters.

Tomato flowers need only motion (usually from breezes) to set fruit. However, during unfavorable weather (night temperatures lower than 55°F or day temperatures above 95°F with drying, hot winds) tomato flowers will drop. Protect plants from low or high temperatures and consider spraying a blossom set hormonal product to help the flowers set fruit.

Harvesting: Pick fruits when they are firm, full size, and fully colored. Tomatoes mature and ripen best at temperatures close to 75°F. When the temperature rises above 90°F the fruits soften and develop poor color. Tomatoes will ripen when picked at their green mature

TOP GARDEN TOMATOES*

Name	Fruit size (ounces), color	Days to mature*	Key features
INDETERMINATE			**LARGE AND PRODUCTIVE PLANTS**
Early season			**Mature in fewer than 70 days**
'Early Girl Hybrid'	4–6, red	52	Dependable, widely adapted. Large yields of solid fruits
'Stupice'	2, red	52	Czech heirloom. Good balance of sweet and tart. Fruits tends to get green shoulders. Disease tolerant
'Early Cascade' Hybrid	4, red	55	Heavy yielding. Disease tolerant, crack resistant
'Moskvich'	4–6, red	60	Tasty, heirloom. Good cold tolerance
'First Lady Hybrid'	4–5, red	66	Produces over a long period. Disease and crack resistant
Midseason			**Mature in 70+ days**
'Cobra Hybrid'	8, red	70	One of best-tasting greenhouse varieties. Crack resistant
'Lemon Boy Hybrid'	8, yellow	72	First full-size yellow. Easy to grow, vigorous, high yields
'Jet Star Hybrid'	8, red	72	Firm, meaty, good flavor
'Better Boy' Hybrid	12, red	72	Classic hybrid. Large yields. Large fruits similar to 'Big Boy', but better disease resistance
'Cherokee Purple'	10–12, purple	72	Tennessee heirloom. Flavorful, soft textured, rose-purple skin, brick red flesh. Highly perishable
'Big Beef Hybrid'	10–12, red	73	Large yields and fruits. Consistent production until frost. Great disease resistance
'Green Zebra'	3, green	75	Amber green with dark green striped skin and light green flesh. Sweet, tangy flavor
'Yellow Stuffer'	4, yellow	76	Shaped like a stuffing pepper, yet with a tomato taste
'Delicious'	16–32, red	77	World record holder for largest tomato (more than 7 pounds). Sweet, meaty fruits ripen over a long period
'Striped German'	16–32, red with yellow stripes	78	Heirloom German variety. Yellow-orange skin and red marbled flesh
'Costoluto Genovese'	8, red	80	Deeply ribbed, Italian heirloom. Juicy, strong tomato flavor. Best in heat
'Brandywine'	12–16, pink	80	The most popular heirloom. Pink-skinned fruits with soft flesh and full flavor. Also in yellow and red versions
'Beefmaster Hybrid'	24–32, red	80	Good slicing variety. Large, meaty deep red fruits. Disease-resistant
'Black Krim'	12, brown	80	Russian heirloom. Dark reddish-brown skin and flesh. Fruit darkens in hot weather
'Pineapple'	16–32, red and yellow	85	Bicolor heirloom. Red and yellow streaks throughout the fruits
'Great White'	10–12, white	85	Heirloom of unusual color. Meaty fruits, mild taste, creamy texture, few seeds
'Big Rainbow'	24–32, orange, red, yellow streaked	90	Large-fruited heirloom. Skin yellow at shoulders, red at blossom end, and golden orange in center. Flesh streaked red, orange, and yellow
Small fruits			**Cherry-size fruits form in clusters**
'Sun Gold Hybrid'	1–2, yellow	57	Very sweet orange fruits. Vigorous
'Juliet Hybrid'	1, red	60	Cherry-size sweet fruits in grapelike clusters. Crack-resistant. Tolerant of late blight and leaf spot
'Grape'	1–2, red	60	Common market variety. Flavorful grape-size fruits. Disease- and heat-tolerant
'Black Cherry'	2–3, black	65	Heirloom of unusual color. Large cherry-size fruits. Black-red skin and flesh. Complex flavor
'Super Sweet 100'	1, red	65	Improved version of classic cherry variety. Vigorous. Large yields. Many fruits. High in vitamin C
'Sweet Million'	1–2, red	65	Better crack tolerance and disease resistance than its predecessor 'Sweet 100'

Name	Fruit size (ounces), color	Days to mature*	Key features
'Sweet Baby Girl Hybrid'	1, red	65	Dwarf indeterminate plant only 3–5' tall. Flavorful, sweet fruits
'Jolly Hybrid'	1–2, pink	75	Peach-shape fruits with pointy tip. 10–14 fruits per cluster
'Red Currant'	½, red	75	Wild species from South America. Vigorous. Many tiny sweet-tart fruits
'Yellow Pear'	1–2, yellow	78	Classic heirloom. Attractive pear-shape fruits
Paste			**Oblong shape and meaty flesh**
'San Marzano'	2–4, red	80	Classic, meaty paste variety. Mild flavor
'Amish Paste'	5–7, red	85	Amish heirloom. Juicy, meaty, very flavorful large tear drop–shaped fruits
DETERMINATE			**PLANTS STAY BUSHY, FRUITS MATURE ALL AT ONCE**
Early season			**Mature in fewer than 70 days**
'Bush Early Girl Hybrid'	6–7, red	54	Compact 2' tall version of popular 'Early Girl' with same size fruits but more disease resistance. Good in containers
'Oregon Spring'	6–7, red	58	Juicy, tender, almost seedless fruits. Tolerant of cool weather
'Cold Set'	4–6, red	65	Sets fruit early. Tolerates light frosts. Good for northern regions
'Heatwave II Hybrid'	6–7, red	67	Sets fruits in heat up to 100°F. Good disease resistance
Midseason			**Mature in 70+ days**
'Bush Goliath'	6–10, red	68	Plants grow only 3–4 feet tall. Fruits 3–4 inches in diameter
'Celebrity Hybrid'	8–12, red	72	Classic, productive, widely adapted variety. Meaty fruits ripen uniformly. Bush form available
'Solar Fire Hybrid'	7–10, red	72	Heat-tolerant variety from University of Florida. Larger fruits than other similarly heat-hardy varieties. Good disease resistance
'Mountain Spring Hybrid'	8–10, red	72	Firm fruits soften as they ripen. Mild flavor. Crack- and blossom end–rot resistant
'Bush Big Boy Hybrid'	10–11, red	72	Classic 'Big Boy' size and flavor but half the height
'Healthkick Hybrid'	4–6, red	74	Plum-shape variety with 50% more lycopene than other varieties
'Rutgers'	6–8, red	75	Highly productive heirloom. Flavorful, meaty fruits. Good for sauce
'Long-keeper'	6–7, orange-red	78	Unblemished fruits gathered before frost can last up to 3 months in storage
'Super Bush Hybrid'	8–10, red	85	Compact 3–4' plant. Large fruits. Good in containers. Disease-resistant
'Ace 55 Hybrid'	12, red	90	Flavorful, low-acid fruits. Protected from sunburn by large leaves
Small fruits			**Cherry-size fruits form in clusters**
'Tumbler Hybrid'	1–2, red	49	Abundant early yields. Small fruits hang off cascading plant. Best in hanging baskets or containers
'Tiny Tim'	1, red	60	18" tall plant. Grows in small containers
'Gold Nugget'	1–2, gold	60	Northwest variety from Oregon State University. Seedless golden fruits. Compact plant
'Window Box Roma Hybrid'	2, red	70	'Roma'-type fruits on 18" plant. Good in containers
'Patio'	3–4, red	72	Flavorful fruits on 2' plant. Attractive deep green leaves. Thrives in containers
Paste			**Oblong shape and meaty flesh**
'Viva Italia'	3, red	75	Italian paste tomato. High sugar content. Good heat tolerance
'Roma'	2–3, red	78	Standard paste tomato. Thick, meaty fruits. Widely adapted. Yellow form available
'Principe Borghese'	1–2, red	80	Small, plum-shape fruits have few seeds. Good for drying

Ranked according to season length

Diverse colors and shapes of tomato

'Big Beef' tomato

stage. Harvest all but the greenest fruits before a killing frost, bring the immature fruits indoors to a 60° to 65°F room, and wrap them individually in a sheet of newspaper. Check the fruits once a week for ripeness and remove any tomatoes that are decayed or not showing signs of ripening. Unripe green tomatoes can also be harvested for pickling and frying. Also, whole plants can be uprooted and hung in a warm, sheltered location, where the fruits can continue to ripen.

Once picked, ripe fruits can be stored for up to two weeks at 55°F. They also can be stored in the refrigerator but will not taste as good as those stored at cool room temperature.

Tomatoes can be dried, canned, or frozen for winter use. To peel fresh tomatoes for a recipe, dip them in near-boiling water for about one minute,

STAKING, CAGING, TRELLISING?

By keeping your tomato plants vertical, you can enjoy a bigger and better harvest. Staking is a good option if your space is limited. Since you'll have to prune staked tomatoes, you'll get an earlier harvest, and the fruits will be easy to see. However, it takes time and effort to install stakes and tie the plants to them. Also, the yields are smaller than with the other methods, and the fruits are sometimes more prone to sunscald and cracking since they don't have as much foliage to protect them.

Cages are easy to set up and reusable, and you don't have the prune the plants. On the downside, cages are more expensive, bulkier, and harder to store than stakes, and the fruits may be slow to mature and ripen in cool climates.

Trellises give you the advantage of planting tomatoes closer together and allowing two or three main stems to develop. However, trellises require more materials and maintenance than either staking or caging.

Bamboo poles as a tomato trellis

depending upon the skin thickness. After that the skin should peel easily.

Pests and diseases: Tomatoes are affected by many insects, diseases, and physiological disorders. Use cardboard collars around tomato transplants to discourage cutworms. Handpick and destroy Japanese beetles. Spray *Bacillus thuringiensis* (Bt) to control tomato hornworms and pinworms. Spray insecticidal soap to control white flies.

Diseases such as verticillium and fusarium wilts and tobacco mosaic virus stunt plant growth and cause plants to die young. Control these diseases by planting resistant varieties. Foliar diseases, such as early blight, late blight, and septoria leaf spot, cause leaves to yellow and drop prematurely. Space plants properly, mulch, and pick off

Straw mulch helps prevent many tomato problems.

newly infected leaves to control these diseases. Avoid planting other tomato-family members (eggplant, pepper, potato, and tomatillo) in the same ground for three years.

Tomato fruits are also affected by physiological problems. Avoid catfacing, cracking, sunscalding, and blossom end rot by keeping the soil consistently moist, planting tolerant varieties, and protecting the plants from the hot sun and cold temperatures.

Varieties: Tomato varieties are usually grouped by the plant's growth habit. Indeterminate plants continue to grow throughout the season because the terminal end of the stem produces leaves instead of flowers. New blossoms appear continuously along the side shoots, and they bloom and produce fruit as long as growing conditions are favorable. Indeterminate plants produce the largest and most fruits of any type of tomato. However, since the plants grow so large, the fruits may be slower to mature. Indeterminate varieties require more space and need to be caged, staked (and pruned), or trellised to grow best. Most heirloom tomato varieties are indeterminate.

Determinate, strong determinate, vigorous determinate, and

Low-acid tomatoes Yellow or golden fruits are not necessarily lower in acid. In practice, low acid means the tomato's

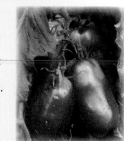

sugar content covers the fruit's tangy, naturally acidic flavor. All tomatoes are acidic, but three tomatoes that are slightly less so are 'Ace 55', 'Beefmaster', and 'San Marzano', (above).

'Persimmon' tomato is an heirloom type.

The white cases on this tomato hornworm are pupae of parasitic wasps that will kill it.

semideterminate plants grow to a compact height and produce clusters of flowers at the growing tips. The plants set fruits along the stem within two to three weeks of one another, and the fruits ripen almost simultaneously, making them perfect for processing. Many paste varieties and early varieties are determinate. Dwarf, or patio, tomatoes are also determinate, producing all their fruits at once on short plants that are ideal for container growing.

A new group of tomatoes called dwarf-indeterminate takes the best traits from the indeterminate and determinate types. These varieties are short, compact plants that produce flowers and ripen fruit all summer long.

Seed packets and seedling tags are often marked with one or more indicating that the variety has been bred for resistance to a specific viral, bacterial, or fungal disease. Combinations of V, F, and N are the most important to look for, but choose cultivars bred for resistance to problems common to your geographic area. Tolerance of a disease means the variety may show disease symptoms but will still be able to produce a good crop.

TOMATO DISEASE ABBREVIATION KEY

ASC	Alternaria stem canker
BC	Bacterial canker
BSK	Bacterial speck
BST	Bacterial spot
BW	Bacterial wilt
C1, C2, etc.	Leaf mold races
CMV	Cucumber mosaic virus
CR	Corky root
EB	Early blight
F1, F2, etc.	Fusarium wilt races
FCRR	Fusarium crown and root rot
LB	Late blight
N	Root-knot nematode
PM	Powdery mildew
PVY	Potato virus Y
Si	Silvering
St	Gray leaf spot
TEV	Tobacco etch virus
ToMoV	Tobacco mottle virus
ToMV	Tobacco mosaic virus
TW, TSWV	Tomato spotted wilt virus
TYLC	Tomato yellow leaf curl
V	Verticillium wilt

Turnip (Brassica rapa Rapifera group)

Type: Biennial grown as a cool-season annual
Edible part: Roots, leaves
Typical yield: 5–10 pounds per 10-foot row
Typical size: 6–12"H×4–6"W

Turnips are grown for their spicy greens and mild-tasting roots, which have white flesh. The large round roots are smooth on the outside and meaty inside. This popular Southern crop tastes good diced fresh in salads, pickled, or cooked in soups, stews, and side dishes. The thin, green, slightly hairy leaves make a tangy addition to salads, casseroles, and stir-fries.

When: Sow seeds four weeks before the last frost date in spring for an early summer crop or 90 to 100 days before the first frost in fall. Turnips grow best with air temperatures between 60° and 65°F.

Planting: Amend the soil with a 2- to 3-inch-thick layer of composted manure. Direct-sow turnip seeds, planting them ½ inch deep and 2 inches apart for large roots and 1 inch apart for small roots, in rows 12 inches apart.

'Hakurei' turnip has smooth white roots.

Growing: Thin turnip seedlings to 3 to 4 inches apart when they are 4 inches tall. The thinnings can be eaten as greens.

Keep the soil evenly moist, applying at least 1 inch of water a week. Cultivate lightly when the roots are young, and apply a 2- to 3-inch thick layer of organic mulch such as straw around the roots to maintain soil moisture, keep the soil cool, and deter weeds. Based on a soil test, at planting apply a complete low-nitrogen fertilizer such as 5-10-10.

Harvesting: If you have planted turnips for greens, harvest the tops as needed when they are 4 to 6 inches tall. Leave the growth point in the center when you're picking individual leaves and the plants will continue to produce greens and roots. Harvest sweet young turnip roots for salads when they are 2 inches in diameter. Allow some roots to mature to 3 to 4 inches in diameter for cooking and winter storage. Turnip roots taste sweeter after being exposed to a light frost. However, don't let the roots grow too large or they will become bitter and woody.

Harvesting 'Purple Top White Globe'

To store turnip roots, trim off the foliage with a sharp knife to within 1 inch of the crown. The roots can be stored for two to four months at 35°F and high humidity. You can also store turnips directly in the garden until the ground freezes by mulching the beds with a 6- to 8-inch-thick layer of straw in fall.

Pest and diseases: Rotate crops and do not plant this or another cabbage-family crop in the same ground for three years to avoid diseases such as club root, anthracnose, and root rot. Control aphids and flea beetles with strong sprays of water or by applying insecticidal soap. Control root maggots with a floating row cover laid over the crop to prevent adult flies from laying eggs on the soil.

Varieties: 'Golden Ball' (60 days) is an heirloom with unique yellow skin and golden flesh. It grows best when allowed to mature during cool fall weather. 'Hakurei' (38 days) produces 2-inch-diameter smooth white roots with a sweet fruity flavor. The dark green smooth leaves are good in salads and steamed. 'Purple Top White Globe' (50 days) is a 3- to 4-inch round root that's white below the soil line, purple above it; it has tender crisp white flesh. 'Scarlet Queen Red Stem' (43 days) produces slightly flattened red-skin roots with mild white flesh. Its red stems are attractive in salads, and it also comes as a green-stem variety. 'Top Star Hybrid' (35 days) is grown primarily for its medium-size lobed, straplike leaves.

Vegetable pear (see Squash)
Wild arugula (see Arugula)

Growing fruit

▲ A private patio is the center of an axis that radiates out to herbs, a half circle of potted lemon trees, and then ornamental shrubs. The garden demonstrates how edibles of all kinds, including fruits, serve aesthetically as well as practically.

▲ Strawberries, black raspberries, and the other fruits of high summer are culinary luxuries that you can harvest from your own garden, given a modest amount of planning, planting, and maintenance.

Eating a sweet, juicy peach plucked fresh from a tree in your own backyard is a wonderfully satisfying experience. Garden-fresh fruits are full of flavor, and growing them successfully provides a sense of accomplishment as well as rewarding you with exceptional flavor. But there are a few obstacles to get past first. Frost or disease can quickly ruin a developing crop, and deer can decimate your efforts in a single evening of feeding.

Avoid common fruit- and berry-growing pitfalls and enjoy these delectable homegrown treats by learning the basics of fruit gardening. The following pages are packed with tips and techniques. From deciding what to grow to site selection to harvest, you'll find key details that will guide you to which fruit plants are a good fit for your garden.

Beyond the many different kinds of fruits that you can choose is a multitude of varieties. If you decide to plant an apple tree, the question is which apple? From flavorful heirloom varieties to colorful, unique modern selections, the choice of varieties can be overwhelming. The detailed descriptions of the individual fruits that begin on page 120 includes general information on growing a particular type of fruit as well as detailed guides to the best varieties for home gardens.

Choosing which fruits to plant

Take your time when selecting plants that are going to live for many years. Look for high-quality varieties that are true to type, are the right size and shape, and have the correct leaf color for your garden. Check the root system for healthy white or light beige roots. If many of the visible roots are brown or black the plant is not thriving.

As noted on pages 16 to 19, climate is critical. In cold-winter areas hardiness is the key factor; be sure to select a variety that will thrive in your plant hardiness zone. In warmer regions chilling requirements—the hours of cool temperatures a plant needs during the winter before it breaks dormancy and starts growing—may be as critical. Read more about both of these parameters on page 19, but also learn from your neighbors, friends, and local experts such as those at your county cooperative extension service.

To know how many fruit plants you should grow, first figure out how you will use and preserve the produce, keeping in mind that the various crops may produce a

▲ In rural areas an ambitious gardener can have a small orchard that will produce enough for a roadside stand.

substantial harvest per plant. A standard apple tree can produce up to 400 pounds of fruit per tree. Pears produce about 200 pounds per tree, blueberries 3 to 10 pounds per bush, and raspberries and strawberries 1 to 5 pounds per plant.

Disease resistance is another important factor. Leave disease-susceptible varieties and crops, such as 'McIntosh' apples, to expert commercial growers and choose disease-resistant varieties for your own garden. You'll be more successful and spend less time, money, and resources.

Dwarf fruit trees

The key to good fruit in the small home garden lies in the effective use of dwarf fruit trees. A standard-size apple tree can grow from 20 to 40 feet high and spread 25 to 40 feet. Dwarf apple varieties, in contrast, can be held to a height of about 10 feet with a 10-foot spread. Standard apricots, peaches, and plums can grow to 30 feet tall with a spread of 30 feet, and pears to a towering 45 feet with a spread as wide as 30 feet. Most dwarf varieties of these trees can be kept to a height of about 10 feet, or even less.

Dwarf trees are produced in nature or through horticultural practices. Natural dwarfs are called genetic dwarfs. Apples, apricots, sweet cherries, sour cherries, peaches, nectarines, and plums all have genetic dwarf varieties.

Among apples, the most common genetic dwarf trees are spur-type apples, so named because on a given amount of wood they produce more spurs, or compressed fruit-bearing branches, than ordinary apple trees. Fruit production can have a dwarfing effect because it uses energy that would otherwise go into the growth of the tree. The heavier crops of spur apples mean slower tree growth; spur apple trees eventually reach about three-quarters normal size. However, all genetic dwarfs can be made even smaller by grafting them onto dwarfing rootstocks.

Dwarfing rootstocks

The easiest and most effective way to produce permanent dwarfing is by grafting the sections of twig or buds of desired varieties onto dwarfing rootstocks. This method offers many advantages. Grafting is one easy way to produce large numbers of plants in a relatively short time. It ensures true reproduction of a desired variety, which is important because seeds do not always breed true to type. And grafted dwarf trees remain uniformly smaller and tend to bear fruit at a younger age than standard trees, sometimes as early as their second year of growth. Grafting can provide the tree with other special characteristics too, such as resistance to insects or diseases, solid anchorage in the ground, as well as fruit production at a younger age. Since the variety is grafted onto the rootstock, you are essentially buying two different plants together— the rootstock that anchors the tree and the variety that produces the fruit.

One advantage of growing dwarf trees is easy care. When the distance from roots to treetop is 10 feet or less, spraying for pests and diseases as well as pruning and harvesting are easier. These advantages increase if you further reduce size by applying various pruning and training techniques.

Grafted dwarf trees are readily available at most nurseries and garden centers. Curious, adventuresome, or enterprising gardeners may want to try grafting their own trees. For more about grafting, see page 119.

The most extensive research on grafting with growth-limiting rootstocks has been undertaken with apples, resulting in the development of the numbered 'Malling' rootstocks. Each has a different degree of dwarfing effect on the apple variety

▲ Fruiting shrubs, such as this gooseberry, occupy an often-overlooked niche in the home landscape.

grafted onto it. There is also a dwarfing rootstock for apples called 'Mark', and the recently developed Cornell Geneva Rootstock series has two apple rootstocks highly resistant to fire-blight: 'CG.16' and 'CG.30'.

Although soil fertility and culture have an effect, the final size of the apple tree depends mainly on the rootstock. It is important to clearly identify the rootstock when purchasing an apple tree since it will dictate the final tree size and the space required for it to grow and fruit.

Fruit trees other than apples can also be dwarfed by grafting. For pears, Old Home × Farmingdale rootstocks provide good fire blight resistance. There are several versions of this rootstock, and you may see it abbreviated as OHF followed by numbers indicating specific combinations. For instance, 'OHF333' performs well in the Northeast and produces trees that are about 10 to 12 feet tall, while pears grown on 'OHF97' are nearly as tall as standard trees but produce fruit sooner. Quince also makes a satisfactory rootstock for dwarfing pears.

Apricots, peaches, nectarines, and plums are dwarfed by grafting them onto 'Nanking' cherry rootstock and cherries onto 'St. Lucie' or 'Vladimir' cherry. Plum trees are commonly propagated on *Prunus* 'St. Julian A' and myrobalan (*Prunus cerasifera*) rootstocks. Myrobalan grows in a wide range of soils, including poorly drained sites. Sweet cherries grow well on 'Giessen' rootstocks.

▲ Fruit trees such as apple, pear, and fig (shown here) readily adapt to training flat against a wall or fence.

▲ Use fruiting vines, such as kiwi, passion vines, or grapes (shown here) over arbors and fences as well as on custom trellises.

▲ A fruitless olive in the foreground provides shade to this patio while a 'Dancy' tangerine in the background adds year-round color and tasty fruits.

Selecting and preparing the site

▲ Most fruit trees are pollinated by insects, and the most common pollinating insect is the honeybee.

▲ Invest in soil before planting by testing it and amending as recommended. The benefits will pay dividends for years.

The most important year for a fruit crop is the year before you plant. Unlike annual crops such as beans and tomatoes, fruit trees, shrubs, and vines are long-term plantings. It's challenging, and sometimes impossible, to amend the soil after planting. The best course of action is to thoroughly prepare the site beforehand.

Begin by choosing a location that receives at least six to eight hours of full sun a day. (Gooseberries and currants are an exception and will do well in part shade.) Good sites have well-drained soil and are protected from weather extremes. Avoid windy sites or ones that are susceptible to late spring frosts.

A site that has been previously cultivated is often preferable to a new one. In such a spot perennial weeds

are often already under control and the soil does not usually have to be amended as heavily. However, some cautions accompany planting in an established site.

Avoid planting strawberries or raspberries where crops that are susceptible to verticillium wilt—such as potatoes, tomatoes, peppers, and eggplants—have grown in the previous three years. If such a site is your only option, grow verticillium-resistant fruit varieties.

Get ready for planting by measuring and modifying the soil pH, adding organic matter to the planting area, and eradicating weeds. If the soil is poorly drained, consider building raised beds because all fruits require soil that drains freely.

Soil sense

As described on page 22, test the soil to determine how to modify it with respect to pH and nutrients. Fruit trees, brambles, grapes, strawberries, gooseberries, and currants grow best when the soil pH is between 6 and

◀ Examine the roots of container-grown fruit trees at the nursery before buying. Avoid those with large, circling roots and those that are poorly developed.

6.5. If your soil doesn't fall within this range, before planting add the recommended amount of lime to raise the pH or sulfur to lower it. Blueberries require acid soil with a pH of about 4.5. You can apply sulfur to lower the pH before planting, but if your soil has a pH of 7 or higher, you're better off planting a crop other than blueberries.

Increase the soil organic matter content and improve soil structure and drainage by incorporating well-decomposed compost into the planting area. Plant a cover crop to provide additional nutrients.

Weed control can be a challenge around established trees and berry bushes. Eliminate perennial weeds before planting by tilling the soil and spraying with a nonselective postemergence weed control. Or solarize the soil by covering the planting area with clear plastic the year before planting. To find out more about solarizing and weed control, see page 196.

For more about soil and soil amendments, see pages 20 to 23.

Planting fruits

Nurseries and garden centers sell plants in three ways: bare root, balled with the root ball wrapped in burlap (B&B), and in containers.

Most deciduous fruit plants are sold bare root. The leafless plant is taken

from the ground in late fall or winter and shipped to the nursery, where it is held in cool, moist conditions. Bare-root plants are fragile and must be kept cool and moist. Plant them as soon as possible after getting them home.

Fruit trees are seldom available as B&B plants, but they are frequently sold in containers made of plastic, pulp, or metal. Keep both B&B and container-grown fruit trees wet and plant them promptly. In most of North America the best planting time is in spring over a four-week period from the time the buds on native trees are just beginning to show green. Once the days get hot, success in planting fruit crops decreases rapidly. It is acceptable to plant them in fall about the time the foliage on native trees begins to color and temperatures become cooler.

The best general guide to planting is to dig the planting hole twice the width of the root ball. Another is always to plant a little high (1 to 2 inches) above the original soil line on the plant. The most fragile part of a woody plant is the crown, that section where the roots branch and the soil touches the trunk. The crown must be dry most of the time. Planting high minimizes crown rot fungus by preventing water from puddling near the trunk. If you were to plant at soil

▼ If the trip home means part of the plant is exposed, cushion the trunk and wrap the leaves to protect them.

▲ If you order any of the bramble berries, they'll likely arrive looking like this: bare-root plants packed in shredded newspaper and wrapped in plastic.

▲ Inspect the roots of bare-root plants thoroughly before planting. Cut away those that are broken or damaged, as well as any that are brittle, dry, or mushy and soft.

▲ After planting a fruit tree, build a low ridge of soil over the outer edge of the root ball to retain water and ensure it soaks into original roots.

level, a depression around the trunk is likely to form as the soil settles.

Be especially careful when planting grafted dwarf fruit trees. Dwarfing rootstocks may blow over unless they are provided a support, such as a stake.

Adjust the plant height so that the bud union or graft union is 2 to 3 inches above the soil line. If the union is buried under the soil, the variety that was grafted on top will root and the benefits of the rootstock will be lost and the tree will grow to full size. The bud union shows as a bulge just above the ground. Some nurseries place the bud of the fruiting variety high on the rootstock, up to 6 or 8 inches above the roots. In that case, plant at or slightly above the original soil line, usually distinguished by darker bark color just above the soil line.

Be careful not to bury the union in soil or mulch at any time during the life of the

tree. Keep mulch a few inches away from it to prevent crown rot.

Watering new fruit plants their first year in the garden is extremely important. Even if you live where summer rains are common, if you haven't received at least an inch of rain a week, it's time to water.

Planting brambles and grapes

Brambles (raspberries, blackberries, and related cane berries) and grapes are sold either bare root in early spring or as container-grown stock. There is usually a line on a bare-root plant that indicates the previous soil level; plant at that same depth. Cut back grape canes to two or three buds. Brambles are normally planted 4 feet apart and grapes 6 to 8 feet apart. Grapes require a trellis, but with brambles a trellis is optional. Refer to the encyclopedia entries on pages 129 and 143 for more details.

Planting blueberries, currants, and gooseberries

These plants are often sold in containers and should be planted at the same depth that they were grown in the nursery. For currants and gooseberries leave only the three strongest branches and cut these back to 8 inches. Space currant and gooseberry plants 3 to 4 feet apart and blueberry plants about 4 to 6 feet apart. For more details see pages 127 and 140.

Planting strawberries

Strawberries are sold in early spring, either in bundles of 10 to 25, or planted in small containers. Be sure to keep the crown above the soil line, and dig a large enough hole to accommodate all the roots.

Strawberries are usually planted in one of two ways: matted row (June bearers) or single (or staggered double) rows (day neutrals). For reasons to choose one or the other and for planting directions, see page 167.

Planting for pollination

Some plants are called self-pollinating or self-fertile, meaning that their flowers can be fertilized by pollen from flowers either on the same plant or another plant of the same kind. Self-fertile plants will produce fruit even if they are planted far away from any other plant of their kind. Among the self-fertile plants are a few types of apples, pears, and plums; most peaches, apricots, and crabapples; and all sour cherry varieties.

Other plants set fruit only when they receive pollen from a plant of a different variety. When a plant's pollen is ineffective on its own flowers, it is called self-sterile. This group includes some peaches, apricots, and crabapples; most apples, pears, plums, and sweet cherries. 'Royal Ann' sweet cherry, for example, must be within 100 feet of another cherry tree with compatible pollen or it will bear no fruit.

The plant that can fertilize a self-sterile plant is called a pollenizer.

Never assume that because you have a bearing fruit tree you can plant a new tree of a different variety nearby and be sure of a crop. Plants must

▲ When planting a bare-root fruit tree, position the bud union above the soil.

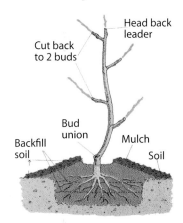

▲ Plant a rooted cane berry or grape with two or three buds above the soil.

bloom at about the same time for successful cross-pollination to occur; for example, an early-blooming self-sterile apple will not bear fruit unless the pollenizer is another early-blooming apple variety.

HERE'S A TIP...
Heeling in bare-root plants
If you must keep bare-root plants for a time before you can plant them, dig a shallow trench, lay the plants on their sides with the roots in the trench, and cover the roots with moist soil. This is called heeling in. Keep the soil moist but not soaked. Try to plant within two to three weeks. If the heeled-in plants begin to leaf out and grow, they will be much harder to plant and will be less likely to survive the transplant.

Pruning and training fruit trees

These two practices improve the quality of a home orchard. Pruning encourages healthy growth and larger fruit, while training a tree to a particular form makes harvesting easier. With just a bit of practice at both techniques you'll feel like a pro.

Pruning and training are fundamental to fruit growing. Pruning consists simply of cutting out branches. Most training involves a lot of careful pruning and a little bit of actual training—that is, tying or propping branches to create desired shapes. Once you have mastered the basics of pruning, you can experiment with techniques for training plants into more elaborate or formal shapes.

Plants will live, grow, and bear fruit without ever being pruned, but experience has shown that good pruning and some training can prevent or remedy many of the problems that arise in fruit growing. Pruning is probably best viewed as the most effective means to head off trouble, improve performance, and keep the plants in excellent condition. Also, training is the area where the craft of growing fruit trees can be raised to an art. Trees can be trained to be beautiful, functional, or even whimsical.

Once fruit trees begin to produce a crop each species should be pruned differently. Pruning methods depend on

▲ The pruning tool you'll use most often is a hand shears, which is why it makes sense to invest in a high-quality, ergonomically designed pair.

▲ Use a compact, folding pruning saw with a narrow blade for those few limbs that exceed the capacity of the hand shears or loppers.

▲ The leverage provided by long-handled loppers allows cutting through 1-inch-thick branches. Loppers are also useful for reaching into thorny brambles.

▲ Pole pruners with an extending handle can reach 10 to 15 feet high, but they do require some coordination and strength to maneuver.

◄ Compared to most fruit trees, peaches (shown here) and nectarines need the most pruning. For the best crops, each winter shorten by two-thirds any branch that produced fruit the previous year.

long run because they last much longer than inexpensive tools.

Pruning 101

In pruning, various plant parts are removed in order to benefit the whole tree. Cutting away any part of a plant directly affects the plant's growth. Depending on how and when it is done, pruning can be used to achieve the following results:
- Produce new growth where it is desired
- Help control growth
- Shape a young plant
- Correct or repair damage
- Help control insects and diseases
- Rejuvenate or reshape an older plant
- Bring about earlier blooming
- Increase the production, size, and quality of fruit.

Good pruning requires knowledge, foresight, and care. As a rule, never make a cut without a clear idea of its probable effect on the plant. On the other hand, don't be so fearful of cutting that you can't get the job done. If you keep in mind that proper pruning is beneficial to plants and then proceed carefully, you'll get good results.

If you find yourself in a quandary about where to begin, remember that you can't hurt a plant by cutting out dead, diseased, or damaged branches as well as branches that cross and rub against other branches (causing wounds that become susceptible to infection). On the contrary, by removing such branches you'll be doing the tree a favor. Eliminating these problems is the first step for both inexperienced and experienced pruners. This initial pruning will open up

the part of the tree that bears fruit, and this differs from one fruit type to another. All bearing fruit trees can be pruned annually, with additional light pruning in the summer to expose fruit spurs to sunlight.

When to prune

In freezing climates prune apples and pears in early spring just as the buds begin to swell, but prune stone fruits after bloom. Avoid pruning early in the dormant season, in November or December, in climates with severe weather. In moderate climates prune all but stone fruits anytime during the dormant period, which is between leaf fall and the beginning of bud swell in the spring.

Pruning tools

The right tools make all the difference in pruning as they do in any other job. Start with a good pair of pruning shears, and if you plan to make cuts larger than shears can handle, you'll need additional tools such as those shown at left. The best-quality pruning tools are generally more expensive but worth the extra cost in the

▲ Pruning directs and controls branch growth. Timing plays a role too. For instance, growth that follows late-winter pruning is much more vigorous than growth that follows summer pruning.

▲ Buds at branch tips, called *terminal* buds, grow much faster than buds behind the tip. But if removed, several buds behind it will begin to grow.

▲ Latent buds—which are smaller and generally just above the scar left by last year's leaf—begin to grow when terminal buds are removed.

▲ Fruiting spurs on apples, apricots, pears, and plums are long-lived, short shoots that produce the particularly fat flowering buds that become fruit.

▲ Leaf or shoot buds are smaller and flatter than terminal or flower buds. Cut just above one to force the branch's growth in the direction the bud points.

▲ Use thinning cuts to completely remove small twigs and branches that weigh down and crowd leaves towards the ends of branches.

▲ Here is the same branch as at left after thinning. When making thinning cuts, cut at an angle facing away from the bud, and leave a stub no longer than ¼ inch.

the tree to more air and light, and it will provide a clearer view of the tree and of the remaining work to be done.

The two basic types of pruning cuts are heading and thinning cuts. Heading is the process of shortening a branch, not removing it entirely. Buds on the remaining portion of the branch are stimulated to sprout when growth above them is removed. Thinning removes a branch entirely and puts an end to growth. All thinning cuts are made to the base of the branch or sucker (strongly upright growing shoot) so that there are no buds left to sprout new growth.

When you cut away part of a plant you leave a wound that is susceptible to pests and diseases. To avoid trouble always make wounds as small as possible. If a new sprout is growing in toward the center of the tree or toward the trunk or threatening to tangle with another branch when it grows longer, pinch it off now to save pruning later. If you see the bud of a sucker down near the soil surface, rub it off with your thumb.

Always make cuts close to a node (point of leaf attachment or branching). Branches grow only at nodes, and if you leave too long a stub beyond the node the stub will die and rot. Cut at a slight angle. A horizontal surface that holds water is more attractive to various diseases and burrowing pests.

Summer pruning

Too-vigorous growth while a tree is young delays fruiting several years. Also, overly robust trees produce many watersprouts—those vertical shoots that spoil the shape of the tree.

Control growth that is too vigorous by pruning in summer. By removing leaves that are creating the tree's nourishment you are weakening the tree. And for the same reason too much summer pruning can damage a tree by weakening it too much. However, summer pruning is the main way to constrain the size of a tree growing in a limited space. Experience will teach you how much pruning is necessary, but here are some guidelines.

In early summer remove only watersprouts. They may suddenly shoot out much farther than any other growth. Cut them off at the base. Also remove any suckers from below the bud union, cutting them to the base.

When the new growth matures and slows its pace, begin snipping it back. The season will vary depending on weather, feeding, and watering, but you can begin to prune some branches in July and finish by early September. Cut off all but about four leaves of the current season's growth on each new branch. Don't thin out any branches. You can do that during winter if necessary.

Fruit tree training methods

Commercial growers train fruit trees to one of three forms, each with its own advantages. Most growers prune their trees into an open center or vase shape; some use the central leader form; and an increasing number are using the modified central leader form, which combines both shapes.

Fruit trees are best trained to one of the forms described here starting when the trees are planted. Such pruning

▶ Avoid cutting at this point on a stem. Doing so will cause both buds to the left to grow, and leave a long stub.

▲ The fast-growing shoots that arise near the base of the tree or from the main scaffold are called watersprouts. They drain energy and mar the tree's shape so are best removed completely to their base.

▲ Root suckers are fast-growing branches like watersprouts, differing only in their origin below the graft union from the tree's roots. Remove them by cutting as close to the ground as possible.

and training will keep the tree balanced in form and—more important—balanced in new and young wood. Left unpruned the tree will become dense with weak, twiggy growth that will be overloaded with small, less healthy fruit. Remember that dwarf trees require less severe pruning than standard-size trees because they are smaller.

Cherries and plums need much less pruning than other fruit trees. Train them to a central leader (most common for sweet cherries and European plums) or to an open center (sour cherries and Japanese and native plums). Once the main structure is developed, prune to keep the tree's shape and thin out branches to allow sunlight in the interior. Annually remove dead, broken, and diseased wood and remove watersprouts and limbs that cross.

● **Open center** Training to an open center creates a broad-spreading, vase-shape tree. The method is used for peaches and nectarines, which bear their fruits on one-year-old shoots. These trees are usually purchased as

3- to 6-foot-tall plants with some lateral branching, or side shoots. See "Training to an Open Center Step-by-Step" at right for details on how to prune these trees.

For larger trees cut the leader back to approximately 8 inches above the uppermost side shoot at planting. Remove any shoots on the bottom 18 inches of the trunk and any stems that attach to the tree at an angle narrower than 45 degrees. Trim the stems that remain to just two buds. As soon as the buds break and the new shoots grow to 4 inches, select three to five of the strongest, best-positioned shoots for the primary scaffold branches; remove all the others. The scaffolds should be spaced evenly around the tree and 4 to 6 inches apart. If other shoots begin to grow during the summer, remove ones with narrow crotch angles or that are growing on the bottom 18 inches of the trunk.

In late spring of the next year, remove the leader just above the top scaffold branch. Head back the scaffold branches, cutting to

TRAINING TO AN OPEN CENTER, STEP-BY-STEP

The open center is probably the most common shape for a fruit tree. The general requirements for establishing this form are given here, but be sure to consult the specific procedures for each type of fruit tree in the encyclopedia that begins on page 120.

A young bare-root fruit tree is normally a whip consisting of a thin vertical shoot and some twiggy side branches. To start the tree on a good course, cut the whip back to about 2 feet above the ground for a dwarf, and 3 feet for a standard tree. Cut just above a bud and then prune any side branches back to two buds.

● **First dormant season** After the new tree has grown through the spring, summer, and fall into its first winter dormancy, choose three or four branches with wide crotches, as shown at the left on page 116. Examining the tree from above, look for branches that radiate evenly around the trunk with almost equal distance between them. You should also try to maintain at least 6 inches of vertical distance between branches, with the lowest

branch about 15 inches above the ground. If there are three such branches, cut off the vertical stem just above the top one. If there are fewer than three good branches, leave the vertical stem and choose the remaining scaffold branches during the next dormant season.

● **Second dormant season** If necessary, choose the remaining scaffold branches and cut off the vertical stem just above the highest selected scaffold. The scaffolds you chose during the first dormant season will have grown side branches. Remove the weakest of these, leaving the main stem and laterals on each branch. Do not prune twiggy growth.

● **Third dormant season** Now is the time to thin surplus shoots and branches. Select the strongest and best-placed terminal shoot near the tip of each scaffold branch as well as one or two other side shoots on each branch. Remove all other shoots on the branch. Leave the weak short shoots that grow straight from the trunk to shade it and help produce food for the tree.

▲ Use notched lengths of wood, called *spreaders*, that push branches apart to make narrow branch angles wider.

▲ Fruit trees such as this dwarf apple that are trained to a modified central leader have two or more tiers of wide-spreading branches radiating off the central trunk.

▲ These peach trees are trained open center fashion. The main stem is shortened, main scaffold branches are chosen, and the center opened so that sunlight can reach all parts of the tree.

buds or side shoots that face outward. Thin the one-year-old shoots so they are 6 to 8 inches apart. Remove any side shoots that are thinner than a pencil. Leave some small shoots in the center of the tree; they will bear the first fruit. When you are finished, the tree should be low, strong, and spreading, with some small shoots in the center.

In the following years, prune to avoid crowding and low-hanging branches and to encourage new growth. For good fruiting, peach and nectarine branches should put on 12 to 18 inches of new growth each year. Head back stems to outward-facing buds or shoots; thin the new shoots to 6 to 8 inches apart.

● **Central leader** Training to a central leader produces a tree with tiers of branches and a pyramidal outline, which allows all branches to intercept sunlight. When you plant a whip, or sapling, in spring, remove any shoots on the lower 18 inches of the trunk and cut the trunk back to about 3 feet from the ground to force several side branches just below the cut to start growing. From these choose one to be the new leader and remove the others.

As this new leader grows, side shoots will branch from it. Select four or five shoots to be scaffold branches. These branches should be evenly distributed around the tree, 4 inches apart on dwarf trees and 12 inches apart on full-size trees. Avoid any that are more than half the diameter of the trunk where they attach to the tree. A branch that joins the leader with a wide angle is best, which is why you'll want to train branches to join the leader at at least a 45-degree angle.

Place clothespins or

TRAINING TO AN OPEN CENTER

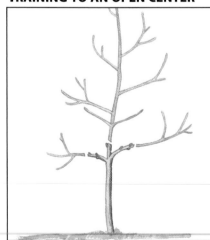

▲ At planting: Head back the main trunk to the desired height; shorten side branches.

▲ Winter #1: Prune to develop the main scaffold branches. Remove all other competing branches.

▲ Winter #2: In the second winter and going forward, remove the weaker and interior-growing stems.

▲ A mature tree that has been trained to an open center is characterized by main scaffold branches that originate low on the trunk and radiate outwards evenly around the tree.

THINNING FRUITS

Reducing the number of fruits on a tree is a form of pruning. Most common fruit trees require thinning in order to produce large, sweet, top-quality fruits. Thinning also moderates a tree's production, which encourages steadier production from year to year. In some cases, thinning will prevent the kind of overbearing that leads to limbs breaking and reduce the tendency for bearing a crop only in alternate years.

Without thinning, nature will produce the most fruit in order to generate the largest number of seeds to perpetuate the species. The tree has only so much food and energy, and you have a choice of harvesting a few large fruit or many small ones. To see how much difference thinning makes, leave a branch unthinned and compare its fruit at harvesttime to that of a properly thinned branch.

Thin to distances of twice the expected diameter of the fruit. For example, if you have an apple tree that should produce 3-inch fruits, leave 6 inches between apples when thinning.

Although each variety has an optimum time for thinning, it is usually best to thin before the natural fruit drop that occurs about three to six weeks after bloom, in early June. When fruits are about the size of a quarter, select the largest, or *king*, fruit and remove the rest. You can do a light thinning after this time, but thinning before the fruit drop means you choose which fruits survive. If your tree loses a lot of fruit you may not want to thin at all. In this case, don't worry if fruits are bunched because total fruit load is more important than spacing.

commercial limb spreaders between the leader and scaffold branches (as shown on the previous page) or hang sandwich bags filled with sand from the branch to weight the new scaffolds into position. Remove the spreaders after several weeks.

Late the next winter cut back the leader by one-third. Let side shoots develop, choose one to be the leader, and remove the rest. Again, when side shoots develop on the new leader, choose four or five scaffolds and attach limb spreaders.

Repeat this process for one more year. From the fourth year onward continue to remove any side shoots that compete with the central leader. Prune off any drooping scaffolds, which produce less fruit and shade lower branches. Get rid of diseased, broken, or dead branches. Take out or break off watersprouts and remove older, less fruitful limbs. Remove stems that grow downward from the bottom of larger branches. Always make large cuts first. Try to avoid heading cuts, which encourage leafy growth. Use thinning cuts instead, removing entire branches or trimming to a vigorous, fruitful lateral.

● **Modified central leader**
This method produces both the strength of a central trunk and the sun-filled center of a vase-shape tree. A single trunk is allowed to grow vertically with whorls of branches in the same manner as the central leader form. At the end of the third or fourth season when the tree is from 6 to 10 feet tall, cut off the main leader at about 3 or 4 feet. Then select main scaffold branches and prune to form a vase shape.

TRAINING TO A MODIFIED CENTRAL LEADER

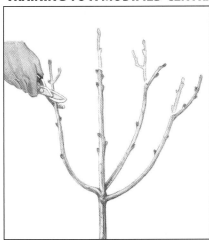

▲ Winter #1: Head back the central leader and all main scaffold branches.

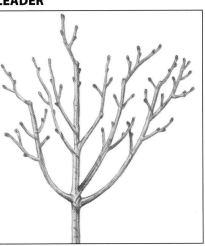

▲ Winter #2: Repeat the previous season's cuts by again heading the central leader and main scaffolds.

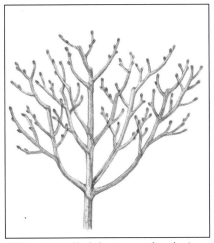

▲ Winter #3: Head back the uppermost branches in order to develop the last tier of scaffolds.

Espaliers and special pruning

Fruit trees can be grown successfully as espaliers or hedges that create garden dividers and boundary plantings. These special training techniques save space and allow the home gardener to grow more varieties than would otherwise be possible.

When training a fruit tree to a special shape or space, pruning continues all seasons and throughout the life of the plant. Be ready to pinch or snip at any time. Major pruning is still a winter task, but in summer you will need to head or thin wild growth and suckers, and you may need to loosen or renew ties or add new ones.

Be sure you understand the normal growth patterns of the plants you intend to train. For example, apples and pears bear fruit in the same places (spurs) for years. Although fruiting spurs may need to be renewed over the years, the growth pattern means that you can confine these trees to formal shapes and keep them that way.

Peaches and nectarines fruit on branches that grew the previous year. Old branches will not bear, and they should be cut away and replaced with new growth from the base of the tree. This heavy pruning makes rigid training patterns impossible. Peaches and

▲ This apple fence was created by training the major limbs of dwarf apple

nectarines can be trained flat over walls or grown as hedges, but they cannot be held to strict geometric shapes.

Grapes are vines and therefore are almost always trained on a wall, wire, or fence. A variety that requires a little more heat than your region normally offers may produce good fruit when grown on a south- or west-facing wall.

You can train brambles flat against fences or walls and treat them something like peaches and nectarines since you must replace all canes that have fruited with canes of the current season.

The poorest subject for limited-space training is the cherry tree. Sweet cherries are normally too large to confine and will not fruit at all without a pollinator close by. They can be trained as an espalier, but your efforts would be better spent on something more rewarding.

▼ For a hedge, space plants 3 feet apart. Position the lower wire 24 inches above the ground. The height of the second wire will vary depending on variety and root stock.

ESPALIERS

Many fruit trees are too large to grow in a standard-size suburban lot, but you can still realize the dream of harvesting fruit from your own tree. Espaliering is a technique that trains a tree to grow flat like a vine, allowing you to fit the tree into a small space. Here's one way to create an espalier:

1. Simple espaliering trains all branches to grow horizontally. Start with either a young whip or branched plant. Cut the main stem to the height you'd like the tree to be. Remove all but four side branches, leaving pairs of branches that grow at the same height.
2. If there are no opposing pairs of side branches, you can create them. Pull two flexible branches up and over to form a circle with the branches heading in opposite directions. Tie the crossover point to a horizontal stake with vinyl tree tape or twine.
3. Secure the ends of the branches to stakes with twine or tape.
4. If one branch of the tree is much shorter than its partner, tie it at a 45-degree angle to force it to grow faster. Once it catches up to the other branch, train it horizontally.
5. Every winter prune side branches to 18 inches long, cutting them to a downward-facing bud.

Budding and grafting fruit trees

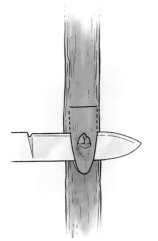

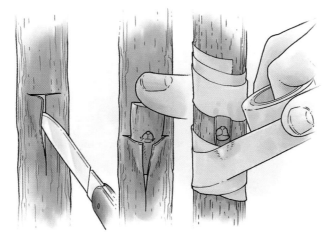

▲ A T-bud graft begins by slicing a viable bud from the desired variety. Cut ½ inch below and ¾ inch above the bud.

▲ Next, insert the bud into the stem that will become the rootstock. Open a T-shaped section of bark to expose the cambium layer. Place the bud under the bark and in firm contact with the cambium layer, and wrap tightly.

▲ Once the inserted bud begins to grow, cut off the old variety, which is the section of the branch above it.

These horticultural techniques effectively splice together the branches of two different but closely related plants. Budding uses a bud from the desired variety, or *scion*, and unites it with a compatible rootstock. Grafting unites a section of twig from the desired variety with a rootstock. Both budding and grafting require practice to be successful. Budding and grafting should be done when the air is still, the humidity is high, and temperatures are cool to prevent drying and killing the cambium tissue. As long as the plants are closely related and the cambium (the thin layer of green, living tissue between bark and wood) align in the splice, the cells will grow together.

Grafting a particular variety of apple, for instance, to a specific rootstock is how dwarf trees are created. It's also the method used to produce multiple varieties of fruits on a single tree.

Almond, apricot, European plum, and Japanese plum may be grafted onto a peach root system.

● **Chip budding** You can use this technique on grapes and many fruit trees. Remove a chip of wood a few inches above the soil from the plant that will function as the root system. Then remove a chip containing a bud exactly the same size from another plant that will form the plant top. Place the bud chip in the chip void on the rootstock. Be sure the green cambium tissues on each part line up. Cover the cut surfaces with budding tape or strips of budding rubber to prevent drying. Avoid covering the bud; wrap above and below it and let the bud protrude. Once the bud starts growing into a new shoot, remove the old stem above the bud to allow the new shoot to become the plant top.

● **Whip-and-tongue grafting** This method involves splicing a 3- to 4-inch-long piece of twig containing one or two buds, onto the root system of another plant. Do the graft in late winter on a dormant bare-root plant using a dormant scion. Make a 2-inch sloping diagonal cut through the stem of the root system about 6 inches above the soil line. Next make a ½-inch-long vertical cut down the stem starting one-third of the way down the slope from the tip. Prepare the scion with cuts of the same shape. Force the two cut surfaces to slide together. A tonguelike projection from each will fit into the other. Be sure the cambium tissues line up as much as possible between the two parts. Wrap the joined area with twine or grafting bands to hold it together, and cover with grafting wax or pruning paint to prevent drying.

● **Cleft grafting** Use cleft grafts on large rootstocks. Cut off the top of the plant selected for the rootstock. Using a hatchet or cleft grafting tool, make a split (cleft) about 4 inches long down the center of the rootstock trunk. Cut wedge-shape ends on two scions ½ inch in diameter. Force a cleft-grafting tool into the cleft to spread it open. Place the wedges of the scions in the cleft with the cambium tissues of the rootstock and scions in direct contact with one another. Remove the spreading device to leave the scions firmly in place. Cover all of the exposed cut areas with grafting wax or pruning paint to prevent drying.

▲ Use a whip-and-tongue graft to join rootstock and scion of equal size.

▲ Cleft grafting is a popular method for apples, cherries, pears, and peaches.

▲ Chip budding is similar to T-budding but has more wood attached to the bud.

Encyclopedia of fruits

Acerola cherry *(see Cherry)*
Amelanchier *(see Serviceberry)*

Apple *(Malus domestica)*

Type: Deciduous tree, Zones 3–10
Typical yield: 50–400 pounds per tree
Typical size: 6–30'H×2–30'W

A sampler of apple varieties

Enjoyed for their flavor, crispness, and utility, apples have a history of cultivation that spans thousands of years. They are the most widely adapted and most widely grown of all the kinds of deciduous fruits. Of the more than seven thousand named varieties of apples that have been recorded, more than two thousand are grown in the United States.

All apples need some cool winter weather, but because of an enormous range in this requirement, varieties are available for any climate except tropical and low-desert regions. The chart on pages 122–123 notes the optimum growing zones for each variety.

When: In most areas plant bare-root trees in late winter or early spring. Plant container-grown trees anytime.
Planting: Choose a sunny, protected site with deep, fertile, slightly acid soil that drains well and is not in a low-lying area where frost may collect. A gentle slope provides the best drainage. Apple trees are intolerant of soils high in salts. A soil test from a commercial soil testing laboratory can provide a measure of soil salt levels.

Make the planting hole wide and deep enough that the roots are not crowded or bent. Plant so the graft is at least 2 inches above the soil to prevent the stem above the graft from rooting. Space trees as far apart as they will be tall when mature, or as close as 6 feet for hedgerows. Columnar varieties can be planted much closer, about 18 inches.

Some apples are partially self-fertile and will set a fair crop in the absence of a pollinator, but they produce a much better crop if another variety is nearby. Plant two or more varieties that bloom at the same time to ensure cross-pollination, though in many neighborhoods the abundance of other apple trees or ornamental crabapple trees is sufficient to ensure good pollination. If you have room for just one apple tree and can't count on nearby trees to pollinate yours, look for a tree with two or more varieties grafted on it.
Growing: Hand weed an area 4 to 6 feet around the trunk. To control weeds and conserve moisture apply a layer of

Solving Apple Disease and Pest Problems

Scab, powdery mildew, fire blight, and codling moth are nearly universal apple problems. Apple maggot and curculio are pests primarily east of the Rocky Mountains. The important times to spray apples are in late winter before buds swell, again just before flowers open, and then after flowers fade. In some cases where pest problems are serious, spraying continues every 10 days or so after that. Late afternoon or evening is a good time to spray because bees are less active and sprays last longer on leaves. Never spray a pest control while flowers are open and being visited by pollinating bees.

● **Scab:** One of the most serious diseases of apples in areas where spring weather is mild and wet, scab causes olive-brown velvety spots 1/4 inch or more in diameter on the leaves and fruit. Spots develop first on the underside of leaves, then on both sides.

The fungus spends winter in infected plant debris on the ground. Beginning at bud break, spores are ejected into the air when the leaf debris becomes wet. Air currents carry the spores to emerging leaves. If a film of water is present on the leaf, the spores germinate and infect it. The infected tissues produce more spores, which in turn infect other leaf and fruit surfaces.

Solution: Planting varieties that are less susceptible or immune to the disease is the best remedy. Removing fallen and spore-carrying leaves and fruit, disposing of them, and treating the soil around trees with lime and compost helps limit the

disease. Organic sprays of liquid sulfur applied when buds show pink require favorable weather to be effective. Check with your local county extension service for approved disease controls.

● **Cedar-apple rust:** This fungus disease affects both apples and certain junipers and red cedars. It causes pale yellow spots to appear on the upper leaf surfaces and on fruit in mid- to late spring. These spots gradually enlarge, turn orange, and develop minute black dots.

The fungus cannot spread from apple to apple or from juniper to juniper but must alternate between the two. In spring, spores from brown and orange galls on juniper or cedar are carried by air up to 3 miles to apple trees. During mild, wet weather the spores germinate and infect the leaves and fruit, causing spotting and eventually premature leaf and apple drop. During summer spores are produced in the small lesions on the underside of apple leaves, which then make their way back to junipers.

Solution: If the disease is common in your area, plant resistant apple varieties. Cedar-apple rust cannot be eliminated from infected apple fruits and leaves. Infected fruits are still edible if affected areas are cut away. Sulfur sprays at the pink bud stage can prevent infections. Check with your local county extension service for approved disease controls.

● **Powdery mildew:** A common plant disease caused by a fungus that thrives in both humid and dry weather, powdery mildew is favored by warm days and cool

nights, reduced light, and lack of rainfall. It causes grayish white powdery patches on the leaves. New growth is often stunted, curled, and distorted. Infected buds may open later than usual, and infected flowers and leaves often turn brittle and die.

Solution: Plant resistant apple varieties. Sulfur sprays at the pink bud stage can be an effective preventive. Check with your local county extension service for approved disease controls. For more about powdery mildew, see page 203.

● **Fire blight:** This plant disease caused by a bacterium commonly affects apples and related plants, such as pear, causing blossoms to turn brown and die. Spurs and branches wilt from the tip down, turn brown, and die, but leaves remain attached. Branch bark becomes water soaked, then dark, sunken, and dry.

The bacterium spends the winter in cankers on the branches and twigs. Just before bloom time it oozes out of the cankers and is carried by splashing rain and insects to the apple blossoms. Honeybees and other insects can spread it from there. Summer storms can spread the disease organism, leading to sudden and severe fire blight outbreaks.

Solution: Prune infected twigs and branches at least 8 inches beyond visible decay and destroy the debris. Disinfect your pruning shears with a dilute solution of bleach between each cut. The following spring, spray with basic copper sulfate before the blossoms open. When 25 percent of the flowers have opened, spray with a disease control containing

mulch in a circle under the canopy but keep it away from the tree trunk. In dry weather water newly planted trees until they are well established. Water mature trees according to your soil type—as often as once a week in areas with sandy soil—and make sure the entire area beneath the canopy is moist to a depth of 12 to 18 inches. Most apple varieties are hardy, but flowers and fruitlets are damaged below freezing. Feed mature trees with compost applied in winter,

TRAINING AND PRUNING APPLES

Any of the training methods described on pages 114 to 117 will suit any apple, but open center is the method most commonly used for standard-size trees. At planting cut back the main stem by about one-third, cutting just above a bud. Cut back any branches by up to one-third to a bud that faces out. Remove any buds growing between branches or in crotches. Cut back by one-third the future main scaffold branches.

In the second and third dormant season, reduce the length of all new growth by one-third, and thin the tree to create a strong, evenly spaced framework of branches. These secondary scaffold branches are the ones that will develop fruit spurs on their lateral branches. The pruning during this period should always be to a bud on the top of a branch that points outward; not to buds that point downward or towards the center of the tree. This will develop the open center.

Semidwarf and dwarf apple trees are stronger and bear earlier if pruned to a central leader system. When planting a bare-root semidwarf or dwarf tree cut back all branches including the top about one-quarter their length or about 5 to 10 inches. Make cuts to a strong outside-facing bud. In the second and third years repeat the process to train the central leader upward and the scaffold branches out parallel to the ground. Maintain the single, upright central leader throughout the life of the tree. Be sure to remove any fruit that forms on this leader because fruit formation will stunt the leader and cause another branch to become dominant.

Prune mature trees during the dormant season because at that time it is easier to see the basic structural framework of the tree. Pruning will encourage spur formation and maintain fruiting wood. Prune to thin out shoots and limbs with the goal of improving light penetration and air circulation. Remove dead or diseased branches, and thin areas of dense growth, remove unproductive branches, and head back shoots at the top of the tree. Prune aggressively to promote more new growth; prune more cautiously to limit new growth. Prune scaffold limbs so that they end in a single shoot.

---

streptomycin. Repeat at intervals of three to five days until the end of the bloom period. The natural bacterium *Bacillus subtilis* is partially effective at blocking fire blight. (For more about fire blight, see pages 202.)

● **Codling moth:** Among the most

Codling moth exit hole

common pests of apples in North America, codling moth larvae feed on the fruits, creating small holes surrounded by dead tissue. A brown crumbly material resembling sawdust may surround the holes, and the interior of the fruit is often rotted.

The moths, which usually fly at twilight, appear in spring when apple trees are blooming. They lay their eggs on the leaves, twigs, and developing fruit. When the eggs hatch, the larvae begin tunneling into the fruit. They feed for several weeks, then emerge. After pupating in sheltered locations on or around the tree, another generation of moths emerges in midsummer. In fall mature larvae spin cocoons under loose bark or in tree crevices. They spend winter in these cocoons, emerging as moths in spring. They may also overwinter on other plants under the trees.

Solution: Two weeks after petal fall, begin spraying the insecticide *Bacillus thuringiensis* (Bt), a bacterium that's toxic only to caterpillars. Remove and destroy all fallen apples and clean up the debris. For more precise spray timing, use pheromone traps (sticky traps with scent attractive to the moths) to monitor moth flights; hang at least two traps per tree. Spray one week after moth catches reach five moths per week. Pheromone traps can also be used to control codling moths without spraying.

● **Apple maggot:** These maggots are the larvae of flies that resemble houseflies. The flies lay eggs in the fruits through

Apple maggot

holes they puncture in the skin. White legless maggots about $3/8$ inch long may be present in the fruit. Infested fruits are dimpled and pitted with brown trails winding through the flesh. The fruits drop prematurely, and mature maggots emerge and burrow in the soil to pupate. They remain in the soil throughout winter, emerging as adult flies in June.

Solution: Maggots cannot be killed after apples are infested. Early varieties are the most susceptible and late ones the least susceptible. Pick up and destroy fallen apples every week throughout summer.

Protect healthy apples from adult flies with apple maggot traps; hang at least two in each tree. These red balls look like ripe apples but are coated with a sticky material that traps adult flies. Spray an insect control product as soon as adult flies appear on the traps. The red ball traps also provide limited control apple maggots without spraying.

● **Plum curculio:** A mottled brown beetle about $1/4$ inch long with a long, curved snout, this pest found east of the Rocky Mountains causes ripening fruit to be misshapen and rotten and to drop prematurely. Adult beetles hibernate in debris and other protected places during winter. In spring when new growth starts, they emerge and begin feeding on young leaves, blossoms, and developing fruit. After five to six weeks the female beetles begin to lay eggs in the young fruit. They make holes about $1/8$ inch wide and deep, leaving crescent-shape scars on the fruit. The grubs that hatch from the eggs feed for several weeks in the fruit. Infested fruits fall, and the grubs inside leave the fruit and bore into the soil, where they pupate. The emerging beetles feed on developing fruit for a few weeks, then go into hibernation.

Solution: Begin treatment at petal fall. Spread a sheet under the canopy and shake the tree to take advantage of the beetle's habit of dropping when startled. Fold up the sheet with fallen curculios and dispose of them. Spray the tree with neem oil or insecticidal soap to repel the pest. Use sprays that contain phosmet.

TOP GARDEN APPLES

Variety	Zones	Ripening season	Fruit (color; flesh; uses)	Pollination*	Disease Resistance**	Key features
'Anna'	8–10	Very early	Green with red blush; crisp, sweet; fresh, cooking	C; 'Dorsett Golden', 'Ein Shemer'	–	Susceptible to scab, especially in the Southeast
'Cox Orange Pippin'	4–8	Midseason	Orange with red stripes; yellow, aromatic, juicy, distinctive, high-quality flavor; fresh, cooking, cider	A; self-fertile	–	Blooms late, missing frosts. Fruits need thinning. Susceptible to scab
'Dorsett Golden'	7–10	Early	Yellow; sweet, firm; dessert, cooking	C; self-fertile	–	Vigorous, upright. Very productive in low desert Southwest, Southern California
'Ein Shemer'	8–10	Early	Yellow with slight blush; crisp, sweet-tart; fresh	C; partially self-fertile; 'Dorsett Golden'	Scab	Strong early-bearing tree
'Empire'	4–7	Early midseason	Attractive, dark red. Firm, dark, waxy; high quality, creamy white, crisp, tart; fresh	B; partially self-fertile	Rust, fire blight	Upright, vigorous, early bearing. Tolerates hot summers. Fruit needs thinning. Ripe fruits hold on trees longer than most
'Freedom'	3–5	Midseason to late	Bright red on yellow; crisp, yellow, aromatic; cooking, cider	B; 'Liberty'	Scab, rust, fire blight, mildew	Immune to scab, rust. Vigorous, spreading. Fruits store into January
'Gala'	4–9	Midseason	Golden with heavy red stripes; crisp, aromatic; dessert	B; partially self-fertile; 'Golden Delicious'	Mildew	Susceptible to rust, fire blight. Good keeper
'Golden Delicious' ('Yellow Delicious')	5–9	Midseason to late	Yellow; crisp, firm, juicy, excellent flavor; dessert, cooking	A; self-fertile	–	Easily trained, naturally wide branch angles. Good pollinator of others. Susceptible to disease. Fruits bruise easily. Bears young and annually
'Golden Russet'	4–5	Late	Gold-bronze with orange; crisp, fine textured, very sweet juice; cider, fresh	A; 'Golden Delicious'	Scab	Vigorous, large tree. Tends to tip bear. Good pollinator. Heirloom
'Goldrush'	4–9	Late	Yellow; rich, tart, spicy, high quality; use fresh or for all-purposes	B	Scab, mildew, fire blight	Tends to develop central leader. Immune to scab, prone to rust
'Honeycrisp'	3–7	Midseason	Mottled red over yellow; distinctive, crisp; fresh	B	Scab	Hardy. Susceptible to fire blight. Good keeper

'Liberty' apple   'Freedom' apple

supplemented with five pounds of 10-10-10 if growth is slow or weak.

Thin the fruit by hand to one per cluster or about one for every 6 inches of stem. Support fruit-laden trees through summer and until harvest by propping a sturdy post under

affected branches so that branches are not broken or their shapes distorted. **Harvesting:** Apples produce fruit on stubby branches called spurs that remain productive for five to seven years. Expect to wait three to five years for your first full harvest. Fruits ripen 70 to 180 days from bloom depending

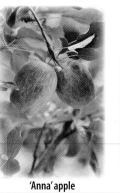

'Anna' apple

Apple bloom with tulips

Variety	Zones	Ripening season	Fruit (color; flesh; uses)	Pollination*	Disease Resistance**	Key features
'Jonagold'	5–8	Midseason to late	Striped red over bright yellow; rich, full flavored, juicy; dessert	D, but not 'Golden Delicious'	-	Vigorous, sturdy, spreading. Susceptible to disease
'Keepsake'	3–6	Very late	Red with white dots; crisp, juicy, yellow, hard, aromatic; dessert	B	Fire blight, rust	Needs full season to ripen. Outstanding keeping quality, until early spring
'Liberty'	3–5	Midseason to late	Red blush; crisp, yellow with red blush; dessert, baked	B	Scab, rust, fire blight	Often requires fruit thinning. Immune to scab. Most disease-free apple
'Mutsu' ('Crispin')	4–8	Late	Yellow; crisp, juicy, spicy; dessert, cider, sauce, storage	D	Mildew	Spreading, vigorous, large, early bearing. Susceptible to scab
'Newtown Pippin' ('Yellow Newtown', 'Yellow Pippin')	5–8	Late	Yellow-green, very russetted; creamy yellow, crisp, aromatic; cider, storage	A	-	Vigorous, large, early bearing. Prone to mildew. Tends to bear heavy crops in alternate years
'Priscilla'	5–8	Midseason	Red over yellow; crisp, mild; dessert, storage	'Honeycrisp'	Scab, rust, mildew	Fruit lasts well on tree, stores 90 days
'Roxbury Russet'	4–8	Late	Green-bronze, russetted; coarse but tender, sweet; all purpose	'Goldrush'	Scab, mildew	Medium to large tree. High-sugar fruit prized for cider. Excellent keeper. American heirloom
'Sansa'	4–8	Early midseason	Bright red stripes on yellow-green; tender, sweet; dessert	B	-	Good pollinator, medium vigor. Flavor similar to 'Gala', one of its parents
'Williams Pride'	4–8	Early	Deep maroon with small white dots, chewy; red-stained; dessert, baked	B; 'Priscilla'	Scab	Vigorous, upright, needs regular pruning. Some resistance to fire blight and mildew
'Winesap'	5–8	Late	Deep red; intense, winey, sweet-tart aroma, juicy; all purposes	D	-	Heavy producer, widely adapted. Good keeper. American heirloom
'Winter Banana'	5–9	Late	Pale yellow with rosy blush; distinctive flavor; fresh, cider	B	-	Vigorous, annual bearer. Fruits bruise easily

*A=Self-fruitful, but improved with pollinator; B=Pollinate with A or any other B; C= Pollinate with another C; D=Not a pollinator, but is pollinated by A or B. Top pollinating varieties for some varieties are noted.

**"Rust" is cedar-apple rust

'Honeycrisp' apple

Harvesting an apple

on the apple variety. Pick apples by hand to avoid bruising them. A ripe apple separates easily from the fruiting spur and has firm flesh. A soft apple is overripe but can still be used in cooking. Late varieties are the best for long-term storage at cool room temperatures. Some types, such as 'Cox', 'McIntosh', and 'Jonathan', decay if stored in the refrigerator.

Varieties: Choosing an apple tree means selecting both a fruit variety and a tree size. Standard apple trees grow 30 to 40 feet high and wide. But by selecting a rootstock you can also choose the tree's mature size.

Semidwarf rootstocks reduce the ultimate size of the tree by 15 to 50 percent. Apple trees on rootstocks MM 106 and MM 111 will reach only 18 to 22 feet high and wide. Trees grafted onto MARK, M26, and M7 stop growing at about 13 feet high and wide.

Dwarfing rootstocks produce trees approximately 30 percent the height of a full-size tree, or about 8 feet high and wide. These rootstocks, which include M9, EMLA27, and P22, are shallow rooted and so aren't as cold-tolerant nor as sturdy to strong wind and rain as other rootstocks.

Genetic dwarf apples, such as **'Babe'** (red) and **'Garden Delicious'** (greenish yellow to red), are not grafted onto dwarfing rootstocks because they are naturally dwarf. At full size they grow about 10 feet high and wide. Genetic dwarfs are more cold tolerant than grafted dwarf apples, and their chilling requirement (hours of exposure to cold temperature required to break dormancy) is moderate. Spur apples produce more of the fruit-bearing short branches called spurs than standard apples. They are naturally semidwarf, rarely growing beyond 20 feet high and wide, but they can be further dwarfed by grafting onto dwarfing rootstocks.

Columnar apple trees develop a polelike single trunk and few side branches. Side branches that do form quickly turn upward as well. Naturally dwarf and upright, the columnar apples grow to 8 feet tall and rarely exceed 2 feet wide. They are hardy in Zones 4 to 8. Plant them 18 inches apart or singly in a large container, keeping in mind that two different varieties are needed for pollination. All are susceptible to disease but to varying degree. Given their size, all are easy to prune, spray, and harvest. Varieties include **'Crimson Spire'** (red), **'Emerald Spire'** (green with yellow), **'Golden Sentinel'** (yellow), **'Northpole'** (red), **'Scarlet Sentinel'** (greenish yellow with red blush), and **'Scarlet Spire'** (red and green).

Crabapples (*Malus* species) are well known as ornamental trees, but many produce excellent fruits too. **'Dolgo'** bears fruits about the size of small plums that are excellent to eat fresh and, given their red flesh, make an attractive sauce. Other crabapples with good fruits are **'Calloway'**, **'Columbia'**, **'Ralph Shay'**, and **'Selkirk'**.

Apple pear (see Pear)

Apricot (Prunus armeniaca)

Type: Deciduous tree, Zones 4–10
Typical yield: 125–175 pounds per tree
Typical size: 6–20'H×6–20'W

Apricot

According to legend, Confucius did his best thinking underneath an apricot tree, and during his lifetime the apricot was already an ancient and revered horticultural treasure in China. In the 18th century apricots found their way to North America. Settlers planted them in Virginia, where they mostly failed to produce crops, but the trees planted by Spanish missionaries up and down California thrived—which tells us much about apricots today too. While the trees are cold hardy enough, they bloom

TRAINING AND PRUNING APRICOTS

In the first dormant season shorten the most promising three or four scaffold branches to 2 to 2½ feet. Leave two side shoots, if they are present, on each of these scaffold branches to form secondary scaffold limbs. Remove all other side shoots. Depending on the growth pattern of the tree, you may need to complete the selection of scaffold limbs and secondary scaffold limbs during the dormant season and the second summer.

Train to an open center with three leaders. Because trees tend to spread, thin horizontal growth favoring upright branches. Prune lightly once a year after bloom to remove old fruiting spurs and control tree height. Thin the branches of shrubby varieties to allow sunlight to penetrate the interior of trees.

Apricot bears mostly on spurs along branches that are up to three years old; many fruits also appear near the midpoint of branches that grew the previous season. As you prune to repair and improve the tree's structure, remove about a third of last season's shoots. Shorten remaining shoots by a third to a half.

Apricots also bear laterally on spurs that usually live for no more than three years. To renew spurs, annually thin bearing trees to upright shoots. Thinning renews fruiting wood and improves light distribution. Don't head remaining branches unless branches are excessively long; head these long branches lightly to contain them.

For more about pruning fruit trees, see page 112.

'Harcot' apricot

early in spring. Wherever late spring frosts are common, the cold will routinely kill the tender flower buds. However, trees thrive and crops are plentiful where spring weather is sufficiently gentle.

Today more than 95 percent of the North American crop is from areas of California where the summers are warm and dry and winters mild. Elsewhere, crops are less reliable. But advances in apricot breeding have made it a realistic option in many locales.

When: Plant bare-root trees in late winter before growth begins. Or plant container-grown plants anytime.

Planting: Choose a sunny site with deep, loose, well-drained, slightly acid soil, and ideally one that is protected from winds and early frosts. In northern regions where adaptability is tricky, plant on a mound of soil to ensure optimum drainage. A north-facing slope, because it's slow to warm up in spring and revive dormant trees, is best if spring frosts are a factor. Space standard size trees about 25 feet apart, semidwarfs 15 feet apart, and dwarfs 6 feet apart.

Growing: Because apricot is an early bloomer, it is susceptible to late spring frost damage, which means no

TOP GARDEN APRICOTS

Variety*	Zones	Fruit	Disease susceptibility†	Key features, disease resistance
'Blenheim' ('Royal')	7–8; 9 in California	Large, pale orange with red flecks, sweet, aromatic	Brown rot	California favorite. Noted for canning quality
'Chinese' ('Mormon')	6–8	Small to medium, orange, juicy	Shot hole fungus, peach twig borer, brown rot	Developed in Utah for areas with late frosts. Medium-size, spreading tree
'Early Golden'	5–8; 9 in California	Large, smooth orange-gold skin, intensely flavored orange flesh	-	Great all-purpose apricot. Attractive tree. Especially suited for Southern gardens
'Garden Annie'	8–9	Medium to large, bright yellow, firm, juicy, good flavor; clingstone	-	Genetic dwarf, grows to 8' high. Low chill requirement
'Goldcot'	5–8	Medium to large, round, thick golden skin, juicy orange flesh, tangy	-	Tree is consistently heavy bearing. Partial resistance to bacterial leaf spot
'Gold Kist'	7–8; 9 in California	Large, firm, excellent flavor; freestone	-	Early ripening. Good for mild-winter climates
'Harcot'	6–7	Medium to large, orange, firm; excellent, sweet flavor	-	Early ripening. Vigorous, productive. Self-fertile. Resists perennial canker, bacterial spot, brown rot
'Harlayne'	6–7	Medium-size, firm, orange with red blush, good texture and flavor; freestone	-	Cold-hardy. Productive. Tolerates perennial canker, bacterial spot, brown rot
'Harogem'	6–7	Small to medium, orange with bright orange blush, firm, good texture and flavor; freestone	Bacterial spot	Tree is consistently productive. Quite upright. Resists perennial canker, brown rot
'Moongold'	4–8	Medium-size, oblong, sweet, tangy	-	Developed in Minnesota. Needs another variety for pollination

* *Most apricots are self-fruitful and do not require pollination by another tree, though production is often enhanced by a pollinator.*
† *Diseases noted refer to notable disease problems. Varieties without diseases noted are not immune to disease.*

'Moongold' apricot

fruiting. If possible, cover trees when a frost is predicted. Apricot trees do not tolerate drought. Keep the soil consistently moist but never waterlogged. Water deeply every week during warm weather. Use tree plant food spikes if growth is less than 1 to 2 feet each year. After normal fruit drop thin to the healthiest fruit on each spur and leave 3 inches between fruits.

Harvesting: The apricot harvest season occurs for two or three weeks anytime from late spring through early summer depending on apricot variety, weather, and regional climatic conditions. For the richest flavor, let the fruits ripen on the tree and pick them once they develop full color with the flesh just starting to soften slightly.

Pests and diseases: Avoid most diseases by choosing resistant varieties and practicing clean cultural habits. Prune out diseased and dead wood immediately, and keep the ground around trees clear of dropped fruit and other plant debris, which harbors pests and encourages disease. Cultivate the soil around the tree shallowly to destroy insect pupae. Avoid using insect controls while trees are in flower to protect pollinators. Use a disease control spray at 10- to 14-day intervals until petal drop and again in autumn after leaf fall to prevent brown rot, twig blight, green fruit rot, and other infections. Spray dormant oil in winter to control scale, mites, and borers. Use netting to protect trees from birds, and trunk wraps in winter to prevent rodent damage. Remove trunk wraps during the growing season to prevent rots from developing under the wrap.

Varieties: Choose apricots grafted to rootstocks that do well in your area and varieties bred for disease resistance. Top varieties of apricots are noted in the chart above. Their chilling requirements vary from 300 to 1,000 hours.

Manchurian apricot (*P. armeniaca mandschurica*) is hardy to Zone 4, but it blooms early leaving it susceptible to late spring frosts. It forms a large shrub or small tree, to 12 feet high and wide, and bears 1-inch yellow-orange fruits.

Japanese apricot (*P. mume*) is a small-fruited species that is used to make plum sauce in Asian cuisines. It has showy red, white, or pink flowers; grows 15 to 30 feet tall; and is hardy to Zone 6. Spring frost will damage the flower buds and destroy the fruit crop.

Hybrids of apricots, peaches, and plums called apriums, peachcots, pluots, and plumcots combine the best features of each species. Read more about them on page 162.

Aprium (see Plum)
Atemoya (see Cherimoya)

Avocado *(Persea americana)*

Type: Evergreen or briefly
deciduous tree, Zones 9–11
Typical yield: 200–500 pounds
per tree
Typical size: 8–60'H×6–40'W

'Sir Prize' ripe avocado

Under the proper growing
conditions these trees provide
an abundant harvest of rich,
buttery fruit. The fruits vary
from round to pear shape
depending on the avocado
variety. They may be as small as
4 ounces or as large as 2 pounds. Because the varieties ripen
in different seasons, there are almost always avocados for
sale at the supermarket.

Avocado trees can become quite large and live 20 or more
years. They bear clusters of yellowish white flowers. Mature
foliage is deep green and leathery; new growth is coppery
red, appearing in flushes throughout the year. The leaves of
Mexican varieties have a scent like anise.

When: The best time to plant avocados is in early fall once
the air temperature has begun to cool but the soil is still
warm. Or plant at any time of the year except in the high
heat of midsummer.

Planting: Choose a protected, sunny location with deep,
rich, well-drained soil. Avocado is adaptable to all slightly
acid soils and will even grow in alkaline soils in Florida and
Hawaii. Space trees so that their canopies will not touch
when they reach their mature size.

Growing: Use a transplant starter solution at the time of
planting, then a balanced plant food every two months
except when the tree blooms and fruits. Hand weed and
water frequently until the roots are established, then water
only during times of drought. Use foliar sprays to correct
mineral deficiencies. Prune to control size. Maintain a
wide circle of organic mulch under the tree canopy but
not touching the trunk.

Harvesting: Grafted trees usually bear one to five years
after planting. Depending on the avocado variety, ripening
requires 6 to 18 months after fruit set. Because the trees
bloom over a long period, fruits will not mature all at once.
Use external coloring as a guide to maturity. Dark varieties
are mature once they look dark; green kinds are ready to
harvest when the skin shows a yellowish tint. Pick the
largest, fullest ones first, using hand pruners to cut the
stems. Fruits will ripen at room temperature in 5 to 10 days.
Hasten ripening by placing an avocado in a paper bag with
an apple or a banana. To preserve half a fruit for later use
leave the seed in, moisten the exposed flesh with citrus juice,
and wrap tightly in plastic
wrap. Store whole ripe
avocados in the refrigerator
for up to a week.

'Hass' avocado

Pests and diseases: Avocado
root rot is a problem in
California. Select certified
disease-free plants and avoid
planting where avocados
previously grew or where soil
drainage is poor. The root rot
disease is easily transported
by equipment, tools, and
shoes from infected soils
to uninfected ones. Deep
mulching (6 to 12 inches of
organic matter such as bark chips) and regular applications
of gypsum (25 pounds per year per tree) help suppress the
disease. Snails can be a problem in California. In Florida
and Hawaii fungus diseases such as scab, anthracnose, and
powdery mildew are common. Read more about these pests
beginning on page 194. Check with your local county
extension service for control measures.

Varieties: The various types of avocado are Mexican,
Guatemalan, and West Indian as well as hybrids of these
groups. The Mexican, Guatemalan, and hybrids of the
two are best adapted to California and cold areas of the
Southeast. West Indian varieties are best adapted to south
Florida and Hawaii. Although there are great similarities
between groups, Mexican varieties are generally hardier, bear
fruit with a smoother and thinner shiny green or black skin,
and are hardy to Zone 9. Guatemalan avocados, which are
restricted almost exclusively to frost-free Zone 10 climates,
bear blackish green fruit with a thick, bumpy rind. West
Indian varieties are the most frost-sensitive and have thin,
smooth, greenish yellow skin.

In the listing that follows, "M" means Mexican, "G"
Guatemalan, "W" West Indian, and "H" hybrid.

California: 'Anaheim' (G) is a large-fruited variety with
fair flavor; fruits are borne on a small, upright tree. **'Bacon'**
(M) has medium-size fruits with good flavor on an upright,
slender tree. **'Fuerte'** (H), bears small to medium-size fruits
on a large, spreading tree.

'Hass' (H) produces small to medium-size fruits with
excellent, nutty flavor; the tree is medium large. **'Zutano'**
(H) has medium-size fruits with good flavor; the tree is large,
and very upright growing.

Florida: 'Booth' (H) bears medium to large fruits with
good flavor on a medium, spreading tree. **'Choquette'** (H)
produces large to very large fruits of excellent flavor on a
medium, spreading tree that resists scab disease. **'Hall'** (H)
has large to very large, green fruits with good flavor; the tree
is medium-size. **'Lula'** (H) bears medium to large fruits of
good flavor; the large, upright tree also does well in south
Texas. **'Miguel'** (H) has large, excellent-quality fruits on a
productive medium-size tree. **'Pollock'** (W) produces large
to very large fruits with very good flavor; the medium,
spreading tree resists scab disease. **'Simmonds'** (W) has
large to very large green fruits with very good flavor; the
medium, spreading tree resists scab disease.

Dwarf: 'Gwen' (H) bears small fruits with good-flavor on
an upright tree to 12 to 14 feet high. **'Wurtz'** ('Wertz', 'Little
Cado') (H) produces small, good flavor fruits on a tree that
reaches 8 to 10 feet high. **'Whitsell'** (H) has small fruits of
excellent flavor; the tree reaches 12 feet high.

Babaco *(see Papaya)*

Banana, plantain *(Musa spp.)*

Type: Herbaceous perennial, Zones 9–11
Typical yield: 75–125 pounds per plant
Typical size: 5–25'H×5–20'W

'Belle' bananas

Throughout much of the
tropics bananas and plantains
are staples. The plants are
extremely decorative, ranking
next to palm trees for the
tropical feeling they lend to the
landscape. They are perennials
arising from underground
stems called rhizomes. The
fleshy stalks sheathed with

huge, broad leaves can rise 5 to 25 feet in as little as six months depending on the banana variety. Each stalk produces one huge flower cluster. After fruits mature the entire stalk dies. New stalks then grow from the rhizome. Fruit size and flavor vary considerably, but most home garden varieties are 4 to 8 inches long and very sweet.

Plantain, red baby banana, baby banana, and regular banana

When: Late spring is the best time to plant.

Planting: Choose a warm, sunny, wind-protected location with deep, moist, rich, slightly acid soil that drains well. Bananas do not tolerate standing water or salinity and will not thrive in sand or heavy soil. Plant suckers or large chunks of rhizome in holes 3 feet wide and 2 feet deep amended with well-rotted compost. Space plants as far apart as they will be tall at maturity.

Growing: Bananas and plantains are heavy feeders, so maintain soil nutrients with plant food spikes and a mulch of compost or composted manure applied monthly in a wide circle under the plant but not touching it. Soil that is infertile or too acid will decrease yields. Mulch is also necessary to conserve soil moisture and control weeds. Keep the soil moist but not waterlogged. In dry climates water deeply a few times a year to leach the soil of excess mineral salts. Bananas have shallow roots but huge leaves (up to 9 feet long and 2 feet wide) that make the plants top-heavy; stakes and supports may be necessary to support fruit-laden plants. Nearly all varieties stop growing in temperatures below 55°F. The plants die back to the ground in freezing temperatures, but the underground rhizomes survive to 25°F. Wrap young plants in blankets if frost is predicted.

Cut off all but one stalk per plant and keep new suckers pruned off at ground level. When the main stalk is six to eight months old, allow one new sucker to develop for the following season. Prop up the fruiting stalk when it begins to bend from the weight of developing fruit. Use a sturdy forked pole or two stakes fastened together to form an "X" to hold the bunch. If there are more than six clusters of fruits, called hands, on a bunch remove the terminal bud several inches below the last hand to encourage fuller fruits. After harvest cut the current season's fruiting branch back to the ground. Banana sap stains so wear gloves and old clothing when pruning (or harvesting).

Harvesting: Harvest once the fruit at the top of the cluster begins to yellow, usually in late summer or fall. Remove the whole cluster and let it ripen at room temperature for one to two weeks. Individual fruits left on the plant will split open as they ripen and the fruit will decay rapidly. Bananas are highly perishable when ripe but can be peeled, cut into chunks, and frozen in plastic bags for later use. They don't refrigerate, but they can be dried. Bananas are preferred for eating out of hand and in desserts; the more nutritious banana relative, plantain, is used primarily in cooking because its flavor is starchy rather than sweet.

Pests and diseases: Few problems develop in home gardens. Control nematodes and banana weevils if they are present.

Varieties: Dwarf varieties such as 'Apple', 'Dwarf Brazilian', 'Dwarf Cavendish', 'Enano Gigante', 'Goldfinger', 'Ice Cream', and 'Williams' all grow 5 to 16 feet tall, ripen in about three months after flowering, and do well in California. 'Gros Michel' is a popular but disease-prone and tall variety for Hawaii. 'Lady Finger' is a tall plant with small sweet fruits that grows well in Florida and Hawaii. 'Macho' is a popular plantain in Florida.

Barbados cherry (see Cherry)
Blackberry (see Brambles)
Blackcap (see Brambles)

Blueberry (Vaccinium spp.)

Type: Deciduous shrub, Zones 3–9
Typical yield: 3–10 pounds per plant
Typical size: 2–7'H×2–10'W

Natives of North America, blueberries are an ideal edible ornamental in those regions where the plants grow well. Depending on the blueberry variety, plants can make good-looking border shrubs, groundcovers, or tall hedges. And of course they produce all those beautiful and delicious berries in late spring and summer. The plants are closely related to azaleas and rhododendrons and so grow best in areas with cool, moist, acidic soils.

The three main kinds available to home gardeners are highbush blueberry (V. corymbosum) rabbit-eye blueberry (V. ashei), and half-high hybrids of highbush and lowbush blueberry (V. angustifolium). All are attractive plants with neat green leaves, dainty spring flowers, enticing clusters of tasty blue fruits that ripen over a three- to four-week period in summer, and brightly colored red to yellow fall foliage.

Highbush blueberries produce the berries found in most markets. Most varieties grow to 6 feet high or more, though varieties that are much lower growing are available. These blueberries thrive in the East (especially around the Great Lakes), the Northeast, and the Northwest. The fruits ripen from late spring to late summer depending on variety. The half-high hybrids grow 2 to 4 feet high and wide. They are best adapted to northern climates.

Rabbit-eye blueberries are grown in climates that are too warm for highbush blueberries, mainly in the Southeast but, if provided the necessary acidic soil, also in parts of Southern California. Rabbit-eye blueberries are taller and more heat-tolerant than highbush types. Their larger berries have a thicker skin and less flavor but ripen over a long period from late spring into summer. There are many varieties of rabbit-eyes with improved qualities.

When: Plant in early spring where winters are cold and in fall where winters are mild.

Planting: Choose a sunny location that has well-drained, preferably acidic sandy loam soil with a pH between 4.5 and 5.5. Plants are available either bare root or in containers. Set bare-root stock at the same depth it was grown in the nursery. Keep the plants continuously moist before planting them. Space highbush and rabbit-eye varieties 6 feet apart, lowbush 2 feet apart, and half-high 3 to 4 feet apart.

Growing: Blueberries are very shallow rooted and lack root hairs, which is why drought and cultivation around roots are particularly harmful. In warm areas without regular summer rainfall, water blueberries weekly in order to keep the top foot of soil moist.

Mulch heavily with shredded bark, sawdust, or composted leaves to about 6 inches deep. The heavy mulch layer maintains even soil moisture, prevents weeds, and reduces the need to cultivate.

Renewal-prune annually to remove old canes. In the first two years of growth remove weak, diseased, and damaged canes only. In subsequent years remove weak, diseased, and damaged canes along with some of the oldest canes. Remove excess young canes to encourage the growth of others, and

TOP GARDEN BLUEBERRIES

Variety	Fruit	Plant	Key features
HIGHBUSH, ZONES 4–8			
'Berkeley'	Large, light blue, mild flavor, firm flesh, resists cracking. Midseason, stores well	Plants are productive and easy to grow	Berries don't fall easily off the bush. Good in the Northwest
'Bluecrop'	Medium to large, light blue, excellent flavor, firm flesh, resists cracking. Midseason	Tall and somewhat drought resistant	The most popular blueberry. More cold hardy and drought tolerant than most. Good for high elevation in the South and Northwest
'Blueray'	Very large, firm flesh, strong flavor and aroma, resists cracking. Early midseason	Tall, upright, productive. Tolerates hot climates	Less flavor than 'Berkeley'. Prune to prevent overproduction, which weakens the plant. Recommended for the high upper South and Northwest. Prone to mummy berry
'Coville'	Very large, aromatic, slightly tart, holds well on the bush, resists cracking. Late-midseason	Vigorous, productive. Canker resistant	Recommended in the Northwest, high-elevation areas of the South
'Darrow'	Large, exceptional flavor. Late	Vigorous, very productive	Consistently productive. Good in the Northwest
'Duke'	Large, light blue, good flavor. Early	Consistently high yielding. Self-fruitful	Developed in New Jersey for fresh and processed market
'Elliot'	Medium size, firm, light blue. Mild flavor. Late	Productive	Attractive, ornamental qualities
'Georgiagem'	Medium to large, firm. Excellent flavor. Early	Consistent yields. Can tolerate higher pH than other varieties	Low-chill, adapted to the South
'Herbert'	Very large, tender, good flavor, resists cracking and dropping. Late midseason	Productive, open spreading	Consistently productive. Good in Northwest
'Jersey'	Medium-size, firm flesh, good flavor, resists cracking, good keeper. Late	Vigorous, hardy	Widely adapted and widely grown

prune to reduce the density of the branches at the top of plants. Careful selection of canes to prune helps to balance the fruit load in the next season. Each mature plant should have 15 to 25 canes of varying ages. Canes decline in productivity after five to six years.

Highbush blueberry harvest

Rabbit-eye blueberries need little or no pruning. Occasional thinning of older plants may be desirable to remove unproductive branches, but too much pruning promotes excessive foliage growth at the expense of fruit production.

Fertilize every year at flowering time with compost or a low-nitrogen plant food for acid-loving plants, such as one designed for rhododendron and azaleas. Excessive nitrogen causes low yields.

Harvesting: Hold a container in one hand and use your other hand to gently loosen berries from the cluster so they drop into the container. Ripening berries turn from green to pinkish red to blue, but not all blue ones are fully ripe. Blueberries are extremely perishable. Store them unwashed in the refrigerator for up to one week. Rinse and dry berries and freeze them in single layers in plastic for long-term

storage, or dry the berries and store them in an airtight container for up to three years.

Pests and diseases: Blueberry plants usually aren't troubled by pests seriously enough to require control. In some locales blueberry maggot, cranberry weevil, and blueberry mite may require sprays. Plum curculio is sometimes a problem. Use disease control products to curb phomopsis canker, root rot, mummyberry, and twig blight. Japanese beetles may feed on blueberry leaves and fruits in the home garden. Keep the ground clean of dropped fruit and other plant debris to discourage fruit flies and maggots. Use protective netting over the entire plant, reflective tape, or noisemakers to protect ripening fruits from birds.

Varieties: Both rabbit-eye and half-high blueberries require cross-pollination. Plant at least two varieties for cross-pollination, which will ensure the best crops. To extend the harvest season choose varieties that ripen at different times.

Other blueberries available to home gardeners include varieties of lowbush types, *V. angustifolium*. As the

'Overton' rabbiteye blueberry

Variety	Fruit	Plant	Key features
'Lateblue'	Firm, light blue, excellent flavor. Late, ripens over short period. Late	Very productive	Simultaneous ripening during periods of hot weather
'Patriot'	Large, tight clusters, excellent flavor. Early	Vigorous, productive, upright and open. Slightly smaller than others	Most berries come in the first picking. Good resistance to Phytophthora root rot. Recommended for the Northeast
RABBIT-EYE, ZONES 6–9			
'Brightwell'	Medium-size, light blue, very firm, excellent flavor and quality. Early	Upright and open. Needs pollenizer	Very good harvest if well watered, well maintained
'Choice'	Medium-size, light blue. Excellent flavor. Late	Vigorous, upright. Needs pollenizer	Produces well in the South
'Climax'	Medium to large, dark blue, good quality. Early	Upright, open, vigorous. Needs pollenizer	Ripens over short period
'Powderblue'	Medium to large, dark blue, sweet, excellent quality. Midseason	Highly productive. Needs pollenizer	Similar, but superior to 'Tifblue'
HALF-HIGH, ZONES 3–7			
'Northblue'	Large, dark blue, excellent quality, superior to many highbush varieties. Wild blueberry flavor. Midseason	High yielding with adequate snow cover. Less than 3' tall	Refrigerates well. Attractive, ornamental qualities. Self-fertile but yield improves if planted with 'Northcountry'
'Northcountry'	Sweet, wild blueberry flavor, early. Small to medium	Good quality. Vigorous, tough. Hardy to −35°F	Good for northern regions, sky blue flowers
'Northsky'	Sweet, excellent wild flavor. Small. Early	Grows 18" high, 36" wide	From University of Minnesota
'St. Cloud'	Light blue, good flavor. Small. Early	Susceptible to winter injury	Requires cross-pollination

name suggests, these grow 1 to 3 feet high and spread 5 feet or wider. The wild blueberry of New England, they are very hardy, to Zone 3, and are often used as a groundcover.

Relatives of blueberry include **huckleberry** (*V. ovatum* and others), which has small, blue berries. It grows best in cool, dry climates. **Lingonberry** (*V. vitis-idaea*), also called cowberry, is a creeping evergreen hardy to Zone 2 that bears small, sour, cranberrylike fruits. **Bilberry** (*V. myrtillus*) is a deciduous shrub that thrives in the Pacific Northwest.

Brambles, blackberry, raspberry (*Rubus* spp.)

Type: Deciduous shrub or vine, Zones 4–9
Typical yield: 5–7 pounds per plant
Typical size: 6–10'H×3–8'W

Delicious and diverse brambles—the closely related blackberries and raspberries—provide sweet treats for snacking or making preserves. The plants may be stiffly erect, semierect, or trailing. Most are thorny; thornless varieties are available, but they are less winter hardy.

Choose raspberry varieties with red, black-blue, purple, or yellow fruit. Blackberries and raspberries are biennial. In each case, canes grow one year, bear fruit the next, and then die. Canes of primocane fruiting raspberries, called everbearing or fall-bearing, begin fruiting the first year in the garden and die the second year. Raspberry canes may be thorny or thornless. Train plants, even small ones, on trellises.

Red and yellow raspberries are genetically similar plants

with 7-foot-long canes. Black raspberries, or blackcaps, are borne on trailing thorny canes that reach 8 feet long; these are the least cold-hardy and productive raspberries, and they are more disease susceptible. Purple raspberries are hybrids of red and black raspberries with canes 7 to 8 feet long.

When: Plant brambles in early spring one month before the last frost date.

Planting: Brambles grow best in areas with long, mild springs and cool summer nights. Select a site away from patios, decks, and recreational areas where bees and dropped fruit can interfere. Plant certified disease-free plants or rooted cuttings in spring, spacing them 4 to 6 feet apart and setting them at the same depth they were grown in the nursery. Plants thrive in all but the most acid soils as long as the drainage is good. They need good air circulation to ward off disease. Avoid planting them in areas where tomatoes, potatoes, eggplants, and peppers have grown in the past three years because the site may harbor verticillium wilt, a disease that can also affect brambles.

Growing: Mulch to reduce weeds and keep plants moist. Remove stray canes to prevent the patch from spreading. Train brambles to a V-shape trellis, which will make it easier to harvest the fruit. Set 6-foot trellis posts so that they are 3 feet apart at the top, 1½ feet apart at the bottom. String two wires between the posts and allow the fruiting canes to grow freely in the middle of the V. Tie the nonfruiting canes to the top and bottom wires.

Because brambles bloom late in spring, frost is not a problem. Blackberries are drought-tolerant and raspberries

TOP GARDEN BLACKBERRIES

Variety, Zones	Fruit	Plant	Key features
ERECT AND SEMIERECT			
'Black Satin' (5–9)	Large, firm, glossy, oblong, sweet	Semierect. Thornless. Good disease resistance. Very heavy yield	Excellent keeper. More productive with pollen from another variety. Good in Pacific Northwest. Not suited for Coastal Plains, Gulf Coast
'Brazos' (5–9)	Large, firm, sweet, juicy, big clusters. High quality	Semierect. Vigorous, productive	Outstanding blackberry for the South (particularly Texas), Gulf Coast
'Chester' (5–9)	Large, very sweet, good flavor. Outstanding quality	Thornless. Very resistant to cane blight	Hardy, productive. Performs well in the South. All-purpose blackberry
'Kiowa' (6–9)	Large, firm, good flavor	Thorny canes are self-supporting	Good Southern performer. From Arkansas. Long harvest season
'Rosborough' (5–9)	Very large, sweet, glossy. High quality	Erect. Does well in extreme heat, drought. Thorny. High yield	Excellent in the South. Similar to 'Brazos' but better flavor, firmness. All-purpose. From Texas A&M
'Thornfree' (5–9)	Large, tangy, tart, glossy, firm	Semierect. Thornless. Vigorous, productive. Disease free	Released by USDA in 2000
'Triple Crown' (5–9)	Large, firm, flavorful	Semierect canes to 15' long. Thornless. High yield	Self-pollinating
TRAILING			
'Boysenberry' (5–9)	Dark red, large-lobed, juicy, nearly seedless. Distinctive, tangy, rich flavor. Long ripening period	Vigorous, productive. Small thorns	An improved loganberry with unique tart flavor. Use or freeze right after harvest. Thornless form produces smaller berries
'Logan' (5–9)	Light red with fine hairs. Distinctive tart flavor. Ripens early	Thornless form is most common. Average productivity	Wild cross between blackberry and red raspberry prized for unique qualities. Adapted to Pacific Coast
'Marion' (7–10)	Excellent flavor, medium to firm, high quality, light blackberry flavor. Ripens midseason over long period	Many large thorns. More productive than 'Boysenberry'	Developed for western Washington, Oregon. Named for Marion County, Oregon. Newer, related varieties include 'Black Butte', 'Black Diamond', 'Waldo'
'Olallie' (4–11)	Large, shiny, firm, sweet, with some wild flavor. Ripens early	Vigorous, productive, thorny	Popular home garden variety in California and Oregon
'Tayberry' (5–8)	Deep purple, cone shape, juicy, firm core, strong tart flavor. Ripens late	Thorny canes grow to 7' high, requires strong support. Very productive.	Excellent for preserves, wine

Red raspberries **Yellow raspberries** **Black raspberries** **Blackberries**

are not, but irrigation results in better yields for both. Blackberries are more tolerant of hot summer weather than raspberries, but mulch both species well to conserve soil moisture, control weeds, and increase yields.

Cane berries sprout new biennial canes each year. Prune blackberries annually or they become invasive. In late winter

Pinching purple raspberries

Removing tip of everbearing red raspberry

or early spring remove and discard injured and diseased canes as well as canes that fruited the previous year. Thin canes to two per linear foot of row. Shorten side branches to 15 inches long. Trim side branches of trailing types to about 18 inches and thin them to six to eight canes per hill in northern regions, fewer in southern regions. The heaviest fruiting may occur at the tips, so avoid cutting canes back severely.

Prune everbearing raspberries twice each season. In spring remove old canes along with any damaged, diseased, or dead canes. Then pinch the tips of canes where the fall crop was borne. The new summer crop fruits on the lower buds of the canes where the previous fall crop developed. Immediately after harvesting the summer crop remove those canes entirely. Prune red and yellow summer-bearing raspberries by removing fruiting canes after harvest, but do not pinch new cane tips. Pinch the tips of black and purple varieties in summer to promote branching. Remove fruiting canes immediately after harvest.

Remove winter-damaged or broken canes. For summer-bearing raspberries, remove spent fruiting canes and thin the remaining canes to three or four per foot of row. For fall-bearing raspberries, remove all canes to the ground in early spring before new canes emerge to stimulate a large late-summer crop.

Pinch 4 inches of growth from the first-year canes of black raspberries when they reach 24 inches tall. In early spring thin one-year-old canes to two to three per foot of row. Shorten side branches.

Harvesting: Harvest ripe berries when they taste sweet and are easy to pull from the plant, preferably in the early morning when fruits and plants are dry and cool. Ripe blackberries are easy to identify: They're glossy, soft, and deeply colored. The fruit's small, soft green core separates from the plant when the fruit is ready to pick. Ripe raspberries will have full color (red, yellow, purple, or black) characteristic of the variety.

Carry harvested berries in shallow trays, because they are easily crushed. They also are highly perishable, so keep picked berries in the shade and move them to a cool location as soon as possible. Harvest often to keep insects such as sap beetles and wasps from infesting fruit.

Blackberries fruit the first year following planting; Raspberries bear a small crop the second year after planting and a full crop the third year, and remain productive for five to eight years.

Pests and diseases: Purchase certified disease-free stock. Uproot and destroy virus-infected plants so that aphids don't transmit the disease to healthy plants. Black raspberries are the most susceptible of the brambles to viruses. If spider mites are a problem in hot, dry weather, dislodge them with the garden hose. Wilted tips are a sign of borers; cut out and destroy the canes. Avoid using insect controls that might harm beneficial and pollinating insects.

Blackberries are sometimes susceptible to phytophthora root rot, particularly where soils are wet. Verticillium wilt, spur blight, crown gall, anthracnose, botrytis fruit rot, raspberry cane borers, fruitworms, crown borers, spider mites, raspberry sawflies, and Japanese beetles are other potential pest problems. Rabbits are troublesome on thornless varieties.

Varieties: The best garden varieties of blackberries and raspberries are noted in the tables on pages 130 and 132–133. Blackberries are divided into two types: erect and trailing. Many fall somewhere between. The erect types grow to 6 feet tall, and the trailing types spread to 15 feet. Trailing blackberries are grown mainly on the West Coast. Raspberries are grouped by fruit color—red, purple, yellow, and black—and by fruiting frequency—summer bearing or everbearing (also called fall bearing.) Summer-bearing varieties produce a crop in early summer, while everbearing varieties produce a crop in spring or early summer and a second, usually heavier crop in fall. Most everbearing raspberries produce either red or yellow fruit.

PRUNING BLACKBERRIES, BLACK AND PURPLE RASPBERRIES

1 Last year's new growth bears fruit in the current year.

2 Post harvest, cut off all canes that bore fruit and all but five new, non-bearing canes.

3 Head the canes at about waist height to promote lateral branch growth.

4 Continue removing tip growth throughout the remainder of the growing season.

5 Head laterals back to 18 inches during winter.

TOP GARDEN RASPBERRIES

Variety, Zones	Fruit	Plant	Key features
RED, SUMMER BEARING			
'Canby' (4–8)	Large to very large, outstanding firmness	Nearly thornless. Very productive. Immune to raspberry aphid, which transmits mosaic virus	Best in cool summers of the Pacific Northwest. Fruit excellent preserved or frozen
'Encore' (5–7)	Notable fruit size and firmness, somewhat dry texture, good flavor	Nearly thornless, sturdy canes	A favorite at local markets, farm stands
'Festival' (5–7)	Large, good-quality, shiny fruit. Midseason	Nearly thornless. Very productive. Canes very short, few branches. Hardy	Slow to start but can last many years. Susceptible to mosaic virus
'Killarney' (3–7)	Large, attractive, high quality, good flavor	Strong, thick, upright canes. Very hardy	All-purpose raspberry. From Manitoba, Canada
'Meeker' (5–8)	Large, firm, rich, excellent flavor. Ripens midseason	Long flexible canes. Highly productive, long lived, vigorous. Some resistance to botrytis fruit rot	Needs well-drained soil. A Northwest favorite
'Prelude' (5–7)	Large, excellent quality, firm. Early bearing	Excellent hardiness. Produces suckers	Harvest is primarily in spring, but continues all season. Good fresh or preserved
'Reveille' (5–7)	Large to very large, outstanding flavor. Ripens early	Upright, vigorous. Hardy, productive. Produces suckers	Tolerates fluctuating winter temperatures. From Maryland
'Titan' (5–7)	Very large, excellent texture	Upright, strong canes. Very productive. Resistant to raspberry aphid and mosaic virus. Very susceptible to crown gall, root rot.	Fresh-eating quality is average. From Cornell University
'Willamette' (5–9 in West)	Large, dark red, excellent tart flavor	Long, sprawling canes	Needs well-drained soil. Disease-resistant. A favorite variety for the Pacific Northwest
BLACK, SUMMER BEARING			
'Allen' (4–8)	Large, glossy black, sweet, juicy. Ripens early, often at once	Very productive. Disease free	Widely adapted, especially in the Northeast. Good for jam and jelly.
'Bristol' (4–8)	Medium large, rich, sweet, firm, high quality	Productive. Some tolerance to powdery mildew, susceptible to anthracnose	Good commercial potential

Cherimoya *(Annona cherimola)*

Type: Briefly deciduous tree, Zones 10–11
Typical yield: 50–75 pounds per tree
Typical size: 15–25'H×15–25'W

Native to mountain valleys of Peru and Ecuador, the cherimoya usually elicits a two-stage response: amazement followed by delight. The amazement is sparked by the unusual appearance of the fruit, which looks something like an artichoke crossed with a pineapple. It is large and heart shape with a thick green skin that seems to consist of overlapping scales. The delight is a reaction to the custardlike texture and tropical flavor reminiscent of pineapple, banana, and papaya.

Cherimoya leaves are about 10 inches long by 4 inches wide, dull green on the top and velvety green on the bottom. According to how the plants are pruned they become either spreading multitrunk trees to about 15 feet high or fairly erect trees to 25 feet high.

Serve cherimoyas chilled and cut in half or quarters; the flesh is eaten with a spoon.
When: The best time to plant is early fall.

Planting: Cherimoya needs a moist but well-drained soil of moderate fertility. Plant young trees 25 to 30 feet apart in holes that are just as deep as the original root ball and at least twice as wide.
Growing: The tree needs consistent moisture during active growth, but not while it is dormant. It is susceptible to root rot in soggy soils, especially during periods of cool weather. A drought-stressed tree will drop its leaves, exposing the fruit to sunburn.

Fertilize regularly. Apply about 2 ounces of an 8-8-8 plant food each month to a young tree during the growing season up until mid- or late summer. Increase the amount by an ounce a year until the tree begins to bear fruit. A mature tree needs 1 pound of 8-8-8 fertilizer per inch of trunk diameter (measured at chest level).

In part to compensate for brittle branches, prune during the dormant period to develop strong, wide-angled limbs that can support the heavy fruit. Also prune to encourage new growth and fruiting near the center of the tree, where the fruits will be protected from sunburn and birds.

Cherimoya production is best when the flowers are pollinated by hand. Where cherimoyas are native there's a beetle that moves pollen around, but not in North America.

Variety, Zones	Fruit	Plant	Key features
'Jewel' (4–8)	Very large and firm, juicy, high quality	Outstanding vigor, reliability. Disease-resistant	Excellent all-purpose raspberry, considered the best by many
'Munger' (4–7)	Large, firm, shiny black, few seeds, sweet, flavorful	Thick canes. Better disease resistance than most	Common commercial variety in Northwest. Good for preservers
YELLOW, SUMMER BEARING			
'Amber' 5–7	Large, slightly conical, sweet, excellent quality. Ripens late	Productive, vigorous. Heavy bearer	One of the sweetest home garden raspberries
PURPLE, SUMMER BEARING			
'Brandywine' (4–9)	Large to very large, firm, glossy, reddish purple, tart, aromatic	Upright, strong, thorny, vigorous, nonsuckering	Outstanding choice for preserves
'Royalty' (4–8)	Very large, firm, sweet, tangy, very high quality. Ripens late	Vigorous, productive. Grows from a single crown. Immune to raspberry aphid, which transmits mosaic virus. Resistant to raspberry fruit worm	All-purpose raspberry. Can be harvested early
RED, EVERBEARING			
'Autumn Bliss' (3–8)	Good size, attractive, firm, mild flavor. Ripens before 'Heritage'	Root rot–resistant	Early-fruiting fall bearer from England that fills the gap between summer and fall. Considered superior to 'Heritage'
'Heritage' (4–9)	Firm, mild flavor	Strong, upright (to 6' high). Suckers. Very productive	Widely adapted. Cut canes to ground in spring for heaviest fall crop. Ripe berries hold well. All-purpose
YELLOW, EVERBEARING			
'Fall Gold' (4–8)	Large to very large, sweet, soft	Vigorous, productive, adaptable	Excellent all-purpose choice. Best for Upper South and nearby mountains
'Goldie' (4–8)	Orange when ripe. Very high quality	Very productive. Strong canes need support when laden with fruit	Mutation of 'Heritage'. From Sonoma, California. Considered superior to 'Fall Gold'
'Kiwigold' (5–7)	Medium to large, good quality and flavor	Good productivity	A sport of 'Heritage' from New Zealand

The plants flower over a long period in midsummer, so if you pollinate every couple of days during bloom the harvest period will extend over several months the following spring.

Harvesting: Cherimoya fruits develop a pale green to creamy yellow color as they reach maturity. Pick them when they are still firm and then allow them to soften at room temperature. They yield to slight pressure when ripe, then turn dark brown when overripe. Harvest the fruits over several days, assuming you pollinated over an extended period. Use pruners to cut them from the tree; don't pull or try to break them off. Store mature fruit above 55°F to prevent chilling injury to the skin and flesh. Ripe fruit will deteriorate quickly but can be stored at temperatures lower than 55°F for short periods.

Pests and diseases: Few problems affect cherimoya. Knock mealybugs off with a stream from a garden hose. Nematodes can be a problem in older trees.

HERE'S A TIP...
Pollinating by hand
Because the insects that pollinate cherimoya don't live in North America, you'll have to distribute the pollen by hand. During the bloom season, collect the anthers and their pollen in a small bottle and immediately daub the pollen on partially open female flowers with a fine artist's paintbrush. (If no female flowers are apparent you can refrigerate the pollen in a sealed container overnight.) Look for flowers just inside the tree canopy because they'll have a better chance of developing mature fruit.

Cherimoya

TOP GARDEN CHERRIES

Variety	Fruit	Tree	Pollination*	Key features
SOUR, ZONES 4–9				
'Balaton'	Large, burgundy, plump, firm, sweet-tart. Long ripening period	Productive. Less hardy than 'Montmorency'	Self-fertile, but larger crops with pollinator	Morello type. Good-quality red juice rich in antioxidants
'Danube'	Large, glossy dark red, firm, juicy, sweet-tart	Prolific crops. A natural semi-dwarf	Self-fertile	Amarelle type. Red juice. Antioxidant rich
'Érdi Jubileum'	Large, very dark purple, firm, sweet-tart	Natural dwarf grows to about 10 feet	Self-fertile	Morello type. Red juice, antioxidant rich. For fresh eating and preserves. From Hungary; may be hard to find
'Meteor'	Large, bright red, oblong, tart, juicy. Meaty flesh, colorless juice. Small freestone	Natural dwarf. Leaves shield fruit from sunscald, birds	Self-fertile	Amarelle type. Early bearing. Grows only 8–12' tall
'Montmorency'	Medium to large, bright red, firm, tart, tangy. Ripens over long season	Large, spreading. Blooms late	Self-fertile	Amarelle type. The standard pie cherry
'NorthStar'	Small, light red skin. Red juice. Small freestone	Natural dwarf grows 8–12' tall. Vigorous. Early and heavy crops.	Self-fertile	Morello type. Crack resistant. Good choice for cold regions
SWEET, ZONES 5–9				
'Bing'	Large, purple, firm, meaty. Excellent flavor	Light bearing	'Black Tartarian', 'Montmorency', 'Rainier', 'Stella', 'Van', 'Windsor'	The standard of good flavor. The favorite sweet cherry in the West. Susceptible to cracking
'Black Gold'	Large, shiny black, firm, high quality	Consistent, heavy crops	Self-fertile	Late blooming. Excellent pollenizer. Resistant to canker
'Emperor Francis'	Large, yellowish with red blush, firm, meaty, sweet	Hardy, productive	'Black Gold', 'Hartland', 'Ranier', 'Stella', 'Sweetheart'	Some resistance to cracking
'Hartland'	Medium to large, round, glossy deep purple	Large, vigorous, hardy. Spreading tree produces heavy crops	'Black Gold', 'Emperor Francis', 'Rainier', 'Stella', 'Sweetheart'	Some resistance to fungal leaf spot, brown rot, and bacterial canker

Varieties: **'Bays'** is a medium-size cherimoya that bears fruits with smooth yellow-green skin and lemon flavor from December to April. **'Booth'** produces small to medium, slightly knobby and yellowish green fruits with papaya flavor and many seeds from November to March.

'Chaffey' is small to medium in size with smooth thick skin and lemon flavor; it ripens January to April. **'El Bumpo'** is medium size and has soft flesh with a knobby skin; flavor is excellent as it ripens December to March. **'Pierce'** fruits range from small to large with knobby, light green skin. They are very sweet with pineapple-banana flavor and few seeds. The plant is partially self-pollinating, and fruits ripen January to March. **'White'** bears large fruits with rough skin and a sweet, papaya-mango flavor from December to March.

Cherimoya relatives include **sweetsop** or sugar apple (*A. squamosa*). It is similar to cherimoya but better adapted to Florida. The fruits are knobbier and the tree slightly smaller, rarely exceeding 15 feet tall. The sweetsop is not hardy below 29°F.

Atemoyas, most popular in Florida, are hybrids of cherimoya and sweetsop that combine the hardiness of the cherimoya with the sweetsop's tolerance of warm, humid climates. **'Gefner'** and **'African Pride'** are often recommended. The trees are hardy to 24° to 26°F. **Soursop** (*A. muricata*) is a tender tree, hardy to only 30°F, that grows upright to 20 feet tall and 15 feet wide. The fruits are covered with long curved fleshy spines. Look for **'Fiberless Cuban'**.

Cherry (*Prunus* spp.)

Type: Deciduous tree, Zones 3–8
Typical yield: 20–50 pounds per tree
Typical size: 8–30'H×10–30'W

Sweet cherries

Whether you like them sweet or sour, cherries are beautiful plants and their flowers are a harbinger of spring. Both sweet and sour types are excellent fruit trees for home gardeners. One or two trees provide a large enough crop for plenty of fresh eating as well as preserves. Both dark- and light-fleshed varieties of sweet cherries are eaten fresh, canned, frozen, dried, or made into maraschino cherries. Sour, or pie, cherries are used in pies and pastries and for juice. On the other hand, cherries are challenging, mostly for the diseases they are subject to. Also, the climates where they thrive are fairly specific, and then there's the competition with birds for ripe fruit.

Sweet cherries are more challenging to grow than sour ones. The trees can be big, up to 30 feet tall and wide or

Variety	Fruit	Tree	Pollination*	Key features
SWEET, ZONES 5–9 (continued)				
'Hedelfingen'	Large, black, firm, very high quality	Vigorous, early bearing, productive	'Ulster'	Good resistance to cracking. Widely planted in Ontario, Canada
'Lambert'	Heart shape, dark red.	Heavy bearing, vigorous	'Angela', 'Black Tartarian', 'Rainier', 'Stella', 'Van'	A bit smaller than 'Bing'. Susceptible to cracking in East, Midwest.
'Rainier'	Large, yellow with rosy blush. Firm, light yellow flesh. Distinctive, fine flavor. Ripens early	Early bearing, vigorous, upright, very productive. Can overbear	'Black Gold', 'Emperor Francis', 'Hartland', 'Stella', 'Sweetheart'	Crack-resistant. Good cooking cherry
'Regina'	Large, deep red, very high quality. Late	Yield may be limited by poor pollination	'Hedelfingen'	From Germany. Crack-resistant
'Royalton'	Black. Exceptional size and quality	Upright vigorous habit requires pruning	'Emperor Francis', 'Hartland'	Crack-resistant
'Skeena'	Large, round, deep red to black, sweet, firm, juicy	Spreading habit. Very productive	Self-fertile	Some crack resistance
'Stella'	Large, heart shape, dark red, sweet, juicy	Vigorous, productive	Self-fertile	Moderate cracking resistance
'Sweetheart'	Large, bright red. Outstanding flavor	Upright, vigorous, heavy bearing	Self-fertile	Very crack-resistant
'Tieton'	Large, firm, dark red	Vigorous, sturdy. Bears consistently	'Bing', 'Rainier', 'Sweetheart'	Similar to 'Bing' but with firmer flesh, larger size. Use more than one pollinator to maximize harvest
'Ulster'	Large, black, crisp, juicy, sweet, very high quality	Productive	'Hedelfingen'	Moderate crack resistance
'White Gold'	Large, red and yellow. Excellent flavor	Consistent heavy crops	Self-fertile	Resistant to cracking and bacterial canker

*Top pollinating varieties for varieties listed.

'Rainier' sweet cherries

more, making maintenance and harvest difficult. Sweet cherries grow best in mild climates. Although the trees can survive temperatures of –20°F, and some can take even colder weather, the spring blossoms are vulnerable to frosts. Moreover, rain during bloom or harvest season causes problems too. (Rain causes brown rot in spring, and fruit splitting at harvest) Further, summer heat over 100°F stops the growth of sweet cherry fruits, and if the heat lasts it will destroy the fruits. But if by virtue of where you live or your own gardening savvy you can beat the odds, then you'll harvest one of the most desirable fruits around. Many sweet cherry varieties require cross-pollination. Most of the commercial sweet cherries in the United States are grown in California and Oregon.

Standard sour cherry trees are smaller than sweet cherries, topping out at 15 to 20 feet tall and wide. They can survive temperatures as low as –35°F and, because they bloom later than sweet cherries, are less likely to be damaged by late spring frosts. Summer rains are less damaging to the fruits too. Most sour cherries are grown commercially in the Upper Midwest, especially in the Great Lakes region. Both sweet and sour cherries are available grafted onto dwarfing rootstocks.

When: In late winter or early spring plant bare-root trees while they are still dormant.

Planting: Choose a sunny location at the top of a slope with deep, fertile, moist, well-drained, slightly acid soil. Avoid soils that are heavy clay and wet, a situation that will provoke the various diseases the trees are prone to. (Bush-type cherries can tolerate heavier and alkaline soils.) If late spring frosts are common in your area choose a cool, north-facing location if possible. That will help keep the trees dormant until frost danger is past. Space standard varieties 25 to 40 feet apart, semidwarfs 15 to 25 feet apart, and dwarfs 8 to 12 feet apart. Situate the bud union 2 inches above the soil. Firm the soil around the roots by hand to make sure there are no air pockets, then water. Do not fertilize at planting.

Growing: Train sweet cherries into a pyramidal, central leader shape, and sour cherries into an open center (see pages 114 to 117 for more about both). After planting cut off all the side branches but leave the leader. In late winter or early spring of the second year choose a branch about 3 feet from the ground for the top scaffold branch, then select a few more shoots at staggered intervals around the tree and not right above one another. Prune out all other branches, trim back the scaffolds to even their lengths, then cut back the leader to a point above the topmost scaffold where you want another one to form.

HERE'S A TIP...
Tangy but Healthful
Much attention has been given to the health benefits of sour cherries, specifically their antioxidant

properties. Antioxidants are vitamins, minerals, and other compounds that help slow down or prevent the oxidation process that damages the body's cells by free radicals.

In the following years prune lightly but continue to develop new scaffold branches and remove any branches that compete. Branches remain fruitful for three to five years; after that prune them out. Thin around the top of the tree to maintain size and improve light penetration. Feed mature trees with fruit tree spikes, and water in dry weather, especially when the fruits are ripening. Remove watersprouts in summer to maintain an open canopy that the sun can pierce. Cut off suckers at ground level as soon as they appear.

Hand-weed an area 4 to 6 feet around the trunk. Use mulch to control weeds and conserve moisture in a circle as wide as the drip line, but keep it away from the trunks of trees. Use nutritional foliar sprays to correct mineral deficiencies. In dry conditions water newly planted trees daily until they are well established.

Harvesting: Sour cherries begin to bear three to four years after they're planted. Fruits ripen about 60 days after bloom, from late May to early July. Sour cherries are normally used only for cooking and are too tart to eat fresh from the tree. But a few varieties will become sweet if left on the tree until completely ripe. Sweet cherries begin best production in their fifth year and bear fruit in July. Store ripe cherries for up to a week in the refrigerator.

Pests and diseases: Humidity and heat encourage fusarium wilt, rots, and molds. Clean cultural practices are essential to the health of cherry trees. Remove and destroy diseased fruits, leaves, twigs, and branches. Choose varieties bred for your weather and soil conditions and with resistance to pests and diseases common in your locale. Varieties susceptible to brown rot are good choices for western, dry-summer climates. Plum curculio, brown rot, fruit flies, leaf spot, and bacterial canker are common problems of cherry trees. (For more about these pests, see page 194; also see page 120.) Cover trees with netting to protect the fruit from birds. Use trunk wraps in winter to protect trees from gnawing rodents.

Varieties: With few exceptions sweet cherries require cross-pollination from another compatible variety in order to set a crop; all sour cherries are self-fertile.

Sour cherries are divided into two types: Morellos have dark skin, red flesh, and acidic juice; the more disease-tolerant amarelles have red skin, yellow flesh, and clear juice. The best varieties are listed in the table on page 134.

For many home gardeners, a dwarf sweet cherry is more practical because it is much easier to manage. Cherries on **'Mahaleb'** rootstock reduce tree height by about one-third, and **'Giessen'** (also called 'Gisela') rootstock reduces tree height by nearly two-thirds. (Actual tree heights are determined by the combination of rootstock and top variety.) 'Mahaleb' is also relatively cold-hardy, and 'Giessen' relatively disease-resistant.

Nanking cherry (*P. tomentosa*) is an extremely cold-hardy shrub that produces tart fruits good for canning or wine making. **Western sand cherry** (*P. besseyi*) varieties **'Amber'**, **'Hanson'**, and **'Black Beauty'** are hardy to Zone 3, and **'Brooks'** grows in Alaska. They are self-fruitful, cold and drought tolerant, and rarely bothered by pests or diseases. Other bush-type cherries that thrive in northern climates are **pin cherry** (*P. pensylvanica*) and **chokecherry** (*P. virginiana*).

The subtropical **acerola** or Barbados cherry (*Malpighia glabra*), hardy in Zones 10 and 11, is a distantly related shrub or small tree. It grows 5 to 20 feet tall, producing pink or red flowers followed by juicy bright red tart fruits resembling cherries; they make excellent sweetened juice and preserves that can be frozen. Acerola blooms throughout the summer and bears several crops of fruit beginning the third or fourth year after planting.

Chinese gooseberry *(see Kiwifruit)*

Citrus *(Citrus spp.)*

Type: Evergreen tree, Zones 8–11
Typical yield: Various (see descriptions)
Typical size: 3–20'H×3–20'W

Harvesting lemons

This attractive group of plants is made up of about 16 species of often spiny evergreen trees with scented white flowers. The glossy foliage is attractive in the landscape or indoors in container plantings. The fruits generally take about a year to mature. Fruit sizes range from 1-inch-diameter kumquats to citrons and pummelos that may weigh several pounds.

When: Plant at any time of the year. Where winters are mild and summers hot, the best time is fall. Elsewhere the optimum time is early spring after the last frost.

Planting: Citrus trees are usually sold in containers, but sometimes they are available balled-and-burlapped. Trees purchased by mail may be shipped bare root. All citrus trees prefer maximum exposure to sunlight, but in desert climates some light shade during the hottest part of the day may

prevent sunburned fruit. In cool climates plant in the warmest possible microclimate such as against a light-color south-facing wall. Avoid low spots where cold air can accumulate. For the best results the soil pH should be between 6 and 7.

Growing: Most citrus trees are easy to care for, requiring minimal pruning and infrequent pest control.

'Delta Valencia' orange

'Cara Cara' pink navel orange

The familiar navel orange (left) compared to pink 'Cara Cara' orange (right)

All they usually need is regular watering and fertilizing.

The plants need adequate soil moisture for healthy growth and good fruit production. Drought during bloom causes the flowers to drop, resulting in poor fruit set. Lack of moisture during the growing season causes fruit drop and low yields. Prolonged drought will defoliate and eventually kill a tree. At the other extreme, standing water and poorly drained soils are almost always lethal to citrus. Plant in well-drained soil and water regularly during dry periods.

Citrus trees need to be fertilized two or three times from February through September. Use 1 pound of 10-10-10 per application per tree the first two years, gradually increasing the amount each year to between 5 and 7 pounds after about eight years. Soils in some areas are also deficient in micronutrients. In these cases the trees will need foliar sprays of micronutrients such as copper, zinc, manganese, and boron. Don't overfertilize. Too much nitrogen increases the likelihood of disease.

Most citrus trees require little pruning, though you might want to prune lemons and other vigorous trees to control their size. Pruning to remove dense growth and open the

COMMON ORANGES

Name	Adaptation*	Fruit	Tree
'Dillar'	DS	Medium-size, sweet, juicy. Few to many seeds. Holds well on tree. Excellent juice orange. Early	Small to medium tree has short, upright branches. Does well in desert. Above-average cold tolerance
'Hamlin'	DS, FL, GC	Small to medium-small, usually seedless, tender and juicy. Low acidity. Very early	Medium to large tree bears heavy, well-colored crop. Produces small fruit in desert
'Marrs'	FL, GC	Medium to large, juicy, sweet. Few to many seeds. Lacks acid, but quality improves if harvest is delayed to later in season. Very early	Small, moderately vigorous, prolific at an early age. Fruit borne in clusters near outside of tree
'Midsweet'	FL, GC	Medium to large, few to many seeds, juicy, sweet, low acid. Very early	Small tree bears heavily at an early age. Fruit borne in clusters near outside of tree
'Parson' ('Parson Brown')	FL, GC	Medium to large, seedy, juicy, sweet. Popular juice orange. Very early	Large, upright, vigorous tree bears heavy crop. Best in Florida
'Pineapple'	FL, GC	Medium-size, moderately seedy. Rich flavor. Named for delicate fragrance. Does not hold well on tree. Midseason	Medium to large, moderately vigorous, thornless tree tends to bear heavy crops in alternate years. Frost-sensitive
'Trovita'	CA, DS	Small to medium, juicy. Pleasant flavor. Few seeds. Midseason to late	Large, upright, vigorous tree bears fruit within dense, dark green foliage. Tends toward alternate bearing
'Valencia'	CA, DS, FL, GC	Medium-size, sweet, juicy. Few to many seeds. Holds well on tree. Excellent juice. Early	Large, upright tree tends to bear heavy crops every other year. Widely adapted

*CA-California, DS-Desert Southwest, FL-Florida, GC-Gulf Coast

NAVEL ORANGES

Name	Adaptation*	Fruit	Tree
'Cara Cara'	CA, DS, FL, GC	Large, seedless. Excellent flavor. Pink flesh. Holds well on tree, but color fades as season progresses. Early	'Washington' sport from Venezuela
'Robertson'	CA, DS	Similar to 'Washington' except smaller and borne in tight clusters near outside of tree. Not as good as 'Washington'	Smaller and more heat-resistant. Fruit ripens 10 to 14 days earlier than 'Washington'
'Summernavel'	CA	Large, flavorful. Similar to 'Washington' but with thicker, rougher rind and ripening later. Holds well on tree	Tree is more vigorous, low, and spreading and has larger leaves than 'Washington'
'Washington'	CA, DS, FL, GC	Large, flavorful, seedless, moderately juicy. Peels and sections easily. Holds well on tree. Early	The original and still the best navel variety. Best in interior California. Drops fruit in dry, hot areas

*CA-California, DS-Desert Southwest, FL-Florida, GC-Gulf Coast

BLOOD ORANGES

Name	Adaptation*	Fruit	Tree
'Moro'	CA, DS	Medium-size, juicy. Distinctive aroma. Almost seedless. Flesh is violet or burgundy. Rind is orange with pink blush. Very early	Medium-size, vigorous. Spreading habit. Fruit borne in clusters at canopy's edge. Tends to alternate bear
'Sanguinelli'	CA, DS	Small to medium, slightly oblong, very juicy. Few or no seeds. Excellent flavor. Flesh is orange with red streaks. Rind is red. Midseason to late	Small to medium, almost thornless tree
'Tarocco'	CA	Medium to large, firm, juicy, excellent raspberry-flavor flesh. Few seeds. Flesh variable, often dark red; rind is yellow with red blush. Midseason	Medium to large, moderately vigorous, open habit. Fruit held inside canopy. Best in interior California

*CA-California, DS-Desert Southwest, FL-Florida, GC-Gulf Coast

MANDARIN ORANGES

Name	Adaptation*	Fruit	Tree
'Changsha'	GC	Small to medium. Seedy, good flavor. Resembles 'Satsuma'. Early	Small tree. Very hardy. Grown in cold areas of Gulf Coast. Bears early. True to type from seed
'Clementine' ('Algerian')	CA, DS, FL, GC	Medium-size, red-orange, sweet, juicy, fragrant. Few to many seeds. Peels easily. Holds well on tree. Early	Small to medium tree has attractive weeping habit, dense foliage. Needs pollinator such as 'Dancy' for best production, but will be seedy
'Dancy'	CA, DS, FL, GC	Medium-size, richly flavored, acidic. Few to many seeds. Peels and segments easily. Does not hold well on tree. Midseason	Medium to large, vigorous tree has few thorns. Traditional Christmas tangerine. Best in Florida
'Fairchild'	DS	Medium-size, sweet, juicy. Many seeds. Holds fairly well on tree. Very early	Medium-size, rounded, nearly thornless tree grows vigorously. Best in low deserts of California and Arizona
'Gold Nugget'	CA	Medium-size, rich, sweet, seedless. Rind light orange, often bumpy. Holds well on tree. Late	Medium-size, upright. Tends to alternate bear
'Kara'	CA	Medium to large, flavorful. Remains tart until very mature. Holds fairly well on tree but becomes puffy. Late	Medium to large, thornless, moderately vigorous. Drooping habit. Large, dark green leaves. Tends to alternate bear. Best in interior California
'Kinnow'	CA, DS	Medium-size, juicy, seedy, richly flavored. Holds well on tree. Midseason	Large, frost tolerant, vigorous, thornless, columnar, attractive. Tends to alternate bear
'Mediterranean' ('Willowleaf')	CA, DS, FL, GC	Small to medium size, juicy, seedy, sweet, aromatic. Late	Small to medium, spreading tree has attractive small, narrow leaves, few thorns. Hardy. Needs heat for best fruit
'Page'	CA, DS, FL, GC	Small to medium, rich, sweet. Few to many seeds. Holds well on tree. Excellent juice. Early	Medium to large, very attractive. Dense foliage. Rround top. Almost thornless. Somewhat alternate bearing
'Pixie'	CA	Small to medium size, light orange, sweet, seedless, easy to peel. Bumpy rind. Midseason	Medium to large, upright tree tends to alternate bear. Good in milder areas
'Satsuma' ('Kimbrough')	CA, FL, GC	Medium-size, mild, sweet, low acid. Holds poorly on tree but stores well. Early	Small to medium, slow-growing, spreading tree has open, dark green foliage. Tough and very cold-hardy
'Sunburst'	FL	Medium-size, seedy. Rich flavor. Smooth, bright orange rind. Early	Medium-size. Somewhat hardy. Tends to alternate bear
'Tango'	CA	Medium-size, seedless. Excellent flavor. Flattened with bright orange rind. Late	Medium size. Known to supermarkets as 'Delite'. 'W. Murcott' is a seedier form

*CA-California, DS-Desert Southwest, FL-Florida, GC-Gulf Coast

center of a citrus tree is also a good way to keep the tree bearing throughout the canopy and prevent the buildup of insect pests. Most citrus types tolerate shearing into a hedge or being trained flat as an espalier.

The bark of citrus trees is thin and susceptible to overheating and sunburn, especially after heavy pruning. Always paint exposed branches and trunks with dilute water-base white paint (1 part paint to 1 part water) or commercially available whitewash after heavy pruning. Also protect the bark of newly planted trees by using trunk wraps, (available from nurseries) or by painting the trunks with diluted water-base white paint.

Harvesting: Citrus fruits mature at various times of the year. Early varieties of oranges and mandarins ripen in October or November of the year in which they bloom. Late varieties of oranges, mandarins, and grapefruits mature

LIMES

Name	Adaptation*	Fruit description	Tree description
'Bearss' ('Tahiti', 'Persian')	CA, DS, FL, GC	Small to medium, acidic, very juicy. Yellow at maturity but usually picked green. Does not hold well on tree	Medium-size, vigorous, spreading. Fragrant blossoms. Hardier and more attractive than 'Mexican'
'Mexican' (Key lime)	CA, DS, FL, GC	Very small, juicy, acidic. Distinctive aroma. The bartender's lime. Yellow when mature but picked when green	Medium-size, twiggy. Dense canopy of small leaves. Many short thorns. (A thornless form is available.) Needs long, hot summers
'Rangpur'	CA, DS, FL, GC	Small to medium, very acidic, juicy. Rind reddish orange when mature. Holds very well on tree	Medium-size, vigorous spreading. Drooping habit. Few thorns. Very cold-tolerant. Not a true lime but good lime substitute. 'Otaheite' is an low-acid, semidwarf form

*CA-California, DS-Desert Southwest, FL-Florida, GC-Gulf Coast

LEMONS

Name	Adaptation*	Fruit	Tree
'Eureka'	CA, DS	Medium-size, highly acidic, juicy, few seeds. Produces fruit all year along coast, in spring and summer inland. Common commercial variety	Medium-size, nearly thornless, moderately vigorous, open and spreading. Short lived. Sensitive to cold, insects, and neglect
'Improved Meyer'	CA, DS, FL, GC	Medium-size, very juicy, slightly sweet, excellent flowery flavor, orange-yellow when mature. Holds well on tree	Orange-lemon hybrid. Small to medium, nearly thornless, moderately vigorous, spreading. Good for hedges, containers. Hardy, productive, and nearly everblooming
'Lisbon'	CA, DS	Medium-size, highly acidic, juicy, few seeds. Best picked ripe; loses acidity if left on tree	Large, vigorous, thorny, upright. Dense foliage. Flowers and new growth tinged purple. Most productive and cold-hardy of lemons
'Ponderosa'	CA, DS, FL, GC	Grapefruit-size, juicy, acidic. Thick, fleshy rind. Holds well on tree	Lemon-citron hybrid. Small, roundheaded, thorny tree with large leaves. Frost-sensitive. Blooms all year. Good for containers and hedges
'Variegated Pink Eureka' ('Pink Lemonade')	DS, GC	Very acidic, juicy, few seeds. Starts green with red and yellow stripes, matures to yellow with green stripes and finally yellow. Interior light pink.	Ornamental with dark green leaves, variegated white. Sport of 'Eureka'

*CA-California, DS-Desert Southwest, FL-Florida, GC-Gulf Coast

'Sanguinelli' blood orange

'Variegated Pink Eureka' lemon

'Dancy' mandarin orange

'Mexican' lime (thornless)

from February to May of the following year. In hot, humid regions such as Florida and South Texas the fruits mature slightly before the same varieties grown in the hot, dry desert regions of the Southwest and well before fruit in the cool coastal areas of California.

The only sure way to determine maturity is to taste the fruit. Color is a poor indication of ripeness because many fruits have fully colored rinds months before they can be eaten. Lemons, limes, and other acidic types of citrus are an exception. They can be picked whenever they reach acceptable size and juice content.

Once mature most citrus fruits can be stored on the tree for several weeks and picked as needed. Mandarins are an

exception. When mandarins have been on the tree too long, they lose their juice, and the pulp dries out. A puffy rind is another indication that the fruit is overly mature.

Most citrus fruits can also be stored in the refrigerator for at least two to three weeks. Under dry conditions at room temperature, fruits develop off-flavor, wither, and become unattractive within 10 days.

Pests and diseases: Citrus plants are sensitive to a variety of environmental problems, the most serious of which are wind and water damage. Proper siting and consistent but not too much moisture are key to their survival. They are susceptible to leaf miners, aphids, scales, and other pests as well as to a host of diseases including viruses, rots, molds, spots, and

GRAPEFRUITS

Name	Adaptation	Fruit description	Tree description
'Cocktail'	CA, DS	Medium-size, seedy, sweet, juicy. Orange flesh. Yellow to orange rind. Midseason	Large and vigorous. Pummelo-mandarin hybrid from California
'Duncan'	FL, GC	Large, seedy, very juicy. White flesh. Excellent flavor. Holds well on tree. Somewhat early	Large, vigorous, productive tree. Attractive habit. Dark green foliage. Reputation as most cold-tolerant grapefruit
'Flame'	CA, DS, FL, GC	Large, seedless. Deep pink flesh. Rind often blushed pink. Midseason to late	Large tree with showy clusters of fruit
'Marsh'	CA, DS, FL, GC	Medium-size, seedless, very juicy. Holds extremely well on tree. Stores well. Late	Large, vigorous, spreading. Requires high summer heat. Attractive clusters of fruit. Glossy leaves
'Melogold'	CA, DS	Large, seedless. Rich, sweet white flesh. Thick rind. Often borne in clusters. Early	Pummelo-grapefruit hybrid. Large. Best in interior California but needs less heat than grapefruit
'Oroblanco'	CA, DS	Medium to large, seedless, extremely juicy. White flesh. Distinctive sweet flavor. Thick rind. Does not hold well on tree. Early	Pummelo-grapefruit hybrid. Large. Best in interior California but needs less heat than grapefruit
'Redblush'	CA, DS, FL, GC	Medium-size. Similar to 'Marsh' except flesh and rind have crimson tinge. Holds very well on tree. Midseason	Large, vigorous. Needs heat to develop red fruit color
'Star Ruby'	CA, DS, FL, GC	Medium-size, seedless, juicy. Deep red flesh. Fruit holds well on tree. Midseason	Medium-size open tree. From Texas. Needs heat. 'Rio Red' is similar and bears more consistently

CA-California, DS-Desert Southwest, FL-Florida, GC-Gulf Coast

'Oroblanco' grapefruit hybrid

anthracnose. Varieties sold for use in your geographic area are bred and grafted to reduce the likelihood of infestation or infection. Ask your local county extension agent or a nursery owner for spraying guidelines specific to the plants you choose and follow directions carefully when using pesticides.

Crabapple (see Apple)

Currant, gooseberry, jostaberry (Ribes spp.)

Type: Deciduous shrub, Zones 2–9
Typical yield: 6–12 pounds per bush
Typical size: 3–6'H x 3–5'W

Currants, gooseberries, and jostaberries are all hardy fruiting shrubs that grow well throughout the cool, humid regions of North America. All have a pleasing, generally tart flavor and make excellent jams, jellies, preserves, and marmalades. Many gardeners enjoy their flavor fresh. But despite their many virtues, the plants aren't nearly as common or popular as they might be, primarily because of their potential to carry and spread white pine blister rust. See White Pine Blister Rust on page 141 for more details about that disease and the role that currants and gooseberries play in it.

Currants grow 3 to 5 feet tall and wide and have attractive 3-inch-wide leaves on thornless stems; the foliage drops in early fall, usually after turning brilliant orange or red. Hanging clusters of creamy white flowers appearing in early spring are followed by midsummer fruits. Gooseberries are similar in every regard but for their larger fruits and thorny stems. A hybrid of black currant and gooseberry, jostaberry has more in common with black currant. Although all are generally self-fruitful, yields improve with cross-pollination. Assuming they remain in good health, plants should be productive for one to two decades.

When: Plant in late winter or early spring as soon as the soil is workable, or set out plants in fall if they are available.

Planting: All types are adapted to a variety of conditions but thrive in rich, moist, well-drained, slightly acid loam that is rich in organic matter and cleared of perennial weeds. The plants do not tolerate soggy soils, so consider planting in raised beds or on soil mounds if your soil is heavy clay or the drainage questionable. Because these shrubs flower early in spring, a sunny northern exposure helps to delay blooming long enough to avoid frost damage and also provides shade for the berries from the hot midday sun in summer. In spring plant vigorous, well-rooted one-year-old plants 4 to 5 feet apart.

Set container-grown plants in the soil at the same level they were growing in the nursery. Plant bare-root stock so that the lowest branch is just above the soil surface, and cut the tops back to about 6 inches above ground level.

Growing: The plants produce well only when watered

Red currant

adequately and regularly. Since they are shallow rooted and do not tolerate drought, you may have to water frequently, but avoid excessive watering. Cultivate little, if at all, to avoid injuring the roots.

Regular feeding is essential. Give the plants nitrogen fertilizer annually in fall or early spring by applying 5 to 10 pounds of composted manure or 4 to 10 ounces of 10-10-10 (less for younger plants) annually in early spring before growth begins.

During the dormant season after the first year's growth,

select six to eight of the strongest and best-positioned stems and remove the others to the ground. A year later choose three or four one-year-old shoots and remove the rest; also choose four or five of the best two-year-old shoots and remove the rest. Always remove broken, twiggy, or misplaced stems. After the third year select shoots so that the bush has three or four shoots each that are one, two, and three years old. In subsequent years remove shoots that are four years old or older. They are less fruitful and are more likely to have disease problems. The best fruit is usually borne on two-year-old canes. Always prune with an eye to spacing the shoots evenly.

Jostaberry

Harvesting: The berries grow in long clusters, ripening over a period of four to six weeks in late summer. When all the berries in a cluster attain full color, they're considered ripe. They gradually become sweeter with ripening, but slightly underripe fruits contain the most pectin. They sunburn easily, so keep freshly harvested berries in a shady spot while you pick. Most gooseberry varieties are thorny; if yours are then wear gloves to pick them.

Pests and diseases: Prune out and destroy diseased or damaged wood, watching for signs of cane borers. To control currant worms pick off any you see or apply *Bacillus thuringiensis* (Bt). Use a spray of water or insecticidal soap to wash off aphids. Cover the plants with netting to protect the ripening fruits from birds.

Varieties: American gooseberry (*Ribes hirtellum*) is generally more resistant to disease than European kinds.

'Captivator' is a cross of American and European varieties with red, pear-shape fruits. It is nearly thornless and is resistant to powdery mildew.

'Hinnonmaki Red' bears medium-size red, high quality fruits with delicate flavor. These mildew-resistant, upright plants are often grown commercially.

'Hinnonmaki Yellow' is similar to 'Hinnonmaki Red', but with greenish yellow fruits. It has light, sweet flavor, and is slow growing, mildew-resistant, and highly winter-hardy.

'Oregon Champion' is exceptional for processing, with medium to large yellow-green berries with a compelling sweet flavor. It is heavy yielding and mildew-resistant. Fruits holds well on the plant.

'Pixwell' bears light green, oval berries that ripen to a rosy pink. Pink-flesh fruits are juicy, tart, and good for pies and preserves. The moderately vigorous, productive, upright plants have good quality glossy leaves that are mildew-resistant.

'Poorman' produces medium-size, green, pear-shape fruits that develop a red bloom when ripe. The vigorous plants are highly productive and less thorny than most gooseberry varieties. It is mildew-resistant and an old favorite considered the best by some.

European gooseberry (*R. uva-crispa*) is relatively larger and more flavorful. Top varieties include:

'Achilles' is old English variety with large, oval, red, sweet, delicious fruit. It ripens late.

'Careless' sets the standard for British production with very large, hairy, white, tangy fruits. It is mildew-resistant and spineless.

'Catherina' bears very large, golden orange, egg-shape fruits that have sweet flavor. The late ripening fruits are excellent quality for fresh eating. The plants have good disease resistance.

'Early Sulfur' produces pale golden, slightly hairy fruit with good flavor early in the season. Although it is a favorite English dessert variety, it is susceptible to powdery mildew.

'Invicta' is one of the best varieties available in North America. It is resistant to powdery mildew, but susceptible to leaf spot. Its huge, sweet white berries are excellent for fresh eating, preserves, and pies.

'Leveller' bears large berries with an unusual pearlike shape. Berries have a meaty texture, and are mellow and aromatic.

Hybrid **Jostaberry** (*R. ×nidigrolaria*) is a fast-growing cross of black currant and gooseberry with reddish black fruits. It produces large clusters of nearly black berries that have a mild black currant flavor, but with berries larger than those of currant. The fruit is good for fresh eating, juice, and cordials. The thornless plant is more vigorous and earlier bearing than either parent, and it is resistant to both mildew and white pine blister rust.

Red currants (*R. silvestre* and *R. petraeum*) are more flavorful than other currants for cooking. They are not typically troubled by diseases, and late flowering assists them in avoiding spring frosts.

'Rovada' is a productive variety with large fruit on long clusters. It is good for preserves; some people enjoy it fresh as well.

White currant, a type of red currant, is the sweetest currant and is less likely to host white pine blister rust. 'Blanca' bears large fruits on a vigorous and highly productive plant; its late bloom time assists it in avoiding spring frosts. The compact 'Primus' produces long clusters of high-quality berries rich in vitamin C. 'White Imperial' is an old favorite with beautiful medium-large translucent white berries with a pink blush and a rich flavor. It is one of the best currants.

Black currant (*R. nigrum*) is most susceptible to white pine blister rust, but both of the following varieties are resistant

WHITE PINE BLISTER RUST

A disease that does little damage to currants or gooseberries, white pine blister rust is devastating to white pine and its relatives. Currants—especially black currant—and gooseberries host a stage of the disease, passing it along to the pines. The disease has caused such serious tree losses that many states have outlawed the planting and growing of all currants and gooseberries. Jostaberry is immune to the disease and so is not included in the ban.

Susceptible pine trees include the bristlecone (*Pinus aristata*), limber (*P. flexilis*), sugar (*P. lambertiana*), eastern white (*P. strobus*), southwestern white (*P. strobiformis*), western white (*P. monticola*), and whitebark (*P. albicaulis*) pines. Nurseries are restricted from shipping all currants and gooseberries into Delaware, Maine, New Hampshire, New Jersey, North Carolina, and West Virginia. Black currants cannot be shipped to Rhode Island in addition to the above states. Other states limit restrictions to disease-susceptible varieties but permit planting red currants, gooseberries, and immune or resistant varieties of black currants. If you live near any of these types of pine trees, check with your county extension service before planting any kind of currant or gooseberry.

Gooseberries

and can be planted where other currants and gooseberries are permitted. **'Crusader'** makes loose clusters of excellent-quality large black fruit that is good for drying, jellies, juice, and wine. Plant it with another variety of black currant for the best fruit set. **'Consort'** produces soft, musky, distinctive black fruits that are excellent dried. The plant is heavy bearing, self-fruitful, and easy to maintain.

Buffalo currant (*R. aureum*) is more closely related to gooseberry and has a broader, weeping habit. It is cold hardy but has a low chilling requirement and tolerates alkaline soils. Resistant to white pine blister rust, it grows well in Southern California.

Clove currant (*R. odoratum*) is a thornless, loosely-branched Missouri native growing 6 to 8 feet tall. It produces either all male or all female flowers, meaning you'll need at least one of each for fruit. The black berry can be used in jellies, preserves, and pies. The rust-resistant **'Crandall'** produces loose clusters of large black fruits of excellent quality for all purposes. Plant it with another variety of clove currant for the best fruit set.

Dewberry (see Brambles)

Elderberry, sweet elder (Sambucus nigra canadensis)

Type: Deciduous shrub, Zones 2–9
Typical yield: 10–20 pounds per plant
Typical size: 6–10'H×5–6'W

Elderberry

Easy to grow and productive, elderberry's only downside is that very enthusiasm—it's big, rampant, fast growing, and rangy, spreading on its own by both seeds and suckers. But plants can be at least partially cleaned up by pruning regularly.

In early summer elderberry bears flat, nearly foot-wide clusters of creamy white flowers. Purple-black berries, whose flavor is reminiscent of blueberries but wilder, replace the flowers by late summer. Both the flowers and fruit are famous for wine, and the berries are also used for juice and pies.

The leaves, stems, and unripe fruits of any elderberry are mildly toxic, usually causing discomfort at most. In general, avoid eating red-berry elderberries because they are similarly toxic even when ripe.

When: Plant in early spring.

Planting: Provide full sun and plenty of space, setting plants at least 6 feet apart. Elderberry tolerates and even thrives in wet soil, but just about any soil will do.

Growing: Elderberry is easy to grow. Cut out dead branches as they appear. Keep plants dense by pruning hard in late winter, removing oldest stems completely and shortening others. Rejuvenate overgrown plants by cutting off all stems just above ground level.

Harvesting: Pick berries once they're ripe by raking through the clusters with your open fingers into a bucket. Use the berries at once for juice, jelly, syrup, or pie, or freeze them for later use.

Pests and diseases: Birds watch the fruits as closely as you do and are good at getting to the ripe ones first. Deploy bird protection just as the berries approach ripening. Wrap the shrubs with bird netting or use bird scare devices. Varieties

that ripen late often suffer the least bird damage.

Varieties: All of the varieties chosen for their berries produce more fruit and are easier to harvest than their wild brethren. **'Adams No. 1'** and **'Adams No. 2'** are strong, vigorous, productive, and hardy varieties that bear large fruit clusters. They ripen late and have been the standard since their release from the New York State Agricultural Experiment Station in 1926. **'Kent'**, **'Johns'**, **'Nova'**, **'Scotia'**, and **'York'** all have large berry clusters on productive plants. 'York' is somewhat more productive and larger fruited than the Adams varieties.

Feijoa (see Pineapple guava)

Fig (Ficus carica)

Type: Deciduous tree, Zones 8–10
Typical yield: 150 pounds per tree
Typical size: 10–30'H×10–30'W

'Brown Turkey' fig

Fig trees have a dramatic presence wherever they are grown. Their silvery gray branches are muscular and twisting, spreading wider than they are tall. The leaves are unusually large (4 to 10 inches across) and bright green with three to five rounded lobes. In winter the trees provide a strong silhouette against cloudy skies; in summer their foliage lends a beautiful tropical feeling.

The fossil record indicates that figlike plants were common throughout the middle and southern part of the Mediterranean basin. Figs, along with dates, grapes, and olives, were among the key fruits cultivated in all the early Mediterranean civilizations.

Besides high marks for beauty, figs are relatively easy to grow and remarkably adaptable. They are productive with or without heavy pruning. Even if the plant freezes to the ground in winter, it can often spring back and bear fruit the following summer. In containers figs are eyecatching specimens in the greenhouse or outdoors.

Though associated with and common to mild-winter climates, fig trees are hardier than citrus trees. Figs are grown commercially mostly in California's inland valleys where winter temperatures remain above 18°F.

Dried figs in supermarkets are usually **'Calimyrna'** or imported **'Smyrna'** figs. Home gardeners have little interest in these because they require pollination from a specific type of wasp that does not live in North America. Instead gardeners grow common figs, which set two crops without pollination. The first crop is borne in spring on last season's growth and is called the breba crop. The second crop is borne in fall on new growth and is known as the main crop. The breba crop is often destroyed by spring frosts in cold regions or intentionally by pruning in any region.

A collection of fresh figs

PROTECTING FIGS IN WINTER

At temperatures between 10° and 18°F fig trees die back to the ground but the roots survive, just like the roots of a deciduous shrub. Therefore, protecting the trunk and branches from drying winter winds allows figs to survive much colder winters. In Zone 7 and the warmer parts of Zone 6, wrapping the main trunk and branches may be enough to get the trees past winter. Here's one way to carry a tree over the winter in Zones 4 and 5:

Once the tree goes dormant in fall, lightly prune and dig partially around the roots until you can lower the tree to the ground. Make a hole on one side of the tree as deep as the root ball is wide, and tilt the root ball into it. With the tree on its side, cover it with a tarp to keep it dry, and put soil over the tarp to keep it in place. Then cover everything with a 2-inch layer of leaves or mulch. In early spring uncover the tree and lift it back into place; it will resume growing.

When: Throughout prime fig territory, planting in fall is optimum. But planting at any time of the year is fine as long as the plant gets sufficient water.

Planting: Choose a sunny location with well-drained soil. Figs grown for drying do best in sandy soil. Space trees 10 to 25 feet apart depending on the fig variety and the soil type. In climates where temperatures fall below 18°F, grow figs in 10- to 15-gallon half barrels or other large containers so you can move them to a protected location for winter.

Growing: Because they bear on new wood, fig trees normally fruit the first year after planting. Shade young trees from the hot midday sun. Apply low-nitrogen plant food twice a year to in-ground trees or use fruit tree fertilizer spikes for trees in containers. Water during hot or dry weather to prevent premature fruit drop, but avoid allowing the trees to stand in water. Stop watering after harvest. When the trees are dormant in fall or winter prune heavily to remove buds of the breba crop and to increase the main crop. Fig trees are fruitful for up to 15 years.

Harvesting: Unripe fruits are gummy with latex, which can irritate the skin, so wear gloves when working with your trees. Most varieties bear two crops each year; the breba crop is generally inferior in quality to the main crop. Ripe fruits become soft. Protect ripening fruit from birds.

Pests and diseases: Protect fig trees from root-knot nematodes with a thick layer of mulch. Prolonged high humidity or drought may invite scale insects. See page 210 for ways to control scale.

Varieties: '**Black Jack**' bears purple-skin fruits with sweet pink flesh. It grows best in California. '**Brown Turkey**' ('Black Spanish', 'San Pedro') produces a breba crop of brownish purple fruits in all fig regions. '**Celeste**' ('Blue Celeste', 'Celestial', 'Honey', 'Malta', 'Sugar', 'Violette') has light purple to purplish-brown skin and reddish amber flesh. It has no breba crop and is adapted to the Upper South. '**Conadria**' fruits are white blushed violet with white to red flesh of fine flavor. It bears a breba crop and is adapted to all fig regions. '**Genoa**' ('White Genoa') develops greenish yellow skin and strawberry-color to yellow flesh. It is adapted to coastal California. '**Kadota**' ('White Kadota') produces fruits with greenish yellow skin and amber flesh in California or Hawaii. '**L.S.U. Gold**' fruits have yellow skin and pink-red flesh. This very large variety is best in the South. '**Osborn Prolific**' ('Neveralla') has reddish brown skin and amber flesh, often tinged pink. Grow it in Northern California or the Pacific Northwest. '**Panachee**' ('Striped Tiger', 'Tiger') bears fruits with greenish yellow skin with dark green stripes and red flesh. It is best in California.

Fraise des bois (see Strawberry)
Gooseberry (see Currant)
Granadilla (see Passionfruit)

Grape (Vitis spp.)

Type: Woody deciduous vine, Zones 4–10
Typical yield: 8–12 pounds per vine
Typical size: 4–10'H×6–12'W

From ancient times to the present day, people have cultivated grapes, in part because the plants are relatively easy to propagate and grow, and in part because there are varieties for virtually all regions. Even though many other fruits are used to make wine, grapes are by far preferred.

Fully ripe grapes vary from extremely sweet to slightly tart and from strong to subtle depending on the grape variety. A given variety is generally sweeter in a climate where summers are hot than where they are cool. Besides providing fresh fruit, grapes are used to make juice, jelly, jam, and raisins.

In North America four types of grapes are grown: American grapes—varieties of *Vitis labrusca*; European grapes—varieties of *V. vinifera*; hybrids of American and European grapes; and muscadine grapes—varieties of *V. rotundifolia*. Each type has distinctive growth characteristics, and each variety has a distinctive flavor. Extensive breeding has created many selections.

American grapes, also called fox grapes or Concord grapes for the main variety, grow well in all but the hottest climates and are adaptable to many soils. The fruits are slipskin—a tough skin that separates easily from the pulpy flesh. American grapes are susceptible to disease and require spraying to obtain high yields of good-quality berries. European-American hybrid grapes are grown primarily for making wine but also are good eaten fresh. Muscadine grapes are the best choice for gardens in the South. They are not as hardy as other grapes but are highly disease-resistant, in part because of their very high concentration of resveratrol, a natural compound with various health benefits that is found in the skin of red grapes. To grow European grapes for wine, choose certified disease-free planting stock grafted to American grape rootstock.

Grapes grow on long-lived woody vines. Though they are most productive when trained to a trellis and pruned heavily, grapevines are attractive and are often used as landscape plants. The handsome large green leaves provide bold texture in summer; in fall they turn red or yellow, often contrasting beautifully with the color of the grape clusters. They can be trained to grow on arbors, pergolas, or trellises.

When: Plant in late winter or early spring.

Planting: Choose a south- or east-facing slope in an area with good air circulation to prevent mildew and rot. Grapes adapt to all soils but do best in deep, well-drained, light, slightly acid to neutral soil. Dig the planting hole 1 foot in diameter, leaving adequate room to place a stake, post, or trellis before the roots are positioned. Position the lowest bud on the trunk even with the soil line. Tamp soil lightly over the roots and flood the hole with water, repeating until the soil settles at ground level.

Growing: Highly fertile soil detracts from the flavor of wine grapes. Irrigation also may be harmful and even illegal for wine grapes but is beneficial for table and raisin grapes. Spread mulch around the base of the vines for protection in cold-winter areas. In extremely cold regions untie the vines and bend them to the ground, then cover them with soil or straw. Uncover and retie the plants to their supports in spring. Provide a windbreak in exposed areas. Rake back the mulch in spring, add new well-rotted compost or manure, and replace the mulch.

TOP GARDEN GRAPES

Variety (Zones)	Fruit, ripening season	Uses	Vine, notes
AMERICAN GRAPE, JUICE			
'Catawba' (5–7)	Dark orange-red, seedless. Spicy flavor. Late	Juice, dessert wine	Vigorous, productive vine. Disease susceptible
'Concord' (4–9)	Dark blue, seedy. Large bunches. Candy grape flavor. Midseason to late	Juice, jelly, jam, preserves	Common and widely grown. Seedless form available. Susceptible to cracking
'Fredonia' (4–8)	Black, large, mild flavor. Seeded. Early	Juice, wine, preserves	Makes deep red juice. Moderately vigorous. Similar to 'Concord' but earlier. Susceptible to downy, powdery mildew
'Niagara' (4–8)	Yellow-green, seedless, large, thick skinned. Sweet, strong "foxy" flavor. Tight, compact bunches. Late midseason	Juice, wine, fresh	Heavy producer. Does well in northern states. Good ornamental quality.
AMERICAN GRAPE, FRESH			
'Canadice' (5–7)	Red, seedless, medium-size. Spicy flavor. Very early	Fresh, juice	Ripens in cool areas. Prune hard or thin the crop. Hardy, productive. Medium resistance to black rot. Bunch rot can be a problem
'Einset' (5–8)	Red, seedless. Fruity flavor. Relatively thick skin. Early	Fresh	Very productive. Stores wells
'Himrod' (5–8)	Gold-yellow, seedless, large. Long clusters. Deliciously spicy-sweet. Very early	Fresh, dried	Vigorous. Good for training on an arbor. Moderate disease resistance. Responds to good culture. Stores well if harvested at full maturity and refrigerated
'Lakemont' (5–8)	Yellow-green, seedless, in large tight clusters. Good, mild flavor. Early	Fresh	Vigorous, productive vine with a tendency to overbear. Susceptible to cracking
'Reliance' (4–8)	Pale red, seedless, in large clusters. Mild, fruity flavor. Early midseason	Fresh, juice	Vigorous, productive, consistent. Resists powdery mildew, downy mildew, and anthracnose
'Vanessa' (6–8)	Red, seedless, firm. Fruity flavor, thin skin. Early midseason	Fresh, dried	Vigorous, moderately productive vine. Tolerates rain. Susceptible to cracking
EUROPEAN GRAPE, WINE			
'Cabernet Franc' (6–9)	Red. Loose clusters. Late	Wine	Vigorous, relatively hardy. Bordeaux wine component. From France
'Cabernet Sauvignon' (7–9)	Red. Strong, distinctive flavor. Very late	Wine	Needs very long season. Bordeaux wine component. From France
'Chardonnay' (7–9)	White. Late midseason	Wine	Cold-hardy, but less than 'White Riesling' or 'Cabernet Franc'. High-quality wine. Early and reliable maturity. Moderate vigor. Relatively high susceptibility to botrytis bunch rot. From France
'Gewürztraminer' (5–9)	Pink-red, small. Spicy flavor. Moderate crops. One of the earliest good-quality white wine grapes	Wine	Very distinctive, spicy aroma. Often blended with Riesling. More cold-hardy than other European wine grapes. High vigor. From Germany
'Merlot' (6–9)	Black, medium-size, round. Late	Wine	High-quality, rich red juice. Bordeaux wine component. From France
'White Riesling' (6–9)	Green-yellow, small, speckled. Late	Wine	High-quality wine grape. One of the hardiest whites. Susceptibile to botrytis bunch rot. From Germany. Widely planted in Finger Lakes region of New York

Variety (Zones)	Fruit, ripening season	Uses	Vine, notes
EUROPEAN GRAPE, TABLE			
'Flame' (7–10)	Red, seedless, sweet, crisp. Light flavor. Loose clusters. Early midseason	Fresh, dried	Vigorous, productive vines need hot summers. Popular commercial fresh grape
'Perlette' (6–10)	Pale green, small to medium, seedless. Thin, crisp, juicy skin. Early	Fresh	More productive than comparable varieties with less heat
'Thompson Seedless' (7–9)	Pale green-gold, seedless, very sweet. Large clusters. Midseason	Fresh, dried	Excellent in long, hot, dry regions of the West and Northwest. Thin clusters for larger fruit. Common market grape
EUROPEAN-AMERICAN HYBRID, WINE			
'Cayuga' (6–8)	Pale green. Large. Compact clusters. Midseason	Wine	One of most productive, disease-resistant vines. Harvest early to make high-quality sparkling white wine with clean, neutral palate-cleansing taste. Good acidity. Pleasant aroma. Anthracnose-susceptible
'Chambourcin' (7–9)	Blue-black. Large clusters. Late midseason	Wine	Claret-type red wine. Very productive vine needs thinning. Relatively disease free
'Chancellor' (6–8)	Jet black, firm. Midseason	Wine	Produces a full-bodied red wine that ages well. Very productive, hardy. Very disease-prone
'Chardonel' (6–8)	Amber. Loose clusters. Late midseason	Wine	Produces high-quality white wine similar to 'Chardonnay', but vine is more cold-hardy. Requires good disease management. No thinning. New York wine grape
'Corot Noir' (4–8)	Red-black. Midseason	Wine	High-quality red wine grape. New from Cornell University
'De Chaunac' (6–8)	Blue-black. Midseason	Wine	Produces good-quality red wine with pleasant taste. Very productive, vigorous, disease-resistant. Good choice for beginning wine grape gardeners
'Frontenac' (4–8)	Blue-black, large. Loose clusters. Midseason	Wine	Produces medium body red wine with fruit overtones; often acidic. Very cold-hardy, disease-resistant. From Minnesota and widely planted there
'Frontenac Gris' (4–8)	Bronze. Midseason	Wine	Sport of 'Frontenac' with the same strengths and weaknesses. Produces high-quality white, rosé, or ice wine,
'Noiret' (4–8)	Red. Midseason	Wine	High-quality red wine grape. New from Cornell University
'Norton' ('Cynthiana') (5–8)	Black, small. Very late	Wine	Produces a very high-quality wine with huge tannins and superior aging potential. Needs a long warm growing season. Remarkable old American red grape
'Traminette' (6–8)	Amber, medium-size. Late midseason	Wine	Produces good semidry, tart wine. Descendant of 'Gewürztraminer' but more cold-hardy and productive. New from Cornell University
'Vidal Blanc' (7–9)	White, small. Medium to large compact clusters. Late	Wine	Produces good-quality wine once the fruit matures. Very productive, vigorous, mildew-resistant
MUSCADINE, FRESH			
'Fry' (7–9)	Bronze, seeded, large. Large clusters. Late midseason	Fresh	Female vine needs pollinator. Yield, vigor, and disease resistance is moderate. Grapes ripen over 6 weeks
'Nesbitt' (7–9)	Black, medium-size. Midseason to late	Fresh	Self-fertile. Productive multiuse grape for fresh market or processing
'Scuppernong' (7–9)	Bronze, large, speckled, thick skinned. Midseason	Fresh, wine	Classic muscadine with distinctive, grape or "foxy" flavor. Female vine needs pollinator
'Southern Home' (7–9)	Black, medium-size. Midseason to late	Fresh, jam, jelly	Hybrid of muscadine and European grape. Self-fruitful. Moderately productive. Developed in Florida
'Southland' (7–9)	Purple-black, seeded, sweet. Midseason	Fresh, jam, jelly	Self-fertile. Pest- and disease-resistant. Recommended for Lower South
'Summit' (7–9)	Bronze-red, relatively thin skin. Early to midseason	Fresh	Disease-resistant, productive. Female vine needs pollinator

To train a grapevine to a wire trellis, begin the winter after planting. Prune off all shoots except the strongest cane to train as the trunk. Tie it loosely to an upright support pole. In the next season when the trunk has grown as high as the first wire (3 feet aboveground), prune out all but two branches to form two main lateral arms, and tie those in either direction along the wire. Each year cut fruiting growth back to three nodes. When the main trunk reaches the height of the second wire (5½ feet above ground), select another pair of strong canes to train as arms similar to the first ones, then cut off the top of the trunk above the wire. In each spring that follows prune out all other canes coming off the trunk and suckers growing from the base.

Spurs and canes grow from the permanent trunk and arms (called cordons) trained to the trellis. Grapes fruit on lateral shoots from the current season's woody growth. Prune all grapes as close to the arms as possible each year to produce the best fruit. Without pruning, the grapes grow increasingly far from the main trunk on the ends of long canes. Cane- or spur-prune wine grapes and muscadines after the first three growing seasons; only cane-prune American and 'Thompson Seedless' grapes.

Cane pruning This method leaves two whole canes from the previous season and two additional canes near the head of the trunk that are cut back to buds. Gather fruiting canes upward and tie them together toward the tip. Let growth from the renewal buds trail. The Kniffen two-arm system leaves canes only on the top wire; the four-arm and six-arm systems leave canes at two or three levels. Use the four-arm and six-arm systems only where vigorous top growth on the higher wire will not shade out the canes on the bottom one.

Spur pruning To spur-train grapes, cut all side branches on lateral arms to two buds in winter. Two new shoots will grow on each remaining spur, and each of those will yield one to three fruit bunches. Space the spurs 6 inches apart. Keep some one-bud renewal spurs to develop for next year's fruiting wood.

In a small garden growing grapes on an arbor is a good way to use vertical space for ornamental as well as edible purposes. To grow vines on an arbor, train and tie one strong cane up a post as a trunk and prune out the side canes. When the trunk reaches the top of the arbor in the second or third season, select a single cane from it to develop as a cordon across the top of the framework. Then begin pruning to train two-bud spurs across the top. Head back all the vines in late winter to a few buds per cane. (Prune muscadines in early winter to reduce sap bleeding.) For large arbors grow vines up opposite posts and train canes to cross one another over the framework. Vigorous vines overproduce; thinning fruit bunches helps the remaining grapes to become sweet.

Table grape clusters must be thinned to produce large grapes free from rot and insect damage.

Harvesting: Vines bear the second or third year after planting. American and table grapes are ready when they reach full variety size and color, in about 150 to 165 days. Leave raisin grapes on the vines to ripen completely before picking. The best time to pick wine grapes depends on the type of wine to be made. Both the sugar (Brix) level and the pH are determining factors. 'Concord' juice grapes are ready to harvest when the sugar level is about 15° Brix; use a digital wine refractometer to measure the level. Muscadine grapes are ready for harvest in about 200 days. Clip grape clusters from the vines with sharp scissors and handle them as little as possible to avoid damage. Picking bunches with grapes of varying degrees of ripeness is desirable for making jelly and jam. Pick grapes for fresh eating and juice two or three times over a period of several weeks as the grapes ripen. Store them in the refrigerator for up to two weeks.

Pests and diseases: Many grape diseases can be prevented with good air circulation and clean cultural practices. Black rot overwinters on infected vines, leaves, and unpicked grapes. Keep vines pruned and trellised so that air circulates well. Choose varieties resistant to botrytis bunch rot, downy

'Himrod' grapes

'Concord' grapes

'Chambourcin' grapes

'Cabernet Sauvignon' grapes

Stake the trunk to a support post.

Prune to two main lateral arms.

Cut fruiting growth back, leaving replacement spurs for each spur removed.

mildew, and powdery mildew. Remove and destroy infected plants immediately. Copper and sulfur fungicides are effective disease controls but may damage the vines. Choose grape varieties resistant to gall phylloxera and pretreated for crown gall. Pick and destroy grape berry moth cocoons and infested grapes and leaves. Spray labeled insect control products for heavy infestations of whiteflies and leafhoppers. Use sticky bands around trunks to control ants. Pick and destroy Japanese beetles. Scrape off loose bark to expose mealybugs. Prune out old wood to control scale. Use netting, reflective tape, or scare balloons to discourage birds, or enclose whole bunches of ripening grapes in paper bags.

Guava, strawberry guava (*Psidium* spp.)

Type: Evergreen tree or shrub, Zones 9–11
Typical yield: 25–50 pounds per plant
Typical size: 6–25'H×5–20'W

The two types of guavas are the tropical guava (*Psidium guajava*) and the strawberry guava (*P. littorale longipes*). The strawberry guava comes in two varieties, one a red-fruit form and the other a yellow-fruit form, which is commonly called lemon guava. Both tropical and strawberry guavas are attractive evergreen plants with shedding bark and fragrant flowers, but they differ in size, fruit quality, and adaptation.

The white flowers, which bloom mainly in spring, develop into 2- to 4-inch-long fruits that ripen primarily in summer and fall. The plants are self-fertile, but fruits may set more heavily in the presence of another guava.

Tropical guava

Tropical guava grows to 25 feet tall and wide and has 6-inch leaves, which may drop briefly in spring. Its egg-shape, 2- to 3-inch fruits have yellow skin and yellow, pink, or sometimes white flesh. The fresh flavor is generally described as musky, and the fruits are commonly processed into jams, jellies, and juices. In Hawaii tropical guava is an invasive weed that thrives at the expense of native plants.

Strawberry guava is a smaller bush, usually 10 feet tall or less and 5 to 7 feet wide. Its leaves are glossy dark green and its bark an attractive, peeling cinnamon-tan, and the overall effect is so striking that the plant is commonly used for its ornamental qualities. Strawberry guava fruits are smaller than tropical guavas, generally 1 to 2 inches in diameter.

When: The best time to plant is midfall once summer temperatures begin to moderate. Planting anytime is fine, as long as the root ball is watered frequently until the roots reach into the surrounding soil.

Planting: Choose a sunny, protected location with soil that drains well. Plant guavas in a north-facing slope if late spring frosts are a problem; otherwise a south-facing slope is best. Space strawberry guavas 6 to 10 feet apart and tropical guavas at least 10 to 15 feet apart. Small varieties adapt well to containers.

Growing: Guavas prefer rich soil, daytime temperatures of 70° to 85°F, and watering during extended drought. Guavas fruit on new growth, so for the best crops prune only to shape the trees and remove suckers. On the other hand, plants are tolerant of pruning, even shearing into a hedge. Rejuvenate old trees by severe pruning.

Harvesting: Guavas fruit two to four years from planting and are productive for at least 15 years. The fruits mature 90 to 150 days after flowering. Leave them on the tree to ripen, but protect them from birds, bats, and fruit flies. Ripe fruits can be shaken from the tree and caught in nets, but they bruise easily. Unripe fruit is hard and gummy, but almost-ripe yellow-green guavas clipped from the tree will ripen in a week at room temperature. Ripe fruits covered with plastic wrap will keep in the refrigerator for up to two weeks. Store guavas away from other fruits and vegetables that release ethylene gas such as apples and bananas.

Pests and diseases: Mites, thrips, aphids, fruit worms, sucking bugs, and fruit flies may cause problems. Damaged fruits are subject to rots. To protect pollinators avoid using insect controls when the trees are in bloom. Use dormant oil spray in winter to control infestations, and keep the ground around trees clean of dropped fruit and other plant debris, which harbors pests and diseases. Control algal spots and anthracnose with labeled disease controls. Use netting and noisemakers to discourage birds and bats.

Varieties: Strawberry guava is available only in the two forms described above. Tropical guava varieties are grown either for fresh eating or for juice. **Dessert:** 'Detwiler', which grows well in California, produces greenish yellow fruits with sweet yellow to pink flesh. '**Indonesian Seedless**' is from Florida and has white flesh. '**Ruby Supreme**', grown mostly in Hawaii, has yellow skin, red flesh, and a strong guava scent. **Juice:** '**Beaumont**', '**Ka Hua Kula**', and '**Waiakea**' are grown primarily in Hawaii.

Jaboticaba (*Myrciaria cauliflora*)

Type: Evergreen tree, Zones 10–11
Typical yield: 15–25 pounds per plant
Typical size: 10–15'H×8–12'W

Unfamiliar to most North Americans, jaboticaba is common in the forests of Brazil, Paraguay, and Bolivia, and—for the last century or so—South Florida and a few corners of California. Its most remarkable feature is the location of its fruits. Rather than at branch tips or along smaller stems, fruits develop along the main trunk and stems. Jaboticaba is related to guavas and pineapple guava.

Low temperature, approximately 27°F, limits where jaboticaba can grow. California Rare Fruit Growers Association reports successful plants as far north as the San Francisco Bay Area. In Florida, plants are currently more common in the far south, but protected areas farther north are often hospitable.

The tree grows slowly, branching close to the ground, with limbs that slant upward and outward so that the dense, rounded crown may attain an ultimate spread as wide as it is tall. The thin beige to reddish bark flakes off much like that of guavas and is quite attractive and ornamental.

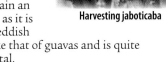
Harvesting jaboticaba

The fruits are like large grapes, but borne singly, with a thicker skin and one to four small seeds. They have a pleasant flavor often compared to muscadine grapes. Eat them fresh or process them into jellies, jams, and wine.

When: Plant at any time of the year.

Planting: Choose a spot in well-drained, acidic soil, and if there's any question about drainage, plant on a soil mound.

Jaboticaba prefers full sun but accepts partial shade. Set out container-grown trees 12 to 15 feet apart. Mulch after planting.

Growing: Water during prolonged drought or once the upper 2 inches of soil are completely dry. Fertilize two or three times a year with ½ to 1 pound of 10-10-10. Prune to remove dead or broken branches and to open the interior of the tree to light where fruits develop.

Harvesting: The fruits are mature when they reach full size and color and are about as soft as a ripe grape. Squeeze the fruit to split it and push the flesh into your mouth.

Pests and diseases: Jaboticaba has few problems, though various animals and birds will browse on the fruits.

Varieties: '**Paulista**' fruits are very large and good quality. '**Sabara**' fruits are small, thin skinned, and sweet. '**Ponhema**' fruits are large and mostly used preserved.

Jostaberry *(see Currant)*
Juneberry *(see Serviceberry)*

Kiwifruit, hardy kiwifruit *(Actinidia* spp.)

Type: Deciduous woody vines, Zones 8–11 (kiwi),
  5–9 (hardy kiwi)
Typical yield: 25–200 pounds per vine
Typical size: 9–12'H×18–30'W

In order to produce fruit the familiar kiwifruit (and sometimes the hardy kiwifruit) needs both male and female plants present for pollination. Kiwifruits, also called Chinese gooseberry, are becoming more popular every year. Although the first large commercial kiwi farms in North America were planted a relatively short time ago, in about 1970, this odd-looking, egg-shape fruit with shimmering emerald green flesh and a delicious berry flavor has found a permanent home on North American tables. The kiwi vine is also working its way into many home gardens. The vines are adaptable to a variety of climates, and close relatives of the kiwi with similar fruit are extremely hardy, extending kiwifruit culture into northern regions. In addition to bearing delicious fruit, kiwi vines also have attractive foliage and flowers and an interesting twining habit.

'Hayward' kiwifruit

Kiwifruits are borne on fast-growing deciduous vines that need heavy annual pruning to keep them productive and within bounds. It is not unusual for a healthy vine to cover an area 18 to 24 feet long and 9 to 12 feet tall. The vines are so heavy that they need a sturdy trellis or arbor. In the commercial orchard kiwi vines are usually trained on wire trellises elevated 6 to 7 feet off the ground. In the garden many more options are available: The vines can be trained over an arbor to shade a patio, tied to a trellis to soften a wall, or allowed to sprawl over a fence or pergola. With any of these methods the fruit will hang from the vine in tantalizing clusters throughout the summer.

The familiar kiwifruit *(Actinidia deliciosa)* has 5- to 8-inch dark green leaves that are round with a fuzzy white underside. The new growth is velvety brown. The yellowish white flowers, about an inch in diameter, are borne in the leaf axils (joints) of the new shoots. The round to oblong fruits have a fuzzy brown, almost leathery skin enclosing soft, bright green flesh dotted with tiny edible black seeds.

'Ananasnaja' hardy kiwifruit

Both male and female plants must be present for pollination if fruit is to be produced.

The hardy kiwifruit *(A. arguta)* looks similar to the more familiar and less-hardy kiwi, but its leaves are slightly longer and more pointed. Its fruit has a kiwi flavor, but because it is smaller and the skin edible it is eaten unpeeled like a grape. Although the fruits need about 200 frost-free days to ripen on the vine, they can be picked when still hard and ripened at room temperature where growing seasons are shorter. Some hardy kiwi varieties may not require a male variety for pollination, but fruiting is better with both male and female plants present.

When: Plant kiwi in fall once summer temperatures begin to moderate. Plant hardy kiwi in early spring as soon as soil is workable, but if you're growing it in a container, wait until late summer.

Planting: Kiwis do best in deep, well-drained loam that is mildly acid and low in sodium. Plants are susceptible to damage from frost and wind, so locate them in a protected area. Space plants 15 to 20 feet apart, and be sure to leave room to erect a trellis.

Growing: The vines require plenty of soil moisture. Water deeply and often when the vines are blooming or fruiting, irrigating in a basin that extends 5 to 6 feet from the trunk. Water-stressed plants drop their leaves, exposing the fruit to sunburn. They also may not flower the following year. Keep the soil moist until harvest, but cut back on water as fall approaches in order to encourage dormancy. Mulch will help maintain soil moisture.

Mature vines need 10 pounds of 10-10-10 fertilizer every year. Because young vines are sensitive to excess fertilizer, apply about 4 ounces the first two years, and increase the amount as the vine grows. Spread the fertilizer evenly under the entire canopy. Feed the plants in spring through midsummer; fertilizer later in the season is likely to delay dormancy and increase cold damage.

Kiwi vines need regular pruning to prevent them from becoming a tangled mess. The two ways to train the vines are the fruiting lateral method and the spur method. The one you choose will depend on how much room you have and how many plants you want to grow.

Most commercial growers choose the fruiting lateral method, in which the vines are trained on a five-wire trellis supported 6 feet above the ground by posts topped with T-shape arms, a structure that looks like a robust clothesline. The fruiting canes develop from permanent arms (cordons) that are trained along the trellis wires.

The spur method is preferable where space is limited. In this case, the short fruiting spurs originate from the main trunk or permanent cordons. The canes that grow from these spurs each season are tied to a fence, wall, or trellis.

Either method requires a strong support. If you build a trellis, construct it with sturdy materials that will last a long time; kiwi vines can remain productive for more than 40 years.

Regardless of the training method you choose, let the

Kiwifruit requires a sturdy trellis.

young plants grow with minimal pruning for a year or two after planting. If a strong main trunk, more than ¼ inch in diameter, doesn't develop the first year, cut the vine back to two or three buds above the ground or graft union the following dormant season. In spring train the most vigorous shoot up the trellis. During the training period direct the plant's energy into developing a strong trunk and arms or spurs. Prune male plants harder than females as their only function is to produce flowers for pollination.

Harvesting: The fruits ripen in November in areas with hot summers or in December in cooler climates. Pick them while they're still hard and let them ripen off the vine like pears or avocados. A change of color from greenish brown to brown is a sign the fruit is almost mature. Also, look for a few fruits beginning to soften on the vine. Pick the largest fruits first, giving the smaller ones a little more time to swell and sweeten. Fruits left on the vine too long will soften and decay, or birds will find them first. Light frosts are not a threat, but lower temperatures will leave the fruit inedible.

Kiwifruits will soften in a few days at room temperature. Unbruised mature fruits may be stored for up to six months in the refrigerator if the air circulation is good and they are kept away from other ripening fruits such as apples or bananas. Check the fruits often while they are in storage and remove any decaying ones.

Pests and diseases: Various insects such as leaf roller caterpillars and scale insects can be troublesome. Treat leaf-rolling caterpillars with *Bacillus thuringiensis* (Bt). Treat scales with neem oil. Careful preparation of a well-drained planting site and proper watering are the best ways to avoid root rot and other stress-related diseases. The kiwi vine's foliage and bark affects cats in the same way as catnip. They may scratch the trunks of older vines.

Varieties: Kiwifruit: '**Hayward**,' the most common kiwi in North America, is easy to grow except in areas with warm winters. Where winters are mildest, plant '**Vincent**'. '**Saanichton**' grows well in the Northwest west of the Cascades. For all three of these female varieties, plant '**Chico Male**' (or simply "male kiwi") for pollination.

Hardy kiwifruit: All need a male pollinator unless otherwise noted. '**Ananasnaja**' produces fruits with sweet-spicy light green flesh high in vitamins. The vine bears reliably and is insect- and disease-resistant but needs protection from drying winds. '**Dumbarton Oaks**' makes sweet fruit of excellent flavor. '**Issai**' is self-fruitful but produces better with pollination. Its flesh is sweet and high in vitamins. '**Ken's Red**' needs minimal chilling to produce its very sweet bright red fruits and thus produces well where winters are mild. '**Red Princess**' ripens to a brick red color and has yellow-red flesh.

Arctic beauty kiwifruit (*A. kolomikta*) has small fruit but is an especially cold-hardy species, thriving throughout Zones 3 to 8. Male plants are popular ornamental vines grown for their variegated leaves. Fruits of the female variety '**Krupnopladnaya**' are sweet and have a pineapple flavor.

Lemon guava (*see Guava*)
Litchee (*see Lychee*)
Loganberry (*see Brambles*)

Loquat (*Eriobotrya japonica*)

Type: Evergreen tree or shrub, Zones 8–10
Typical yield: 35–300 pounds per tree
Typical size: 15–30'H×15–30'W

The loquat is an easy-to-grow plant with boldly textured foliage and clusters of small orangish yellow fruit 1 to 2 inches in diameter. Each fruit contains three to five large seeds surrounded by sweet, tangy, and aromatic flesh. Depending on the loquat variety the flesh may be orange, yellow, or white.

Loquat trees are often grown as ornamentals. Their large prominently veined leaves contrast well with the smaller,

Loquat

softer leaves of many other plants. The underside of the leaves is light green and often covered with a soft down. The new growth is sometimes tinged with red. Mature trees are roundheaded and can be used to shade a patio. Loquats also make attractive espaliers.

Small white fragrant flowers are borne at the ends of the branches in fall or early winter. Before they open, the flower clusters have an unusual woolly texture. In full bloom, the trees are alive with honeybees.

The best fruit comes in areas with mild winters and summers. Although the tree is quite hardy, temperatures near 28°F usually damage the flowers and ripening fruit. Prolonged high summer temperatures can inhibit flowering. Intense heat and sunlight during winter usually result in sunburned fruit. White-flesh varieties are better adapted to cool coastal areas; varieties with yellow flesh need more warmth to produce sweet fruit.

When: The best planting time is in fall, but anytime is fine.
Planting: Loquats are adaptable to all moderately fertile soils that drain well. Plant them 20 to 30 feet apart.
Growing: Water when the flower buds swell and again several times during harvest season. Thin the flowers and fruits to increase the size of the remaining fruit. Enclose fruit clusters in paper bags to prevent sunburn, which shows as purple staining in hot climates. Fertilize during periods of active growth with 1 pound of 10-10-10, or mulch with composted manure. Prune after harvest to prevent alternate bearing. Weed around young trees by hand and around mature trees by light hoeing.
Harvesting: Loquats typically bloom in fall and fruit in spring. The fruits mature about 90 days after flowering. The best indication of ripeness is full color. Use a clean sharp knife or hand pruners to cut the fruits; leave their stalks attached to avoid tearing the skin. Store at room temperature for up to 10 days or refrigerate for up to two weeks.
Pests and diseases: Caribbean fruit fly is a problem in Florida; keep the area underneath and around the tree cleared of fallen fruit. Fire blight is a problem in the Southeast; pear blight bacteria in the West. Remove and destroy any affected branches at least 8 inches below the visible infection using loppers; between cuts sterilize the tool with diluted bleach or rubbing alcohol. (See pages 120 and 202 for more about fire blight.) Pick off and destroy any caterpillars. Codling moth (see page 121) may be a problem in California; scrape the cocoons off the bark in late winter, and spray with dormant oil. Tie the developing fruits in paper bags to prevent moths from laying eggs on them. Spray dormant oil in winter to combat aphids and scales. Cover trees with netting to protect fruit from birds.
Varieties: In the Southeast, try '**Tanaka**,' which is partially self-fertile and more cold-hardy than average. '**Advance**' is a late-fruiting, blight-resistant natural dwarf about 5 feet tall, often used as a pollinator for other varieties. In California '**Golden Red**' is popular.

Lychee *(Litchi chinensis)*

Type: Evergreen tree, Zones 10–11
Typical yield: 50–200 pounds per tree
Typical size: 30–60'H×25–50'W

Lychee

A lychee tree in full fruit is a stunning sight. Large clusters of bright red fruit dangle among shiny, leathery dark green leaves divided into four to eight leaflets. Lychees are also eyecatching in spring, when huge sprays of yellowish white flowers adorn the tree.

The fruits are encased within a brittle, warty shell. Inside this shell is a sweet, translucent, gelatinous delicacy that the Chinese have enjoyed for more than 2,000 years. Lychee trees branch to the ground and produce a dense crown. Under ideal conditions they may reach 40 feet tall, but they are usually much smaller. In some areas lychees have a tendency for alternate bearing.

The trees require seasonal temperature variations for optimum flowering and fruiting. Lychee grows most satisfactorily where summers are hot and wet and winters are cool with low amounts of rain and no frost. Varieties differ in how much chilling they need, but most need between 100 and 200 hours between 32° and 45°F. Lychee trees become hardier as they age. Young trees may be killed by a light frost, but mature trees have survived temperatures as low as 25°F when fully hardened. Lychees are best adapted to parts of Hawaii and Florida, but they have also been grown successfully in frost-free coastal areas of California.

When: Fall is the best planting time, but any time of the year is all right as long as the root ball is kept moist until the roots reach into the native soil.

Planting: Lychee is adaptable to a wide range of soils, including clay and alkaline ones, and can tolerate brief flooding but not salinity. It does best in a nice acid loam. Space trees at least 30 feet apart and 40 feet from other trees and structures that might shade them.

Growing: Protect young trees from wind and high heat. Prune them to a central leader and remove any low and narrow-angle branches. Add continuous-feed fertilizer to the planting hole, and fertilize once a year early in the growing season until the tree is large enough to bear fruit, then fertilize only immediately after harvest. Bearing trees need less phosphorus than developing trees, and too much nitrogen causes the fruit to crack. Lychees require insects for good pollination, primarily honeybees, so avoid spraying pest controls. Water during hot, dry months. Heavy rain or fog and hot, dry winds during flowering can cause blossoms to drop and fruit to split. Shaded portions of a tree will not bear fruit.

Harvesting: Trees begin fruiting two to five years after planting, and they continue to bear for many decades. The fruits mature four to five months after flowering. Harvest every few days over a period of a few weeks. Yields vary with environmental conditions, variety, tree age, cultural practices, and availability of pollinators. Fruits are ripe when they reach the full variety color. The aromatic oval fruits are red, pink, or amber and look like strawberries hanging in clusters. The swelling of maturing fruits causes the warty bumps on the skin to flatten out somewhat. Use a pruning pole to cut clusters with some stems and leaves attached;

pulling fruit off the branches will break the skin.

Fresh lychee flesh is juicy and white, grayish white, or pinkish white. The seed comes out easily and is not edible. The fruit dries naturally; the skin turns brown and brittle, and the flesh dark brown and wrinkly. The dried flesh is dark and rich, similar to a large raisin. Eat lychees fresh out of hand or peeled and pitted and added to salads, baked goods, and sherbet. Store fresh fruits in a cool, dry location with good air circulation to prevent rotting.

Pests and diseases: Lychee trees are susceptible to algal leaf spot, leaf blight, dieback, and mushroom root rot. Avoid planting them where oak trees once grew. Birds, bats, and bees can damage ripe fruits. Raccoons and rodents are attracted to the aroma of ripe fruit. Use netting if necessary to protect the fruit from invaders.

Varieties: Some lychees leak juice when the skin is broken. Those that don't, such as the following, are the most desirable and are referred to as "dry and clean." **'Brewster'**, **'Peerless'**, and **'Bengal'** withstand light frosts and are good choices for Florida; they fruit midseason. In Hawaii **'Kaimana'**, **'Kwai Mi'** ('Mauritius'), and **'Groff'** are popular varieties that fruit in August and September. 'Groff' and 'Kwai Mi' are also popular in California, as is spring-ripening **'Amboina'**.

Mango *(Mangifera indica)*

Type: Evergreen tree, Zones 10–11
Typical yield: 400–500 pounds per tree
Typical size: 30–60'H×20–40'W

To millions of people living in the tropics the mango is of far greater significance in the diet than the apple is to North Americans. Mangoes are also becoming increasingly popular in America, where they are available in supermarkets nearly year-round. Some of these come from commercial orchards in Florida, Hawaii, and California, but most supermarket mangoes in winter are from Brazil, Peru, and Venezuela, and

'Keitt' mango

in spring and summer from Mexico, Haiti, and the Philippines. Mangoes are also imported from India, where there are more than a thousand commercial varieties.

Although dozens of species of mango grow throughout the tropics, only 17 of them bear edible fruit. All have thick, leathery, pointed leaves that are a foot or more long and about 3 inches wide. They are normally dark green but emerge brownish red. The new growth occurs in flushes, usually in spring and summer, and sometimes only on one part of the tree at one time. The fruits dangle at the ends of 6- to 8-inch-long stalks.

Reflecting their complex origins the fruits vary widely in size, shape, color, and flesh qualities. Mangoes may be round, oblong, or kidney shape. Sometimes the fruit has a small pointed beak. They can weigh as little as 4 to 5 ounces or as much as 4 pounds. The skin color can be green, yellow, red, or purple, but usually it is a combination of several shades. The flesh is more or less fibrous, and when perfectly ripe it is yellow to orange and has the texture of a peach. The

TOP GARDEN MANGOES

Variety	Fruit	Ripening months	Tree	Anthracnose susceptible
HAWAII				
'Ah Ping'	Large, yellow and orange, fiberless. Small seed	July	Upright	Yes
'Edwards'	Large, dark yellow, fiberless. Small seed	June to July	Spreading tree bears lightly	Yes
'Julie'	Small, dark green and red, some fiber	August to September	Small	Yes
'Pirie' ('Pairi', 'Paheri')	Small, green and yellow, fiberless	July	Spreading tree bears lightly	Yes
'Zill'	Small, yellow and crimson, fiberless. Small seed	June to July	Dome-shaped	Yes
FLORIDA				
'Earlygold'	Medium, pink and yellow, fiberless. Most are seedless	May to June	Upright tree, light producer	No
'Irwin'	Medium, red, fiberless. Small seed	June to July	Small	Yes
'Keitt'	Large, green and pink, firm. Small seed	August to September	Long, arching branches	Partial
'Kent'	Large, green, red, and yellow, fiberless. Small seed	July to August	Upright	Yes
'Sensation'	Medium, pink and red, some fiber. Small seed	July to August	Moderately open. Tends to bear in alternate years	Yes
'Tommy Atkins'	Large, red and yellow, firm. Small seed	June to July	Dense, rounded	Partial
CALIFORNIA				
'Aloha'	Small to large, red, almost fiberless. Small seed	November to December	Spreading. Bears lightly	Yes
'Edgehill'	Small to medium, green with red blush, nearly fiberless	December to February	Upright	Yes
'Manila'	Small, yellow, fiberless. Small seed	October to December	Bushy growth. Seedlings true-to-type	Yes
'Piña'	Small, yellow and orange, nearly fiberless	November to December	Upright. Seedlings true-to-type	Yes
'Reliable'	Small to large, red and yellow, nearly fiberless. Small seed	December to January	Dome-shape	Yes
'T-1'	Medium to large, red, yellow, and green, fiberless. Small seed	December to January	Upright, rounded	Yes
'Thomson'	Small to medium, yellow, fiberless. Small seed	December to January	Spreading	Yes
'Villaseñor'	Medium, light green with pink blush, fiberless. Small seed	December to January	Spreading	Partial
'Winters'	Small to medium, red and yellow, fiberless	October to November	Dome-shape. Bears lightly. Seedlings true-to-type	Yes

flavor also resembles that of the peach, but it also has a distinctive tropical sweetness.

Mangoes are generally categorized as one of two types: Indian and Indo-Chinese. Indian mangoes usually have brightly colored fruit, are susceptible to anthracnose, and produce seeds that do not grow true to type. These are the kinds most often grown commercially in Florida. Indo-Chinese mangoes usually do not develop brightly colored fruit, but the trees are resistant to anthracnose disease. Moreover, Indo-Chinese mangoes also usually produce seeds that do come true to type. But many mangoes do not fit neatly into either group.

Mangoes grow only in frost-free climates. Flowers and small fruits are killed at temperatures below 40°F. Young trees may be seriously damaged if the temperature drops below 30°F, but mature trees may withstand very short periods of temperatures as low as 25°F. Nighttime temperatures above 55°F are required for pollination; mango trees are self-fruitful.

Warm, dry weather is needed for mangoes to set fruit well. In California the first bloom of the season usually occurs during spring when the weather is often cool and wet, which causes poor fruit set. Later in summer the second growth flush and bloom produce a crop that ripens in fall and winter.

When: The best time to plant mangoes is in fall once

Mango

daytime high temperatures become more moderate, although planting at any time of the year is all right.

Planting: Mangoes grow well in almost any moderately acid soil but not in heavy clay or wet soils. Wear gloves while working with mango trees; the leaves and fruit skins contain a toxic sap that can cause a painful dermatitis. Plant at the top of a slope for the best drainage and good air circulation, and provide a windbreak or stake young trees. In the desert, plant mangoes in the shade to keep the fruits from sunburning. In cooler zones plant on the south side of the house for maximum sun and warmth.

Growing: Keep the soil consistently moist until the fruit is harvested. That usually means weekly irrigation during warm weather, though in the desert trees may need daily watering until harvest. Trees tolerate slightly drier soil when not in fruit.

Fertilize mango trees regularly from February through July; apply composted manure around the trees every two weeks until July. Don't overfertilize; too much nitrogen increases the likelihood of disease.

Prune in winter or early spring to control the tree's size and shape. To avoid alternate-year bearing, remove some flower clusters in years when blooms are too abundant. Thinning the fruit also helps to encourage annual bearing.

Harvesting: The fruits mature 100 to 180 days after the flowers bloom. Tree-ripened fruits have the best flavor, but pick all fruits from late-bearing trees if temperatures fall. The fruits will ripen indoors; place them with the stem ends down in trays covered with a damp cloth to prevent shrinkage. Keep mangoes at cool room temperatures not below 50°F. Ripe fruits will keep in the refrigerator for up to three weeks.

Pests and diseases: Anthracnose is a problem primarily summer-humid Florida. Choose resistant varieties or use copper spray or another disease control. Too much nitrogen causes shriveling at the fruit apex, a condition called soft nose. Control fruit flies and sand weevils by picking up and destroying all dropped fruit and other plant debris around the trees. Use dormant oil or insecticidal soap to control scale, mites, and mealybugs.

Varieties: Given the tremendous diversity of mangoes, varieties are likely to grow better or produce superior fruits in one region or another, but not everywhere. See the table on page 151 for variety recommendations for the three main growing regions of the United States.

Mango

Marionberry (see Brambles)
Mexican apple (see Sapote)
Nanking cherry (see Cherry)
Nectarine (see Peach)

Papaya, babaco (Carica spp.)

Type: Perennial, Zones 10–11
Typical yield: 75–300 pounds per plant
Typical size: 6–25'H×3–6'W

Papaya

The papaya is an unbranched, single-stemmed perennial that grows to a height of 6 to 20 feet. Its deeply lobed dark green leaves have a boldly tropical look and reach 2 feet wide under ideal conditions.

There are three types of papayas and two main species: Hawaiian and Mexican papayas (both *C. papaya*) are the papayas available in markets. Babaco (*C. ×heilbornii pentagona*), which is native to high-elevation areas of Ecuador, is somewhat more adaptable to cooler regions.

Hawaiian papayas are pear-shape fruits that weigh about a pound and have a yellow skin when ripe. The flesh is bright orange or pinkish, depending on the papaya variety, with small black seeds clustered in the center.

Mexican papayas are much larger than Hawaiian types. They weigh up to 10 pounds and grow to more than 15 inches long. The flesh is yellow, orange, or pink. The flavor is less intense than that of Hawaiian papayas but is still delicious and extremely enjoyable. They are also slightly easier to grow than Hawaiian types.

Babacos are long, seedless fruits with yellow, melon-flavor flesh. They need warm winters and part shade in areas with hot summers. Given their short stature, babacos are ideally suited to container culture.

Papaya pollination is unusual. Plants may produce only female flowers, only male flowers, or both. To complicate matters, the plants may change from one form to another during their life cycle. In any case, male and female flowers must be present to produce fruit. The best practice is to plant three or four papayas in a group to ensure pollination. However, some varieties have a propensity for producing certain types of flowers. For example, 'Solo' seedlings have flowers of both sexes 66 percent of the time, meaning two out of three plants will produce fruit, even if planted singly.

Papayas have exacting climate requirements for vigorous growth and fruit production. They must have warmth throughout the year and are damaged by light frosts. Cold, wet soil is lethal. Cool weather will alter fruit flavor. Because of this papayas are limited to south Florida, moderate locations of Southern California, Hawaii, and greenhouses anywhere.

When: Plant in late winter or early spring.

Planting: You can grow papayas from transplants or start your own plants indoors from seeds that you save from fruits. Germination takes three to five weeks, but washing the seeds in water to remove the gelatinous membrane before planting saves a week or two. Babacos are seedless and so must be started from transplants.

Choose a planting site that is warm and sunny. If possible, plant along a south-facing wall. Provide a windbreak if planting in an open area.

Plant carefully to avoid breaking the root ball. Set the plants a little high to allow for settling. Use mulch, but keep it away from the trunk. A plastic mulch will help keep soil warm and dry in wet-winter areas, but remove it as soon as the weather becomes warm.

Papaya in landscape

Set plants 8 to 10 feet apart in light, well-drained soil not overly rich in organic matter. Papayas require excellent drainage; excess moisture can kill them. Plant on hillsides, on soil mounds, or in raised beds to ensure the proper drainage. Many gardeners go to great lengths, such as installing drain tiles and planting on beds of perlite.

Growing: Watering is the most critical aspect of raising papayas. The plants should be kept on the dry side to avoid root rot, but they also need enough water to support their large leaves and fruit development. Papayas require regular applications of nitrogen. Add 1 ounce of continuous-feed plant food such as 14-14-14 to the planting hole, then feed monthly once the plant is established and growing. When the plant is a year old, fertilize with 1 pound of 10-10-10 every three months; adjust the rate according to the plant's response. Papayas do not need to be pruned, but some growers pinch the seedlings or cut back established plants to encourage multiple trunks. To ensure cross-pollination and high-quality fruit, plant three or four plants and replace them every four years. Seedlings usually begin flowering 9 to 12 months after they germinate.

Harvesting: The fruits of spring transplants are ready for harvest by November, when most of the skin is yellow-green. After several days of ripening at room temperature, they should be almost fully yellow and slightly soft to the touch. Dark green fruit will not ripen properly off the tree, even though it may turn yellow on the outside, nor will it contain viable seeds. Fully mature fruit will have edible dark brown to black seeds, the size of small peas, completely filling the internal cavity. The seeds have a spicy flavor that complements many sauces and salad dressings. Mature fruits can be stored at 45°F for about three weeks.

Pests and diseases: Use sulfur to combat powdery mildew and other disease controls as appropriate for ring spot, black spot, blights, anthracnose, and other diseases. Control mosaic virus with clean cultural practices and pest control products labeled for green citrus aphids. Spray whiteflies with insecticidal soap. Spray *Bacillus thuringiensis* (Bt) on webworm larvae and other caterpillars. If there are just a few caterpillars, knock them into a bucket of soapy water to kill them. Remove and destroy any branches infested with scales, then wipe off any scales on the trunk with an insecticidal soap solution.

Varieties: 'Solo' bears the small papayas often sold commercially, and 'Blue Solo' has similar fruits on a low-growing hybrid; both do well in Florida and Hawaii. 'Sunset' and 'Vista Solo' are also recommended for Florida. Pink-flesh varieties for Hawaii and California include 'Sunrise', 'Sunset', and 'Thai Dwarf'.

Passionfruit, purple granadilla (*Passiflora* spp.)

Type: Evergreen or semi-evergreen vine, Zones 10–11
Typical yield: 6–15 pounds per plant
Typical size: 10–50'H×6–10'W

Passionfruit is a member of a large family of vining plants, many of them prized for their beautiful flowers and delicate leaves. Several species and varieties produce edible fruit, but the most widely available is the purple granadilla (*P. edulis*).

The passionfruit vine was named by Spanish missionaries to whom its intricate and strikingly beautiful flowers represented the passion of Christ.

Plants are self-fruitful, producing 1- to 2-inch egg-shape fruits that are dark purple when ripe. The rind is inedible. The orange pulp surrounds small black seeds, which are usually strained from the pulp prior to its use as a juice or flavoring.

Fruits of passionfruit

An attractive vine, passionfruit bears delicate, three-lobe leaves with serrated edges and a glossy light green sheen. Its tendrils cling to almost any support. Extremely fast growing, the vine requires heavy pruning to keep it in bounds. It grows best in frost-free climates, although it may survive for short periods at temperatures below freezing. The vine may lose some of its leaves in cool winters, and the roots may resprout if the top is killed. Passionfruit vine does not grow well in intense summer heat.

The vine has naturalized in Hawaii to such a degree that it is a pest. Plant it there with caution, if at all.

When: Planting in either fall or spring is preferable, but any season is fine.

Planting: Choose a sunny location (partial shade in very hot areas) protected from strong winds. Excellent drainage is absolutely necessary; passionfruit is highly susceptible to root and crown rots. Plant adjacent to an existing fence, trellis, or arbor that is strong enough to support the vine. The soil should be rich in organic matter and low in salts. Because the vine is shallow rooted, it benefits from a thick layer of organic mulch. If you're planting several vines, space them at least 4 feet apart and as much as 8 feet apart.

Growing: Plants must have consistent moisture or harvest and fruit quality will be reduced. They grow fast and thus need regular applications of a fertilizer such as 10-10-10. Too much nitrogen, however, results in vigorous foliage growth at the expense of flowers.

Prune to keep a vine within bounds, to make harvesting easier, and to maximize productivity. In mild-winter climates prune immediately after harvest. In areas with cool winters prune in early spring. Fruits develop in the leaf axils (joints) of the current season's growth; prune to maintain vigorous growth from the main branches and thus keep the plants productive. As a rule, remove all weak growth and cut back vigorous growth by at least one-third. Unpruned passionfruit vines become rampant and produce fruit well out of reach.

Harvesting: Fruits quickly turn from green to deep purple when ripe and then fall to the ground within a few days. They can either be picked when they change color or gathered from the ground each day.

Passionfruit flesh is orange and combines various tropical flavors including citrus. Extract the juice or use a spoon to from a halved fruit.

Ripen yellow passionfruits at room temperature in plastic bags to retain humidity. Store unwashed fruits in plastic bags in the refrigerator for up to one week.

Pests and diseases: Snails can be a serious problem in California. They can completely strip a vine of leaves and bark, killing young plants or predisposing them to disease. Passionfruit vines are also susceptible to nematodes and viruses as well as the diseases that thrive in cool soils, such as fusarium.

Varieties: Yellow passionfruit (*P. edulis flavicarpa*) produces yellow fruits that are larger, more acidic, and less juicy than those of the purple-fruit species. Hybrids of the two combine the best attributes of both: purple-fruit **'Edgehill'** and red-fruit **'Frederick'**, **'Kahuna'**, and **'Red Rover'**. The fruits of 'Kahuna' are especially large. Yellow passionfruit is also used as a rootstock because of its resistance to nematodes and soil disease problems.

Pawpaw (Asimina triloba)

Type: Deciduous tree, Zones 5–8
Typical yield: 50–400 pounds per tree
Typical size: 10–20'H×6–10'W

Pawpaw

Pawpaw is a small shade-tolerant ornamental tree native to North America. Mature trees flower in sun or shade. Although not as well-known as other indigenous fruit, pawpaw is easy to grow. It is often found growing wild in hardwood forests or along the shady, protected edges of old-growth forests. It does well in urban settings, providing tropical-tasting fruit in climates where true tropicals do not grow. Pawpaw has unusual and attractive foliage and flowers, and its open branches droop. Exotic dark red to purple blossoms hang upside down among the long dark green leaves in early spring. The large, heavy, distinctive butter yellow fruits are extremely high in vitamin C, potassium, iron, calcium, and magnesium. They taste like banana and caramel with a hint of citrus or berry and have a custardlike texture and large dark seeds.

The tree is found from southern Michigan to the Gulf Coastal plain; most named varieties are from the Midwest. Almost all pawpaws are self-incompatible, and natural pollinators are scarce and undependable, so plant more than one variety for successful pollination.

When: Ideally plant in early spring, although fall planting is also successful.

Planting: Choose a shady, fertile, well-drained location that is protected from wind and where the soil can be prepared deeply. Because of pawpaw's long taproot, container-grown trees have the best survival rate. Plant young dormant trees 8 feet apart. Keep the planting consistently moist but not wet. If you prefer you can plant from seed, although seed-grown trees will not be identical to their parents. Sow seeds 1 foot deep and 1 inch deep in a nursery bed; thin seedlings to the healthiest specimens.

Growing: Protect transplants and young seedlings from the sun until they are three years old. Apply a liquid soluble plant food, such as 20-20-20, every few weeks through the first half of the growing season. Hand-pollinate flowers with a small brush or swab to ensure fruit formation. Prune out dead or damaged limbs and remove suckers.

Harvesting: Trees grown from seed fruit in five to eight years; grafted trees bear in as few as three years. The fruit ripens approximately 180 days after flowering—in late summer to early autumn depending on the pawpaw variety and your zone. Ripe fruit is noticeably fragrant and comes off easily by hand or by shaking the tree gently. The skin of a ripe pawpaw is medium to dark green, often mottled with dark brown or purple streaks like a banana; it becomes darker if stored after picking.

Eat pawpaws fresh or on ice cream. Or process the pulp for use in pies and other baked goods (it can be used in place of persimmon pulp). Don't eat unripe fruits, seeds, or skin—they're mildly toxic, though sensitivity varies. Pawpaws can be stored for a week in the refrigerator. If you intend to plant the seeds in spring, store them in a plastic bag on an open shelf in the refrigerator; they should not freeze or dry out.

Pests and diseases: Pawpaws have few significant pests because natural compounds in the leaves and bark have insecticidal properties. Caterpillars, specifically the peduncle borer, may cause the flowers to drop before the fruits set. The larvae of zebra swallowtails also like pawpaws, so sharing may be in order. Raccoons and squirrels eat the fruits as they ripen.

Varieties: **'Davis'** has small fragrant fruit and refrigerates well. **'Sunflower'** bears large sweet fruit with banana and custard flavors; pollinate it with 'Davis'. **'Taylor'** fruits are green with yellow flesh. **'Taytoo'** is favored by many for its vanilla custard flavor.

Peach, nectarine (Prunus persica)

Type: Deciduous tree, Zones 5–10
Typical yield: 135–200 pounds per tree
Typical size: 6–16'H×6–18'W

Few fruits are more evocative of summer's peak, or simply more pleasurable, than a tree-ripened peach or nectarine (which is merely a smooth-skinned peach). And at least a part of the preciousness of these fruits is their cultural exclusivity. In the South and parts of the West, they couldn't be easier. Elsewhere, growing peaches is a matter of some attention, skill, and luck.

After the apple the peach is one of the most widely distributed tree fruits. Its range is somewhat more southern than that of apple because the trees are less hardy; on the other hand, there are more varieties of peach adapted to mild-winter climates than there are of apple. Also, unlike apples, peaches thrive in sunny, hot weather during the growing period.

Several peach or nectarine varieties that ripen at different times can be budded or grafted onto the same tree. In a small garden a multivariety tree is an ideal way to have fruit over many weeks. Peaches and nectarines begin bearing large crops when 3 or 4 years old and typically reach peak production between 8 to 12 years old.

Breeding programs have greatly extended the range of peaches and nectarines. As a rule, the trees are killed at temperatures of –15 to –20°F, and the flower buds at –10° to –12°F. These temperatures aren't absolute. Trees that are not fully acclimated to cold won't be as hardy. These temperature limits, in addition to the threat of a late spring frost damaging flowers, establish the boundaries of peach and nectarine culture.

Peach and nectarine varieties can be divided into those with flesh that clings to the pit inside the fruit, called clingstone, and those with flesh that separates easily from the pit, called freestone. Freestone varieties are easier to use for cooking and preserves.

Most varieties have yellow flesh, but white-fleshed types are also available. Both peaches and nectarines tend to turn brown when sliced. Although the discoloring does not affect flavor, many people find the fruit objectionable and so varieties that resist browning have been bred.

When: Plant dormant, bare-root trees in late winter or early spring as soon as soil is workable. Container-grown trees should go into the ground in fall in hot-summer areas, but they can be planted anytime where summers are cooler.

Planting: Find a sunny, protected location. A south-facing slope is the best site, although a spot on the north side of your property is advisable if late spring frosts are a problem in your area.

Peaches and nectarines grow best in rich, moist, well-drained, slightly acid soil. If your soil drains slowly or is high in clay—the trees do poorly in either situation—plant on a mound of soil or in a raised bed. Allow 18 to 24 feet between standard-size trees, 5 to 8 feet between dwarfs.

Choose one-year-old trees about 4 feet tall and at least ½ inch in diameter grown on a rootstock suitable for your climate. Prune out any dead or damaged wood, and cut away any roots that encircle the root ball. Remove any wires and ties, and allow for stakes if they are needed. The holes should be large enough to accommodate the roots without crowding or bending. Plant so that the graft union is several inches above the soil surface. The top layer of soil should be light and friable so the crown (juncture of the trunk and roots) will dry quickly, thus deterring disease. Make a shallow trench around the tree 8 to 12 inches from the trunk to catch water.

Growing: Of all deciduous fruit trees, peaches and nectarines benefit most from regular applications of nitrogen fertilizers. A yearly application of 1 to 1½ pounds of actual nitrogen ensures vigorous growth and annual renewal of fruiting wood. A healthy tree grows 12 to 24 inches a year; if yours does not, have the soil tested to determine its needs. Unnecessary feeding encourages excess succulent growth, which is susceptible to frost damage and insect infestation. Keep the soil consistently moist but never waterlogged.

High humidity increases the likelihood of brown rot. Spread several inches of well-rotted manure or mulch around the tree but away from the trunk to avoid pest and fungal damage and to control weeds.

Peaches and nectarines need heavy pruning every year to stimulate the new growth that will bear fruit the following season. Early each spring as new growth is just starting and after basic structural and corrective pruning, remove up to two-thirds of the shoots that fruited the previous year and leave the thicker of the new growth, heading the longer shoots back about halfway. Prune harder in the upper, outermost parts of the tree to force fruiting on stouter wood. Since lower shoots on peach trees are easily killed by shade, thin the branches so that ample light reaches the scaffold limbs. Prune the trees to an open center (see page

PEACHES FOR COLD AND WARM REGIONS

In colder climates consider one of the many numbered selections of the Flamin' Fury series of peaches such as 'Flamin' Fury PF 23'. All are results of the Paul Friday peach breeding program in Michigan, are well suited to northern conditions, and are hardy to Zone 4.

In warmer regions look for any of the Florida series, such as 'Flordabelle', 'Flordacrest', and 'Flordadawn'. These come from the Florida Agricultural Experiment Station breeding program, which offers excellent varieties for the South. Some, such as 'FlordaKing', are well adapted to the Deep South, and others, such as 'Flordaprince' have become popular in California and Arizona.

115), and space shoots so air can circulate through the tree. Remove any watersprouts and suckers.

Thin the fruits to 6 inches apart once they reach 1 to 1¼ inches in diameter and after normal fruit drop. Thin early varieties and heavy producers to 10 inches apart. Prop up any sagging fruit-laden limbs to keep them from breaking under the heavy fruit load.

Harvesting: Peach and nectarine trees begin bearing two or three years after planting. Fruits ripen from midsummer to midautumn depending on the peach or nectarine variety and your zone. Pick them when all green coloration is gone. Ripe fruits come off the tree readily with a slight upward twist, but handle them gently because they bruise easily. Store ripe fruits in the refrigerator for a few days. Pressure-can fruits for long-term storage. Sliced fruits bathed in lemon juice to retard discoloration can be stored in the freezer for up to six months.

Pests and diseases: Prune out sick and damaged wood immediately, and keep the ground around the trees cleared of dropped fruit and prunings, which potentially harbor pests and diseases. Avoid most diseases by choosing resistant varieties, and practice clean cultural habits to keep pests away. Spray lime-sulfur in late winter or early spring to prevent peach leaf curl (see page 203). If necessary spray dormant oil during winter to control serious infestations of peach tree borer, scale, and mites; spray *Bacillus thuringiensis* (Bt) at bloom time and in summer to control caterpillars, and lightly cultivate the soil around the tree to destroy their pupae. To protect beneficial bees and other pollinators avoid using insect control products while the trees are in flower. Nectarines are more susceptible than peaches to plum curculio and brown rot. Use netting to protect fruit from birds, and trunk wraps in winter to prevent rodent damage.

Varieties: Unlike many stone fruits, most peach and nectarine varieties are self-fruitful.

Most peach trees need 600 to 900 hours of chilling to set fruit, but many varieties need only 100 to 300 hours of chilling. These can be grown in Southern California and parts of Florida.

Peaches and nectarines are among the smallest deciduous fruit trees. Properly pruned standard-size trees are easily maintained at 12 to 16 feet high. For even smaller trees, about 6 to 8 feet high at maturity, choose ones grafted onto dwarfing rootstocks. Many genetic dwarf varieties are available. Peach and nectarine trees are compact and bushy, beautiful in bloom, and handsome additions to gardens in addition to being well suited to containers.

Hybrids of peaches, apricots, and plums called apriums, peachcots, pluots, and plumcots combine the best features of each species. Read more about them on pages 162 to 165.

TOP GARDEN NECTARINES

Variety (Zones)	Fruit, ripening	Tree, pests	Key features
YELLOW FLESH			
'Desert Dawn' (6–8)	Red, semifreestone. Medium to large. Firm, sweet, juicy. Early	Heavy producing. Susceptible to brown rot, peach leaf curl, Oriental fruit moth	Good quality in warm western climates. From California
'Durbin' (5–9)	Red, semifreestone. Large. Firm, sweet, melting. Late midseason	Good disease resistance	Excellent quality. From North Carolina
'Flavortop' (6–8)	Red over yellow, freestone. Large, egg-shape, firm, smooth textured. Midseason	Vigorous, productive. Susceptible to bacterial spot	Excellent quality. Showy flowers. Good choice for California
'Mericrest' (5–8)	Dark red, freestone. Medium. Firm, juicy, sweet-tangy. Late midseason	Blooms late. Precocious. Resists brown rot, bacterial leaf spot	High quality. Hardiest nectarine. From New Hampshire
'Nectared 4' (6–8)	Red over yellow, semifreestone. Medium-large. Midseason	Highly productive and consistent	Requires heavy, early thinning
'Necta Zee' (6–8)	Red. Yellow clingstone flesh. Medium size. Midseason	Vigorous. Genetic dwarf	Grows 6' tall
'Pocahontas' (6–8)	Red, semifreestone. Medium to large. Early	Vigorous, productive. Resists brown rot	Good quality. Tolerates light frost
'Red Gold' (5–8)	Red, freestone. Very large, glossy, blemish free. Firm, juicy, deep-colored flesh. Late	Vigorous, productive. Crack-resistant. Susceptible to mildew, bacterial spot	Hardy. Outstanding color, flavor. Holds firmness. Stores well. Grows only 12–15' tall. From California
WHITE FLESH			
'Goldmine' (6–8)	Red over white, freestone. Small to medium, sweet, juicy, aromatic. Midseason	Vigorous, productive	Old favorite in California and Oregon
'Morton' (6–8)	Red, semiclingstone. Small to medium, thick skinned, firm, juicy. Midseason	Productive	Hardy. Good quality, attractive fruit
'Nectacrest' (6–8)	Yellow with bright red, freestone. Medium to large, sweet. Late	Vigorous, productive	Hardy to -15° F. Very dwarf, growing to only 10' tall

Yellow freestone peach

White freestone peach

'FlordaKing' peach

Ripe peaches ready to harvest

Hand thinning peaches

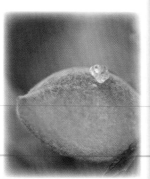

Early curculio damage to peach

'Mericrest' nectarine

Genetic dwarf peach in bloom

TOP GARDEN PEACHES

Variety (Zones)	Fruit, ripening	Tree, pests	Key features
YELLOW FLESH			
'Brighton' (6–8)	Yellow with red, semifreestone. Medium-size, round, firm, juicy. Early	Vigorous, productive	Reaches high quality while firm. From New York
'Canadian Harmony' (6–8)	Yellow with red, freestone. Large, round, firm. Midseason to late	Bears heavily	Excellent for freezing. From Harrow, Ontario
'Cresthaven' (5–8)	Yellow with red, freestone. Medium-large, nearly round, firm, juicy. Late	Vigorous, productive. Tends to overset. Some resistance to bacterial spot. Subject to cracking	Holds well on tree. From Michigan
'Dixie Red' (5–8)	Red, clingstone. Large. Firm. Early	Productive. Precocious	Holds well on tree. Very high quality for an early variety
'Elberta' (5–9)	Yellow with red blush, freestone. Juicy. Midseason	Vigorous, compact, self-fruitful. Good pollinator	Good all-purpose peach. Commercial variety. Ships well. Widely grown, available, and adapted
'Harrow Diamond' (4–9)	Yellow with red blush, freestone. Large. Sweet, juicy. Early	Productive. Medium vigor. Resists bacterial spot, brown rot. Some tolerance of perennial canker	High quality
'Redhaven' (5–8)	Bright red, little fuzz, freestone. Medium. Firm. Early	Vigorous, productive. Some resistance to leaf spot. Susceptible to leaf curl, brown rot, fruit moth, twig borer	Heavy fruit set needs thinning. Good for all purposes, and the standard for early peaches. Recommended for lower Midwest. From Michigan
'Veteran' (5–8)	Yellow with light red blush, freestone. Large. Round, skin peels easily. Early midseason	Large, vigorous. Precocious. Produces reliably in cool, wet weather	Excellent for all purposes. Attractive flowers. From Canada
WHITE FLESH			
'Belle of Georgia' (5–8)	White with red blush, freestone. Large, firm, highly flavored flesh with red streaks. Midseason	Consistent producer. Very bud hardy. Very resistant to bacterial spot. Partially resists brown rot	Excellent for every purpose. An old favorite in the South. Fruits fall when ripe, bruise easily
'Blushingstar' (6–8)	Pink-red, freestone. Medium-size. Firm, pink-tinged flesh with very distinctive flavor. Midseason	Heavy producer	Ships, stores well
'Eden' (5–8)	White with red blush, freestone. Large, firm, sweet, rich, juicy. Midseason	Vigorous, productive	Hardy. Flesh browns slowly
'Raritan Rose' (6–8)	Red over white, freestone. Medium to large, round, tender, juicy. Early	Vigorous, productive	Very high quality. Good fresh, frozen. Excellent roadside market peach. From New Jersey
'Strawberry Free' (6–8)	Creamy white with pink blush, freestone. Large. Very sweet, aromatic. Early	Vigorous. Requires thinning, pruning. Grows 20' tall	Old favorite, especially in Northern California
'White Lady' (6–8)	Red, freestone. Medium to large, firm. Midseason	Large. Vigorous and productive	Good commercial variety. Stores well. From California

Pear *(Pyrus* spp.)

Type: Deciduous tree, Zones 3–9
Typical yield: 200 pounds per tree
Typical size: 10–40'H×8–25'W

A soft, perfectly ripe pear with cheese or in a salad or fruit bowl is one of life's great pleasures. That's the appeal of pears, their way of elevating the ordinary to the special.

Most pears originated in southwestern Europe and came to North America with the earliest settlers. These large pyramidal, long-lived trees are varieties of *P. communis*, and the shape of their fruits provides the definition of the descriptive pear shape. The types that ripen early and don't store well are called summer pears. Those that ripen late and can be held in storage for several months are called winter pears.

A principal limiting factor of European pears is the bacterial disease fire blight. Where spring is warm and wet the

Pears trained as espalier

disease can kill a tree in a single season. Because such weather is more common east of the Rocky Mountains, most commercial pears in North American are produced in the arid West.

Asian pears are descendants of two Asian species: *P. pyrifolia* and *P. ussuriensis*. These are smaller trees, growing to 30 feet tall at most, and perhaps half that with pruning. Asian pear trees are more resistant to fire blight than their European counterparts. The fruits of Asian pears, in contrast to those of European pears, are nearly round with crunchy flesh like an apple—the reason for their other name, apple pear. In fact, the greatest difference between the two types of pears is flesh texture: European pear flesh is variously described as soft, creamy, buttery, smooth, melting, and so on, while the flesh of Asian pears is crisp.

Hybrids between European and Asian varieties, called Asian hybrid or hybrid pears, are also available. They are similar in appearance to pears of European heritage but are generally more fire blight–resistant. Many need less winter chill than European pears and are popular on the Gulf Coast and in the mild-winter West, but others such as 'Ure' are very cold hardy.

Generally European pears are hardier than peaches but less hardy than apples. Some varieties are productive in the South and mild-winter West, and others are hardy in cold climates. All pear trees are attractive garden trees with bright green leathery leaves and brilliant white spring flowers. And

'Bosc' pear

'Bartlett' pear

'Hosui' Asian pear

'Comice' pear

TOP GARDEN PEARS

Variety (Zones)	Fruit	Tree	Use, pollination, notes
EUROPEAN PEARS			
'Bartlett' (5–8)	Large, golden yellow with brownish red blush. Juicy. Ripen off the tree for several weeks for best flavor	Highly productive, early bearing and vigorous	Fresh, preserves, canning. Keeps for 3 months if held near freezing. Pollinate with one of several other varieties. Partially self-fruitful.
'Blake's Pride' (5–9)	Large, attractive, yellow-gold skin. Flesh aromatic, rich, sweet, and juicy	Reliable production. Fire blight-resistant	High-quality dessert pear. Pollinate with 'Bartlet'. New from USDA.
'Bosc' (5–8)	Medium to large, dark yellow russeted brown, long neck. Tender, juicy, fragrant, rich flavor	Reliable, productive, slow growing	Excellent quality for eating and baking. Requires pollinator, such as 'Bartlett'. From Belgium
'Comice' (5–8)	Large, yellow lightly russeted, with red blush, broad based, narrow neck. Flesh sweet, juicy, melting. Excellent flavor.	Large, very vigorous. Inconsistent crops. Good fire blight resistance	Outstanding dessert pear. Ripen in cool storage for one month. Pollinate with 'Bartlett'. From France
'Flemish Beauty' (3–8)	Large, round, clear yellow. Firm, sweet, aromatic	Vigorous, productive, cold-hardy	Good for drying. Requires cross-pollination. Originally known as 'Fondante de Boise'
'Gorham' (5–8)	Large, bright yellow, smooth, similar to 'Bartlett'. Melting sweet	Slightly more resistant to fire blight than 'Bartlett'. Needs nitrogen fertilizer	Similar to 'Bartlett' but ripens later and keeps longer.
'Harrow Delight' (5–8)	Medium-size, yellow, red blush, attractive. Smooth flesh, no grit	Hardy, productive. Excellent fire blight resistance	Fresh and dessert. Pollinate with 'Bartlett' or 'Moonglow'.
'Magness' (6–9)	Medium-size, oval, greenish yellow, lightly russeted, tough skin. Sweet, soft, juicy, free of grit	Vigorous, spreading. Resistant to fire blight. Tough skin resists insects	Keeps well. May take several years to come into bearing. Needs cross-pollination
'Moonglow' (5–8)	Medium-size, yellow with pink blush. Mild, soft. Excellent flavor, little grit	Fire blight-resistant	Excellent for all purposes. Keeps well. Requires cross-pollination
'Packham's Triumph' (5–8)	Large, yellow, plump bottom with bumps. Sweet, crisp, flavorful flesh. Needs cold storage to ripen.	Vigorous, early bearing, late ripening. Susceptible to fire blight	Good storing winter pear. Requires cross-pollination. 'Bartlett' type from Australia
'Potomac' (5–8)	Medium-size, light green. Fine, buttery, pleasing mild aroma	Moderate vigor. Excellent fire blight resistance	High quality. Good for all purposes. Requires cross-pollination

all are more productive if another, compatible variety is nearby for cross-pollination.

Pear trees usually mature at about 25 feet high and as wide. Pears on dwarfing rootstocks are one-half to one-quarter as large.

When: Plant dormant bare-root trees in late winter or very early spring.

Planting: Choose a sunny, well-drained location. Pears are more tolerant of fine-texture, slow-draining clay soils than are most other fruit trees. Plant in a north-facing location to delay blooming in areas where late spring frosts are possible.

Plant a one-year-old tree at the same depth it grew in the nursery, then cut back the top to about 3 feet. Space standard-size varieties 16 to 20 feet apart, dwarf varieties 10 to 12 feet apart.

Growing: Keep the soil consistently moist; lack of moisture causes fruit to drop. In areas with hot summers shade the developing fruits from sunscald and keep the soil moist. Fertilize only if a soil test indicates the need because excess nitrogen encourages succulent growth that is susceptible to fire blight.

Train young pear trees to either a central leader or open center (see pages 115–117). Open center is easier and may reduce the extent of damage in the event fire blight strikes. Begin by selecting three main shoots the first summer and pinching back all others between them. Leave lower shoots to fill in the base of the tree. Leave side shoots alone until they produce flower buds, then at bloom time shorten the branches to where the flower buds begin.

Like apple trees, pears produce fruit on stubby branches called spurs that remain productive for five to seven years. Prune mature trees to control their height, and thin out the branches so that light can reach the fruiting spurs. Remove crossing limbs, deadwood, and any watersprouts. Prune hardest in the upper, outermost parts of the tree so that most fruit is borne on the lower, stronger limbs.

A clothespin forces wide-angle branching on pears.

Pear trees are easily espaliered: Trained flat, the trees bear well, are ornamental, and take up little space. For more on espalier pruning, see page 118. Dwarf varieties can also be grown as hedges. After normal fruit drop, thin the remaining fruits to one fruit every 6 to 8 inches for best size.

Harvesting: Standard pear trees begin to bear fruit in five or six years, dwarf trees in three or four years. The fruits ripen in August through September. Pick pears by hand one to two weeks before they are completely ripe. Lift the fruit upward with a twisting motion, or cut it, until the stem separates from the spur. If the stem doesn't snap off, leave the pear on the tree to ripen further.

Variety (Zones)	Fruit	Tree	Use, pollination, notes
EUROPEAN PEARS (continued)			
'Taylor's Gold' (5–8)	Large, russet, smooth. Creamy, juicy, tender, rich, sweet, perfumed	Slightly more vigor than 'Comice'. Spreading growth habit	Late-ripening winter dessert pear. Good in Northwest. Pollinate with 'Packham's Triumph' or 'Harrow Delight'. Strain of 'Comice' from New Zealand
ASIAN PEARS			
'20th Century' ('Nijisseiki') (6–9)	Medium-size, yellow with greenish mottling, long stems, thin skin. Juicy, crisp, mild	Very productive. Requires fruit thinning. Disease-prone	Excellent fresh. Stores well. Most common Asian pear. Partially self-fruitful. Pollinate with 'Bartlett'
'Kikusui' (6–9)	Medium-size, greenish yellow, smooth. Sweet, crisp, juicy	Very productive, vigorous, early bearing. Drooping, spreading habit	Keeps well. Pollinate with '20th Century' or 'Bartlett'
'Niitaka' (6–9)	Large, greenish with brown russet. Mild, sweet, crisp, juicy	Very productive	Good to very high quality if tree ripened. Keeps well. Becomes sweeter in storage. Not suitable as a good pollinator
'Shinko' (5–8)	Medium to large, oval, bronze-russet. Rich, distinctive flavor	Early and consistent bearer. Resistant to fire blight, codling moth	Pollinate with '20th Century' or 'Bartlett'
PEAR HYBRIDS			
'Fan Stil' (5–9)	Medium-size, yellow with light red blush. Crisp. Midseason	Vigorous, upright. Bears large crops consistently. Fire blight resistant	Fresh, cooking. From Texas
'Kieffer' (4–9)	Medium to large, green-yellow with red blush. Grainy, average flavor. Late	Fire blight resistant	Canning, cooking. From Pennsylvania
'Monterrey' (5–9)	Large, yellow. Good flavor. Midseason	Fire blight resistant	Fresh, canned. From Mexico
'Orient' (5–9)	Large, yellow, russeted. Juicy, grainy. Mid- to late-season	Very productive	Canning, cooking. Keeps well. From California
'Ure' (3–7)	Small (2"), round, green-yellow. Sweet, juicy. Early	To 18' tall. Sturdy branches. Fire blight resistant	Fresh, canned. From Canada

Fire blight can be a serious problem on pear trees.

Pick European pears when they reach full size but are still hard and green, and ripen them off the tree at room temperature. If they are left on the tree too long, they become soft and mushy around the core before the outside is ready to eat.

Early-maturing summer varieties are best about a week after harvest when kept at room temperature. Or store them for several weeks before ripening. Keep late-maturing winter pears in cold storage for four to six weeks before ripening them at room temperature. Or to store them for a longer time, keeping them near freezing. Otherwise the pears are likely to spoil without ripening.

Harvest Asian pears when they develop their characteristic color and when the stem separates easily from the tree. They need no further ripening but can be held in cold storage in a ripe edible condition much like apples.

Pests and diseases: Pears are susceptible to pear scab, mildew, bacterial blossom blast, and fire blight (see pages 120 and 202). Only fire blight is a serious problem.

Insects such as codling moth (see page 121) and pear psylla are serious pests. Sprays that kill both pests often also kill beneficial insects and predators of them, which allows the pests to rebound. Pear psylla can be controlled with a precisely timed dormant oil spray in late winter or early spring; ask your local county extension agent for help determining when treatment will be most effective. Control of codling moth requires insect control sprays timed to coincide with the hatching of newly laid eggs. Remove watersprouts to reduce the number of aphids. Rake up and destroy dropped fruits and other plant debris to control pear scab and insect pests. Use hardware cloth or plastic guards around the lower part of tree trunks to prevent rabbits and mice from eating the bark.

Persimmon (Diospyros spp.)

Type: Deciduous tree, Zones 5–10
Typical yield: 300–500 pounds per tree
Typical size: 15–60'H×10–20'W

Two species of persimmon are grown in North America. Japanese or Oriental persimmon *(D. kaki)* is the better known: It's the persimmon available in many markets, especially in fall and winter. It grows well in Zones 7 to 10. Although Texas, Florida, and southern Georgia have some commercial orchards, California produces the vast majority of the North American crop. Most of the world crop is grown in China and Japan, where the fruit is well known and highly prized. Japanese persimmon trees are also valued for their brilliant red and orange fall leaf colors in areas where winters are mild and fall color limited.

American persimmon

The American persimmon, or possomwood *(D. virginiana)*, is native to much of the Southeast. Although the tree resembles that of Japanese persimmon, it is much more cold hardy (Zones 5 to 9) and its fruits are smaller, about 1½ inch in diameter or roughly half the size of a Japanese type. The earliest settlers wrote about its

'Fuyu' Oriental persimmon

high-quality flavor, but for various reasons commercial trade has never developed. But the tree is perfect for gardens. American persimmon is often used as a rootstock for Japanese persimmon.

The Japanese species is self-fertile, but American persimmon needs pollination by another tree.

Persimmon fruits are either astringent or nonastringent. The former are eaten only once the fruits are soft-ripe; otherwise they are inedible. Nonastringent persimmons can be safely consumed once they're firm-ripe. Judge the readiness of a nonastringent persimmon just like you would an apple. All American persimmons bear astringent fruit, and Japanese persimmons have one or the other depending on the variety.

The fruits begin to ripen in late September and October. Frosts will hasten the loss of acidity in astringent varieties.

When: Where winters are mild, plant in fall once summer temperatures begin to cool. Elsewhere plant in spring as soon as the soil is workable.

Planting: Persimmons adapt to any fertile soil as long as it drains well. Space trees 20 feet apart.

Growing: Young trees need consistent moisture to develop properly, and where growing seasons are normally dry mature trees need water. Thinning the fruit is unnecessary and impractical for large trees but can help to reduce cleanup around smaller trees. Remove any weak or willowy branches in late winter. Prop up fruit-laden branches to keep them from breaking. Some types may bear fruit only in alternate years.

Oriental persimmon in fall

Harvesting: Trees begin to bear fruit after three to ten years and remain fruitful for many decades. Eat ripe Japanese persimmons out of hand or cut them in half and eat the flesh with a spoon, with or without lemon juice or sugar. The fruit tastes best chilled. Add the flesh to salads, ice cream, or yogurt, or use it to make jams. The puréed pulp is used in baked goods and can be frozen for up to two years. Freeze whole ripe fruits or dry them for long-term storage. Peel whole, unripe, astringent Japanese or American persimmons and dry them.

Pests and diseases: Persimmons in the home garden are relatively disease- and insect-free, although birds and raccoons eat the fruit. Keep debris from trees raked and composted to avoid pest infestations.

Varieties: Oriental: 'Fuyu' has large, round, somewhat flattened, glossy orange-red nonastringent fruit. Eat them when firm; flesh is crunchy, sweet, and mild. It keeps several months in cool storage. The self-fruitful tree is attractive and pest-free, but in the East needs pollination. **'Hachiya'** bears large, astringent acorn-shape fruit. Allow fruits to soften after harvest. It is good for drying while still firm. Vigorous trees are self-fruitful and highly ornamental. **'Saijo'** produces small yellowish orange fruits of excellent quality that are astringent and largely seedless. It is a consistent, heavy bearer, and is self-fruitful.

American: 'Early Golden' has large, sweet fruit with very good quality, although it is not as productive as some of the other varieties. Plant with another variety to encourage heavier fruiting. **'Garretson'** has outstanding flavor, particularly in northern areas. Fruits have tender light orange skin with a red blush, and soft flesh. The tree is a heavy bloomer; fruits ripen in early October. **'John Rick'** is the most widely grown American persimmon. It bears large, attractive fruits late in the year. Pollinate it with **'Yates'**, an early ripening, prolific variety with large fruit of fine flavor.

Pineapple *(Ananas comosus)*

Type: Perennial, Zones 9–11
Typical yield: 2–3 pounds per plant
Typical size: 3–5'H×4–5'W

Pineapple

The pineapple plant is a South American bromeliad that produces a flavorful, sweet fruit. Pineapples grow so well in Hawaii that they have become an important commercial crop there. Plants also grow successfully outdoors in south Florida and somewhat less so in Southern California. However, they can grow and fruit anywhere, even in cold-winter climates, as long as they are brought indoors in winter.

When: Plant at any time.

Planting: Start with crowns (from a pineapple fruit from the grocery store) or offsets from an existing plant. Space them 4 to 6 inches deep and 12 to 18 inches apart in acidic, well-drained sandy loam that is high in organic matter. As an alternative, grow them in containers. Prepare the crowns by either cutting or twisting off the leaves. Remove any fruit flesh that remains because it will rot and destroy the crown. If there are any lower leaves pull them off. Let the crowns dry for two days, then either plant them in loose potting soil in a container or set them in a cup of water until roots form. In summer move the rooted plants in containers outside to a sunny, warm location.

Growing: Pineapples need frequent watering and feeding, especially with nitrogen. Plant food containing magnesium and iron is beneficial. Use either continuous-feed or liquid or soluble fertilizers such as 14-14-14.

Harvesting: After growing for two years a plant produces knobs of reddish flower clusters over a period of two to three weeks. Each flower produces one fruitlet; eventually the fruitlets merge into a single fruit, the pineapple. Test for ripeness by pulling on leaves near the crown; they will be loose on mature fruit. Cut the stalk with a sharp knife a couple of inches below the fruit, then store the fruit whole until you're ready to eat or cook it. A pineapple is sweetest near the base, so the day before you intend to use it, cut off the top and turn the fruit upside down in a shallow bowl in the refrigerator to let the sweet juice filter down through the whole fruit.

Pests and diseases: Mealybugs, scales, and mites are the most common pests. Remove them by washing the leaves in a mild soap solution and rinsing well. Hot sun will usually kill nematodes. Treat rots with a disease control product labeled for pineapple.

Varieties: **'Smooth Cayenne'**, one of the most common varieties, has sweet, highly acidic bright yellow flesh that keeps well. **'Red Spanish'** produces pale yellow to white flesh and is best eaten fresh.

Pineapple guava, feijoa
(Acca sellowiana, formerly Feijoa sellowiana)

Type: Evergreen tree or shrub, Zones 8–11
Typical yield: 25–50 pounds per plant
Typical size: 8–15'H×8–15'W

Pineapple guava

An attractive South American native, pineapple guava bears delicious fruit with an unusual and refreshing pineapple-mint flavor. The round to elongated pear-shape fruits have a waxy, dull blue-green skin. They are best eaten fresh; most people simply cut the fruit in half and scoop out the sweet flesh with a spoon. The seeds are small and edible, and the flower petals are a refreshing addition to spring salads. Pineapple guava grows well in subtropical climates with low humidity.

Pineapple guava doubles as a practical landscape shrub. Its leaves are soft green on top and silvery underneath, flashing nicely in a breeze. In late spring the plant is covered with inch-wide white flowers with scarlet stamens. It responds well to pruning or shearing, but wait until early summer—after you've enjoyed the flowers. When planted close together pineapple guavas make a nice hedge, screen, or windbreak. It also can be espaliered or trained as a small tree with one or more trunks.

For information about tropical, strawberry, and lemon guava, see page 147.

When: Fall is the best time to plant, though planting in any season is all right.

Planting: Choose a partially shaded site to protect the tender fruits from the hot midday sun. Pineapple guava does best in rich, organic acid loam that is well drained. Plant large varieties 15 to 20 feet apart; space smaller ones 10 to 12 feet apart.

Growing: Cool weather improves the flavor of the fruit. Some varieties are more heat tolerant, but all types need watering during extremely hot or dry weather to develop fruit and prevent internal decay. The root system is shallow, so weed by hand or hoe carefully. Use a low-nitrogen plant food for fruit at flowering. Prune lightly after harvest to encourage new growth; fruit sets on young wood. Thinning branches helps air circulate and makes harvesting easier. Remove low-hanging limbs to keep fruit at least 12 inches off the ground. In Zone 8 protect plants from spring frosts.

Harvesting: Plants propagated by air layering or grafting will begin to bear fruit the second year, and plants grown from seed in the third to fifth year. Fruits drop to the ground when ripe. Once fruit drop begins spread a tarp underneath the plant and shake the branches. Almost-mature fruits can be picked and allowed to finish ripening at room temperature but will decay after only a few days. Keep unbruised fruits for up to a week in cool storage.

Pests and diseases: Scale may cause sooty mold. Use dormant oil in winter if infestations are heavy. Fruit flies are attracted to the strong aroma of ripening fruit. Keep the ground beneath and around the plant cleared of dropped flowers, fruits, and other debris.

Varieties: If you have room for just one pineapple guava, plant **'Edenvale Improved Coolidge'**, a self-fertile variety. **'Beechwood'**, **'Coolidge'**, **'Mammoth'**, **'Nazemetz'**, and **'Trask'** are self-fruitful, but cross-pollination will stimulate a better crop.

Plum, prune, plum hybrids (*Prunus* spp.)

Type: Deciduous tree, Zones 2–9
Typical yield: 50–100 pounds per tree
Typical size: 8–25'H×10–20'W

Of all the stone fruits none is more varied in origin, size, color, and flavor than the plum. The many types range from small native plums to comparatively giant Asian varieties. Despite their many differences all are clearly plums with pits that either separate easily from the flesh (freestone) or don't (clingstone).

There are five main groups of plums and hundreds of varieties and hybrids. European plums are varieties of *P. ×domestica*. They have dry, sweet yellow-green freestone flesh and blue or purple skin. Enjoy European plums fresh, canned, dried, or frozen.

Varieties: Plums that are so sweet they don't ferment near

European plum

the pit as they dry are called prunes. European plum trees bloom later than Asian plums and are hardy enough for Michigan and New York, but their need for winter cold limits them from prospering in mild-winter areas. Most European plums are self-fruitful and do not need pollination by another tree (exceptions are noted in the table beginning on page 163.)

One category of European plum is the institia or damson (*P. ×domestica institia*). Originating in the Middle East, the trees are smaller, more compact, and more cold hardy; they grow wherever apples thrive. Their fruits are smaller, nearly round, and usually blue but sometimes yellow. The damsons interbreed freely with all European plums.

Japanese plums are varieties of *P. salicina*. They have large sweet, juicy fruits with red skin. Excellent eaten fresh, they may also be canned or made into jams and jellies. Japanese plums thrive throughout much of North America, but the highest-quality fruit develops in areas with warm, dry summers. They grow well in California (but not southernmost Florida). Because they flower early, Japanese plums often lose crops to late spring frosts along the northern edge of their range. Some Japanese plums are self-fruitful, but most require another Japanese plum variety nearby for pollination.

Native plums make up another category; some half-dozen types are in commerce. These fast-growing trees, which are

'Green Gage' plum

hardy and pest free, thrive in just about every soil and climate. Many produce large quantities of fruits that birds and wildlife depend on and that people use primarily for jams and jellies. Native plums have been crossed with Japanese plums, creating entirely new sorts of fruits that combine the hardiness of the native with the high fruit quality of the Japanese varieties.

The final group consists of the plum hybrids, which resulted from crossing plums

Asian plum variety

with other stone fruits such as apricots and peaches. The result is completely new fruits, with different varieties reflecting various degrees of one parent or another. Most plum hybrids require another tree as a pollinator, but many nurseries offer multiple, pollen-compatible varieties grafted onto a single tree.

Plum trees are relatively small. A height of 12 to 15 feet is typical if the tree is pruned annually. Many tend to be somewhat wider. Some varieties are genetically small, and some are available on a semidwarf rootstock, which produces a slightly smaller tree. Most trees are productive for 10 to 15 years.

When: Plant bare-root trees in late winter or early spring. Fall planting of container-grown trees is fine where winters are mild.

Planting: Choose a sunny, protected location with deep, rich, fertile loam. If late spring frosts are a problem in your area plant on the north side of your property; otherwise a south-facing slope is the best site. Plant the tree at the same depth it grew in the nursery. Space standard-size trees 20 feet apart, semidwarf trees 15 feet apart, and dwarf trees and shrubs 8 to 10 feet apart.

After planting the tree cut it back to 3 to 4 feet. Spread a layer of well-rotted manure or compost under the canopy and cover that with a couple of inches of mulch to the drip line, but keep both away from the trunk.

Growing: Because European plums have deep roots they can tolerate heavy soils. With their shallower roots Japanese plums can't withstand waterlogged soil, but they are drought-resistant.

Established European plums should grow 12 inches a year, and Japanese plums up to 20 inches. If your trees put on less growth, have your soil analyzed to determine the nutrient deficiencies before adding any fertilizers. Overfeeding encourages new succulent growth, which is susceptible to pests and diseases.

Train European plums to a central leader, and Japanese plums and all shrub types to an open center (see page 115). Prune after flowering to remove dead or diseased wood. The fruits develop on long-lived spurs. European fruits develop toward the interior of the tree, so thinning the branches promotes ripening. Thin the branches of native plums, which are shrubby, to make harvesting easier.

Thin the fruits by hand after normal fruit drop, leaving only the best plum on each spur and 4 to 6 inches between fruits. Red-fruit varieties need more thinning than blue ones, and heavily fruiting branches may need to be propped up.

Black knot disease of plum

Harvesting: Plums are ready to harvest when they come off in your hand with a gentle twist. Sample a few from different parts of the tree before harvesting a significant amount. European plums must ripen on the tree but should be picked before they are mushy. Ripe plums left on the tree will rot; dry them for use as prunes. Pick Japanese

TOP GARDEN PLUMS

Variety (Zones)	Fruit	Tree	Uses, pollination, notes
EUROPEAN PLUMS AND PRUNES	*Prunus ×domestica*		
'Castleton' (5–9)	Medium to large, blue, egg-shape. Firm, yellow-green flesh. Rich flavor	Consistent heavy production. Spreading tree	All uses. Nonfragmenting pit. Self-fruitful
'Damson' ('French Damson') (5–7) *P. ×domestica institia*	Small, dark blue. Tart, juicy, yellow flesh	Vigorous, productive	Canning. Self-fruitful
'Green Gage' ('Reine Claude') (5–9)	Small to medium, yellow-green. Sweet, juicy, smooth textured	Low branching, productive	Dessert, all other uses. Self-fruitful but better with pollinator
'Laxton Gage' ('Early Laxton') (4–9)	Medium-size, pink-orange, freestone. Meaty yellow flesh	Very productive, upright. Low maintenance	Dessert, cooking. May be a hybrid of 'Green Gage' and 'Mirabelle'. Self-fruitful. High in vitamin C
'Longjohn' (4–9)	Very large, long teardrop shape, dark blue. Amber flesh, freestone, prune-type.	Crops early to bear. Requires fruit thinning. Vigorous, productive, spreading	Partially self-fruitful, but heavier crops with pollination
'Mirabelle' (4–9) *P. ×domestica institita*	Small, dark golden-orange skin with red spots. Smooth textured, sweet, flavorful	Spreading, very productive. Harvest by shaking tree and collecting fruits in a net	Fresh, jams, pies, tarts, wine, brandy. A European favorite. Needs pollinator
'Oullin's Golden Gage' ('Reine Claude d'Oullin') (4–9)	Medium-size, golden yellow. Very succulent green-yellow flesh. Excellent flavor	Moderate vigor. May bear only alternate years. Late flowering	Excellent dessert. Ideal for preserves. Self-fertile. Subject to brown rot. From France
'President' (4–9)	Very large, blue-black to maroon, freestone, Fine-textured, yellow flesh. Late	Vigorous, very productive	Keeps well. Pollinate with 'Stanley'
'Richard's Early Italian' ('Early Italian') (5–9)	Medium to large, purple, freestone. Flesh greenish	Vigorous, productive	Fresh, canning, drying. Self-fertile
'Seneca' (5–9)	Large, reddish blue, freestone. Flesh yellow, crisp	Vigorous, upright. Consistent bearer	High dessert quality. Self-fruitful. Crack- and brown-rot resistant
'Stanley' (4–8)	Medium to large, dark blue skin. Flesh yellow-green, firm, sweet, rich flavored	Early bearing and consistent. Heavy annual production	Excellent all-purpose, fresh, dried, canned. Self-fertile but yields heavier with pollinator
JAPANESE PLUMS	*Prunus salicina*		
'Au Rosa' (5–9)	Small to medium-size, red. Firm, sweet yellow flesh	Needs thinning for best fruit size	Disease-resistant. From Alabama
'Black Amber' (6–9)	Large, dark purple to black, freestone. Flesh, yellow, sweet, firm. Early	Grows vigorously. Heavy bearing	Requires pollinator such as 'Satsuma', 'Santa Rosa'
'Burbank' (5–9)	Large, yellow-red, clingstone. Flesh yellow, sweet. Early	Low growing, drooping	Requires pollinator such as 'Early Golden'
'Early Golden' (5–9)	Large, yellow with red blush. Golden flesh	Tends to alternate bear	Good quality. Requires pollinator such as 'Burbank'
'Friar' (6–9)	Large, dark purple to black, freestone. Flesh, yellow, firm, sweet	Tends to overbear. Fruit needs thinning	Partially self-fruitful. Better pollinated by 'Black Amber', 'Santa Rosa', or 'Wickson'. Resists cracking
'Methley' (5–9)	Medium to large, reddish purple. Juicy, mild, sweet. Distinctive flavor	Early blooming, attractive, vigorous, upright. Does well in many soil types	Fresh or jellies. Excellent all-purpose plum. Low chill. Self-fruitful
'Santa Rosa' (5–9)	Large, dark red, clingstone. Yellow flesh, firm, tart-sweet. Midseason	Large, vigorous, productive	Fresh, canned. Produces well in West. Self-pollinating. Low chill
'Satsuma' (6–9)	Large, dark red. Flesh red, firm, meaty. Excellent, distinctive flavor. Small pit	Vigorous, upright	Fresh, cooking, canning, preserves. Partially self-fruitful. Better pollinated by 'Santa Rosa' or 'Wickson'

Chart continued on next page

TOP GARDEN PLUMS (continued)

Variety (Zones)	Fruit	Tree	Uses, pollination, notes
'Shiro' (5–9)	Medium to large, yellow with pink blush, clingstone. Flesh yellow, mild, sweet	Spreading habit. Bears consistently. Requires thinning	Fresh, cooking, canning, preserves, dessert. Low chill. Pollinate with 'Early Golden', 'Methley', 'Santa Rosa', or 'Satsuma'
'Vanier' (6–9)	Medium-size, red with yellow blush, clingstone. Yellow flesh is firm, meaty, improves with storage	Vigorous, productive, upright	Fresh. Excellent for keeping. Cross of 'Wickson' and 'Burbank'
'Wickson' (6–9)	Large, heart shape, greenish yellow. Firm, sweet flesh	Medium-size, upright, vigorous	Fresh, cooking. Partially self-fruitful. Better pollinated by 'Friar'
CHERRY, NATIVE, AND HYBRID PLUMS			
American plum, *P. americana* (2–9)	Small, red and yellow	10–20' tall. Good fall color	Fresh, jams, jellies, preserves. Excellent wildlife food. 'Newport', 'Fairlane', 'Manet' named varieties
Beach plum, *P. maritima* (4–8)	Very small, black, blue, red, or yellow	To 6' in sandy soil. Tolerates salinity. Can be used as a hedge or grown in a container	Fresh, cooking, canning, jams, preserves. 'Grant' (1", blue), 'Red' (red), 'Flava', (yellow), and 'Dunbars' (red freestone) are hybrids
Canada plum, *P. nigra* (2–8)	Small, oval, red	To 10' tall	Preserves
Chickasaw plum, *P. angustifolia* (4–9)	Small, red. Tart flesh	Fast to 12–25' tall. Bears alternate years. Best pruned to central leader	Jellies
Delight cherry plum, *P. salicina* ×*P. cerasifera* (5–10)	Small to medium-size. Blue-black skin and yellow flesh. Flavorful, tangy, clingstone	To 10' tall. Heavy crops. Very productive, even under adverse conditions	Hybrid of cherry plum and Japanese plum. Pollinate with 'Sprite'
'Pipestone' (2–7)	Small, red with yellow flesh. High quality	Vigorous, productive	Jams, jellies. Hybrid of Japanese with native plum. Requires native plum pollinator. From Minnesota
Sloe plum, *P. spinosa* (2–9)	Very small, dark blue.	4' tall and wide	Bitter fresh, but excellent jams, jellies. Also used to flavor gin.
'Sprite' cherry plum, *P. salicina* ×*P. cerasifera* (5–10)	Small, black, freestone. Flesh yellow, sweet, flavorful	To 10' tall	Fresh. Holds well on tree. Self-fruitful, but better pollinated with 'Delight'

Yellow plums

Red plums

'Dapple Dandy' pluot

Beach plum

plums before they are completely ripe; they will continue to ripen off the tree. Native plums are ready to harvest when they are soft. Store all types of ripe plums for up to two weeks in the refrigerator. All sweet-flesh varieties are excellent eaten out of hand or added to fresh fruit salads, and they also can be used for cooking and canning. Tart varieties are good in jams, jellies, preserves, baked goods, and wine.

Pests and diseases: Plums are susceptible to black knot, a fungus that produces hard black bumps on twigs and branches. Prune out infected areas in winter by cutting the wood well below the knots and destroying the cuttings; sterilize your pruning tools between cuts. Use a labeled disease control product to prevent brown rot. Prune away diseased and damaged wood immediately, and keep the ground around trees clear of dropped fruit and other plant debris, which harbors pests and encourages diseases.

Avoid most diseases by choosing resistant varieties and practicing clean cultural habits to keep pests away. Spray dormant oil in winter to control aphids, scale, and borers.

Variety (Zones)	Fruit	Tree	Uses, pollination, notes
CHERRY, NATIVE, AND HYBRID PLUMS *(continued)*			
'Superior', *P. salicina* ×*P. americana* (3–9)	Medium-size, dark red, clingstone. Yellow flesh.	Bears heavily at an early age. Showy spring flowers	Pollinate with 'Toka' or other Japanese plum. From Minnesota
'Toka', *P. americana* ×*P. simonii* (2–7)	Medium to large, red-bronze, freestone. Flesh yellow, firm, meaty, sweet, spicy	Vigorous, upright, vase shaped, to 15' tall. Needs pruning. Bears heavily	Self-fertile. Excellent pollinator for many plums
'Underwood', *P. salicina* 'Shiro' ×*P. americana* (2–7)	Large, dark red, smooth skin, clingstone. Pale yellow flesh. Rich flavor	Vigorous. Bears annually	Fresh, jam. Pollinate with 'Toka'
PLUM, APRICOT, AND PEACH HYBRIDS			
'Dapple Dandy' pluot (6–9)	Large, maroon-yellow, mottled, freestone. Flesh pale pink to red, firm. Excellent flavor	Requires hot summer to reach full flavor	Pollinate with 'Flavor Supreme'. Use to pollinate any other pluot
'Flavor Delight' aprium (6–9)	Medium to large, yellow. Flesh yellow, firm like apricot. Unique flavor	Vigorous, upright, apricotlike. Maintain to 10' tall	Self-fertile, but better pollinated by any apricot
'Flavor Grenade' pluot (6–9)	Large, elongated, green with red blush. Flesh crisp. Excellent flavor	Requires hot summer to reach full flavor	Ripens over 6 weeks. Pollinate with any Japanese plum
'Flavor King' pluot (6–9)	Large. Red. Flesh red, sweet, flavors of both plum and apricot	Requires hot summer to reach full flavor	Excellent quality. Pollinate with 'Flavor Supreme' or 'Santa Rosa'
'Flavor Queen' pluot (6–9)	Large. Green-yellow. Flesh sweet, juicy. Apricot aftertaste	Requires hot summer to reach full flavor	Pollinate with 'Mehley' or 'Santa Rosa'
'Flavorich' pluot (6–9)	Large, purple. Flesh yellow-orange, firm, sweet, apricot aftertaste	Vigorous, upright	Excellent quality, plumlike. Pollinate with any other pluot
'Flavor Supreme' pluot (6–9)	Large, maroon and green mottled. Flesh red, very sweet. Distinctive flavor	Requires hot summer to reach full flavor	Pollinate with any Japanese plum or other pluot, and use to pollinate any other pluot
'Honey Rich' aprium (6–9)	Medium to large, bright orange. Flesh orange, firm, acidic, sweet-tart	Large, vigorous, semispreading. Consistent, heavy production	Hangs well on tree. Delicate skin discolors easily. Pollinate with any Japanese plum
'Plum Parfait' plumcot (4–8)	Large, orange-pink, freestone. Flesh marbled red and orange. Flavorful	Small, to 15' tall. Requires annual pruning	Self-fruitful
'Tri-Lite' peach-plum (7–9)	Large, red, clingstone. Flesh white. Peach and plum flavors. Early	Very productive. Showy pink spring flowers. Tolerates both hot and mild summers	Fresh, canned. Peach-plum hybrid. Self-fertile

Use insect controls on heavy infestations of plum curculio; to protect bees and other beneficial pollinators, avoid spraying when trees are in bloom. Use netting to protect fruit from birds, and trunk wraps in winter to prevent damage from rodents. See page 194 for more information about pests.

Varieties: If you have room for just one tree, choose either a self-fruitful variety or a tree with several varieties grafted onto it.

Pomegranate *(Punica granatum)*

Type: Evergreen or deciduous tree or shrub, Zones 8–11
Typical yield: 10–20 pounds per tree
Typical size: 10–20'H×10–20'W

A shiny-leaf plant native to Iran and northern India, pomegranate grows around the world in Mediterranean climates as well as in hot valleys and deserts. Its red flowers, reminiscent of carnations, bloom for several weeks. Its large roundish fruits, which may be 3 to 5 inches across, are yellow overlaid with pink or red and contain sacs of seedy, sweet-tart, juicy pulp. The fruits are quite showy, especially in autumn, when they turn bright red. The plant is self-fruitful, requiring no pollinator.

Where adapted, pomegranate is easy to grow and few pests or diseases bother it. The plant does well in a wide range of soils, including somewhat saline types, and does not need much water or fertilizer. It can be trained as a tree by selecting one or more strong shoots or can be grown as a shrub or espalier.

When: The best time to plant is in fall once temperatures begin to moderate, but planting in any season is fine.

Planting: Choose a sunny, warm location with moist, well-drained soil. Plants may produce less and poor-quality fruit in sandy and clay soils, but they are tolerant of alkalinity. Space plants 10 to 20 feet apart.

Pomegranate

Growing: Pomegranate does best where winters are cool and summers hot and dry. It is drought-tolerant, but yields improve when the soil is consistently moist. Water young plants until they are established, and mature ones with ripening fruit. Fertilize mature plants with a 10-10-10 plant food once in spring for the first two years. Apply a mulch annually, but keep it from touching the trunk. Plants can be pruned to a few trunks or trained as fountain-shape shrubs for ornamental value. For multiple trunks select five or six suckers to develop, then remove all the others. Fruit forms on the tips of the current year's growth, so prune young trees and shrubs to encourage new shoots on all sides. After the third year prune out only deadwood and suckers.

Harvesting: The fruits ripen 180 to 220 days after flowering, from July through September. Ones that are ready for harvest make a slight tinny or cracking sound when tapped. Allow them to ripen on the plant, but clip them off before they become overripe and crack; flavor will improve in storage. Fruits can be kept for six months in cool but not freezing temperatures and high humidity. Extract the juice by reaming halved fruits in a juicer. To eat a pomegranate fresh, cut it into sections, peel the rind, and eat the seeds.

Pests and diseases: Apply a forceful water spray periodically to prevent spider mites. Excessive moisture causes heart rot. Cover ripening fruits with netting or bags to protect them from birds.

Varieties: '**Ambrosia**' has large fruits with a pink rind and purple pulp. '**Eversweet**' fruits are nearly seedless and the juice doesn't stain. Early-ripening '**Granada**' bears pink flowers followed by fruits with a dark red rind and sweet pink pulp. '**Sweet**' is greenish with a red blush when ripe but much sweeter than other varieties. '**Utah Sweet**' has pink skin and pulp and soft seeds. '**Wonderful**' bears large dark purple-red fruit with juicy deep red flesh.

Possomwood *(see Persimmon)*
Raspberry *(see Brambles)*

Sapote, white sapote *(Casimiroa edulis)*

Type: Evergreen tree, Zones 9–10
Typical yield: 300–1,000 pounds per tree
Typical size: 15–50'H×15–50'W

The sapote is a distinctive, large tree with glossy bright green leaves. It produces an abundance of round yellow or green fruit, 3 to 4 inches in diameter, with a delicious flavor reminiscent of peach or banana. The smooth-texture flesh contains three to five large seeds. Varieties with green skin have white flesh, and those with yellow skin have yellow flesh. A mature sapote tree produces such a huge crop that it is almost impossible for one family to pick all the fruits, let alone consume them. Unpicked fruits can be a problem because they drop from the tree as they ripen, making a mess and attracting bees and other insects.

When: The optimum planting time is fall, but any time is acceptable.

'McDill' Sapote

Planting: Sapote succeeds anywhere that orange trees do. Plant in any well-drained soil away from patios or other areas where bees, flies, and ants would be a nuisance and where fallen twigs and fruit would make a mess. After planting the tree pinch out the terminal bud at the tip of the main stem to encourage branching.

Growing: The tree is drought-tolerant but does best with regular deep watering to discourage surface roots that ruin lawns or break through pavement. An established tree tolerates wet roots and some frost to 25°F. Sapote requires regular applications of nitrogen fertilizer to maintain healthy growth. In years when the tree carries a heavy crop apply a little extra nitrogen to help offset its tendency to bear crops in alternate years. As the tree matures prune it to encourage compact growth and to control size.

Harvesting: Grafted trees bear fruit in three or four years. The apple-size fruit ripens six to nine months after the flowers bloom, from midsummer to February depending on the sapote variety and your locale. Tree-ripened fruit has the best flavor but is likely to fall first; the fruit bruises easily and the flesh beneath the bruise turns bitter. Handle the fruits gently and as little as possible. Clip mature fruits with short stems attached; the stems will fall off when the fruit is ready to eat. Store ripe fruits in the refrigerator for up to two weeks. Eat fresh fruit out of hand or in salads, or mash and freeze the pulp to use in ice cream or baked goods. Avoid eating the peel, which is bitter, and seeds, which are toxic.

Pests and diseases: Temperature extremes cause a temporary loss of leaves, and winds can cause fruit drop. Control weeds, which can harbor insect pests, and use snail baits against snails. Discourage fruit flies by collecting and destroying fallen fruit and other plant debris. Prune and destroy branches infested with black scale. Spray mealybugs with insecticidal soap. Control aphids with a sharp spray from the garden hose; use insecticidal soap for heavy infestations. Birds eat the fruit; be prepared to share it.

Varieties: '**Bravo**', '**Lemon Gold**', '**Louise**', '**McDill**', '**Suebelle**', '**Michele**', and '**Vernon**' are nearly everbearing small to medium-size trees that grow well in California. '**Denzler**' is grown in Hawaii.

Serviceberry, shadbush, saskatoon
(Amelanchier spp.)

Type: Deciduous tree or shrub, Zones 2–9
Typical yield: 5–10 pounds per plant
Typical size: 6–30'H×3–30'W

Allegheny serviceberry

A small native understory tree or shrub, serviceberry goes unnoticed most of the year. But after a long, cold northern winter, suddenly in early spring, ahead of most other plants, serviceberry bursts into life with a cloud of white flowers. In the woods and along river banks it's the plant in bloom so it is very obvious and prominent.

This timing of spring bloom largely accounts for many of its various common names. It was called serviceberry (sometimes pronounced "sarvisberry") because its flowers were the only ones available for the services held by traveling preachers who reached settlers after a long winter (or so one story goes). The name shadbush supposedly notes the coincidence of the tree's bloom with the migration of shad up Atlantic coastal rivers. Juneberry and sugarplum refer to the sweet berries, which usually are compared to black currants or blueberries. Early natives and settlers combined the berries with meat to make pemmican. More often today the fruits are used just like raisins and other dried fruits, or in jams, puddings, and jellies. Saskatoon refers to the city in Saskatchewan, Canada, which is in a region where the berries are grown commercially.

Serviceberry trees are highly variable, some being low shrubs and others growing to 25 feet or taller. All have thin, pale gray limbs and pointed leaf buds. The hard and strong wood was used by natives to make bows. The leaves emerge pale pink and coppery bronze just after bloom. The berries appear early, by June in most areas. In fall the shiny green leaves shift to shades of brilliant red, orange, and brown.

When: Plant in late winter or early spring as soon as the soil is workable. Or plant in late summer once weather cools.

Planting: To protect crops from late spring frosts, plant serviceberry on the cooler, north side of your property. Avoid low spots where cold air will collect. Any well-drained soil is acceptable. Plants grow about a third to a half as wide as tall; allow about 8 feet in each direction for tree types, and for a hedge about 5 feet.

Growing: Keep the soil around a new plant moist the first year, and mulch to help sustain the moisture. An established serviceberry needs little additional water. Maintain soil fertility by spreading a thin layer of compost around the plant in late summer. For best crops, prune in mid summer after harvest. Remove weak, diseased, damaged, and low branches, and also thin crowding and old, unproductive branches from the center of the tree.

Harvesting: Serviceberry crops begin within two to four years. The berries develop on growth that is at least one year old, but the best fruit is borne on the youngest, most vigorous branches. Before picking sample a few berries to check for ripeness, then rake the small berries off the branches with your hands.

Pests and diseases: Fire blight is the most significant pest. Powdery mildew and rust sometimes occur. For more about these diseases, see page 202.

Varieties: North America is home to three or four serviceberry species, and confusion arises because they hybridize freely. The species best known for its fruits is *A. alnifolia,* called **saskatoon**. It grows to 20 feet tall and has several named varieties. **'Pembina'** and **'Smoky'** both have excellent fruits similar to blueberries. **'Indian'** and **'Shannon'** bear large crops of relatively large fruits. The berries of **'Success'** and the 8-foot-tall **'Dwarf Mountain'** are black when ripe. **'Regent'** grows to only 6 feet tall.

The tall serviceberries include **shadblow serviceberry**, *A. canadensis,* and Allegheny or **smooth serviceberry**, *A. laevis,* both of which grow 25 feet tall or more. **Apple serviceberry**, *A. ×grandiflora,* a natural hybrid of *A. arborea* and *A. laevis,* has named varieties selected for their ornamental qualities. All are ornamental, and produce edible fruits that birds love.

Soursop *(see Cherimoya)*

Strawberry *(Fragaria ×ananassa)*

Type: Perennial, Zones 3–10
Typical yield: ½ to 1½ pounds per plant
Typical size: 6"H×18"W

Given the many varieties of strawberries, often tailored for specific regions, just about any gardener in any climate can produce a crop, which is one reason strawberries are the most popular garden berry. The other reason has to do with strawberries themselves, especially ripe, red, juicy ones. The only downside to strawberries is the bending over required to harvest them. But you can beat that too by growing them in raised beds, containers, or even hanging baskets.

'Honeoye' strawberry

Growing about 6 inches high, strawberry plants have pretty semi-evergreen leaves made up of three oval leaflets with toothed edges.

Strawberries varieties are either June-bearing (also called spring-bearing) or day-neutral (also called everbearing). June-bearing types respond to the lengthening days and shorter nights of spring by flowering and setting a crop that matures in late spring or early summer. In some climates June-bearers may also set another, much smaller crop during the short days of fall. Day-neutral strawberries flower and produce fruit anytime temperatures are between 35° and 85°F. Instead of one main crop in early summer, the harvest is spread through the summer into fall. The main disadvantage of day-neutrals is that they don't ripen as many fruits at once for preserving.

'Tribute' strawberry

Row cover to protect strawberry crop

Strawberries ready to harvest

Strawberry plants are short-lived but continually renew themselves. The renewal happens mostly in summer when the plants produce runners. Renewing the patch consists of removing older plants and replacing them with healthy young plants. However, various diseases conspire to wear down plants so that many gardeners simply remove the entire patch and replace it with new plants every four or five years.

Before purchasing bare-root plants inspect them for signs of winter injury, mold, and root rot. Any plants that show evidence of winter injury, such as brown or orange coloration inside the crown, are likely to die if the weather quickly turns hot and dry after planting. Heavy mold on the roots and crowns indicates that the plants weren't stored properly. If plants are moldy, don't purchase them. Store healthy plants in a refrigerator until you are ready to plant.

When: Plant in early spring where winters are cold but in either late winter or fall where winters are relatively mild.

Planting: Choose a warm, sunny, elevated location for good surface drainage. A well-drained loam or sandy loam is preferable. Amend the soil with well-rotted manure or compost. If your soil is predominantly clay, plant in raised beds that are least 6 inches deep. If the soil is still frozen when bare-root plants arrive, or when they're available at nurseries, refrigerate them until the ground has thawed. To plant dig a hole large enough so that the roots can extend vertically, then cover the plants with soil to just below the crown. Do not bury the crowns. You may need to cut the roots back to 4 inches before planting to avoid J-shape root systems. During the first few weeks after planting make sure the plants

SOLVING STRAWBERRY DISEASE AND PEST PROBLEMS

● **Botrytis fruit rot (gray mold):**
Prevalent during prolonged rainy and cloudy periods just before or during harvest, botrytis is the most common and serious fungus disease of strawberry plants. Under favorable conditions healthy fruit can rot within two days of picking. Infection begins as soft, light brown areas. Later a gray dust of spores covers the fruit as it shrivels. Handling diseased fruit while picking spreads the fungus.
Solution: Prevent the problem with good weed control and by not overfertilizing with nitrogen.

● **Red stele:** Most common in low-lying, poorly drained areas, red stele can spread throughout an entire strawberry patch, especially during cool, wet springs. Infected plants are stunted, lose their shiny luster, and fail to send out runners; the plants quickly wilt and die with the first hot, dry weather of the season. To identify red stele as the culprit, dig up ailing plants and look at their roots. Infected plants have few new roots compared with healthy plants, whose roots are thick and bushy. Peel away the outer portion of the white roots and the central part (stele) appears pink to red or brownish red instead of the normal yellowish white.
Solution: The best way to control red stele is to plant only resistant varieties.

● **Slugs:** For details on controlling these well-known pests of many garden plants, see page 210.

● **Strawberry bud weevil:** The dark reddish brown weevil cuts flower buds and severs stems, causing blossom loss. It comes out of hiding in spring when temperatures approach 60°F. Damage is most likely near woodlots, where the weevil overwinters. Injury is often evident before and during bloom. Late varieties usually suffer the most harm.
Solution: Row covers will protect the plants but only until the covers are removed to allow pollinators in. An insect control product may be necessary to stop the pest. Clean up and remove debris at the end of the growing season.

● **Tarnished plant bug:** This pest appears in the strawberry patch when the plants start to bloom. The brownish adults are about ¼ inch long and marked with yellowish and black spots. Injured berries remain small, have a woody texture, and fail to mature. Seediness around the fruit tip, called button berry, occurs when the bug punctures young fruits before they fully develop. The tarnished plant bug is more troublesome in fields bordered by woods and fencerows or where weeds are plentiful.
Solution: If you confirm its presence consider using an insect control product to prevent the damage it causes.

● **Verticillium wilt:** In new strawberry plantings this disease often appears about the time runners form. With older plants symptoms appear just before the berries ripen. Although the symptoms vary, the outer older leaves turn reddish or dark brown at the margins and between the veins. Affected plants wilt and die.
Solution: To minimize the disease start off with healthy plants and do not plant them in low-lying, wet areas. Sterilize your garden tools before using them in the strawberry patch.

have adequate water.

Strawberry plants are also available as container-grown plants at many garden centers and nurseries.

Plant June-bearing strawberries in a matted-row pattern. Set plants 12 to 24 inches apart in rows 48 inches apart. Remove the flowers the

Matted-row planting system

first season to encourage the growth of runners, which will produce daughter plants at their ends. Choose six to eight daughter plants to fill out a row 12 to 18 inches wide. Mulch immediately after planting.

Because day-neutral strawberries do not send out as many runners as June-bearers, manage them differently. Plant them in either single rows or staggered double rows. For single rows space plants 5 to 9 inches apart in rows about 42 inches apart. For double rows stagger plants 10 to 18 inches apart in two 8-inch-wide rows that are 42 inches apart. To maximize the yield of berries remove all runners that form the first season. Mulch right after planting and remove any flowers that form for several weeks.

Growing: About six weeks after planting June-bearers, apply 2 pounds of 10-10-10 fertilizer per 100 linear feet of row. Apply another 2 pounds in early September before flower buds form. Sprinkle the fertilizer evenly over the row but not on the plant leaves. Avoid cultivating since the shallow roots are easily damaged.

Strawberry plants need about 1 inch of water each week. Water at times other than late evening to avoid keeping the plants wet for long periods and encouraging disease.

Remove mulch in early spring.

Keep the strawberry patch weed free, especially in the first few months after planting. In fall cover the plants with a mulch of clean straw to prevent injury from low temperatures. Apply the straw when nighttime temperatures approach 20°F, and cover the plants 2 to 6 inches deep. Remove the mulch in early spring after the threat of severe cold weather has passed. Move the mulch between the rows to help smother weeds and to keep mud from splashing onto the fruit.

Renovate June-bearers immediately after harvesting to reduce diseases, stimulate vigorous new growth, and prolong the life of your planting. Mow or clip the plants to a height of 3 inches. Collect your clippings in the mower bag or rake them off and take them to the compost pile. Till between the rows to incorporate the straw. Apply 5 pounds of 10-10-10 fertilizer per 100 feet of row.

Fertilize day-neutral strawberries with 3 to 6 pounds of 10-10-10 per 100 feet of row each month from June through September in the first year, and from May through September in subsequent years. Day-neutrals produce best

Mow after harvest to renovate.

their first season, but you can overwinter them by covering them with straw just as you would do with June-bearers.

Harvesting: Begin harvesting June-bearing strawberries the year after planting—about 14 months from planting in northern climates and 9 months in warmer regions. Day-neutral plants will be

Till between rows to control weeds.

TOP GARDEN STRAWBERRIES

Variety (Zones)	Fruit	Plant	Pests, growing
JUNE-BEARING			
'Allstar' (4–8)	Large, light orange-red. Flesh red, firm, sweet. Late	Large, vigorous. Produces many runners	Excellent disease resistance. Very reliable, productive. Good in Northeast
'Cabot' (4–8)	Very large, bright red, firm. Late	Reliable producer	Good disease resistance except susceptible to gray mold. Good in Northeast. From Nova Scotia
'Cavendish' (3–8)	Very large, dark red. Good flavor. Early to midseason	Tremendous yields. Many runners	Red stele disease-resistant. Good in Northeast. From Nova Scotia
'Earliglow' (4–8)	Large, shiny, dark red, firm. Outstanding flavor. Early	Vigorous, productive. Many runners	Excellent disease resistance. Recommended for mid-Atlantic, North, Northeast. Fruit size diminishes as season progresses. From Maryland
'Honeoye' (3–8)	Large, bright red, slightly tart. Long picking season begins early	Vigorous, very productive, dark green leaves. Many runners	Susceptible to soilborne diseases. Tolerates leaf spot and scorch, fruit rot. Best in New England, Great Lakes region
'Jewel' (4–8)	Rich red. Excellent flavor. Large berry size all season. Late	Compact, dark green. Moderate number of runners	Widely grown. Low fruit rot. Susceptible to verticillium wilt and red stele
'Lateglow' (6–8)	Very large, deep red, glossy, firm, sweet, aromatic. Good quality. Late	Reliable producer. High yielding, medium-size. Many runners	Susceptible to leaf blight and anthracnose. Excellent for extending harvest
'Northeaster' (4–8)	Large, dark red, firm. Strong flavor, aroma. Slight grape aftertaste. Early	Very productive	Best adapted to Northeast. Higher quality than 'Earliglow'. Resists red stele. Susceptible to powdery mildew
'Sable' (4–8)	Large, dark red. Excellent flavor. Early	Productive. Flowers open very early	Best for direct retail and u-pick. Red stele–resistant. From Nova Scotia
DAY-NEUTRAL			
'Seascape' (4–8)	Large, bright red, firm, sweet. Early summer to fall	Vigorous, medium-size, high yielding	Virus-resistant, widely adapted. From California
'Tribute' (3–10)	Medium-size, bright red. Pleasing acidic flavor. Summer to fall	Provides crops when others don't but requires more effort	Widely available. Good disease resistance. For upper South, Pacific Northwest
'Tristar' (3–10)	Similar to 'Tribute' but smaller and sweeter. Summer to fall	Provides crops when others don't but requires more effort	Widely available and adapted. Good disease resistance. Attractive in hanging baskets
ALPINE (F. VESCA)			
'Rugen' ('Improved Rugen') (3–9)	Large, dark red, tangy, flavorful. Midsummer to fall	Vigorous, low growing. Produces no runners	Hardy. Tolerates some shade and grows well in containers

ready to harvest about 90 days after planting. The highest yields will come from the youngest plants. The berries will be ready to pick about a month after the plants bloom. Regardless of size berries are ripe when they attain full color for their variety. Ripe berries left on the plants will quickly become overripe and start to decay and attract pests, so collect all the ripe berries each time you pick. Harvest as often as every other day. Pinch the stems between your thumbnail and forefinger, leaving the leaf cap and short stem attached. Store unwashed berries in the refrigerator for up to a week. Enjoy fresh berries out of hand; sliced, sugared, and served with milk or cream; in salads and on breakfast cereal; and as the essential ingredient in strawberry shortcake. Use them in pies and other baked goods; for juice, jam, jelly, and marmalade; and added to ice cream, yogurt, and smoothies. Freeze strawberries for up to a year for use in cooked recipes.

Pests and diseases: Because strawberries carry hard-to-manage virus diseases, it's important to buy only dormant, virus-indexed plants from a reliable nursery. Several other pests and diseases (listed on page 168) damage plants and fruits. Birds, rabbits, raccoons, and chipmunks seek out strawberries. Chicken wire or bird netting is the only reliable protection.

Varieties: Strawberries are bred to succeed in specific climates and conditions. Select June-bearing or day-neutral varieties grown for your locale.

Alpine strawberry (F. vesca), also called fraise de bois and wood strawberry, is day-neutral. Most alpine varieties are propagated from seed and are often grown as ornamental plants, although some are grown for their fruit. The plants produce most heavily in late summer, tolerate some shade, and grow well in containers; they do not create runners, but spread by self-seeding.

Strawberry guava (see Guava)
Sugar apple (see Cherimoya)
Sugarplum (see Serviceberry)
Sweetsop (see Cherimoya)
Tayberry (see Brambles)
Tropical guava (see Guava)
White sapote (see Sapote)

Growing culinary herbs

◄ Herb gardens are surprisingly productive and will yield baskets full of fragrant or useful leaves, flowers, stems, or roots.

▼ A basket of mint, marjoram, and sage is more fragrant than many flower bouquets, and convenient to the kitchen or barbecue.

Fill your life with herbs. They will bring beauty to your yard and luscious flavors to your meals. Some can improve your health and appearance, and others will fill your home with fragrance.

More than a thousand plants are considered herbs, so you'll find quite a few candidates for your garden. In this chapter the focus is on culinary herbs, and you'll learn how to recognize, grow, and use those classic herbs that are the most flavorful, beneficial, and fragrant.

So what exactly is an herb? More than 12 centuries ago Emperor Charlemagne, who compelled his citizens to grow herbs, answered this question by saying, "An herb is the friend of physicians and the praise of cooks."

Not much has changed since then, except that the definition has expanded from the fields of medicine and cooking to include plants valued for their household, fragrant, or economic uses. Because herbs have played a valued role in civilizations since the earliest times, they also provide interest through their wealth of history and folklore.

And how is the word "herb" pronounced? Derived from the Latin *herba*, meaning vegetation or green plant, the letter "h" was originally pronounced. The "h" was dropped as the romance languages—Italian, Spanish, and French—evolved, and it even was omitted in the spelling for a while. By the Middle Ages, the "h" was in place again, both in the written and spoken word in England. The French, however, chose to keep the "h" muted. Today the British sound the "h," while most Americans do not. Ultimately, how you pronounce "herb" is less

► Because fresh herbs are less potent than dried, increase by fifty percent or more the amount specified by recipes.

important than including culinary herbs in your garden and home.

Growing and using herbs

Cultivating and using herbs are not particularly difficult, but to derive the greatest benefit, pleasure, and success from your effort, consider these key points.

● **Know your herbs**
Minimize mistakes and confusion by knowing—before setting any plants in your garden—how each herb grows, the conditions it needs, and how to use it after harvest. Take this book with you when plant shopping, then keep it handy in your home. Label the herbs growing in your garden and the dried ones stored in your pantry.

● **Provide the right conditions** Herbs grow best when light, soil, drainage, and climatic conditions meet their individual requirements for healthy growth.

> **HERE'S A TIP...**
> **Dried herbs stronger than fresh**
> If you're substituting fresh herbs for dried ones, increase the amount called for in the recipe. For example, if the recipe calls for 1 teaspoon of dried thyme, use about 1 tablespoon of fresh thyme. Conversely, use a third of the quantity when substituting dried herbs for fresh ones. When herbs are dried their flavors concentrate, which is why you don't need to use as much.

◀ It's easy to find room for a few pots of the culinary herbs you use most often, perhaps mixed with some flowers.

● **Give the proper care**
Watering, pruning, pinching, harvesting, and providing winter protection for tender plants help ensure healthy, vigorous herbs.

● **Experiment in the kitchen**
Don't let culinary herbs intimidate you. If an herb is new to you, nibble on it; then let your imagination fly with all the possibilities the herb can bring to your meals. Start with small quantities until you feel sure of yourself. And remember, it's hard to fail with fresh herbs.

● **Use the right herb in the proper manner** Herbs can be potent or benign. Use herbs throughout your home. Besides filling your kitchen cabinets, herbs can bring fragrance and beauty to every room of the house. Use them in potpourris, wreaths, and other aromatic handicrafts.

● **Enjoy the beauty of herbs**
For centuries gardeners have enjoyed the peaceful quality that herbs impart to gardens. Strolling and sitting among herbs will regenerate and lift your spirit.

Herbs in the garden

To obtain the most benefit and pleasure from growing herbs, make them a part of your everyday life, not something reserved purely for special occasions. To do this, your herbs must be easy to get to. The ideal—and traditional—place for growing culinary herbs is right outside the door nearest the kitchen.

If you cook outdoors a lot, you'll find it convenient to have some herbs planted near the deck or patio. Before you plant, though, remember that most culinary herbs need well-drained soil and at least six hours of sunlight if they are to grow well. Try incorporating them into flowerbeds and borders.

One of the easiest ways to create a small culinary herb garden is to make a raised bed either 4×4 feet

▲ Harvest tender herbs such as basil as you would flowers, by submerging the cut stems immediately in water.

or 4×8 feet. Even in these small spaces, you'll be able to grow about one to two dozen different herbs. For many herbs, a single plant will supply plenty of harvests. But if you really like a particular herb, consider planting extras.

The vegetable garden is another logical place to plant herbs, especially the ones you want in quantity. In fact, some herbs, including anise, cilantro, and dill, are best started by direct seeding into the garden, so allow space for several 2- to 3-foot rows when planning your vegetable garden.

If space or sunshine is at a premium, containers offer an ideal alternative. A pot 18 to 24 inches in diameter can hold a number of small plants. Mix trailing and upright growers for the greatest effect.

Create a mini garden by surrounding a large mixed container planting with smaller pots of various sizes containing individual herbs.

▲ Low-growing herbs such as golden oregano make excellent border plants.

▶ Shrubby sweet bay can be trained to a treelike form. In cold climates grow it in a container to restrain its size and to make it easier to move indoors for protection from winter cold.

Types of herbs

▲ Herbs and vegetables are natural companions, each complementing the other in numerous ways.

When deciding which herbs to grow and how best to use them in the landscape, you'll find it helpful to know something about the different types of plants and their growth habits.

● **Annuals and biennials** Annuals germinate, grow, flower, and die in one growing season, whereas biennials germinate and grow the first season, become dormant to survive winter, then flower the second growing season before dying. Basil is an example of an annual herb, and parsley a biennial.

● **Shrubs** are woody plants that grow smaller than trees, with multiple stems and many branches starting near the base of the plant. Their leaves may be deciduous or evergreen. Rosemary and lavender are popular shrubby herbs.

● **Perennials** Plants that usually die back to the ground in winter and then send out new growth in spring are perennial. Most have soft, herbaceous stems, but some develop woody stems. Sage is an example of a perennial herb.

● **Trees** These are woody plants, usually with a single main stem but sometimes two or three stems. The branches form well above the ground, and the leaves may be deciduous or evergreen. None of the herbs in this book is a tree. Sweet bay (*Laurus nobilis*) is an example of a tree with leaves used as an herb.

Plant parts used as herbs

Not all parts of all herbs have herbal properties. Be sure to choose the correct part of the herb in question.

● **Leaves and stems** Lovage and lemongrass are examples of culinary herbs with stems used in cooking.

● **Flowers** The flowers of various herbs are used in cooking, and the flower buds of caper are considered a culinary herb as well.

● **Roots** One herb that's a root is horseradish.

● **Seeds and fruits** Some plants, such as dill and coriander, produce seeds that are naked, or exposed. Others develop seeds in a fleshy fruit, which in the case of roses are called hips and are considered an herb.

● **Essential oils** These are the concentrated, aromatic oils of plants. Lavender and mint produce essential oils.

▲ A stone wall through and over which trailing and creeping herbs can creep and spill is an ideal herb companion.

▲ A nearly wild, naturalistic look is easily achieved with herbs by allowing plants to take their natural shape and size.

▲ Herbs are a smart option for geometric, formal spaces that naturally organize and restrain their exuberant growth.

▲ Nasturtiums are annuals in most areas that you start from seeds or nursery seedlings each spring.

▼ Many herbs serve well as groundcover or low shrubs, and many have attractive silvery leaves that combine will with other ornamentals.

▼ A container of rosemary is surrounded by 'Purple Ruffles' basil, 'Tricolor' sage, thyme, and lavender.

COMMON HERBS AND THEIR USES

Herb	Parts used	Flavor	In the kitchen	In the garden
Anise	Seeds, leaves	Licorice	Use seeds to flavor bread, pastry, liqueurs; leaves in salads, pasta sauce	Attracts beneficial insects. Self-sows. Annual
Basil	Leaves, flowers	Variable: sweet mint, spicy, anise, citrus	Sauces, soups, salads, vinegars	Easy-growing addition to vegetable garden. Annual
Caper	Flower buds	Mustard, pepper	Component of many Mediterranean recipes	Drought-tolerant, low shrub. Tender perennial
Caraway	Seeds, leaves, roots	Cumin- licorice-anise	Add to breads, especially rye; cook with cabbage	Grow like carrot. Annual and biennial types
Chervil	Leaves	Sweet licorice	Use with chives, tarragon, and parsley to make *fines herbes*; béarnaise sauce	Soft, delicate, fernlike leaves. Best in cool, moist weather. Annual
Chives	Leaves, flowers	Mild onion	Salads, fish, soups, eggs, butter, vinegars, *fines herbes*; garnishes	Colorful borders. Divide crowded clumps. Perennial
Cilantro (leaves), Coriander (seeds)	Leaves, seeds	*Leaves:* pungent, waxy, citrus *Seeds:* sweet, citrus with tones of sage and clove	*Leaves:* salsa, guacamole, ceviche *Seeds:* curry	Attracts beneficial insects. Self-sows. Annual
Dill	Leaves, seeds	Sharp version of caraway	Cream cheese, omelets, salmon, potato salad, pickles	Tall. Attracts beneficial insects. Self-sows. Annual
Edible flowers	Flowers	Variable	Color in salads; garnishes	Colorful additions to any herb garden
French tarragon	Leaves	Sweet licorice	*Fines herbes*; salads, marinades, and sauces; vinegar	Low-growing, tender perennial
Horseradish	Roots	Sharp mustard	Bitter herb; meat accent	Hardy, potentially invasive weed. Perennial
Lavender	Leaves, flowers	Lavender	Cakes, cookies, jellies, teas, vinegars, fruits, eggs	Mounding perennial with fragrant, attractive flowers
Lemon balm	Leaves, flowers	Subtle lemon	Teas, fruit salads, green salads, custards	Mounding, hardy. Perennial. Potentially invasive
Lemongrass	Leaves, stems	Lemon	Curries, stir-fries, especially Thai cooking	Clump-forming, tall grass. Perennial
Lemon verbena	Leaves	Lemon	Teas, drinks, vinegar, dressings, sauces	Gangly, tender perennial
Lovage	Leaves, stems, seeds, roots	Celery-lemon	Green salads, soups, potato salad, candy	Tall. Yellow flowers. Perennial
Marjoram	Leaves, flowers	Spicy sweet; mild oregano	Eggs, lamb, vegetable dishes, soups	Low growing. Borders and beds. Tender perennial
Mint	Leaves, flowers	Various, mostly menthol	Teas, vinegars, jellies, syrups, sauces	Most are low growing. Perennial. Can be invasive
Oregano	Leaves, flowers	Pungent, peppery, hot, spicy	Eggs, tomato sauces, meats, beans, shellfish, soups, vinegars, pasta	Low growing. Perennial
Parsley	Leaves	Mild, grassy	Salads, eggs, vegetables, meats, soups, stews, *bouquet garni, fines herbes*	Low growing, lustrous dark green. Biennial
Rose	Flowers, fruits (hips)	*Petals:* flowery *Hips:* slightly acidic	*Petals:* salads, teas, syrup, sugar, butter, vinegar *Hips:* jellies, jams, tea, syrup, sauce	Various, mostly woody, thorny shrubs. Perennial
Rosemary	Leaves, flowers	Pine, lemon	Pork, lamb, poultry, fish, eggs, breads, soups; stems on grill	Tender woody shrub for hedges, containers
Sage	Leaves, flowers	Mint with camphor, juniper, pine	Vegetables, breads, pork, poultry, sausage, stuffing	Gray-green leaves. Perennial
Savory, summer and winter	Leaves, flowers	Pepper and thyme	Meats, stuffing, beans	Low-growing mound. Annual, perennial
Thyme	Leaves, flowers	Sweet clove	Salads, stocks, *bouquet garni, fines herbes*	Low growing. Spreading, tiny leaves. Perennial

Choosing and starting herbs

You can easily begin an herb garden either by buying seedlings at a garden center or by starting the plants from seed at home. Many herbs are simple to grow from seeds; sow them directly into the garden or germinate them indoors.

Buying and planting

Buying herbs as seedlings rather than starting them yourself from seed saves time, money, and the effort involved in raising your own transplants, especially if you want just one or two plants of each herb. Also, some herbs, like French tarragon or named cultivars of other herbs, either do not produce seeds or do not come true to form from seed and can be propagated only from cuttings or by division.

Not long ago herb plants were difficult to find. Now the most common herbs are readily available in spring at garden centers, hardware stores, and garden sections of home stores.

When looking for some of the more unusual herbs, among the best sources are specialized herb nurseries, local herb society plant sales, and mail order sources (listed on page 214). If you are unfamiliar with a specific mail order company, it is best to make your first order

▲ Young plants of thyme, basil, and parsley can thrive on a sunny windowsill.

small. Immediately open boxes of mail-ordered plants and water the plants well. Place the new arrivals in indirect light, then gradually move them to the garden or repot them within the next several days.

To review the process of acclimating seedlings to the garden and actually getting them into the ground, see page 39. Although that discussion is about vegetable seedlings, the same process applies to herbs.

Many herbs are easy to start from seeds sown indoors or out. Use the same techniques as described for vegetables; see page 36.

Winter protection

Herbs that are marginally hardy in your area can succumb to cold if planted in a windy spot or in poorly

▲ A garden that survives winter is particularly useful when it comes to herbs, which are mostly annual and biennial plants. The permanent layout means that you don't have to reinvent the design from scratch each spring.

▲ Parsley in a raised bed will remain vigorous well into fall. But if mulched with pine boughs or weed-free straw it will survive cold winters and return in spring.

▼ If your local nursery doesn't offer the kinds or varieties of herbs that you seek, you can obtain them by mail order. They'll arrive looking something like this and ready to plant in your garden.

draining soil. Plan ahead by establishing windbreaks and making sure the drainage is good. Plants grown in areas with cold winters but little snowfall can be pushed out of the ground by alternate periods of freezing and thawing unless they are protected. Dead foliage and stems left on perennial herbs may look messy and provide shelter for pests, but they help to protect plants in winter. A more attractive alternative is to trim back plants and mulch them loosely with pine boughs, oak leaves, or other organic mulch. Avoid using leaves that mat down, such as those of maples. Be sure to remove any fallen tree leaves on evergreen or prostrate plants like thyme. Leaving them could cause the plants to rot.

Herbs in containers

Cultivating herbs in containers is not new. Records show that ancient Greeks, Romans, and Egyptians grew herbs in clay pots, and the Moors of southern Spain used potted herbs lavishly in their courtyards. Gardens in 12th-century Britain, in 15th- and 16th-century Italy, and in the Victorian and Edwardian ages all had them too.

▲ Basil stems are soft enough to prune and harvest by pinching between thumb and forefinger.

HERBS IN A STRAWBERRY JAR

A planting of herbs in a strawberry jar is spectacular, especially when the herbs are placed in the individual pockets and allowed to cascade down the jar as they grow. Good candidates for cascading include creeping thyme, marjoram, oregano, and creeping rosemary. Put small upright-growing plants, such as parsley, chives, short varieties of basil, and savory, in the top.

The challenge when growing herbs in a strawberry jar is to adequately water all the plants. An ingenious solution is to create a conduit for the water: Insert into the center of the jar a length of PVC plumbing pipe that you have drilled with small holes, then fill the pipe with pea gravel.

1 Drill ⅜-inch holes in a length of PVC pipe that equals the pot's depth.

2 Place the pipe in the center of the pot, add some soil, and begin planting.

3 Fill the pot and finish by placing a plant on top that covers the pipe.

For today's busy lives, nothing beats having a tub of culinary herbs near the kitchen door. Even if you have plenty of garden space, herbs in containers add beauty to your yard. And for those whose gardening is confined to a balcony or patio, pots of herbs are indispensable.

To successfully grow herbs in containers, provide a fertile, fast-draining potting soil and keep it adequately watered and fertilized during the growing season. Also be sure to meet the herbs' light requirements.

Container choice is a matter of personal preference, with each material having pluses and minuses. The only requirement for containers is that they have drainage holes.

For more details about container gardening, see pages 32 and 33.

● **Terra cotta** The pots have a natural beauty but are heavy and difficult to move. They also break. You must shelter these pots in winter to avoid freezing, cracking, and breaking.

● **Wood** Containers of wood are also heavy, but they can stand up to winter weather. The longest-lasting wood containers are made from redwood or cedar. When growing herbs and other edible plants, don't use

▶ Harvest flowering lavender on dry days and in the morning after dew dries. To keep flowers fresh, submerge the cut stems in water after cutting.

containers made from treated wood, which could leach chemicals into the potting soil.

● **Plastic containers** are a lightweight alternative to terra cotta and wood. Prices range from cheap to rather expensive, and there are many sizes, styles, and colors to choose from.

Most individual herbs are best planted in pots that are 12 to 14 inches across. For mixed plantings, choose larger containers that are at least 24 to 36 inches across.

▼ A bright, south- or west-facing window is enough to sustain these two potted rosemary plants, both of which are trained as standards.

Propagating herbs

Multiplying herbs by cuttings, layering, or division is easy and inexpensive. It also provides you with an opportunity to share favorite plants with your friends.

Cuttings

Rooting cuttings taken from the stems of woody herbs is a simple way to get many new plants. The following are the three main types of stem cuttings.

● **Softwood cuttings** These are spring and early-summer cuttings from new growth that has not yet hardened.

● **Semihardwood cuttings** Taken midsummer, these cuttings are from growth that has hardened at the base.

● **Hardwood cuttings** These sections of fully hardened wood that are taken late in the season

For all three types, cut 4- to 6-inch-long sturdy pieces of stem, making the cut just above a leaf. Next pinch off the lower third of the leaves, taking care not to tear the stem. Dust or dip the stripped end in a powder or liquid rooting hormone.

With a pencil or chopstick, make a hole in a pot of moistened, sterile potting mix, perlite, or horticultural vermiculite. Insert the stem up to the bottom of the leaves, and firm the potting medium around it. Add more cuttings to the pot, about 2 inches apart. Insert a label with the name of the plant and the date. Cover the pot with a plastic dome or bag, making sure it does not touch the leaves. The dome holds in moisture and keeps cuttings from wilting, but it also can cook plants by holding in heat. Keep the pot out of direct sunlight, and open the dome a crack to let heat escape.

Set the pot in a spot with bright indirect light and keep the medium moist. Placing the pot on a heating mat speeds rooting. When the cuttings show signs of growth, usually after four to six weeks, remove the dome. When you tug on a cutting and it resists being pulled out of the pot, it is developing roots. How long that takes varies with the species of herb. Once it has roots, pot up the plant, harden it to outdoor conditions, and then plant it in the garden.

Many herbs, including mint, basil, rosemary, oregano, and thyme, will root in water if they are not too woody. You can try developing roots that way instead of setting the cuttings in potting soil, vermiculite, or perlite.

Layering

Layering is a good way to propagate low-growing or creeping plants that are difficult to root from cuttings. With layering, rooting occurs while the stem is still attached to the plant.

Bend a shoot to the ground. Scoop out a small hole in the soil where the shoot touches the ground, then hold the stem in place with an old-fashioned peg-type clothespin, a hairpin-shaped piece of wire, or a U-shape drip tubing stake. Cover the pegged section with soil and gently firm.

Keep the area moist until new growth develops; then cut the newly rooted plant from the main plant, and transplant it immediately.

▲ Herbs such as lavender readily propagate by layering. Select a lower stem and pin it to the soil.

Dividing

Many perennial herbs, such as oregano and lemon balm, send out an ever-widening circle of growth. These new plants crowd the original plant, which then declines. Dig up an overgrown clump and cut or break it apart. Or, depending on the herb, you may be able to dig up small plants from the edge of the clump. Early spring and fall are the best times to divide plants.

Harvesting

Gathering herbs, either for fresh use or for preserving, is among the most pleasurable aspects of growing the plants. Take the time to enjoy their intoxicating fragrances as you work. Gather only as much as you can process at one time, and keep different kinds of herbs separate and clearly labeled.

When using herbs fresh, simply cut what you need when you need it. A side benefit of regular snipping is that it keeps a plant lightly pruned. However, if you are harvesting to preserve an herb, do it in a way that maximizes the herb's essential oils. The timing and method depend on the part of the plant you are harvesting.

● **Leaves** The concentration of essential oils in leaves is highest just before flowers begin to develop. The best time to collect leaves is in the morning, after the dew has dried and before the day

▲ Propagate herbs that grow in expanding clumps, such as these chives, by digging and dividing the clump.

▲ Use a heavy utility knife to slice the mat of roots and soil into as many pieces as you require.

▲ Cuttings of rosemary root easily and will be identical to the parent plant. In fall, snip 3- to 4-inch tips from new growth, cut off lower leaves, coat the bottom ¼ inch in rooting powder, and place in potting soil. Keep humidity high around cuttings by covering them with plastic or by misting. Roots form in about three weeks.

warms up. Cut stems or leaves with sharp scissors or pruning shears, and lay them gently in a gathering basket.

● **Flowers** Gather just-opening flowers at midday. For flowers on stalks, such as calendula, snip off the entire stem. When preserving individual flowers, pick each one separately. Avoid touching the petals, and do not harvest damaged or wilted flowers. Gently place flowers in a gathering basket.

● **Seeds** Harvest seeds on a warm day when they are fully ripe but haven't begun to fall. Usually this is when all the seeds are hard and the pods are paper-dry and colored beige, brown, or black with no green showing. Cut the seedheads from herbs such as dill, coriander, chervil, and fennel directly into a box or paper bag.

● **Roots** Dig up the roots in fall when the top of the plant begins to die. Carefully dig the entire plant, and cut off and compost the top. If desired, save a few clumps for replanting. The roots of perennial herbs such as horseradish may need two or more seasons to reach usable size.

Preserving

Although drying may immediately come to mind when you think of preserving herbs, in fact herbs also can be frozen. If you grow more herbs than you can use fresh, either dry or freeze some—or try both techniques.

● **Drying** The several ways to dry leaves include hanging them, spreading them on a

▼ Most herbs dry readily given typical indoor humidity and good air circulation.

screen drying rack, and using a dehydrator. The room where you dry herbs, as well as where they are later stored, should be dark, dry, warm, and well ventilated.

● **Leaves and flowers** Discard old or damaged foliage and blooms. If any harvested material has been splashed with soil, rinse it off in cool water and then let it dry. Otherwise, do not wash the collected herbs.

Strip leaves of large-leaf herbs, such as basil and mint, from the stem. Spread them on the drying screen in a single layer. Cover basil with a sheet of newspaper to preserve its color.

To dry herbs by hanging, gather small bunches together, secure their ends with a rubber band, then hang the bunches upside down. If you use a dehydrator, follow the manufacturer's directions; stripping the leaves from the stems will speed the process.

Herbs are dry when the leaves or flowers are brittle like cornflakes. If any leaves have been dried on the stems, gently strip them off and place them on dry paper before storing them. With some herbs, such as lavender, you may want to leave the flowers on the stems.

● **Seeds** Gather several stems of seedheads into a bunch, and tie them loosely together. Hang the bunches over a box or paper bag with the seedheads facing down or cover the seedheads with a piece of cheesecloth or muslin. When they are completely dry and the seeds are falling out, gently rub the heads to remove any remaining seeds. Remove any nonseed plant parts by either shaking the seeds in a fine sieve or gently blowing away the debris.

● **Freezing** This method is particularly effective for preserving herbs that lose their flavor when dried and for herbs with soft leaves. Among the herbs you should

▶ Freezing a water slurry of soft-leaved herbs, such as chervil, in ice cubes keeps flavors of delicate herbs fresh.

STORING DRIED HERBS

Once herbs are fully dry, crumble leaves into small pieces and store in airtight, labeled containers.

First and foremost when storing dried herbs, make sure they are totally dry; otherwise they will mold in the jars and be unusable. A good rule is to check jars for condensation after about a week. If you immediately attend to moisture, sometimes you can salvage part of the contents by redrying the herbs.

Glass jars, preferably dark-colored ones, are best for storing dried herbs. Although you can store more herbs in a smaller space by crushing them, you will sacrifice some flavor. It's best to leave herbs whole and to pack jars loosely.

Cover the jars with tight-fitting lids: It's important to keep air out of the jars. Label each jar with the name of the herb and date, and store the lot in a dark pantry or closet.

Dried herbs lose much of their flavor or active constituents after a year. Use older herbs in potpourris or add them to the compost pile.

consider preserving by freezing are chives, chervil, tarragon, basil, parsley, dill, fennel, and mint.

To freeze herbs, put clean, dry individual leaves or sprigs into plastic freezer bags, seal the bags, and label them. Double-bagging will reduce dehydration and preserve flavor better. If freezing many different kinds of herbs, collect the plastic bags in a larger container to make organization easier.

Another method of freezing herbs is to puree the herbs in a blender with a small amount of water. Then pour the slurry into ice cube trays and freeze it. After the slurry is solid, remove the herbal ice cubes and transfer them to labeled plastic freezer bags. You can add a cube or two to a dish to give it an almost-fresh flavor.

▲ Ordinary distilled white vinegar is transformed by several sprigs of herbs and a fine container.

Encyclopedia of herbs

Anise, sweet alice (Pimpinella anisum)

Type: Annual
Edible part: Seeds, leaves, flowers
Typical size: 2'H×1–2'W

Like other members of the carrot family, anise has rounded

Flowering anise

to toothed lower leaves and finely divided upper leaves. Clusters of creamy white flowers are followed by oval seeds ⅛ inch long.

Anise adds a licorice flavor to foods. Use whole, crushed, or ground seeds in baked goods, apple dishes, pickles, curries, eggs, soups, stews, fish, and liqueurs. Chew toasted seeds to freshen your breath and aid your digestion. You can also use flowers and leaves in fruit salads.

When: Where winters are cold, plant in late spring; where summers are hot and winters mild, plant in fall. Plants need 120 days of warm weather to produce a crop of seeds. Where seasons are shorter than that, sow seeds indoors a month or two before the last frost, then set out plants after frost danger passes.
Planting: Grow anise in average, well-drained, slightly acidic soil. Direct-sow fresh seeds or set out transplants. Plants quickly develop a taproot that prevents easy transplanting. Space plants 6 to 8 inches apart. Anise is excellent in containers.
Growing: Plants may need staking or protection from wind.
Harvesting: Collect leaves throughout the growing season, and harvest flowers as they open. Harvest ripe seeds as they turn gray-green, and store them in a paper bag to catch seeds. Preserve harvested material by drying it.
Pests and diseases: Few insects or diseases bother anise.

Basil (Ocimum spp.)

Type: Annual
Edible part: Leaves, flowers
Typical size: 1–3'H×1–3'W

A delightfully aromatic and flavorful herb, basil is a favorite choice of gardeners. Use fresh, snipped leaves in salads, tomato-based recipes, and pesto (a paste made of basil, garlic, nuts, and oil and used on pasta, pizza, and bread). Cut large leaves or add small whole ones to cooked dishes just before serving to preserve basil's spicy flavor. For a tangy treat, substitute basil leaves for lettuce on sandwiches.
When: Sow seeds indoors in early spring for planting outside after danger of frost is over. In areas with a long growing season, sow seeds directly in the garden. Space seeds or seedlings 12 to 36 inches apart.
Planting: Choose a sunny location with rich, moist, friable,

slightly acid soil that drains well. Basil is highly adaptable and grows well almost anywhere, including raised beds and containers. It does well when interplanted with tomatoes.

Basil, several varieties combined

Growing: Basil is very tender; growth slows in cool weather, and leaves may wither and discolor if nighttime temperatures are consistently below 45°F. Keep plants inside cloches or cold frames in cool zones or anytime frost is predicted. Pinch out the tops of newly planted tall seedlings to about 6 inches to promote root growth. Cut or pinch off flowers as they appear to encourage bushier growth. Keep the soil around plants consistently moist and weed free. Fertilize with well-rotted compost, and use mulch to conserve soil moisture.

'Spicy Bush' basil as edging

Harvesting: Begin harvesting basil as soon as the plant has at least four sets of leaves. Pinch out the topmost set of leaves and any flowers as needed for use in food preparation. Store unwashed basil as you would lettuce, but only for a day or two; basil begins to decay as soon as it is picked. Preserve fresh leaves and flowers by hot packing them in sterilized bottles with vinegar and olive oil. Basil can also be processed with oil and stored in the freezer for up to two years or in the refrigerator for up to three months. If you use only part of what you have stored, cover any unused portion with more oil. Basil can be dried but is not as flavorful and colorful as when it is preserved with oil.

At the end of the growing season in temperate climates, pull up the plants by their roots and harvest any remaining leaves before the first frost. In hot climates cut basil back to 6 inches tall and regrow several times in one year before the final harvest.

Basil 'Siam Queen'

TOP GARDEN BASILS

Name (All are *O. basilicum* unless noted)	Plant size (H×W in inches)	Leaf length (inches)	Scent/flavor	Days to harvest (from seed)	Key features
'Ararat'	25×15	2	Mild	60	Leaves splotched green and purple
'Aroma 2'	24×15	3	Sweet	70	Classic 'Genovese'-type with fusarium resistance
'Fino Verde'	20×15	1	Spicy, sweet	63	Excellent in containers
'Genovese'	24–30×18	3	Spicy	68	Slow to bolt (develop flowers)
'Genovese Compact Improved'	18×12	3	Spicy	74	Familiar basil in compact form. Suitable for container
'Greek'	6–9×6–9	¼–½	Sweet, pungent	70	Smallest basil
Holy basil (*O. tenuiflorum*)	20×12	1½–2	Camphor, clove, mint, cinnamon	95	Slender purple and green leaves, purple flowers
'Italian Large Leaf'	30×18	4	Sweet, less clove than 'Genovese'	78	Medium dark green leaves
Lemon basil (*O. ×citriodorum*)	20×15	2½	Lemon	60	Intense flavor. White flowers
'Lettuce Leaf'	30×18	5	Licorice, cinnamon	85	Use large leaves like lettuce
Lime basil	20×14	1–2	Lime, cinnamon, camphor, lavender	60	White to lavender flowers
'Magical Michael'	10–14×8	2	Sweet, fruity	62	Red-veined green leaves, burgundy flowers
'Mexican Spice'	24×18	1–2	Cinnamon	70	Reddish brown stems and flowers
'Napoletano'	15×10	4	Spicy	75	Frilly light green leaves
'Nufar'	24–30×18	4	Sweet	77	'Genovese'-type with fusarium resistance
'Purple Ruffles'	24×20	3–4	Cloves, licorice	85	Purple-black ruffled leaves
'Osmin'	18×12	2	Sweet, fruity	80	Leaves glossy, slightly ruffled. Lavender flowers
'Red Rubin'	20×14	3	Sweet	76	Bronze-tinged purple leaves
'Siam Queen'	36×30	2–4	Spicy, licorice	80	Purple stems
'Spicy Bush'	12×12	1	Spicy, sweet	70	Ideal in containers or to edge beds
'Spicy Saber'	14×12	2–3	Spicy	75	Bright green, lance-shaped, frilled leaves
'Sweet Dani'	30×15	3	Lemon	61	Olive green leaves
'Sweet Thai' ('Thai Magic')	12–18×12	2	Spicy, anise, clove	59	Reddish purple stems and flowers

Pests and diseases: Many insects are attracted to basil, but no common insect control is labeled for use on edible herbs. Discourage pests by keeping mulch from touching the plants, and remove and destroy any leaves that look unhealthy. Spray water from a garden hose to knock aphids and mites off plants.

Japanese beetles sometimes feed on leaves; remove them by hand. Basil is susceptible to fusarium wilt in hot, humid weather; look for cultivars bred for resistance and plant them in soil that drains well. Remove and destroy infected plants, including the roots and surrounding soil.

'Red Rubin' basil with dill

'Genovese' basil

Bee balm (*see Edible flowers*)
Bergamot (*see Edible flowers*)
Calendula (*see Edible flowers*)

Caper (*Capparis spinosa*)

Type: Sprawling shrub, Zones 9–11
Edible part: Flower buds
Typical size: 3–5'H×5–8'W

Caper shrub in flower

A Mediterranean native, the spiny caper shrub thrives in dry, rocky, poor soils and along sandy shorelines where temperatures do not fall below 20°F. Its fragrant, attractive flowers resemble those of cleome. The edible capers are the immature flower buds. Pickled, the buds are prized for the peppery zing they add to cooked dishes, especially in combination with tomatoes, garlic, and olive oil. Use preserved buds in fresh salads.

When: Plant in fall so that roots can establish during the cool part of the year.

Planting: Space transplants 8 feet apart in a location where they can sprawl or perhaps be draped over a wall. Mulch heavily to conserve soil moisture. Keep the roots of transplants moist until they are established. Caper plants are slow to germinate from presoaked seeds; propagate using stem cuttings taken in late winter or early spring or graft productive clones onto seedling rootstocks.

Growing: Caper prefers dry heat and bright sunlight, and it needs excellent drainage. Remove the mulch as soon as a plant is well rooted. Fertilize caper until its roots are established. Avoid pruning until the third year, then cut the plant to the ground late in the year; on a mature plant, flower buds develop on one-year-old branches.

Harvesting: The caper bush begins producing buds in its fourth year and lives 20 to 30 years. One plant can produce about 4 pounds of capers each year. Pick the buds early in the morning just before they are about to flower. The smallest buds are considered the most desirable: Harvest them when they are about ⅛ to ¼ inch in diameter. Soak the buds in a brine solution for 30 days, and then pickle them in salted vinegar and store them in glass jars for up to 6 months. Pickling brings out their peppery flavor, which comes from a type of mustard oil in the plant tissues.

Pests and diseases: Use clean cultural practices to avoid introducing any viruses

Caper flower buds, pickled

when taking cuttings or grafting plants. Sterilize your pruning tools between cuts. Pick off weevils and cabbageworms by hand or treat serious infestations with *Bacillus thuringiensis* (Bt) or an insect control labeled for food plants. Water plants from underneath to avoid mold and botrytis.

Varieties: '**Josephine**' and '**Nocellana**' are bred to be spineless, and they may also be more pest resistant.

Caraway (*Carum carvi*)

Type: Annual or biennial, Zones 4–11
Edible part: Seeds, leaves, roots
Typical size: 12–18"H×18"W

Like other carrot relatives, caraway produces finely cut, feathery leaves on floppy stems. White flowers appear on flat heads. Its ridged ¼-inch-long crescent-shape brown fruits are commonly referred to as seeds. Caraway has been a flavoring and medicine for more than 5,000 years. Use

Caraway plants in flower

caraway seeds in breads, cakes, cookies, soups, sauces, stews, pork, beef, goose, fresh vegetables, pickled vegetables, sauerkraut, cheeses, eggs, grains, apples, and liqueurs. The young leaves are tasty in fruit or green salads, herb cheeses, and butters. The roots are eaten as a vegetable.

When: Sow seeds directly in the garden where you want the plants to grow. Fall is the best time, but you can also seed in early spring.

Planting: Grow caraway in full sun and provide deeply tilled, average, well-drained soil. Thin seedlings to 8 inches apart. Caraway adapts well to containers.

Growing: Mulch the plants in winter.

Harvesting: Pick young leaves as needed, and seedheads as they turn brown; preserve them by drying. Harvest the roots in autumn after collecting the seeds.

Pests and diseases: Few insects or diseases bother caraway.

Carnation (*see Edible flowers*)

Chervil (*Anthriscus cerefolium*)

Type: Annual
Edible part: Leaves
Typical size: 1–2'H×1'W

A relative of carrots and parsley, fresh chervil is the essential ingredient, along with parsley, thyme, chives, and tarragon, in the French mix called *fines herbes*. It is rich in vitamin C, beta-carotene, iron, and magnesium. Chervil's faintly licorice flavor is excellent paired with salmon, asparagus, eggs, cream soups, cottage cheese, butter, mayonnaise, carrots, peas, or potatoes.

When: Because chervil does not transplant well, sow seeds directly into the garden in early spring or, where winters are mild, in fall. Broadcast seeds several times throughout the

Pinching out chervil flower stalk

Chives, in flower

spring and fall to have a continuous supply of leaves. **Planting:** The seeds need light to germinate, but the plants grow best in light shade. Interplant chervil among taller crops that will provide the shade it needs. **Growing:** Keep the root zone continuously moist. Thin seedlings for kitchen use. As the plants develop, pinch out flower stalks to promote foliage growth. Mulch around the plants so the roots remain cool and moist. Overwinter chervil in a cold frame or grow it in a pot indoors for year-round use.

Harvesting: Plants are ready for kitchen use 30 to 40 days after sowing. Snip bits of chervil from the outside edges of a plant as needed and use immediately. leaves lose their flavor rapidly and should not be cooked.

Pests and diseases: Few insects or diseases bother chervil.

Chervil growing in garden

Varieties: Chervil comes in flat and curly-leaf types. Some growers think that curly chervil has a slightly bitter taste. **'Brussels Winter'** is larger and slower to bolt than standard chervil varieties.

Chinese parsley *(see Cilantro)*

Chives *(Allium* spp.)

Type: Perennial, Zones 3–10
Edible part: Leaves, flowers
Typical size: 8–18"H×8–12"W

Chives are grassy, clump-forming onions with hollow leaves, essentially tiny onions grown for their leaves, not their bulbs. Almost spherical purple flowers appear in spring. Along with being an excellent edging plant, chives are well suited to growing in a pot near the kitchen door. Cut off leaves, chop then into narrow sections, and include them in salads, sauces, and quiches; add chives to baked potatoes and egg dishes at the end of cooking to preserve the onion flavor. The fragrant small pinkish purple flowers are also edible and can be used as a garnish.

When: Sow seeds in early spring or, in mild-winter areas, in fall. Plant divisions or nursery transplants anytime.
Planting: Plant in average, well-drained soil in beds or pots.
Growing: Chives need average moisture and light. They are

somewhat drought-tolerant and don't require plant food or much attention besides regular cutting. The plants are evergreen in warm climates but die back to the ground in cooler zones in winter. The clumps eventually become overcrowded, so dig and divide them every few years and plant the divisions in new locations. Deadhead spent flowers to prevent chives from self-seeding and spreading throughout the garden.

Harvesting: Chives are ready to cut in 75 to 85 days when grown from seed. Snip chive leaves as needed by cutting

Harvesting chives with scissors

through them just above the soil with scissors or a sharp knife. Chives can be dried but retain their color and flavor better when frozen.

Varieties: *A. schoenoprasum* is the standard species. Two outstanding cultivars are **'Forescate'**, with rose red flowers, and **'Ruby Gem'**, which has gray-green foliage and red flowers. Chinese or **garlic chives** (*A. tuberosum*) grows taller than common chives, produces flat leaves and white flowers, and can be invasive. As the common name suggests, the leaves have a mild garlic flavor.

Pests and diseases: Few insects or diseases seriously affect chives. They may experience some of the same pests and diseases as onions.

Cilantro, coriander, Chinese parsley

(Coriandrum sativum)

Type: Annual
Edible part: Leaves (cilantro); seeds (coriander)
Typical size: 5–24"H×4–10"W

Similar in appearance to and easy to mistake for flat-leaf Italian parsley, this plant is notable for the two different flavors it contributes to foods. One is the pungent, distinctive tang of its leaves that some love and others abhor; the other is the spicy-citrus taste of its ground seeds. The flavor of cilantro leaves is essential to south Asian and Mexican foods, such as ceviche and guacamole. The ground seeds, called coriander, are commonly used in many Middle Eastern and European foods, such as regional cuisine stews, sausages, and cakes.

When: Sow seeds in early spring after the last frost. Where

Harvesting cilantro

Flowering dill with fernlike foliage

winters are mild and summers extremely hot sow seeds in fall. Plants that become established and are allowed to scatter seeds will self-sow. **Planting:** Plant seeds in well-drained, slightly acid soil in a sunny or partially shady location where plants can remain; they have a deep taproot and are not tolerant of transplanting. Keep the seeds and seedlings evenly moist. Gradually thin seedlings to about 1 foot apart. Interplant with peas, beans, peppers, and tomatoes.

Growing: Water during dry weather. Plants tend to bolt in hot, dry conditions, so make successive plantings two to four weeks apart to maintain a steady crop all summer long. Plant again in autumn for spring harvest in warm climates. Try overwintering some cilantro in a cold frame in northern gardens. It will also grow well indoors sown directly into deep pots.

Harvesting: Thin out whole plants as needed, or begin picking leaves from the lower part of the plant when several stems have developed. The lower leaves, called cilantro or Chinese parsley, look similar to flat-leaf Italian parsley and have more of the desired spicy flavor than the upper foliage, which resembles dill. The flowers are tiny white or lavender umbels and are edible; however, their presence indicates that the plant is past its flavor peak. Add leaves to cooked foods just before serving; heat dissipates the flavor. The leaves can be dried for later use, but the flavor is much milder. Leaves are best used fresh and can be stored for up to two weeks in the refrigerator. Cut the heads when the seedpods begin to turn brown. Hang the heads upside down in paper bags to catch the seeds. Use some seeds whole or ground as coriander, and save some for the next planting.

Pests and diseases: Few insects or diseases bother cilantro.

Varieties: 'Santo' is among the most popular cultivars for fresh leaves because it is slow to bolt.

Cuban oregano *(see Oregano)*

Dill *(Anethum graveolens)*

Type: Annual
Edible part: Leaves, seeds
Typical size: 12–36"H×6–24"W

Just about everyone knows about dill, if only from dill pickles. In the garden it is an easy-to-grow annual with delicate, fernlike leaves and flattish clusters of yellow flowers in summer. The seeds mature in late summer and fall. Beyond making pickles, you can use fresh chopped dill leaves to add flavor to many other foods, everything from potato salad to salmon.

Strictly from a gardener's perspective, dill is an important garden plant because it is a key food of various beneficial insects, such as lacewings (see page 205). With dill there will be fewer aphids in your garden, a favorite main course of lacewings. Dill is also a host (along with its relative parsley)

to one of the most beautiful butterflies, the black swallowtail.

When: In spring—or in fall in hot-summer areas—sow seeds where you want the plants to grow. Established plants will self-sow.

Planting: Broadcast seeds in nutrient-rich, moist, well-drained soil, and cover them with a fine layer of sifted compost. Choose a location that receives full sun. Thin plants when they are large enough to use in the kitchen.

Growing: Sow seeds once a month for a continuous supply of ferny new growth. Hand weed around young plants. Remove flowers to encourage foliage and prevent self-sowing, or let some plants flower and go to seed for new crops. Dill is adaptable but does best in consistently moist soil. Feed plants monthly with a high-nitrogen, water-soluble plant food. Tolerant of cool weather, dill is often the last herb standing in a late-autumn garden.

Harvesting: Dill is ready for leaf harvesting 30 to 55 days after seeding. It goes to seed in 75 to 100 days. Snip leaves as needed or pull whole stems for thinning. To save seeds, cut 4 inches below the flowerheads when the seeds are turning brown, and hang the heads upside down inside paper bags to catch the seeds as they ripen. Leaves can be air-dried or

Dill seeds falling from dried flower

frozen for long-term storage. Fresh leaves add flavor and visual interest in salads, sauces, soups, breads, pesto, potato salad, and egg dishes. Use the dried seeds in pickling brine.

Pests and diseases: Parsley worms feed on dill, but they're worth leaving alone. Handpick them if absolutely necessary.

Varieties: 'Bouquet', the most commonly grown variety, has large seedheads. 'Fernleaf', a dwarf blue-green variety with a high leaf yield, is excellent in kitchen gardens and containers. 'Long Island Mammoth' is widely grown for both leaves and seeds. 'Superdukat' produces abundant foliage and is high in essential oils and thus flavor.

Edible flowers

Type: Annuals and perennials; Zones variable
Edible part: Flowers
Typical size: Various

Nasturtium flowers come in a range of warm colors.

'Pink Delight' bee balm is beautiful in bloom.

Use edible flowers as a garnish and to add color to foods, especially salads. Flavor is a bonus, the flowers often contributing distinct new tastes to foods. Most edible flowers are used fresh, but many are employed in a host of ways, from vinegars to candy. Many kinds of flowers are technically edible; the following are a selection of favorites.

Bee balm, bergamot, oswego tea *(Monarda didyma)* Bee balm is a perennial (Zones 4 to 8) that grows 3 feet tall and wide and produces shaggy pink, lavender, or flaming red flowers that are quite aromatic. In salads the flowers have a minty, sweet-hot flavor. Bee balm doesn't grow well where winters are warm and humid. It tolerates some shade but prefers full sun and grows best in humus rich soil that's kept moist. Bee balm is slow to start from seed, so buy nursery stock or propagate by division. Cut back flowerheads the first year before they bloom to increase strength in the plant. The roots are very shallow, so exercise care in weeding. Prune almost to the ground in fall.

Calendula *(Calendula officinalis)* The flowers of this annual are slightly bitter, but its yellow or orange color adds brilliance to salads. Calendula enjoys a long flowering season: In warm regions it blooms in winter and spring, and elsewhere in summer and fall. The plant produces angular, branched, hairy stems to 2 feet tall with 4-inch-wide flowers. Flowers of hybrids are in the same color range but richer. Most gardeners start with transplants from the nursery. Provide full sun, ordinary soil, and routine care. Propagate from seed.

Nasturtium *(Tropaeolum spp.)* Peppery-tasting flowers of this climbing or sprawling annual make colorful additions to summer salads. The pungent leaves are also edible, and the buds and seeds can be pickled as substitutes for capers. The spurred blossoms come in orange, yellow, red, creamy white, salmon, and deep mahogany. Grow nasturtium in full sun and well-drained soil. If the soil is too rich or overfertilized, plants will produce much lush foliage but few flowers. Watch for aphids, which seem to thrive on nasturtiums, and spray plants with a strong blast of water to remove the pests. Propagate from seed.

Pink, carnation *(Dianthus spp.)* The clovelike quality in the scent of these species, most of them perennial, is also expressed in their flavor. Plant choices range from low-

Calendula adds sunny yellow-orange color to salads.

Flowers of 'First Love' pink add clove flavor to salads.

Sweet violet flowers are a springtime treat.

growing miniature pinks with small flowers to the tall florist's carnation. They are perennial and hardy in Zones 3 to 9. The flowers come in every shade of pink and red as well as white. Carnation *(D. caryophyllus)* also blooms in shades of yellow, orange, lavender, and purple. Both pinks and carnations come with striped and variegated petals. The evergreen foliage is often gray-blue. All need full sun, although some will bloom in partial shade. The soil should be well drained and slightly alkaline.

Sweet violet *(Viola odorata)* The flowers brighten salads, and their deliciously sweet scent is important to connoisseurs of herbal fragrances. A hardy perennial (Zones 3 to 10), sweet violet spreads from creeping roots and forms an attractive ground cover of heart-shape leaves with crinkled edges. Flowers of deep violet, pink, or white appear in late spring. The species is native to wooded areas and should be planted in partial shade and fairly rich soil that is kept evenly moist. Propagate from rooted offshoots or root division.

Fennel *(see Florence fennel, page 70)*

French tarragon *(Artemisia dracunculus sativa)*

Type: Perennial, Zones 5–9
Edible part: Leaves
Typical size: 12–24"H×12–18"W

French tarragon

A classic French herb used to season béarnaise sauce and fish, the name "tarragon" is derived from the French word for little dragon. The plant is a low shrub with glossy, lance-shape leaves on slender stems that sprawl outward before sending up shoots. The leaves have a distinctive aniselike fragrance and flavor.

When: Set out plants in spring, or do so in fall in areas with mild winters.

Planting: Plant rooted cuttings or young plants 18 to 24 inches apart in fertile, well-drained soil in

Transplanting French tarragon

a location with good air circulation and full sun to partial shade. Allow the soil to dry between waterings. Tarragon can be grown either indoors or outside in containers.

Growing: Remove flowers to encourage foliage growth. Plants will grow vigorously if cut regularly. Cut them back in fall and mulch for winter protection. Plants rarely produce seeds and must be replaced every few years; propagate new plants from cuttings or divisions. Take cuttings in late summer for overwintering indoors in containers, or wait until spring to divide plants or take cuttings.

Harvesting: French tarragon's anise-flavor leaves are used to season a wide variety of salads, soups, and fish and poultry dishes—and are the key to a perfect béarnaise sauce. Snip leaves as needed from the tops of stems. Add leaves just before hot foods are served to enjoy the most flavor. Store leaves in vinegar or freeze them. Essential oil of tarragon is used commercially in mustards, vinegars, and other foods, as well as in some cosmetic products.

Pests and diseases: Few insect pests or diseases bother French tarragon.

Varieties: Although **Russian tarragon** *(A. dracunculoides)* can be sown from seed and is hardier than French cultivars, it does not have the flavor desired for culinary uses. **Mexican mint marigold** *(Tagetes lucida)* has similar, though somewhat inferior, flavor but is more heat tolerant than tarragon.

Garlic chives *(see Chives)*
Greek oregano *(see Oregano)*
Hardy marjoram *(see Marjoram)*

Horseradish *(Armoracia rusticana)*

Type: Perennial, Zones 3–9
Edible part: Roots
Typical size: 1–4'H×1–2'W

The pungent roots of horseradish are an important addition to the culinary garden. The plant has glossy green leaves and profuse small white flowers. It's a hardy perennial but in most gardens is best treated as a short-lived perennial. Plant where its spread is restrained; left to its own for too long it is likely to become a spreading weed.

When: Set out plants in spring after the last frost; for mild-winter climates, plant in fall.

Planting: Although horseradish thrives in cool climates, it is not fussy about location and grows so vigorously that it can

Horseradish plants form a spreading clump in the garden.

become invasive if left unattended. Choose a spot where the soil can be prepared a foot or more deep. A raised or otherwise isolated bed helps to keep horseradish from spreading too far. In addition to producing edible roots, the plant has large dark green leaves that provide vertical interest at the back of an herb bed. Horseradish is highly adaptable but does best in soil that can be kept consistently moist.

Growing: Set out plants or root cuttings 3 inches deep and 12 inches apart. Thin overcrowded plants in autumn by harvesting. If the roots seem small and underdeveloped, add potassium to the soil, working it in as deep as possible. To encourage large taproots, remove a few inches of topsoil in midsummer and trim the fine lateral roots off the main root, then replace

Cut off lateral roots of horseradish to promote the taproot.

the soil. Start new plants from lateral root cuttings taken from near the top of the taproot.

Harvesting: Cuttings planted in spring produce mature roots in 180 to 240 days, but for the best flavor leave the roots in the ground until after a few frosts have sweetened them. Roots may need two or more seasons to reach usable size. Loosen the soil with a pitchfork and pull up the roots by hand, using those that are 6 to 12 inches long and replanting the smaller ones. Save some cuttings for next year's crop, or simply leave the plants in the ground and mulch

Mature, harvested horseradish roots

them for winter protection. Store unwashed harvested roots in plastic bags in the refrigerator as you would carrots. Horseradish root is ground and used as a condiment with meat. The flesh smells and tastes quite sharp—too piquant for some palates. Grate washed and peeled roots with a ginger grater or in a food processor and serve fresh, or mix the grated roots with a small amount of vinegar and store in the refrigerator for up to six months.

Pests and diseases: Few insects or diseases seriously affect horseradish.

Varieties: 'Bohemian' is popular because of its hardiness and high-quality roots. **Wasabe** (*Wasabia japonica*), a distant relative that produces highly aromatic, spicy rhizomes used in Asian foods, is grown in streams in mild climates.

Indian mint *(see Oregano)*

Lavender *(Lavandula* spp.)

Type: Perennial, zones variable
Edible part: Flowers, leaves
Typical size: 1–3'H×1–3'W

'Munstead' lavender is attractive in a mixed border.

Lavender with its seductively fragrant flowers in early summer is a delight for the senses. It is a bushy shrub that becomes dense and woody with maturity. The smooth-edge silver-gray leaves grow to 2 inches long, and the small lavender-purple to deep purple flowers form 6- to 8-inch-long terminal spikes for nearly a month in early summer. The whole plant is aromatic, releasing fragrance when you brush against it. Both its tiny purple or gray-white flower spikes and its foliage are fragrant. On a warm day the scent wafts throughout the garden. The clump-forming plants grow in a mound of gray foliage at a slow to moderate pace. Use fresh or dried flowers sparingly in cakes, cookies, muffins, jellies, black tea, vinegars, fruits, or eggs. Plant lavender along paths, where its perfumelike fragrance can be most appreciated.

When: Set out plants in spring or, where winters are mild, in fall.

Planting: Plant in full sun and average, well-drained soil. Space plants 1 to 3 feet apart.

Growing: Lavender tolerates drought, heat, and wind, but not high humidity, wet soil, or poor drainage. Cut back older plantings after they have flowered to rejuvenate them.

Shear plants after bloom to remove spent flowers and to promote density and repeat bloom. In spring wait until new growth has begun before cutting plants back; never cut them down to the ground. Propagate by seeds or tip cuttings in spring.

TOP LAVENDERS

Name	Flower color, scent, season	Height (feet)	Leaves	Features; Zones
L. ×allardii	Violet-blue clusters spread out on long stems. Slightly acrid. Late summer.	3½	Gray-green	Heat & humidity tolerant; 8–10
English lavender, L. angustifolia 'Alba'	White. Sweetly fragrant. Early to midsummer	2	Gray-green	5–10
L. a. 'Hidcote Blue'	Dark blue. Strong fragrance. Midsummer	1½	Gray-green	5–10
L. a. 'Irene Doyle'	Pale violet. Sweet scent. Repeat bloom in early and late summer	2	Gray-green	5–10
L. a. 'Lavender Lady'	Lavender blue on short stems. Early summer	1	Gray-green	Variable seed-grown strain; 5–10
L. a. 'Munstead'	Lavender blue. Pungent. Popular culinary variety. Early summer	1½	Green	5–10
French lavender, L. dentata	Purple spikes topped with bracts. Fragrant. Long blooming	3–4	Green to gray-green	8–10
L. 'Goodwin Creek Grey'	Dark purple on long stems. Strong scent. Long blooming	3	Light gray	Heat & humidity tolerant; 8–10
Lavandin, L. × intermedia 'Grosso'	Violet on long stem. Very strong lavender scent	2½	Gray	Heat & disease resistant; 7–10
Spanish lavender, L. stoechas	Dark purple on short stems, very aromatic. Summer	2–3	Gray-green	5–10

Harvesting: Cut flower stalks before the last bloom in the spike has opened. Hang the stalks in bundles upside down in a dark, airy place. Use lavender in potpourris.

Pests and diseases: Occasionally lavender is troubled by root rot or southern blight, particularly when it's not in an ideal site. Mulch with pea gravel to promote rapid drying around the crown.

Lemon balm (Melissa officinalis)

Type: Perennial, Zones 4–11
Edible part: Leaves
Typical size: 2–3'H×2'W

This old-time favorite bears leaves that give off an intense minty lemon fragrance, and its flowers attract bees. Lemon balm is excellent in cooked vegetables and fruit salads, and it also makes a tasty tea. The plant is bushy with heavily veined, heart-shape foliage. The lemon flavor and flower scent are more intense on plants grown in poor soil. Lemon balm is more tolerant of shade and moisture than most other herbs.

When: Set out plants in early spring.
Planting: Plant in full sun or partial shade and moist, rich, well-drained soil. Space nursery plants 2 feet apart, or start your own plants from seed. Lemon balm is excellent in containers.
Growing: Plants may be thin the first year but will fill out quickly. Harvest leaves before the plant flowers. Lemon balm reseeds and spreads readily, sometimes to the point of becoming a weed. Cut plants back in midsummer to prevent

Lemon balm leaves

self-sowing, and mulch in winter.
Harvesting: Collect leaves as you need them for fresh use. Preserve them by drying, although dried leaves lose much of their fragrance. To keep the leaves from turning black, dry them quickly on a rack, and store the dried leaves in an airtight container.
Pests and diseases: Powdery mildew is occasionally a problem, particularly in sites with poor air circulation.
Varieties: 'Aurea' has gold-tinged leaves.

Lemongrass, West Indian lemongrass
(Cymbopogon citratus)

Type: Perennial, Zones 9–11; annual elsewhere
Edible part: Leaves, stems
Typical size: 3–6'H×5–8'W

This strongly lemon-scented grass is the most desirable member of a small group of aromatic grasses native to tropical Southeast Asia. Its dark green, slightly ridged leaves are 3 feet long and ½ inch wide; it rarely blooms. The leaves and stalks are used for adding lemon flavor, especially in Thai food. Citral, commercially extracted from the plant's essential oil, is used in perfumes and cosmetics and to flavor soft drinks.

When: Set out plants or divisions in spring. Or if you live where winters are mild, plant in fall.
Planting: Grow lemongrass in full sun and sandy or other well-draining, fertile, slightly acid soil. Space the plants about 4 feet

Lemongrass leaves

Cut near the leaf base to harvest lemongrass.

apart. Cut back the tops of transplants to encourage root growth.

Growing: Maintain plants at the desired size by frequent pruning and harvesting. Divide plants in four to eight years to restore their vigor. Water in dry climates and during periods of drought. Protect plants from frost. In Zone 9 plants may go dormant during the winter; water them occasionally if there has been no rain. Dig a clump to bring indoors for winter use and to ensure a plant for next season just in case. Where lemongrass is not hardy, grow it as an annual.

Harvesting: Cut leaves at the base anytime, or dig up a whole section to use the entire stalk. Steep the leaves for an herbal tea or add them to soups and stocks as you would bay leaves. Chop the tender white bulbous ends for use in Asian cuisine and baked goods; the chopped pieces can be frozen for up to a year. Hang leaves upside down in a dark room to dry them for later use.

Pests and diseases: The plant's volatile oils are a natural pest control that repels insects; they also have natural antimicrobial and antifungal properties.

Varieties: East Indian lemongrass (*C. flexuosus*) matures faster and has a higher content of citral, the essential oil that gives lemongrass its distinctive lemony aroma. However, West Indian lemongrass is the type most commonly grown for culinary use. Its stalks are more numerous and its bulbous ends larger.

Lemon verbena (*Aloysia triphylla,* syn. *Lippia citriodora*)

Type: Perennial, Zones 9–10; annual elsewhere
Edible part: Leaves
Typical size: 6'H×6'W

A tropical shrub from Chile, lemon verbena has a sharp, intensely lemony fragrance and flavor. The essential oil has been used in perfumes since the 18th century. The leaves are added to sauces, marinades, salad dressings, teas, drinks, vinegars, fruit desserts, jellies, cakes, and ice creams. The plant's narrow, almost viny branches are covered in pale green leaves 3 inches long and ½ inch wide. The plants lose their leaves in cold winters and are semi-evergreen in milder climates. Flowers come in open sprays of tiny white-and-purple flowers.

When: Plant in spring after the soil is warm and the threat of frost is past.

Planting: Set the plant in full sun in average but well-drained soil, or in a

Lemon verbena leaves

container. Prune it flat against a wall or lattice or, with a central stake for support, as a standard.

Growing: Provide winter protection to keep the plant evergreen, or if it is in a container bring it indoors before the first frost. Lemon verbena may drop leaves during winter chills. In spring prune to maintain plant shape and size. Fertilize plants growing in containers during the summer. Propagate by softwood cuttings.

Harvesting: Collect leaves as needed for recipes, and chop any tough leaves finely when using them fresh. Preserve leaves by drying them.

Pests and diseases: Few insects or diseases significantly affect lemon verbena.

Lemon verbena tea

Lovage (*Levisticum officinale*)

Type: Perennial, Zones 3–9
Edible part: Leaves, stems, seeds, roots
Typical size: 2–4'H×2–4'W

Lovage is a relative of celery and on casual comparison looks like celery on steroids. The flavor is very similar, but discriminating palates note various differences. Unlike celery, in the garden lovage is a hardy perennial. Though its leaves and stems die to the ground in winter, its roots persist and produce new growth the following spring. In summer the dark green leaves are topped by small pale yellow flower blossoms that are very attractive to beneficial insects. The flavor of lovage complements sour pickles and vinegars, beef stock, and potato dishes. In northern coastal Italy lovage is popular in tomato sauces, often combined with oregano. The dried seeds are used in pickles.

When: Sow seeds directly in the garden in fall or early spring, or sow them indoors in late winter for transplanting in spring. Divide the roots of established lovage plant in spring or fall.

Planting: Plant in deep, fertile, consistently moist soil. Transplant seedlings when they are 3 to 6 inches tall and set them 4 feet apart, or use just a few plants and place them toward the back of the garden where their height will be useful.

Harvesting lovage

Growing: Lovage grows well in full sun or partial shade and in soil that is moist, fertile, and well drained. Plants will self-sow if flowers go to seed. Mulch lovage for overwintering in cold climates.

Harvesting: Begin collecting lovage leaves about three months after sowing seeds. Removing flowers as they appear will give you more leafstalks. Letting some flowers develop will invite beneficial insects into the garden and allow you to collect dried seeds. Pick the tender leaves and stalks anytime during the growing season and use them fresh in salads. Blanch the leafstalks as a vegetable side dish, or chop them and use them in cooking as you would celery. When dried or frozen, leaves hold their flavor about one year. Collect seeds by cutting off the nearly mature seedheads and hanging them upside down in bunches in paper bags.

Pests and diseases: Maintain adequate space between plants to help avoid blights. If any stems rot or leaves turn yellow or reddish, pull and destroy the whole plant and sow seeds in a new location.

Marjoram, sweet marjoram *(Origanum majorana)*

Type: Perennial, Zones 8–11; annual elsewhere
Edible part: Leaves, flowers
Typical size: 12–18"H×12–18"W

Marjoram

Like its relative oregano, marjoram is a primary herb in Italian cuisine, but marjoram leaves have a sweeter, milder flavor and aroma than oregano. Use marjoram in place of oregano, and because of its spicy sweetness you can also use it in soups, herb butter, and egg dishes as well as to flavor spinach, beans, and other vegetables. Try it in addition to or in place of sage in poultry stuffing and pork sausages. The plants are low growing and clump forming, producing tiny white, pink, and red flowers in mid- to late summer. The most tender of the *Origanum* species, marjoram is grown as an annual beyond mild-winter regions.

When: Set out plants after all danger of frost has passed.
Planting: Choose a sunny, well-drained location. Marjoram is adaptable but does best in light, fertile, slightly alkaline soil. Space plants about 12 inches apart. Propagate by division or by taking stem cuttings; plants are slow to start from seed.
Growing: Marjoram is well suited to container growing and looks especially attractive in hanging baskets. Cut the trailing stems frequently to encourage bushier growth. Protect plants from midday sun in hot climates. Marjoram dries out quickly, so keep the soil consistently moist but not waterlogged. To stimulate new growth, dig and divide plants every few years when they become woody. Overwinter plants where they are hardy by covering them with mulch, or dig

and divide plants in autumn and pot some for use indoors.
Harvesting: Snip freshly harvested leaves into salads or cooked dishes just before serving. Hang the stems upside down to dry in a cool, dark location with good air circulation. Pull the leaves from the stems when they are completely dry, crumble them, and store them in airtight glass jars. Dried marjoram retains its flavor better than dried oregano.
Varieties: **'Max'** is a tall, upright marjoram with yellow-green leaves. **'Erfo'** has pale grayish green leaves with a balsamlike fragrance. **Hardy marjoram**, sometimes sold as Italian oregano *(O. ×majoricum)*, is a cold-tolerant hybrid (Zones 6–9) of wild oregano and sweet marjoram that is both pungent and sweet. **Pot marjoram** *(O. onites)*, typically grown as an ornamental, is not as flavorful as sweet marjoram. It is hardy in Zones 8–11.

Mint *(Mentha* spp.)

Type: Perennial, zones variable
Edible part: Leaves, flowers
Typical size: 1–4'H×1–4'W

Plant mint in a pot to restrain its spread.

As fragrant and flavorful as they are unfussy, mints are welcome members of the garden, especially if you enjoy mint tea or mint julep. (Peppermint, *M. ×piperita*, is the classic tea mint, and spearmint, *M. spicata*, the one for mint julep.) Mint is one of the most common commercial flavors, and various mints are traditional remedies for fevers and especially stomachaches. Add fresh leaves to brewed tea while it is still hot, or snip leaves into fruit salad, ice cream or sherbet, and any dish containing peas. Mint is also made into sauces and jellies as an accompaniment to lamb and game meats, and it is a key ingredient in many Asian, Mediterranean, and Middle Eastern dishes. One little-known virtue of mints is that rodents are repelled by their strong scent, the reason they were known as "strewing" herbs, meaning stems were strewn about houses. There are numerous species of mint, and they are notorious

Variegated pineapple mint

TOP GARDEN MINTS

Name	Flavor	Size (H×W) in inches	Zones, varieties
Corn mint, field mint, wild mint, *M. arvensis*	Menthol	6–24"×12–40"	4–10
Japanese mint, *M. a. piperascens*	Peppermint	20"×36"	4–10
Ginger mint, red mint, *M. ×gracilis*	Mint and ginger	18"×24"	6–10; 'Madalene Hill'
Peppermint, *M. ×piperita*	Peppermint	12–30"×18"	3–8; 'Chocolate', orange mint, *M. × p. citrata*
Corsican mint, *M. requienii*	Sweet mint	½–1"×12"	7–10
Spearmint, *M. spicata*	Spearmint	12–26"×24"	4–10; *M. s. crispa*, 'Kentucky Colonel'
Apple mint, *M. suaveolens*	Mint and apple	18–36"×36"	5–10; pineapple mint, *M. s.* 'Variegata'

Wood edging prevents the spread of spearmint.

for cross-pollinating with each other and creating new types. The chart at above shows the best mints for home herb gardens.

When: Establish plants from cuttings or nursery stock in spring.

Planting: Plant mints in full sun or part shade and moist, rich, well-drained, slightly acid soil. Northern climates get the right amount of sun for the best mint oil production. Plant rooted stem cuttings or runners 3 inches deep and 2 feet apart. Space different types as far apart as you can to avoid cross-pollination.

Growing: Frequent cutting will keep large areas of mint looking attractive. Remove flowers as they appear, and pinch back the stems to encourage bushier growth. Keep the area around mint free of weeds and grass, which reduce yields and may affect flavor. Divide mints every few years. Cut the plants to the ground in late fall. Mints can spread far beyond the bounds you establish, so try growing them either in pots or containers sunk into the ground to prevent the roots from spreading too far. Or set boards 12 inches deep in the soil around the plants. All mints adapt well to containers.

Harvesting: Cut the leaves and the flower tops when the plants start to flower; hang them upside down to dry in small bundles, or spread them loosely in a shallow tray. When the stems are brittle, remove the leaves and flowers and store them in airtight containers. Freeze fresh leaves to retain their bright color.

Pests and diseases: Verticillium wilt, mint rust, mint anthracnose, spider mites, flea beetles, root borers, cutworms, root weevils, and aphids are occasionally troublesome. Knock off mites and aphids with a spray from the garden hose, being careful to spray the undersides of leaves. Plant mint in containers to avoid soil-borne diseases such as verticillium wilt. Provide good air circulation to thwart foliar diseases.

Nasturtium *(see Edible flowers)*

Oregano *(Origanum vulgare)*

Type: Perennial, Zones 5–11
Edible part: Leaves, flowers
Typical size: 12–24"H×24–40"W

An essential ingredient of Mediterranean cuisine, oregano is a low, sprawling shrubby perennial sporting aromatic leaves and small purple, pink, or white tubular flowers. The flavor of its leaves is widely appreciated in a wide range of dishes, combining well with eggs and cheese, not to mention garlic, basil, and olive oil.

When: Set out transplants or divisions in spring after frost danger is over.

Planting: Choose a sunny location with well-drained soil. Oregano is adaptable but does best in light, fertile, slightly alkaline soil. The more sun it receives, the more pungent the flavor of the leaves. Space plants 24 inches apart.

Growing: Divide plants every few years when they become woody. To obtain two large harvests, cut the whole plant back to 3 inches just before it flowers, then again in late summer. Avoid root rot by watering only during periods of drought. Propagate oregano by division or from stem cuttings; growth is slow from seed.

Harvesting: Oregano's flowers attract bees and butterflies, but the leaves are best picked just before the buds open. Cut succulent stems as needed, and snip fresh leaves (or flowers) into salads or cooked dishes just before serving them. Hang stems upside down to dry in a cool, dark location with good air circulation. Pluck the leaves from the stems when they are completely dry, crumble them, and store them in airtight jars. Fresh leaves can also be frozen for later use.

Varieties:

'**Aureum**', which is sometimes sold as creeping golden marjoram, has yellow-green leaves and white flowers.

'**Aureum Crispum**' bears curly golden leaves and pink flowers.

'**Compactum**' is a low-growing aromatic and edible groundcover that rarely blooms.

'**Kaliteri**' has spicy silver-gray leaves.

'**Thumble's**

Oregano

Harvesting Greek oregano

Variety' forms low, small mounds of gold- and-green variegated foliage. **'Roseum'** has green leaves and rose flowers. **'White Anniversary'** ('Polyphant') is a tender cultivar with variegated green-and-white foliage.

Greek oregano, *(O. v. hirtum,* formerly *O. heracleoticum)* looks similar to common oregano but has more and larger oil glands, resulting in more intense flavor. Most commercial dried oregano is from this plant. **Italian oregano** *(O. ×majoricum)* is a hybrid of wild oregano and sweet marjoram that is both pungent and sweet but also hardy. **Cuban oregano** *(Plectranthus amboinicus)* is an African plant that shares many of the flavor qualities of oregano. Also known as Spanish thyme and Indian mint, it grows about 1 foot high and 3 feet wide. Grow it as an annual anywhere; it doesn't withstand cold. **Mexican oregano** *(Lippia graveolens)* grows 4 feet high and wide and is perennial in Zones 9 to 11. Its flavor and intensity are similar to those of common oregano, and some people actually prefer it.

Oriental garlic *(see Chives)*
Oswego tea *(see Edible flowers)*

Parsley *(Petroselinum crispum)*

Type: Biennial grown as an annual
Edible part: Leaves
Typical size: 8–24"H×8–24"W

Valued for its vitamin content and unique mildly grassy flavor, parsley is excellent for fresh use and in sautés, soups, salads, and herb butter. The dark green leaves are divided into feathery sections and may be flat or curly.

When: Sow seeds or set out transplants in early spring. Parsley seed is slow to germinate. Warm the seedbed with black plastic or use a cold frame over the bed to concentrate heat. Keep the soil evenly moist and weed free.

Planting: The planting location should have rich, moist, friable, well-drained, acid to neutral soil. Space transplants and seedlings 10 to 18 inches

Italian flat-leaf parsley

apart. Parsley also grows well in a pot, outdoors or indoors, in a sunny spot.

Growing: For a steady supply, sow seeds in spring and fall. When seedlings develop their first leaves, thin to 10 inches apart. Use a soluble vegetable plant food on mature plants once a month. Use mulch around curly parsley to keep soil particles from gathering in the leaf crevices. To keep parsley productive, snip the full length of the stems regularly; remove flower stalks as soon as they begin to form. Late in the season allow a plant to develop flowers and form seeds.

Harvesting: Harvest parsley as needed, and encourage new growth by cutting outer stems at least 1 inch above the soil. The whole plant can be cut before winter or mulched for overwintering in the garden. Plants kept in an insulated cold frame will continue to produce new stems until the following spring. Parsley can be refrigerated for up to one month or frozen for up to one year. To dry parsley, hang the stems upside down or spread them in a single layer on screens in a cool, shady, well-ventilated location. Use leaves, fresh or dried, in cooking. Its mild flavor blends well with many foods.

Pests and diseases: Knock off aphids with a strong spray of water from the garden hose. Carrot weevils may overwinter on parsley or nearby carrot foliage. Parsley attracts the

'Moss Curled' parsley with red and orange zinnias

swallowtail butterfly. Its caterpillars will eat some parsley leaves, but not enough to damage the plant, so the insect is best admired rather than controlled.

Varieties: **'Moss Curled'** is the most popular curly-leaf parsley. **'Giant of Naples'** is a flat-leaf Italian type. Turnip-rooted or **Hamburg parsley** *(P. c. tuberosum)* is grown for its fleshy, parsniplike root that tastes like a combination of parsley and celery; sow seeds in spring and harvest roots in fall.

Pinks *(see Edible flowers)*
Pot marjoram *(see Marjoram)*

Rose *(Rosa spp. and hybrids)*

Type: Shrub, Zones 2–10
Edible part: Flowers, fruits (hips)
Typical size: 2–8'H×3–5'W

No other flower has stirred people's passions through the ages like the rose. As an herb, rose petals are valued for their fragrance and are used in salads, sweets, and beverages. The edible fruits, or hips, are a rich source of vitamin C. If the aroma of old roses has ever enthralled you, chances are you've already added one to your garden. The fragrances are heavy and lingering. Old roses are easy to grow, quite hardy and very pest free. The petals, which may be delicately single or heavily double, come mostly in shades of pink, rose, and white, with some yellows. Roses are deciduous or evergreen

Rugosa rose hips

shrubs, depending on climate, growing from less than 2 feet to 8 feet and taller. The leaves are composed of pairs of oval, pointed, toothed leaflets on woody, thorned stems. Flowers with five to dozens of petals in various colors are borne singly or in clusters. Some types bloom once in late spring; others flower throughout the growing season. The hips ripen to red, orange, or yellow.

When: Plant bare-root roses in late winter or very early spring, as soon as the soil is workable. Set out container-grown plants anytime.

Planting: Choose a location in full sun and where the soil is rich, moist, and well drained. Space plants 3 to 5 feet apart. In cold climates set the bud union of grafted plants 2 inches below soil level. In other regions set at the same level as the plant grew at the nursery.

Growing: Prune to shape the plant and remove deadwood in spring. Water as needed to keep the soil moist. At least once in spring feed plants with compost, manure, or a fertilizer designed for roses. Propagate by stem cuttings.

Harvesting: Collect the petals as the flowers open, preserve them by drying, and use them in salads, teas and other drinks, syrups, vinegars, fruit pies, cookies, and sorbets. Rose petals also can be candied. Collect hips when they ripen after flower petals drop, and use them in jellies, jams, teas, syrups, and sauces.

Pests and diseases: Aphids, spider mites, and Japanese beetles are common rose pests. Wash them off with a spray of water, or use insecticidal soap. Good sanitation and air circulation discourage black spot and powdery mildew. Plant varieties resistant to these fungal diseases.

Varieties: The species and older varieties have the best culinary properties. Consider the **white rose** (R. ×alba), Zones 5 to 10; **dog rose** (R. canina), Zones 3 to 10; **cabbage rose** (R. ×centifolia), Zones 6 to 10; **damask rose** (R. ×damascena), Zones 5 to 10; **gallica rose** (R. gallica), Zones 6 to 10; and **rugosa rose** (R. rugosa), Zones 2 to 10. Many named varieties of each are available. Some with abundant hips are dog and rugosa roses; **eglantine rose** (R. rubiginosa), Zones 5 to 10; and **apple rose** (R. villosa), Zones 5 to 10.

Making rose hip jelly

Rosemary (Rosmarinus officinalis)

Type: Shrub, Zones 6–10; annual elsewhere
Edible part: Leaves
Typical size: 1–6'H×2–4'W

A clipped rosemary hedge fronts roses.

Pruned into topiary or allowed to become bushy, rosemary is a favorite of gardeners and cooks alike. It is an evergreen shrub with scaly bark and narrow dark green leaves that have a distinctive, pungent, piney scent. In spring and early summer the plants are loaded with pretty little blue flowers. Upright and creeping varieties of rosemary are available. Use the aromatic leaves with meats and in recipes that include potatoes, tomatoes, eggplant, or peppers as well as in soups, stews, and marinades. Insert a few fresh stems into a bottle of vinegar or olive oil.

When: Set out transplants or container plants in fall or, in Zones 6 and 7, in spring after frost danger is past.

Planting: Choose a sunny, protected location that drains well. Rosemary grows well in average garden soil as well as in containers indoors and out. It is drought-tolerant.

Growing: In cold climates, grow rosemary in containers and bring them indoors in winter. Grow the plants in a greenhouse or place them in a sunny, cool window. Rosemary must have high humidity to overwinter well indoors. Regularly harvest a few stems throughout the season to encourage bushier growth. In warm-winter areas protect rosemary from harsh winds that may dry it out. Grow new plants from cuttings or by layering. Rosemary responds well to pruning and shearing.

Harvesting: Cut a few succulent stems above woody growth as needed throughout the growing season. Strip the resinous leaves from the stems and chop or grind them. Tie harvested stems in small bunches and hang them upside down in a cool, airy space to dry. In northern climates pull the plants up before the first frost and hang them by their roots to dry. Pull the dried leaves from the stems and store them in an airtight container for up to two years. Pulverize them before adding them to foods; the whole leaves can be chewy. Rosemary also can be frozen for long-term storage but loses its rich color.

Varieties: All are hardy to Zone 8 unless otherwise noted: **'Arp'** has gray-green foliage and blue flowers; Zone 6. **'Athens**

Rosemary sprig flavors lamb chops.

'**Blue Spires'** grows upright to 6 feet; Zone 7. **'Blue Boy'** is a dwarf, only 12 inches tall by 8 inches wide; it does well in containers. **'Prostratus'** grows 2 feet tall, 8 feet wide, hugging the ground and draping over walls. **'Lockwood de Forest'** looks like 'Prostratus' but with brighter green leaves. **'Madalene Hill'** has dark green leaves and pale blue flowers; Zone 6. **'Majorca Pink'** has an intermediate habit—upright but spreading with some trailing stems. **'Rexford'** is a warm-climate cultivar with especially good flavor; Zone 9.

Sage (*Salvia officinalis*)

Type: Perennial, Zones 4–10
Edible part: Leaves
Typical size: 12–24"H×24–36"W

Sage leaves

Cultures around the globe have valued sage for its medicinal properties. Today it's enjoyed for its flavor, which is a featured favorite in poultry seasoning. Sage is an evergreen shrub in mild climates and winter-deciduous in cold regions. It has square, woody stems and long gray-green leaves. In early to midsummer mauve-blue tubular flowers bloom on 3-foot-tall stems rising above the leaves.

Cutting back sage in spring

When: Transplant container-grown plants in spring.
Planting: Sage is adaptable to most soils but does best in rich loam that drains well.
Growing: Trim to shape a plant after it has finished blooming, but leave the woody stems to resprout new growth. To have fresh leaves through winter, dig plants in late autumn and pot them in containers.
Harvesting: Cut about 6 to 8 inches of succulent growth above the woody stems two or three times before the plant blooms in summer. For the best flavor snip stems in the morning after the dew has dried. Clean the stems and dry them in a dark, airy space either by tying them together in small bunches and hanging them upside down or spreading them on screens. Crumble the dried leaves off the stems and store them in airtight jars up to three years. The fresh leaves are delicious snipped into egg and

Purple-leaved sage

'Tricolor' sage in hanging basket

cheese dishes.
The dried leaves are outstanding added to poultry stuffing and ground into a dry-rub powder for meats.
Varieties: **'Dwarf White'** is a good choice for small gardens and container growing. Its silver-white foliage and white flowers are aromatic, and the plant grows only to 12 inches tall. **'Extrakta'** has smooth green leaves and is exceptionally flavorful. **'Icterina'** is variegated green-and-gold. **'Tricolor'** leaves are variegated green, cream, and purple.

Savory, summer and winter (*Satureja* spp.)

Type: Annual (summer savory) and Perennial (winter savory), Zones 5–8
Edible part: Leaves, flowers
Typical size: 3–18"H×2–24"W

With a flavor similar to thyme and sweet marjoram, the leaves and flowers of both winter and summer savory add great flavor to bean, egg, vegetable, beef, pork, and poultry dishes. Summer savory (*S. hortensis*) is a sweet-flavored, upright annual with long gray-green leaves and small white or pink flowers. Its flavor is more delicate than that of winter savory (*S. montana*), a semievergreen spreading perennial with trailing stems and petite white to lavender flowers. Along with a stronger flavor, it has a stronger pine scent than summer savory. Both plants bloom in summer.
When: Set out plants of either type in spring, or plant winter savory in fall where winters are mild.
Planting: Savory is adaptable to most soils. Start winter savory seeds indoors four to six weeks before the last frost date, or plant transplants or rooted cuttings after the soil warms in spring. You can direct-sow seeds of summer savory

Summer savory

Winter savory

A patchwork of gold- and green-leaved thyme

When: In spring, plant divisions in well-drained soil.
Planting: Space nursery plants or divisions 8 to 12 inches apart. Starting with divisions is the best way to establish specific varieties. Or start seeds indoors or sow directly into the garden.
Growing: Water when needed to maintain soil moisture, but do not overwater. Clear weeds by hand. Shear off the tiny flowers after plants finish blooming to keep energy concentrated in the leaves. Plants may lose vigor and need replacing in a few years; grow new plants by division, from cuttings, or by layering.
Harvesting: Strip the leaves from the stems and use them fresh. To dry thyme, harvest handfuls of the stems, tie small bundles together, and hang them upside down in a cool, airy room. When the leaves are completely dry, crumble them off the stems and store them in airtight glass jars for up to two years.

Harvesting common thyme

Pests and diseases: Overwatering and slow-draining soil invite root rot.
Varieties: Caraway thyme (*T. herba-barona*) has a caraway scent, shiny green leaves, and lavender flowers. **'Lemon Carpet'** is low growing with wiry stems and a lemony caraway flavor. **Common thyme** (*T. vulgaris*) has a strong thyme fragrance. **'Orange Spice'** creates a dense groundcover mat. **Lemon thyme** (*T. ×citriodorus*) has dark green foliage, a lemon scent, and an upright habit. **'Archer's Gold'** is highly scented and retains its color. **'Argenteus'** has silver-edged leaves, and **'Aureus'** has gold-edged leaves. **'Silver Queen'** produces silver-splashed foliage. **Orange thyme** (*T.* 'Fragrantissimus') has a spicy orange scent and flavor. **Portuguese thyme** (*T. carnosus*) is more upright growing with lilac, pink, or white flowers.

Drying bunch of thyme in paper bag

after the last frost date in spring in northern climates or anytime during the growing season in mild-winter zones. Plant the seeds ½ inch deep and 1 inch apart. Interplant them with beans, beets, eggplant, or cucumbers. Winter savory can be transplanted from cuttings in spring.
Growing: Savory needs full sun and average, well-drained soil. Keep the soil consistently moist but not waterlogged. Hand weed around young plants. Trim summer savory regularly to encourage new growth. Prune winter savory to a miniature hedge, if desired.
Harvesting: Summer savory is ready to harvest in 60 to 70 days after sowing seeds. Winter savory can be trimmed the first time 50 days after planting cuttings or 75 to 100 days after planting seeds. Cut stems from either plant for drying when flowers begin to form. Spread them on screens or tie them in small bunches and hang them upside down in a dark, airy space. When the leaves are completely dry, strip them from the stems, making sure to remove any woody parts. Store the leaves in airtight containers for up to two years.
Varieties: Summer savory: 'Aromata' is a peppery cultivar bred for high leaf yields. **Winter savory: 'Nana'** is an extremely cold-hardy dwarf variety only 3 inches tall and spreading to 2 feet. **African savory** (*S. biflora*) has a spicy lemon aroma and flavor that blends well in sweet or savory dishes, but it is a tropical plant suitable only for Zones 9 to 11.

Spanish thyme (*see Oregano*)	**Sweet marjoram** (*see Marjoram*)
Sweet alice (*see Anise*)	**Sweet violet** (*see Edible flowers*)

Thyme (*Thymus* spp.)

Type: Perennial, Zones 4–9
Edible part: Leaves, flowers
Typical size: 3–12"H×18"W

The biggest decision when growing thyme is which of the 40 or more species and cultivars to plant. All are small creeping plants with many woody stems. The aromatic leaves are ½ inch long. The small bluish purple to pink flowers open in summer and attract bees. Use the leaves and flowers in salads, soups, stews, stuffings, vinegars, and vegetables. Thyme blends well with almost any beef, pork, poultry, or seafood dish and adds a sophisticated flavor to cheese and egg dishes.

Winter marjoram (*see Oregano*)

Solving plant problems

▲ Gardens that include many different kinds of plants and are obviously well-maintained are the gardens with the fewest pest problems.

▲ Looking closely, sometimes with a magnifing glass, is necessary to properly identify some pests, such as these flea beetle holes in radish leaves.

Gardens are dynamic environments that are subject to innumerable interactions among plants, weather, soil, insects, spiders, birds, lizards, toads, and other living things, including humans. Most organisms contribute positively to the health of plants. Insects, for instance, pollinate flowers, without which we'd have fewer fruits, not to mention seeds for next season.

A pest is an insect, disease, animal, or weed that is causing problems for cultivated plants. Always observe pests in your garden before intervening; don't assume an unfamiliar insect is a pest. The web of relationships in the garden seeks balance, and in many circumstances nothing is required of the gardener.

Most insects and diseases thrive in specific seasons or temperature and moisture levels. Changes in weather or predation by birds and insects will often knock out pest populations before they are a problem. For example, if aphids are sucking plant sap on tender new growth, watch carefully for a week or so. It is likely that green lacewings or ladybugs will soon appear. Their larvae feed voraciously on aphids.

The best thing a gardener can do to prevent pests from gaining the upper hand is to grow healthy plants. Research shows that healthy plants have strong immune systems. They react to pest outbreaks by releasing chemicals that help withstand the attack. The key to growing healthy plants is simple: Provide the sun exposure, soil conditions, moisture levels, and nutrients that the plants require, and they will reward you with vigorous growth.

Integrated pest management

Integrated pest management (IPM) is an approach that promotes good gardening practices as the first and most effective step. It views all the elements in the garden—plants, weather, soil, insects, and the gardener's actions—as part of an interconnected system. The goal of IPM is to solve a problem with the least toxic effect on all involved.

If a problem does arise,

IPM encourages the gardener to look at all the options. Blending a variety of good gardening practices and pest control techniques is more effective over the long term than reliance on pest control products alone. IPM does not preclude the use of pest control products. However, in most instances, a combination of other methods will alleviate the problem without chemicals. IPM uses common-sense gardening practices, most of which you probably do already.

Here are the key concepts of IPM, ranked in order of most fundamental to more involved practices.

● **Prevent problems** Healthy plants and sound gardening techniques and habits are the first steps in an effective home garden IPM program.

● **Identify symptoms and pests** This step requires vigilance in the garden. As you work in and enjoy your garden, look for signs of stress or disease, such as yellowing, wilting, puckering, discoloration, and holes in or chewed edges on foliage. Look around to try to identify the cause. For tiny insects, such as mites, aphids, and the crawler stage of scales, hold a piece of white paper under a leaf and tap the leaf. Then look for specks crawling on the paper. You'll find that a magnifying glass is helpful.

Accurately identify what you find. Use reference books

or put a sample of the insect and the plant damage in a plastic bag or jar and take it to a nursery or county cooperative extension office. Identification is essential before attempting any control method, especially spraying.

● **Monitor the situation** If you think a plant has a pest, watch to see what changes take place over the next few days, or perhaps longer if minimal changes occur. Are there signs of damage to the foliage? Does the entire plant show signs of decline? Has another insect arrived on the scene, perhaps to consume the first? Depending on the type of insect, plant material, and weather conditions, as well as your goals for specific plants, you may decide to take action quickly, before all the strawberries disappear for example. Conversely, if changes are slow and the plants are experiencing minimal damage, you may not need to intervene at all.

● **Decide if control is required** Only a small percent of insects are potential pests. Determine if the damage is sufficient to warrant control. Gardeners have different tolerances for what is acceptable and must make that determination for their own circumstances.

● **Choose control methods** Choosing which (if any) control methods to use is the backbone of an effective IPM program. A successful solution integrates all factors, including the pest, plant, growing conditions, weather, gardener's needs, potential control methods, and cost. This is where you can have significant impact on your surroundings by starting with the least toxic control methods before advancing to other options, using chemical pest control products as a last resort.

● **Keep records and evaluate results** This final step is sometimes neglected. However, because insects are usually seasonal, your records will help you make changes in your plant care routine. Jot down the type of insect, what plant it was on, the type of

damage (if any), weather conditions, the time of year, and control methods and their effectiveness.

Best garden practices

These techniques are fundamental steps that help ensure healthy plants.

● **Cultural controls** Cultural techniques start with selecting plants appropriate for your growing conditions and maintaining them properly. If plants look stressed, changes in care often improve the situation.

● **Make disease resistance a priority when selecting plants** Disease resistance is noted as an acronym at the end of cultivar names. For example, 'Celebrity' VFNT tomato is resistant to verticillium (V), fusarium (F), nematodes (N), and tobacco mosaic virus (T), all problems that can plague tomatoes. Catalog descriptions and seed packs contain disease-resistance information.

● **Adequately space plants** Encouraging air circulation and sunlight penetration helps prevent common fungal diseases such as powdery mildew.

● **Crop rotation** Members of the same family of plants should not follow each other in a planting rotation. For example, eggplant, pepper, and tomato are in the nightshade family. If possible, allow at least three years before replanting a member of the same family in a particular location.

● **Water right** Avoid over- or underwatering plants. If necessary, increase the time interval between irrigating to keep roots from rotting in wet soil. Water deeply to soak the entire root area and if necessary, to leach salts beyond the root zone. As a guide, water should soak 1 foot deep for shallow-rooted plants, such as annuals and perennials, 2 feet deep for shrubs, and 3 feet deep for trees. Apply water directly to the soil with a soaker hose or drip system. Overhead watering leaves foliage wet, which encourages fungal diseases.

▲ Picking up and removing fallen apples and leaves is an essential step in limiting diseases such as scab, and insects such as codling moth.

● **Use an organic mulch** Spread mulch around the base of plants (but away from the trunk or main stem) to maintain soil moisture, decrease soil temperature, inhibit weed germination, and add nutrients to the soil over time.

● **Feed only when needed** Overfeeding leads to an overabundance of tender new growth, which attracts insects, such as aphids, that like to feed on plant sap. Follow fertilizer label instructions precisely for application rates and methods.

● **Pull weeds** Remove weeds before they flower and set seed. Toss them on the compost pile as a source of nitrogen. If you pull weeds that spread by tenacious underground runners, discard them in the trash.

● **Clean up the garden** Pick up fallen fruit and nut hulls, which can harbor pests. Promptly remove dead, broken, or diseased branches. Always use sharp tools and make clean cuts when pruning. Disinfect tools with rubbing alcohol or dilute chlorine bleach between plants or between cuts on the same plant if you suspect disease. Clean up all branch trimmings and debris after pruning. Applying sealants to cuts is unnecessary. Research shows that sealants interfere with a plant's natural healing mechanism.

▲ Learn to recognize different stages of some pests. These larvae of Colorado potato beetle only feed for about three weeks, but will damage leaves severely.

▲ Praying mantids are the *Tyrannosaurus rex* of the garden. They'll eat anything smaller than they are that they can catch.

▲ Pests such as aphids have such a tenuous grip on their host that a strong spray of water is usually enough to wash them off.

▲ Preventing cabbage moth with a row cover, coupled with frequent close inspections, heads off trouble allowing you to harvest a perfect crop.

Managing garden weeds

Most gardeners would agree that weeds are the most time consuming and persistent garden problem. Efforts to eliminate them early payoff later. Spending one or two growing seasons diligently removing every weed before it makes seeds can reduce the need for future weed control to a minimum because fewer weeds will sprout.

Weeds can be divided into two categories. The first includes weeds that produce

▲ Use the sun's energy to heat soil sufficiently to kill most weeds, weed seeds, and many diseases.

enormous quantities of seeds. These weeds are often easy to kill, either with weed control products or with a hoe, but new ones keep appearing. Weeds in the second category are hard to kill, often because they have persistent

▲ Raised beds surrounded by heavily mulched paths prevent most weeds.

underground parts that can sprout into new plants. A few especially troublesome weeds, such as dandelions, have both of these characteristics.

The first category of weeds is most easily controlled by keeping the seeds from sprouting. Begin the battle in the spring, or whenever seeds germinate, by applying a mulch. The mulch alone will prevent many seeds from sprouting. Then, once a week throughout the growing season, hand pull every weed that appears in your yard. As weeds are pulled the mulch will begin to mix with the soil and weed seeds are brought to the surface. For the mulch to remain an effective weed barrier, refresh it.

In lieu of a mulch, use an oscillating hoe. Working the top few inches of soil to dislodge the weeds easily kills young seedlings of this type of weed. Repeat this light weeding every week or so until the vegetables are large enough to shade out any new weeds.

The second category are weeds that are harder to kill. On the other hand, once they are eliminated they're less likely to return. Killing these weeds requires more drastic effort. Dig out perennial weeds, such as quackgrass and dandelion, to remove as much of the root system as possible. For this purpose use a taproot- or Cape Cod–type weeder. Another way to deal with perennial, tough weeds is to cover them with a mulch of black plastic or old carpet. Or, if you're preparing a new, weedy area for a garden, perhaps you might choose to use a weed control product such as glyphosate.

Solarizing soil

Using the sun's energy to heat and partially sterilize your soil is an effective way to eliminate many weeds as well as some other pests. The process entails covering your garden area with clear plastic for four to six weeks during

▲ A cover crop of buckwheat is planted in summer to reduce weed problems, and to improve availability of phosphorus.

the hottest part of the year. Some pests are killed within a few days, but a month or more is required to assure control of most pests. Essentially a ground-level greenhouse, the plastic traps the sun's energy and raises the temperature of the top several inches of soil sufficiently to kill weed seeds.

Soil solarization is an especially useful technique where summers are hot and you can plant a garden in the fall. Where summer high temperatures are not reliably in excess of 80°F solarization is not effective. And where winters are cold and the growing season is short, solarizing your soil requires sacrificing most of the growing season.

To solarize your soil use clear plastic. Black or colored tarps will not allow the soil to heat to the highest possible temperatures. For most gardeners, 1½- to 2-mil clear plastic is best.

Before laying the plastic, cultivate and level the soil, remove all weeds, plants, debris and large clods of soil, just as if you are preparing the soil for planting. Maximum soil heating occurs when the tarp is close to the soil; air pockets caused by clods, debris, or furrows decrease the effectiveness of the treatment. Water thoroughly so that soil is moist 6 inches deep.

Solar heating can effectively control annual bluegrass, nightshades, mallow, pigweeds, mustards,

▲ A mulch of black plastic blocks weeds and maintains soil warmth. Set a soaker hose underneath to ease watering.

and other winter annual weeds. To a somewhat lesser degree, soil solarization can eliminate bermudagrass. Crabgrass and purslane are only partially controlled.

Cover Crops

Cover crops provide many benefits, among them reducing weeds. Because they grow fast, cover crops outcompete weeds in the struggle for light and nutrients. Once the cover crop is cut off and left on the surface, it acts as a mulch to shade the soil and prevents germination of weed seeds.

Cover crops can also suppress weeds chemically. Some plants release natural chemicals, either while they are growing or while they are decomposing, which prevent the germination or growth of other plants. Researchers have effectively used cover crops of wheat, barley, oats, rye, sorghum, and sudangrass to suppress weeds. Weed suppression has also been reported from residues of crimson clover, hairy vetch, and other legumes. See page 24 for more about using cover crops.

Mulch

Mulch is one of the easiest and most effective ways to suppress weeds. A mulch is a layer of material—compost, plastic, spun landscape fabrics, paper, or whatever— that covers the soil and excludes sunlight. Since most

◄ Dandelions are perennial and have deep taproots. To handpull, extract the entire taproot, using a tool to pry it out.

▲ Use a hoe to cut off annual weeds at the soil level, such as lambsquarters, without exposing weed seeds to light.

weeds need sunlight to germinate, shading the soil surface prevents weed seeds from germinating.

Compost makes an ideal mulch. Three to four inches deposited on the soil surface will eliminate most annual weed growth, allow good water penetration, and provide a desirable soil conditioner once the mulch is incorporated into the soil. Organic mulches of any kind gradually decompose and gradually become part of the soil and create a positive benefit in the process. Find more about compost and making your own on page 23.

Leaf mold and pine needles increase the soil's acidity more than most other organic mulches. Where soils are naturally alkaline, such as in most of the West, this is a benefit. In the East where soils are naturally acidic be aware that using these kinds of materials for mulch means using more limestone to counteract their acidity.

Black polyethylene and spun polypropylene plastic are the most common manufactured mulches. By excluding light from reaching leaves, black plastic starves plants trying to grow beneath it. Besides providing good weed control, black plastic warms the soil at shallow depths in the spring, which can help warm-season crops get an early start. Set the transplants or seeds through holes cut in the plastic after laying it in place. Plastic mulches of various other

colors—specifically green, red, and white—are recommended for specific vegetable crops for their beneficial effect on growth. These mulches are included in the descriptions of the crops they benefit.

Mulches created from spunbonded polypropylene fabric are preferable in many situations because they allow water to pass through while excluding light. They are also more resistant to puncture than plastic.

Weed control products

While weed control products are useful weed control tools in some situations, they are rarely used in food gardens. Toxicity to crops, difficulty in applying products accurately, and the potential for toxic residues are the main reasons for avoiding them.

Glyphosate is one possible exception because it can kill some of the most persistent weeds you're likely to encounter, such as Bermudagrass, bindweed, and dallisgrass. You might decide to use glyphosate to help clear a new garden area, or once every few years to eliminate weeds particularly resistant to other measures. Even though glyphosate will easily control many annual weeds, using it for that purpose is less easily justified.

As for any weed control product, apply glyphosate carefully. For instance, don't try to use a hose end type applicator because it's too difficult to control the spray. Pressurized, pump-type sprayers are the easiest devices to control and generally provide the safest application.

Apply glyphosate with care because of its potential hazard to surrounding plants. A few drops of it can severely injure young trees, and it can kill lawn or herbaceous plants if their leaves come in contact with the spray.

New kinds of weed control products are made of natural materials such as fatty acids, which are soap-like, and acetic acid, otherwise known as vinegar. The fatty acids work by dissolving the waxy covering over leaves so that the exposed tissues dry up and die. These products will kill crabgrass, spotted spurge, and many other annual weeds, though they are less effective on perennial weeds or weeds that are well established. Sprays containing 10 percent acetic acid readily kill young weeds; older weeds more often need 20 percent solutions to be effective. Spray and thoroughly soak weeds such as dandelion to kill them with vinegar. Even though these weed control products are made of what are familiar ingredients, both can damage desirable plants they contact.

Glyphosate, fatty acids, and acetic acid are kinds of post-emergence weed control products, meaning they are applied to existing, growing weeds. Another category of weed killer is called pre-emergence, meaning it is applied to soil to prevent weed seeds from germinating. Corn gluten meal is a popular pre-emergence weed control product derived from corn. Synthetic pre-emergence weed control products that are sometimes used in edible gardens are pendimethalin and trifluralin. Use any kind of pre-emergence with caution in a vegetable or herb garden, or where you might be soon planting seeds. Read product labels carefully before applying any weed control product.

▲ Weeds growing in mulch are loosely rooted and easy to dislodge.

▲ Use a shallow cultivator to turn soil over and kill weeds while they're small.

▲ Powered cultivars are available to make quick work of weedy beds.

▲ Weeding by hand, a little each day, is how to manage weeds within crops.

▲ Use a narrow profile cultivator to work in close quarters.

Gallery of common weeds

Bermuda grass

Bermuda grass (*Cynodon dactylon*) is a perennial grass with a vigorous creeping habit. The vigorous roots may grow several feet deep, making the plants drought- and heat-tolerant and also difficult to kill. Bermuda grass spreads by seeds as well as above- and belowground stems.

Control: Smother with a heavy layer of fabric or black plastic for several months. Apply glyphosate any time the grass is actively growing.

Common chickweed

Common chickweed (*Stellaria media*) prefers damp, shady areas with rich soil. It is a winter annual that grows from seeds that sprout in the fall. The ½- to 2-inch heart-shape leaves are attached to the stems by a slightly hairy stalk. The creeping stems root at their joints wherever they touch the soil. Small, white, starlike flowers bloom in clusters on the ends of the stems from spring through fall.

Control: Hand cultivation and a 2-inch-thick mulch layer together provide most of the control needed in home gardens. Soil solarization will kill seeds.

Crabgrass

Crabgrass (*Digitaria* spp.) is a grass, annual weed that grows fast in hot, dry weather. The blades are 2 to 5 inches long and ⅓ inch wide. Seed heads are 1 to 3 inches across (smooth crabgrass) or 4 to 5 inches across (large crabgrass). The seeds remain dormant over the winter and then sprout in the spring. The plants are killed by the first fall frost.

Control: Use a mulch and spread out irrigations, watering only as often as necessary. Frequent cultivation and weed control products that contain acetic acid also can control crabgrass. Use a pre-emergence weed control product containing corn gluten meal.

Dandelion

Dandelions (*Taraxacum officinale*) are rosette-shape perennials that have thick, fleshy taproots that may grow 2 to 3 feet deep in the soil. The yellow flowers bloom primarily in spring but continue until frost. Wind carries the seeds. The taproot survives winters.

Control: Pull roots from moist soil. Take care to extract the entire taproot; even a small piece is enough to regenerate the plant. A mulch will prevent seeds under it from germinating and make any that do manage to grow easier to pull. Smother dandelions under a heavy mulch or black plastic. Or use a weed control product that contains glyphosate.

Field bindweed

Field bindweed (*Convolvulus arvensis*) thrives in rich, heavy soil. The stems may be 3 to 9 feet long with arrow-shape leaves 1 to 2 inches long. White to pink funnel-shape flowers the size of a quarter bloom and produce seed from May to September. Bindweed reproduces by seeds and pieces of the rhizome. Any rhizome pieces left behind after hand pulling will sprout into new plants.

Control: Spray glyphosate when bindweed is growing vigorously, usually midsummer.

Lambsquarters

Lambsquarters (*Chenopodium album*) grows 1 to 4 feet tall from a short, branched taproot, and is common in gardens. The plant is a host for the beet leafhopper, which transmits curly top, a virus disease of beets. Leaves are 1 to 3 inches long with toothed edges. Seeds remain dormant over the winter and sprout in the spring.

Control: Hand pull or remove by hoeing. A 2-inch-thick layer of mulch will prevent seeds from germinating, and solarization can kill dormant seeds. Prevent the seeds from germinating in vegetable gardens with a pre-emergence weed control product containing corn gluten meal, pendimethalin, or trifluralin.

Nightshade

Nightshade (*Solanum* spp.) grows in rich, moist soil and frequently creeps into home gardens from surrounding fields. The stems may grow up to 9 feet long, creeping along the ground or twining on fences and plants. The stems frequently root where they touch the soil. Dark green to purple leaves, 1 to 4 inches long, have varying shapes. Blue, violet, or white flowers with yellow centers resemble tomato flowers and appear May to November. The flowers are followed by green berries that turn red or black when ripe. Birds spread the yellow seeds from inside the berries.

Control: Hand pull and dispose of the vining stems as well as any berries that are formed. Remaining pieces of stem will root, and seeds inside the berries germinate readily.

Nutsedge

The two most common troublesome nutsedges are yellow nutsedge and purple nutsedge (*Cyperus* spp.). Yellow nutsedge is found throughout the United States, and purple nutsedge is primarily a problem in the southeastern United States and in coastal California. All nutsedges prefer poorly drained, rich soil. They thrive in frequently watered garden areas. The grasslike, yellow-green leaves grow on erect triangular stems. Seedheads are purple or yellow, appearing from July to October. Nutsedges reproduce by seeds, underground stems, and nutlike tubers. The tubers store food and are drought-tolerant.

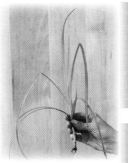

Control: If there are only a few clumps of nutsedge in your garden, may be worth it to dig up the plants, taking care to dispose of the soil in order to also dispose of the tubers. Solarization is not effective. Glyphosate applied when the plant is actively growing is effective.

Purslane

A common annual weed in vegetable gardens, purslane (*Portulaca oleracea*) thrives in hot, dry weather. Leaves are ½ to 1½ inches long, succulent, and wedge-shape. Small yellow flowers open only in full sunlight from midsummer to frost. The seeds may remain viable in the soil for many years and will sprout in warm weather when brought to the surface during tilling or cultivating. The

thick, reddish stems grow vigorously, forming a mat that roots wherever it touches the soil. The stems and leaves store water that enables purslane to survive drought periods.

Control: Because purslane grows low to the ground, an oscillating hoe is often effective, though uprooted plants left in place may reroot. A mulch effectively prevents residual seeds from germinating. Solarization is effective against seeds and plants. Either fatty acid or acetic acid weed control products are useful for spot treating.

Quackgrass

Quackgrass (*Agropyron repens*) is a perennial grass weed in the northern United States. Its extensive fibrous root system consists of long, yellow-white roots that may grow 5 feet or more in a single growing season. The narrow bluish green blades grow on stalks

1 to 3 feet tall. Wheatlike spikes produce seeds from May to September. Seeds may survive in the soil for up to four years, but most germinate in the spring within two years. The underground creeping rhizomes also send up new shoots, increasing the infestation. Quackgrass tolerates any type of soil. Its roots are extremely competitive, crowding out and inhibiting growth of desirable plants.

Control: Glyphosate is the quickest way to kill quackgrass.

Redroot pigweed

Redroot pigweed (*Amaranthus* spp.) is an annual with oval or egg-shape leaves. Flower spikes bloom and produce seeds from July to October. Each plant may produce thousands of seeds, which sprout spring

through summer. Pigweed prefers hot, dry weather and dry soil.

Control: Hand pulling or cultivating is the best way to remove existing plants. Mulch and solarize soil to kill dormant seeds or prevent their growth. In edible gardens, prevent growth of redroot pigweed with corn gluten, pendimethalin, or trifluralin. Apply to the soil two weeks before the last expected frost.

Shepherdspurse

Shepherdspurse (*Capsella bursa-pastoris*), an annual weed that grows throughout the United States, tolerates most types of soil but will not grow in the shade. Lobed or toothed leaves form a rosette at the base of the plant. Arrow-shape leaves and tiny white flowers grow on stems 3 to 18 inches tall. Flowers bloom and produce seeds in triangular pods from March to December. The seeds

fall to the soil and may remain dormant for several years before germinating in the spring. Fall frost kills the plants. In warm-winter areas, seeds may germinate in the fall. The plants then grow through the winter until the next fall.

Control: Hand pull or cultivate to remove existing plants. Mulch and solarize soil to kill dormant seeds or prevent their growth.

Sow thistle

Sow thistles (*Sonchus* spp.) are annual weeds that grow throughout the United States but are most common in the South and along the West Coast. The reddish stems arise from a short taproot and grow upright 1 to 6 feet. A milky sap oozes from the stems when the stems are broken. The upper branches may be covered with hairs. From July to September, yellow flowers, ½ to 1 inch in diameter, bloom on branches at the top of the

plants. In Florida, Texas, and California, the plants may germinate or bloom year-round. The seeds these flowers produce are contained in brownish seedheads. They germinate either that fall or the following spring. Sow thistles prefer rich soil.

Control: Pull or cultivate to kill weeds, but wear gloves so the plant's fine hairs don't irritate your skin. Follow up by applying a mulch. Seeds are susceptible to solarization.

Spotted spurge

Spotted spurge (*Euphorbia macula*) is an annual weed that thrives in most soils. It grows in vegetable gardens and orchards as well as in cracks in walkways and driveways. Spurge forms dense mats up to 2 feet in diameter. Leaves are oval, ¼- to ¾-inch long, and pale to dark green

with a purple spot. The slender reddish stems ooze a milky-white sap when broken. Small pinkish-white flowers bloom and produce seeds from May to October.

Control: Hand pulling or cultivating is usually sufficient to control spotted spurge. Plants and seeds are susceptible to solarization.

Managing diseases

Diseases are caused by fungi, bacteria, and viruses. Fungi are tiny organisms that live on plants, causing the symptoms we see. Insects, water, and wind are typical ways they spread. Bacteria are single-cell organisms that live on various kinds of organic matter. Unable to survive in the open environment, they live inside plants and are transferred plant-to-plant by insects, water, and hands. Viruses are the smallest of the three and the most difficult to control. They are usually

▲ Plant varieties of plants, such as this 'Bloomsdale Long Standing' spinach, that are resistant to disease.

▲ Reduce overwintering disease spores at season's end by removing crop residue and cleaning supports.

▲ Strawberry anthracnose causes oval, sunken spots on fruits and girdling and death of runners.

▲ Downy mildew is promoted by excessive irrigation, often spreading from crop residue and nearby weeds.

▲ Prevent seedling damping off by sowing in sterile or heat-treated soil.

spread by insects, though some are spread by seeds and tools. Some plant problems grouped with diseases for convenience are actually caused by environmental factors, such as weather, or nutrient imbalance in the soil.

Generally for a disease to occur, organisms must be transported to a susceptible host. This may be done by unintentionally planting infected seeds or plant material, planting in contaminated soil, or more often by wind, water, animals (including humans), or insects. Environmental conditions favorable to the causal agent must be present for the organism to infect and thrive in or on the plant. Effective disease control requires knowledge of the disease life cycle; time of likely infection, agent of distribution, plant part affected, and the symptoms produced by the disease.

Disease control methods

Apply the decision-making process known as IPM, described on page 194, to all plant problems, including disease. In addition here are some specific steps you can take to prevent, minimize, or eradicate disease.

● **Site selection** Establish your garden in a sunny location with well-drained soil and good air circulation. Remove weeds not only from the garden area but also from surrounding areas because weeds harbor many disease organisms.

● **Resistant varieties** The home gardener's first line of defense from plant disease is to plant varieties of plants bred to be resistant or immune to important diseases whenever possible.

● **Cultivate deeply** Whether by hand or with equipment, cultivate as deeply as possible in order to completely bury remnants of the previous

crop and any disease organisms that are attached to them.

● **Weed control** Certain weeds, particularly those botanically related to the vegetables in your garden, may harbor viruses or other diseases that could move into your garden with the aid of insects that feed on both plants.

● **Solarize soil** Heating the soil as described on page 196 will destroy various

▲ Prune out limbs killed by fire blight, cutting 8 inches beyond visible damage, and disinfect tools between cuts.

▲ Drip irrigation systems that do not wet leaves help prevent disease spread.

▲ Cucumber beetles spread bacterial wilt by feeding on the plants.

▲ Black sooty mold feeds on the honeydew secreted by aphids.

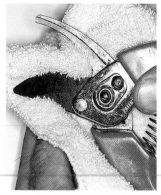

▲ Disinfect shears between cuts by wiping blades with disinfectant.

DISEASE CONTROL PRODUCTS

Name	Diseases controlled*	Cautions
OILS		
Jojoba oil	Powdery mildew	Do not apply within 2 weeks of a sulfur spray
Horticultural oil	Powdery mildew	Do not apply within 2 weeks of a sulfur spray
Neem oil	Powdery mildew	Do not apply within 2 weeks of a sulfur spray
SULFUR		
Lime sulfur	Anthracnose, apple scab, peach leaf curl	Apply during dormant season. Wear eye and skin protection
Wettable sulfur	Powdery mildew	Can damage some squash and melons. Apply when temperatures are below 90°F.
COPPER		
Copper oleate, metallic copper	Apple scab, brown rot, fire blight, peach leaf curl	Toxic to fish
Copper soap	Anthracnose, downy mildew, early blight, late blight, powdery mildew, rust	Avoid inhaling spray mist. Wash hands after use
Bordeaux mixture	Downy mildew, fire blight (as dormant spray), peach leaf curl, powdery mildew	Corrosive, toxic spray mixture
BICARBONATES		
Potassium bicarbonate	Powdery mildew and others	Combined with oil to enhance effectiveness. Can injure plants. Use with caution
BIOLOGICAL		
Ampelomyces quisqualis	Powdery mildew	Safe to use
Bacillus subtilis	Bacterial blight, downy mildew, early blight, fire blight, and powdery mildew	Safe to use
Bacillus pumilus	Downy mildew, powdery mildew, rust	Safe to use
Streptomyces griseoviridis	Damping off, early blight, late blight	Apply as a seed treatment. Safe to use
SYNTHETIC		
Captan	Vegetable seeds; apple scab, anthracnose, brown rot, damping off, downy mildew	Don't use with or soon after oil
Chlorothalonil	Downy mildew, early blight, late blight, peach leaf curl, rusts	Very toxic to fish. Don't use with or soon after oil
Myclobutanil	Apple scab, brown rot, powdery mildew,	Toxic to aquatic invertebrates

*Specific products vary—check the label to confirm both diseases and crop.

disease agents as well as weeds and insects. The process can take 4 to 6 weeks. Assume that you can kill most nematodes in the root zone with temperatures at 130°F; most fungi at 140°F; and most bacteria between 160° and 212°F. Use a soil temperature probe set about 6 inches deep to measure the temperature the soil reaches.

● **Start disease-free** Nursery transplants, seeds, potato starts for example, can all carry diseases, meaning problems are guaranteed before you start. Shop for healthy, disease-free transplants and certified disease-free seed potatoes.

▲ Fusarium wilt of melons girdles the main stem causing the plant to wilt.

▲ Stunted, yellow, mishapen, or forked carrots are caused by nematodes.

▲ Yellow, older, lower leaves indicate nitrogen deficiency.

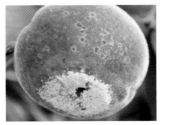
▲ Removing fallen and hanging fruit "mummies" helps prevent brown rot.

▲ Control peach leaf curl by spraying before buds swell in late winter.

▲ Sunlight plus not over fertilizing helps prevent powdery mildew of peas.

Managing diseases *(continued)*

Paying slightly more if necessary for the highest quality seeds, plants, and transplants pays significant dividends.
● **Observation** Spend time in your garden inspecting your plants. That way you'll spot problems while they're small and easy to manage.
● **Crop rotation** Rotating crops works because different kinds of diseases attack different kinds of plants. Planting the same crop in the same location year after year allows various pathogens to accumulate in the soil such that control is difficult if not impossible. While crop rotation is challenging in small gardens you'll notice benefits especially if diseases have been a problem.
● **Disease control** You can sometimes prevent or limit disease damage with the timely use of a specific product. Proper identification of the disease coupled with use of the proper material at the right dose and time is essential. See the table on page 201 for descriptions of common disease control products.

COMMON DISEASES OF GARDEN AND ORCHARD

Name	Vegetables	Fruits	Herbs	Type, symptoms*, remedy†
Anthracnose	Beans, chayote, cherimoya, cucumber, eggplant, melons, pepper, rutabaga, squash, tomato, turnip	Brambles, mango, papaya, strawberry	Cilantro	Fungus. Distinct dead spots of stem, leaf, or fruit, usually yellow, water-soaked. Spores spread by water. Plant disease-free seeds and plants. Mulch. Remove and destroy infected plant parts. Avoid overhead watering. Clean up end-of-season residue. Rotate crops
Bacterial blight	Bean, celery, sweet corn	-	-	Bacteria. Small leaf spots, watersoaked, eventually with yellow border. Plant disease-free seed. Don't work around or touch wet plants. Spray *Bacillus subtilis*
Bacterial wilt	Bean, corn, cucumber, melon	-	Cilantro, sage	Bacteria. Plants wilt at any stage, are often stunted. Plant disease-free seed. Avoid plant injury. Bacteria is spread by insects, usually striped or spotted cucumber beetle (page 209). Control beetle. Plant resistant varieties
Blossom drop	Beans, pepper, tomato	-	-	Environmental. Occurs when nights are below 58°F or days above 85°F. Use row covers to raise night temperatures.
Blossom-end rot	Cucumber, pepper, squash, tomato, watermelon	-	-	Environmental. Blossom end of fruit is water-soaked, sunken. Caused by lack of calcium in developing fruit. Mulch to maintain soil moisture. Avoid fresh manures and high-nitrogen fertilizers.
Brown rot	-	Apricot, cherry, nectarine, peach, plum	-	Fungus. Causes fruits to rot. Fungus survives in rotted fruits on tree or ground. Plant resistant varieties. Remove cankers, blighted twigs. Clean up and destroy old fruits around tree. Spray sulfur, chlorothalonil
Damping off	Beet, broccoli, cabbage, kale, sweet corn, tomato, and most other vegetable seeds	-	Fennel, parsley, sage, and many others	Fungus. Sudden collapse of seedlings, or failure to germinate. Plant when soil is at optimum temperature. Presoak seeds to speed germination. Use sterile potting soil and containers. Allow soil to dry between watering
Downy mildew	Beet, broccoli, cabbage, cucumber, endive, escarole, lettuce, lima bean, melon, onion, pumpkin, radish, rutabaga, spinach, squash, turnip, watermelon	Blackberry, grape, strawberry	Cilantro, horseradish, sage, tarragon	Fungus. Dark spots on lowest leaves gradually expand. A white mold appears on leaf undersides. Spray *Bacillus subtilis*
Early blight	Celery, potato, tomato	-	-	Fungus. Irregular spots with concentric rings. Causes dark, sunken spots on potato tubers. Most severe late season. Destroy infected tubers. Avoid overhead watering. Plant certified potatoes. Rotate crops. Spray copper, *Bacillus subtilis*
Fire blight	-	Apples, apricot, blackberry, cherry, pear, plum	-	Bacteria. Shoots wilt, appear scorched by flame. Occurs in spring, in moist weather. Plant resistant varieties. Remove dead stems 8 inches beyond symptom, and disinfect pruners with bleach between cuts. Spray copper, *Bacillus subtilis*
Fusarium wilt	Asparagus, celery, cucumber, melon, pumpkin, radish, southern pea, squash, tomato	-	-	Fungus. Lower leaves yellow, wilt, die, followed by upper shoots. Often one side of plant dies before the other. Fungus enters roots, spreads up plant. Plant resistant varieties. Solarize soil

▲ At high temperatures blossoms of pepper drop without forming fruits.

▲ Sunscald develops on peppers when ripening fruits are exposed to hot sun.

▲ Avoid blossom end rot on tomato by mulching and watering regularly.

▲ Avoid verticillium wilt of tomatoes by planting resistant varieties.

Name	Vegetables	Fruits	Herbs	Type, symptoms*, remedy†
Late blight	Celery, potato, tomato	-	-	Fungus. Brownish, water-soaked spots on leaves. Brownish-purple spots on potato tuber. Cause of potato famine and still most serious potato disease. High humidity and heavy dew promotes it. Plant disease-free, certified potatoes. Avoid overhead watering
Mosaic	Bean, beet, celery, cucumber, endive, escarole, lettuce, melon, pepper, pumpkin, rutabaga, soybean, spinach, squash, tomato, turnip	Blackberry, peach	-	Virus. Mottled yellow, slightly puckered, deformed leaves, stunted growth. Remove infected plants. The virus lives in many kinds of weeds. Spread by aphids, cucumber beetle. Plant resistant varieties. Control vector insects
Nematodes	Many; usually bean, carrot	Many	Many	Parasites. Microscopic worms cause poor growth, such as wilting during the day from which plants recover at night. Plant resistant varieties. Solarize soil
Nitrogen deficiency	All	All	All	Environmental. Lower leaves yellow while newest leaves remain green. Spray with foliar fertilizer
Peach leaf curl	-	Nectarine, peach	-	Fungus. Affects primarily leaves, causing them to pucker and deform. Prune while dormant and then spray with product containing copper or lime-sulfur
Powdery mildew	Bean, cucumber, melon, pea, pumpkin, squash	Apple, cherry, grape, papaya, strawberry	Cilantro, horseradish, mint, sage, tarragon	Fungus. White patches coalesce on leaves causing plant to look dusted with flour. Thrives in both humid and dry weather. Plant resistant varieties. Spray *Ampelomyces quisqualis*, *Bacillus subtilis*
Rust	Asparagus, bean, cherimoya	Apple§, blackberry	Anise, mint, sage	Fungus. Causes powdery, red spots, usually on underside of leaf. Plant resistant varieties. Destroy infected plant parts
Scab	-	Apple, apricot, avocado, citrus, mango, nectarine, peach, pear	-	Fungus. Causes brown, velvety spots on leaves and fruits. Infected fruits are edible after peeling. Plant resistant varieties. Remove and destroy fallen fruit and leaves. Spray sulfur, captan, myclobutanil
Scab, common	Beet, carrot, parsnip, potato	-	-	Bacteria. Corky scabs or pits on potato tubers. Rotate crops. Avoid manures. Spray *Bacillus subtilis*
Sooty mold	-	Citrus	-	Fungus. Black coating on leaves isn't parasitic on plants but grows on honeydew secreted by aphids and similar insects. Wash black fungus from leaves. Control insects
Sunscald	Pepper and tomato fruits	Bark of citrus and others	-	Environmental. A section of fruit becomes soft, wrinkled, light in color, dry. Cause is sunburn. Maintain enough foliage to shade fruits, or shade exposed fruits artificially
Verticillium wilt	Eggplant, okra, pepper, potato, tomato	Strawberry	Cilantro, horseradish, mint, sage	Fungus. Causes sudden wilting. Fungus grows in vascular tissue, clogging it. Older, lower leaves die first. Plant resistant varieties. Solarize soil

*Symptoms vary with plant. †Read and follow product labels; check with local cooperative extension for more information.
§Cedar-apple rust

Managing insect pests

▲ Cultivating soil in the fall in order to disrupt overwintering insects, and removing all the weeds and debris from the season's growth, prevents many kinds of insect pest problems.

▲ A pest-free crop such as these potatoes is usually more than luck. It begins by knowing the pests to expect and taking preventive measures to thwart them.

▲ Beautiful gardens have fewer pests in part because flowers such as these zinnias attract beneficial insects.

In nature a balance of natural predators and a healthy environment normally keeps pests under control. Many plant pests are avoided simply by using good gardening practices, for instance keeping plants healthy and gardens clear of weeds and plant debris.

Despite efforts to cope, a tolerable balance can be thrown off. Weather—unusually mild winters or rainy summers, for example—is a common cause. Those are opportunities for pest populations to explode. When preventive measures are not enough, turn first to the simplest control measures available. That's the principle of IPM as described on page 194.

There are three main ways to out maneuver the pests in your garden: physically, biologically, and chemically.

Physical Controls

Use physical controls to prevent insects from accessing plants or remove insects that reach plants.
- **Your fingers** Remove leaves that are heavily infested with insects or larvae. Dispose of the leaves in the trash rather than composting them. Handpick larger insects such as beetles, tomato hornworms, or cabbage loopers. Toss the infested foliage and insects into a bucket of soapy water or stomp them before discarding them.
- **Water** Dislodge insects from infested plants with a sharp blast of water from a hose. Be sure to spray the entire plant, including the underside of foliage. This works well against smaller insects, such as whiteflies, aphids, or spider mites. Repeat treatment as often as needed, which may be daily. If the pest population is tenacious, you will need to move on to stronger controls.
- **Barriers** Floating row covers are lightweight woven materials that keeps flying insects, such as leafhoppers and moths, from landing on plants to feed or lay eggs. Cardboard collars around seedlings prevent cutworms from reaching and chewing through stems.
- **Traps** Sink plastic, pint-size tubs or other similar small containers into the soil near plants susceptible to snails or slugs. Fill with beer or a mixture of sugar, water, and yeast. The sweet concoction attracts slugs, which fall in and drown. Commercial sticky traps attract insects such as leafhoppers, flea beetles, and whiteflies with their yellow color. Note that many insect traps perform best as monitoring devices, alerting you when pests arrive in the neighborhood; they are less effective at killing sufficient numbers to make a dent in pest populations.

Biological controls

Biological control is what nature does all by itself, but control may not happen soon enough or thoroughly enough to suit your needs. This is augmenting nature's own methods. Predators are insects that seek out and dine on other insects, notably the ones that feed on our plants. Parasites use garden pests as hosts, usually to lay eggs upon, a process that ends with the demise of the pest.

Some beneficial insects are specific about their target and the temperature in which they thrive, so if you do decide to buy beneficial insects, be sure to match the species correctly to your climate and particular pest problems. Pathogens are other kinds of organisms that prey on garden pests. The most common is a bacteria.

Beneficial organisms: predators

- **Assassin bugs** These well-named predators attack with fast-acting spiny legs to trap and hold prey while stabbing it with a long, thin beak. Both nymphs and adults target large insects such as caterpillars and beetles, as well as many other insects. Adults are brown or black and about ½ to 1½ inches long and ¼ inch wide. They have long, narrow heads and obvious antennae. Nymphs resemble the adults.
- **Big-eyed bugs** Another descriptively named predator, this beneficial has bulging eyes that seem to protrude from the sides of its head. These small gray or brown bugs are ⅛ inch long and wide. Nymphs look similar to adults but lack wings. Both adults and nymphs consume aphids, caterpillars, leafhoppers, mites, thrips, whiteflies, and insect eggs.

▲ Both larvae and adults of striped cucumber beetle feed on plants, but adults also transmit disease.

● **Damsel bugs** With their narrow bodies and long antennae, damsel bugs may be mistaken for assassin bugs, but they are not as large, growing only about ³⁄₈ inch long. They are brown or gray and do not display the colorful markings that some assassin species do. Nymphs appear similar to the adults but lack wings. Both adults and nymphs consume aphids, small caterpillars, mites, leafhoppers, and insect eggs.

● **Decollate snails** Important predators of brown garden snails, they grow to 1½ inches long, live for about two years, and dine regularly on small snails. They are omnivorous and feed on soft plant growth, especially if it's near the soil. But their effectiveness as snail predators exceeds by far any damage they cause to plants. However, in some areas their

HERE'S A TIP...

Use plants to attract beneficial insects
The adults of many beneficial insects require a diet of carbohydrate-rich nectar and pollen. To attract these insects into your garden, grow plants that produce such pollen in clusters of small flowers. Herbs in the parsley family are among the most attractive plants to various beneficial insects. These are: Cilantro (*Coriandrum sativum*), page 181; dill (*Anethum graveolens*), page182; fennel (*Foeniculum vulgare*), page 70; and parsley (*Petroselinum crispum*), page 190.

release is prohibited for the damage they cause to endangered mollusk species. Check with your local cooperative extension.

● **Green lacewings** Pale green adults have delicately veined wings and golden or coppery eyes. Nectar is their primary food source. It is their larvae that make short work of eliminating pests, greedily devouring 40 to 60 pests, primarily aphids, per hour. Green lacewing larvae are pale cream, tan, or grayish in color with brown markings. They are tapered at the ends and wider in the middle, resembling an alligator's shape in miniature. Lacewings are one of the most effective predators, remaining in the garden from spring through fall.

● **Ladybugs** Many ladybug species with varying colors and markings exist. Most have red, orange, or yellow bodies with dark spots. The larvae have a tapered shape similar to green lacewing larvae but have black or dark bluish gray coloring with orange flecks. The black and orange pupae are round in shape and resemble bird droppings. Both adults and larvae consume small insects, such as aphids, mealybugs, mites, and scale insects, as well as insect eggs.

● **Minute pirate bugs** So small (⅛ inch or less) they may go unnoticed, these insects hide in flowers to attack thrips, which awards them another common name, flower bug. Adults are black with white wing patches, which create a triangular pattern when the wings are folded at rest. The soft-bodied nymphs are orange or yellow and may be mistaken for aphids, although they are more active than aphids.

● **Praying mantis** Adults grasp and hold prey upright with their strong forelegs. Most praying mantis are 2 to 3 inches long, but they can range from ½ to 6 inches long. Nymphs resemble adults. Praying mantis have much less of an effect on pest populations than their reputation suggests. They

▶ A common beneficial insect, both larvae and adults of green lacewings feed on a variety of small, soft-bodied insect pests.

feed indiscriminately, devouring beneficial insects, pollinating bees, and one another, as well as a few pests.

● **Predatory ground beetles** There are many species of ground beetles, most of which mature at ½ to 1 inch long. Their shiny bodies are black, brown, or a dark metallic color. They are night patrollers, scurrying across the soil in search of cutworms, grubs, slugs, snails, and tent and gypsy moth caterpillars. They also consume eggs and larvae of ants, aphids, Colorado potato beetles, spider mites, and thrips. The larval stage is light brown and wormlike and remains underground, feeding on soil insects.

● **Predatory mites** Predatory mites are a bit bigger than pest mites, and they move faster. Scientifically speaking, mites are not insects; they are related to spiders. Predatory mites thrive in hot, humid environments rather than in dry conditions. They eat pest mites, thrips, fungus gnats, and eggs of other pest insects. Adult predatory mites consume pests in all life stages; nymphs mainly eat pest eggs and nymphs.

● **Spiders** Eight-legged spiders are classified as arachnids, rather than insects. They are especially capable predators. They control a wide variety of insects, including annoying household pests such as cockroaches. About three thousand spider species reside in North America alone. Only a few have potentially dangerous venom, including the black widow, brown recluse, and Arizona brown spiders. Many spider species construct webs to trap flying insects.

● **Spined soldier bugs** Shaped like a shield with a sharp spine projecting on each side, these insects are sometimes called stinkbugs. (The true stinkbug is a pest, so make sure you've correctly

identified the insect.) Adults are pale brown and about ½ inch long; the round, wingless nymphs are orange with dark markings. Both nymphs and adults consume numerous pests, including gypsy moth caterpillars, corn earworms, armyworms, Mexican bean beetles, and cabbage loopers, as well as eggs of these species.

● **Syrphid flies** The maggotlike larvae of syrphid flies consume vast quantities of aphids. Adults resemble bees or wasps; however, they have one set of wings rather than two and do not sting. Most syrphid fly species are considered beneficial, but the larvae of one species, narcissus bulb fly, feeds on daffodil bulbs.

Beneficial organisms: parasites

● **Braconid wasps** Some of these species target aphids, depositing a single egg within the body.

▲ This tomato hornworm larva is carrying the white egg cases of trichogramma wasps. When the eggs hatch, the wasp larvae feed on the hornworm, killing it.

• **Nematodes** Several species of these microscopic worms attack and parasitize soil-dwelling pests such as grubs.

• **Tachinid flies** These beneficial insects resemble gray or brown bristle-covered houseflies. They parasitize beetles, caterpillars, and other insects by laying an egg on the pest's body.

• **Trichogramma wasps** Common in a garden, they may go unnoticed because of their tiny size ($\frac{1}{100}$ to $\frac{1}{25}$ inch). They parasitize caterpillar species, including cabbage loopers, codling moths, tomato hornworms, and corn earworms, by laying their eggs on the pests' eggs. The wasps are much too small and uninterested to sting people.

Beneficial organisms: pathogens

• **Bt** *Bacillus thuringiensis* (Bt) is probably the most commonly applied pathogen in the garden. It works only on caterpillars, destroying their

digestive systems. Bt is sprayed on susceptible plants; caterpillars feed on the foliage and eventually die. Over 30 types of Bt target different species of butterfly and moth larvae. For example, *B.t. tenebrionis* controls Colorado potato beetle.

Chemical controls

Chemical controls are typically the last resort in an IPM strategy. You may turn to these controls after a combination of other attempts have failed and you have determined that the damage warrants intervention. Spraying pest control products routinely as a prevention program is seldom needed in the home landscape. Most pests appear seasonally when specific temperatures and humidity conditions occur and will disappear when those conditions change. Learn which pests may cause problems in your region on the plants you grow and whether preventive spraying is a viable option. Your county extension service can provide these details.

A pest control product is any substance that kills a pest. Pest control products are classified by the type of pest they control, such as miticides, insecticides, fungicides, or herbicides. Pest control products are often further classified as being botanical, mineral-based, microbial, or synthetic products.

• **Botanical pest control products** Derived from plants, these include pyrethrum, made from the pyrethrum daisy, and neem, obtained from the Indian neem tree.

• **Mineral-based pest control products** Derived from mined substances, these include sulfur, copper, and diatomaceous earth.

• **Microbial pest control products** These naturally occurring microbes kill specific pests. Bt, which

▲ Three of the most useful organic pest control products are insecticidal soap (left), iron phosphate snail and slug bait (center), and horticultural oil. Using these materials, organic gardeners can defeat many of the most common insect pests.

targets caterpillars and is harmless to other creatures, is an example. These are also classified as biological controls.

• **Synthetic pest control products** Synthetically produced and contain carbon and hydrogen in their structure. Examples include malathion and pyrethrin.

Organic versus synthetic

Some gardeners prefer to use only organic substances in the landscape. Organic has a variety of definitions, and farmers who sell organic produce must follow legal definitions. For most home gardeners, organic pest control products are simply

HERE'S A TIP...

More about pesticides
If you have a question about using, storing, or disposing of a pesticide, call the manufacturer's telephone number, which is listed on the product label, or the National Pesticide Information Center (NPIC) at Oregon State University, Corvallis, OR, at 800-858-7378; or visit their website: http://npic.orst.edu/map.htm. The NPIC is a telephone hotline, partly funded by the EPA for answering consumer questions concerning pesticides, pesticide ingredients, uses, storage, and disposal. Note the EPA's Code Number on the product label to speed assistance. Of course, in case of an emergency, call your local poison control center (call 4-1-1 information for that number), or call the national emergency telephone number: 9-1-1.

▲ Dilute concentrated pest control products, such as horticultural oil, with all the precision you can muster, and follow all the safety precautions noted on the label.

Common Pest Controls*

Name	Insects controlled	Type, cautions
NATURAL ORIGIN		
Azadirachtin (neem)	Many	Botanical
Bacillus thuringiensis	Caterpillars	Microbial pathogen
Bacillus t. tenebrionis	Colorado potato beetle	Microbial pathogen
Beauveria bassiana	Aphids, armyworms, Colorado potato beetle, cutworms, leafhoppers, loopers, mites, thrips, whiteflies	Fungus pathogen
Citric acid	Aphids, cabbage looper, caterpillars, cucumber beetles, cutworms, earwigs, flea beetles, Japanese beetle, scales, slugs, snails, spider mites, whiteflies	Botanical
Copper strips	Slugs, snails	Physical
Diatomaceous earth	Aphids, cutworms, flea beetles	Mineral
Garlic	Aphids, cutworms, earwigs, earworms, hornworms, leaf miners, spider mites, thrips, whiteflies	Botanical
Horticultural oil	Aphids, scales, spider mites, whiteflies	Oil. Do not apply if temperatures will exceed 90°F and fall below 45°F within 24 hours
Insecticidal soap	Aphids, scales, spider mites, thrips, whiteflies	Soap. Repeat applications needed
Iron phosphate	Slugs, snails	Mineral toxin
Kaolin clay	Squash bug	Mineral repellent
Nematodes (**H**eterorhabditis, **S**teinernema)	**H:** Colorado potato beetle, Japanese beetle; **S:** cucumber beetles	Parasites
Nosema locustae	Grasshoppers	Protozoan pathogen
Pepper (capsaicin)	Aphids, leaf-miners, scales, spider mites, thrips, whiteflies	Botanical
Pyrethrins	Aphids, cucumber beetles, earwigs, flea beetles	Botanical
Saccharopolyspora	Beetles, caterpillars	Fungus extract
Traps (**Y**ellow sticky, **O**ther—see text)	**Y:** flea beetles, leafhoppers, whiteflies; **O:** earwigs, slugs, snails	Physical
Volatile herb oils (citrus, rosemary, mint, wintergreen, others)	Aphids, cabbage looper, caterpillars, Colorado potato beetle, cucumber beetles, cutworms, earwigs, flea beetles, Japanese beetle, scale, spider mites, thrips, whiteflies	Botanical
SYNTHETIC ORIGIN		
Carbaryl	Many insects	Carbamate insecticide. Very toxic to honeybees, spider mite predators
Metaldehyde	Slugs, snails	Molluscicide

See page 204–206 for information about predators and parasites

naturally occurring pesticides derived from plants, animals, or minerals that may have minimal adverse effects on users or the environment. Organic pest control products often break down fairly quickly and leave no long-term residues. Still, organic pesticides must be used with caution; they are toxic materials.

Synthetic pest control products are manufactured products and are not accepted for use by organic gardeners. Synthetics sometimes take longer to break down after use than organic products. However, researchers are currently developing synthetic pest control materials that break down more quickly.

Using pest controls responsibly

Whether you use organic or synthetic pest control products, it is essential to select the appropriate product for each situation. Grabbing any can on the shelf is likely to do more harm than good if the product is not formulated for the particular pest and plant. If you have a choice, select a target-specific product that acts against a limited number of species. Avoid those that kill a wide range of insects, including beneficial insects.

When applying any pest control, wear protective clothing, including gloves, long sleeves and pants, eye protection, and a dust mask. Use thick neoprene rubber gloves, not cotton or leather, which can absorb the pest control product. Follow dilution rates exactly. These amounts have been carefully determined after considerable research to control the pest without causing plant injury or contamination from excess residues. Use measuring utensils designated for garden use only rather than estimating or guessing the proper amounts.

Never pour unused pest control product on the ground or down the drain. Take it to a household hazardous waste disposal site. Call your local sanitation department for information on locations.

Gallery of common insect pests

Aphids

Pale green, yellow, purple, or black soft-bodied insects cluster on the undersides of leaves. Leaves turn yellow and may be curled, distorted, and puckered. Plants may be stunted and produce few fruits.

Aphids on chard

Aphids are one of the most common pests in the garden. They do little damage in small numbers, but they are extremely prolific, and populations can rapidly build up to

Pepper leaves curled by aphids

damaging numbers. Aphids usually prefer tender young leaves. Severely infested plants may be stunted and weak, and aphids may also spread plant virus diseases. Aphids feed on nearly every plant in the garden and are spread from plant to plant by wind, water, and people. They exude a sticky substance, called *honeydew*, which ants feed upon, and which is the reason ants are often present where there is an aphid infestation.

Control: Wash aphids off plants with sprays of water. Encourage beneficial insects, many of which feed on aphids. Spray insecticidal soap, or if safe for the plant, apply horticultural oil.

Borers

Foliage on a branch or at the top of the tree is sparse; eventually the twigs and branches die. Holes or tunnels are apparent in the trunk or branches. Sap or sawdust may be present near the holes. The bark over the tunnels may die or slough off, or knotlike swellings may be on the trunk and limbs. Weakened branches break during high winds or snowstorms. Weak, young, or newly transplanted trees may be killed.

Raspberry cane borer damage

Borers are the larvae of beetles or moths. Many kinds of borers attack tree and cane fruits. Trees weakened by mechanical injuries, disease, poor growing conditions, or insect infestation are more susceptible to borer attack.

Squash vine borer is a common pest of squash, pumpkins, gourds, and especially 'Hubbard' squash. Destroy vines after harvest and cultivate in fall to destroy overwintering cocoons. Cover vines with soil at leaf joints to promote supplemental rooting.

Control: Cut out and destroy all dead and dying tree branches, and remove severely infested young trees.

Maintain tree health by watering and fertilizing regularly and controlling insects and disease-producing organisms. Inspect squash vines for damage; slit them open with a sharp knife to remove the borer, then cover that area with soil.

Sap oozing from peachtree borer exit hole

Cabbageworms

Leaves have round or irregular holes. Green worms up to 1½ inches long, with light stripes down their backs, feed on the leaves or cabbage heads. Masses of green or brown pellets may be found between the leaves.

Cabbage butterfly on kale

Several worms attack lettuce; the most damaging is the cabbage looper, which attacks all varieties of lettuce, as well as members of the cabbage family. The other is the imported cabbageworm. It attaches yellow, bullet-shape eggs to the

Cabbageworms

undersides of leaves of plants in cabbage family. The white butterflies are frequently seen around these plants in the daytime. The brownish cabbage looper moth lays pale green eggs on the upper leaf surfaces.

Control: The most effective action is preventive, namely row covers placed over susceptible plants that prevent the moths from reaching plants. Spray or dust with bacterial *Bacillus thuringiensis* (Bt) while the caterpillars are small. *Saccharopolyspora* is effective. Repeat this treatment at weekly intervals if the plants become re-infested. Clean all plant debris from the garden to reduce the number of overwintering pupae.

Colorado potato beetle

Yellow-orange beetles with black stripes, about ⅜ inch long, eat the leaves. Fat, red, humpbacked larvae with two rows of black dots may also be present.

The Colorado potato beetle can devastate potato, tomato, eggplant, and pepper plants. Both adults and larvae damage plants by devouring leaves and stems. Small plants are most severely damaged. The beetle is native to the Rocky Mountains

Colorado potato beetle larva

but spread eastward long ago. Only California and Nevada are still free of them. The beetles lay their yellow orange eggs on the undersides of leaves as the first potato leaves emerge from the ground in the spring. The larvae that hatch from these eggs feed for two to three weeks, pupate in the soil, and emerge one to two weeks later as adults, which lay more eggs. One generation is completed in a month. One to three generations occur per year.

Control: Floating row covers keep beetles away from potatoes. Rotate crops, planting as far from last year's crop as possible. Potato beetles are developing resistance to many insecticides, so control may be difficult. Early-maturing potato varieties mature and are harvested before the beetles are at their worst. Spray or dust with *Bacillus thuringiensis tenebrionis*. It's only effective against larvae, primarily young ones; apply when the larvae are newly hatched. Spray *Beauveria bassiana*. It's effective against both larvae and adults. Apply when temperatures are between 70° and 80°F. Beneficial nematodes of the *Heterorhabditis* species kill larvae and adults in the soil.

Cucumber beetles

Cucumber beetles, both striped and spotted, are common pests of cucumbers, melons, squash, and pumpkins. They chew holes in the leaves, leafstalks, and stems. Plants may wilt and die. It is important to control these beetles because they carry two serious diseases that

Spotted cucumber beetle

damage and may kill cucurbits: mosaic and bacterial wilt (see page 202). The adults survive the winter in plant debris and weeds. They emerge in the early spring and feed on a variety of plants. As soon as cucurbits are planted in the garden, the beetles attack the leaves and stems and may totally destroy the plant. They lay their yellow orange eggs in the soil at the base of the plants. The grubs that hatch from these eggs eat the roots and the stems below the soil line, causing the plant to be stunted or to wilt. The slender white grubs feed for several weeks, pupate in the soil, and emerge as adults to repeat the cycle.

Control: Remove plant residues and cultivate deeply in fall to discourage overwintering pupae. Cover plants with row covers. Rotate crops. Apply a thick mulch around plants to deter egg laying and to limit larvae climbing from soil to fruits. Handpick when possible. Encourage beneficial insects such as braconid wasps, tachinid flies; use *Steinernema* nematodes (for soil larvae). Spray spinosad or carbaryl.

Cutworms

Young plants are chewed or cut off near the ground. Gray, brown, or black worms, 1½ to 2 inches long, may be found about 2 inches deep in the soil near the base of the damaged plants. The worms coil when disturbed.

Several species of cutworms attack plants in

Cutworms

the vegetable garden. The most likely pests of lettuce plants in the spring are surface-feeding cutworms. Cutworms hide in the soil during the day and feed only at night. Adult cutworms are dark, night-flying moths with bands or stripes on their forewings.

Control: Cultivate the soil thoroughly in late summer and fall to expose and destroy eggs, larvae, and pupae. Place a collar around individual seedlings to prevent the cutworm from reaching the stem. Apply *Steinernema* nematodes to soil. Dust soil around seedlings with diatomaceous earth.

Earwigs

Dark, reddish brown insects up to ¾ inch long with pincers projecting from the rear of the body feed at night and retreat to cool, dark hiding places for the day. They scurry for cover when disturbed, and they chew holes in leaves and blossoms.

Although seen in most gardens, earwigs are only minor pests of vegetables and berries unless populations are high, when they can become major pests. They feed predominantly on decaying plant material and other insects. Earwigs feed at night and hide under stones, debris, and bark chips in the

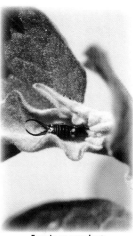
Earwig on eggplant

daytime. Earwigs are beneficial when they feed on other insect larvae and on snails. They sometimes invade homes.

Control: Because earwigs typically cause only minor damage, control is seldom needed in the vegetable garden. Eliminate hiding places, or place traps from which you can collect them in the morning. Scatter diatomaceous earth around seedlings. For severe infestations, use carbaryl dust, if your crop is listed on the label.

Flea beetles

Leaves are riddled with shot holes about ⅛ inch in diameter. Tiny (1/16-inch) black beetles jump like fleas when disturbed. Leaves of seedlings and eventually whole plants may wilt and die.

Flea beetles jump like fleas but are not related to fleas. Both adult and immature flea beetles feed on a wide variety of garden vegetables,

Flea beetle damage to eggplant

including radishes and potatoes. The immature beetle, a legless gray grub, injures plants by feeding on the roots and the lower surfaces of leaves. Adults chew holes in leaves. Flea beetles damage young plants most. Adult beetles survive the winter in soil and garden debris. They emerge in early spring to feed on weeds until vegetable plants sprout. Grubs hatch from eggs laid in the soil and feed for two to three weeks.

Control: Clean all plant debris from the garden after harvesting to eliminate overwintering spots for adult beetles. Protect seedlings with row covers. Dusts of diatomaceous earth discourage them. Sprays containing insecticidal soap, neem, or pyrethrum are often effective.

Japanese beetle

Japanese beetle

Leaf tissue has been chewed between the veins, giving the leaf a lacy appearance. Metallic green-and-bronze beetles, ½ inch long, feed in clusters on the foliage, especially on the tender new leaves.

Japanese beetles are a major pest in the eastern United States. They feed on hundreds of different plant species. The adult beetles are present from the beginning of summer to early fall. They feed only in the daytime, rapidly defoliating plants. Leaves exposed to direct sun are the most severely attacked. The larva of the Japanese beetle, a white grub, feeds on grass roots, frequently killing entire lawns.
Control: Watch for beetles daily and handpick those that you see, dropping them into a container of soapy water. Most Japanese beetle larvae overwinter in sod, so treating your lawn for grubs may help. Treat garden (and lawn) with *Heterorhabditis* nematodes.

Leafhoppers

Lettuce leafhopper

Variously colored and marked insects up to ⅛ inch long hop, move sideways, or fly away quickly when a plant is touched. The leaves are stippled. Cast-off skins may be found on the undersides of leaves.

Leafhoppers feed on many vegetables and small fruits, generally on the undersides of leaves, sucking the sap, which causes stippling. Severely infested vegetable and small fruit plants may become weak and produce few edible fruits. Leafhoppers at all stages of maturity are active during the growing season. They hatch in the spring from eggs laid on perennial weeds and ornamental plants. Where the winters are so cold that the eggs cannot survive, leafhoppers migrate in the spring from warmer regions.
Control: Clean up and compost plant debris in fall after harvest, and eliminate nearby weeds. Protect young plants with row covers. Predators such as ladybugs and lacewings consume leafhopper eggs and larvae. Diatomaceous earth and insecticidal soap will reduce populations.

Leaf miners

Leaf miner damage to tomato

Light-color, irregular blotches, blisters, or tunnels appear in the leaves. Tiny black specks are found inside the tunnels. A tiny black or yellow adult fly lays its white eggs on the undersides of leaves of many vegetables. When the eggs hatch, cream-color maggots bore into the leaf. They tunnel between the upper and lower surfaces of the leaf, feeding on the inner tissue.

The tunnels and blotches are called mines. The black specks inside are the maggot's droppings. In the case of beets, the leaves are no longer edible, but the root is. Several overlapping generations occur during the growing season, so larvae are present continually from spring until fall.
Control: Clean up end-of-season debris and cultivate soil to destroy overwintering pupae. Protect plants with row covers. If practical, destroy infested leaves. Trap adults with yellow sticky traps.

Scales

Scale on lemon shoot

Crusty, waxy, or smooth bumps up to ¼ inch in diameter are found on the trunk, stems, foliage, and sometimes fruit. Often leaves turn yellow and drop. Fruit may also drop. In some cases, a sticky substance coats the leaves on which sooty mold grows.

Many species attack citrus. Some of the most damaging are California red scale, Florida red scale, brown soft scale, black scale, and citrus snow scale. Scales spend the winter on the trunk and twigs of the tree. They lay eggs or bear live young in spring to midsummer. The young scales, called crawlers, move about and settle on the leaves, on twigs, and sometimes on developing fruit. The tiny (¹⁄₁₀-inch), soft-bodied young resemble aphids. They feed by sucking sap from the plant. As they mature, the legs usually atrophy, and a hard crusty or waxy shell develops over the body. Some species excrete honeydew.
Control: Some ladybugs and parasitic wasps attack scale insects. Check with companies that provide the parasitic wasps in order to match the scale with the predator or parasite. Spray horticultural oil.

Snails and slugs

Snail damage to broccoli

Stems and leaves may be sheared off and eaten. Holes are often found in ripening berries, especially under the berry cap. Silvery trails wind around on the plants and soil nearby. Snails or slugs may be seen moving around or feeding on the plants, especially at night.

Snails and slugs are mollusks and are related to clams, oysters, and other shellfish. They feed on a wide variety of garden plants. Like other mollusks, snails and slugs need to be moist all the time. For this reason, they avoid direct sun and dry places and hide during the day in damp places, such as under flowerpots or in thick

Slug on cabbage

groundcovers. They emerge at night or on cloudy days to feed. Snails and slugs are similar except that the snail has a hard shell into which it withdraws when disturbed. Slugs lay white eggs encased in a slimy mass in protected places. Snails bury their eggs in the soil, also in a slimy mass. The young look like miniature versions of their parents.
Control: Inspect the garden for them at night by flashlight, and remove them by hand. Use traps as described on page 204. Surround garden beds with copper strips. Surround seedlings with diatomaceous earth. Introduce predatory decollate snails (where permitted). Use baits containing iron phosphate or metaldehyde.

Spider mites

Spider mite damage to beans

Leaves are stippled, yellowing, silvered, or bronzed. There may be webbing over flower buds, between leaves, or on the lower surfaces of leaves. The fruit may be roughened or russet colored. To check for certain species of mites, examine the bottoms of the leaves with a hand lens. Or hold a sheet of white paper underneath an affected leaf and tap the leaf sharply. Minute specks the size of pepper grains will drop to the paper and begin to crawl around.

Spider mite webbing and mites on leaf underside

Mites, related to spiders, commonly attack fruit trees and other garden plants. Certain mites, such as the twospotted spider mite, are large enough to be detected on white paper. Smaller mites, such as plum and pear rust mites, are microscopic and cannot be seen without the aid of a strong hand lens or microscope. Mites are favored by hot, dry weather (70°F and up).
Control: Spray plants frequently to wash mites off and keep leaves clean. Use predatory mites. Spray horticultural oil or insecticidal soap. Dust with sulfur.

Squash bug

Squash bugs

Squash and pumpkin leaves wilt and may become black and crisp. Bright green to dark gray or brown, flat-back bugs, about ½ inch long, cluster on plants. Both the young (nymphs) and adult squash bugs attack squash and pumpkins and other plants of the same family. In the course of feeding, they inject a toxin that causes plants to blacken and wilt, and possibly a virus as well. They injure and kill the plants by sucking sap from leaves and stems. Seedlings are especially susceptible. Dark brown adults emit a disagreeable odor when crushed. They lay brick red egg clusters on leaves in the spring. Although only one generation occurs per year, all stages are found throughout the summer.
Control: Remove leftover plant parts after harvest, or cultivate them into the soil, and rotate crops. Plant varieties that are resistant to squash bugs. Handpick the bugs and crush egg masses. Use row covers and trap adults by laying boards on the ground and destroying bugs that congregate under them during the day. Insecticidal soap and neem are partially effective on immature squash bugs. Apply carbaryl around the base of plants just before and two weeks after eggs hatch.

Squash bug eggs on leaf underside

Whiteflies

Whiteflies on underside of squash leaf

Tiny, white, winged insects $\frac{1}{16}$ inch long feed mainly on the undersides of leaves. Nonflying, scalelike larvae covered with white waxy powder may also be present on the undersides of leaves. When the plant is touched, insects flutter around it. Leaves may be mottled and yellow. In warm-winter areas, black mold may cover the leaves. Adults lay eggs on the undersides of leaves. Both larval and adult forms suck sap from the leaves.
Control: Protect vulnerable plants with row covers. Partially control whiteflies with yellow sticky traps, insecticidal soap, or horticultural oil.

Wireworms

Wireworms feeding on sweet potato

Plants are stunted and grow slowly. Hard, jointed, shiny, cream- to rust-color $\frac{5}{8}$-inch-long worms drill holes into the base or roots of the plants.

Wireworms feed on carrots, corn, beets, peas, potatoes, turnips, and many other plants. Infestations are most extensive in soil where lawn grass has previously grown, in poorly drained soil, and in soil that is high in organic matter. The adult is known as the click beetle because it makes a clicking sound when turning from its back to its feet. Adults lay their eggs in the spring. Wireworms feed for two to six years before maturing into adult beetles, so all sizes and ages may be present in the soil at the same time. Infestations are often spotty.
Control: Cultivate prior to planting to make soil less favorable to egg-laying adults. Plant after soil is fully warmed as larvae are more active in cool soils. Use carrots and potatoes as traps: Place a carrot or half a potato under garden soil as though it was growing. Check it every other day or so and discard any wireworms attached to it. Some beneficial nematodes will partially control wireworms.

Gallery of animal pests

Pets can help discourage some animal pests.

Welcome visitor or a gardener's worst nightmare? Animals in the garden can be both. Over the centuries, gardeners have developed a multitude of ways to repel animals, but often the results are inconsistent: They work one year, but not the next. Deer in populated areas even learn which dogs to fear and which are harmless nuisances.

Barriers are usually the most effective way to control animal pests. These range between a fence around the garden to a sheet of hardware cloth laid over a vegetable bed.

When animal pests need to be removed, traps are usually more effective than poisons, although in some cases poison baits work well. Traps let you see that you have caught the animal, for one thing. If you don't want to kill the animal, you can catch it in a live trap and release it in a nearby wilderness area. Local regulations may govern this. Consult your county agricultural commissioner's office about the rules in your area.

Birds

Many types of birds feed on seeds, seedlings, fruit, and berries in the garden. Birds scratch away at soft soil to unearth newly planted seeds. They peck at seedlings and young leaves. Birds are especially damaging to berries, grapes, and soft fruit.
Control: Once birds develop the habit of feeding in your garden, you will probably have to exclude them with wire or fabric cages. Make wire cages out of 1-inch-mesh chicken wire. If birds have not yet developed the habit of feeding in your garden, you may be able to repel them. Set up stakes around the plantings you wish to protect and tie crisscrossing strings between the stakes. Attach strips of aluminum foil to the strings. Birds will not readily fly through the crossing strings and will avoid the shiny aluminum. Remove protective devices once plants have produced several sets of mature leaves or, in the case of

Netting thwarts birds from eating blueberries.

Floating row cover protects strawberries.

berries, after you've harvested all of the fruit. To prevent birds from digging up seeds, lay hardware cloth (¼-inch mesh) over the seedbed. It must be removed before the plants are too large to slip through the mesh.

Deer

An enclosed garden excludes deer.

Deer can cause severe damage to gardens in rural and suburban areas. They feed on many vegetables and fruits, stripping off new growth and often eating the entire plant. Deer may also browse on the tender bark, leaves, and twigs of shrubs and trees. Usually they feed on tree buds and bark during the winter or when other sources of food are scarce. Males may damage trees by rubbing their antlers on trunks and branches. While feeding, they may trample on plants.
Control: The best way to prevent deer damage is to fence the animals out. Deer are strong and agile jumpers; to be effective, a vertical fence must be at least 8 feet high. Enclose all areas of the garden that are accessible to deer. The fencing material should be woven wire mesh. Stretch it between wooden or steel posts placed 10 to 12 feet apart. The wire mesh should fit tightly along the ground to prevent deer from forcing their way under the fence. If the ground is uneven, secure the mesh to depressions in the ground, or fill in the depressions with soil, rocks, or other material.

A fence of plastic mesh is not only effective, but less visible than other fences, especially in wooded or brushy country. It's lightweight, inexpensive, and easier to install than metal fencing, and can be attached to trees in wooded areas.

Electric, baited fences using poly tape or poly rope are effective in many situations. These are convenient to set up and move: set the wire 2½ feet above the ground between posts 50 feet apart. Spread peanut butter or molasses on the tape or rope as bait so that deer are sure to touch the electrified tape and so learn to avoid the area. Electrified fences need regular maintenance.

Sprays containing tetramethylthiuram disulfide, egg solids, and hydrolyzed casein protein powder also have repellent properties and are useful in some situations.

Gophers

Gophers are burrowing rodents that live and feed primarily underground. They eat roots, bulbs, and plants that they pull down into their burrows. They can kill vegetables, herbs, and especially young fruit trees by chewing on roots and girdling the underground part of the trunk or stems. The crescent-shape mounds of soil they leave on the surface are excavated from new runs.
Control: Gophers are best controlled by trapping. Find the main runway by probing with

Buried wire along a bed excludes gophers.

a sharp rod about 1 foot deep near a fresh mound or an eaten plant. Dig a hole to intersect the run, and insert two wire or box traps in the run, one facing in each direction. Tie the traps together or to a stake above ground. To keep soil from falling on the traps, cover the hole with sod or a board, and sprinkle with soil to block out all light. Check and move the traps daily. Protect new fruit trees or perennial herbs or vegetables where gophers are present by planting them in a cage of hardware cloth.

Rabbits

Rabbits are often very damaging pests of gardens. They are active all year long, mainly during the day. In the summer, they feed on tender young plants, especially vegetables. During the winter, they gnaw on bark, twigs, and buds. They are especially destructive to young fruit trees in the winter. Rabbits bite off twigs cleanly as if with a knife, without creating ragged edges. Rabbits can also clip off twigs on older trees up to 2 feet above snow or ground level.

Trunk wrap protects fruit trees from rabbits.

Control: The best way to keep rabbits out of a vegetable garden or small orchard is to enclose it with a 1½-inch-mesh chicken wire fence. The fence should be 2 feet tall or above the snow level. The bottom should be buried 3 to 4 inches under the soil, with the wire lying away from the garden. Or build portable cages to place over small garden plots. To protect single trees, build a cylindrical chicken wire fence 2 feet tall around the trunk. Chemical repellents, cats, dogs, or live traps may also be used to protect the garden from rabbits.

Raccoons

Use a fence to exclude raccoons.

Raccoons are omnivorous, feeding on insects, small mammals, fish, fruits, nuts, grains, and vegetables; they are especially fond of corn. Raccoons are nocturnal, foraging at night and returning to their dens during the day. They are agile climbers and climb trees to feed on fruit or nuts, often knocking many to the ground.

Control: Raccoons are intelligent, inquisitive animals that can be difficult to exclude. You can discourage raccoons from invading your vegetable garden by erecting a 4-foot-tall chicken wire fence, with its top extending 18 inches above the fence post. As the raccoon climbs up onto the unattached portion of the fence, his weight will pull the fence down to the ground. Low-voltage electric fences are also effective in excluding raccoons from the garden. To keep raccoons from climbing between trees or from a building to a tree, keep the limbs pruned so

that they do not touch each other or make contact with the roof. Prevent raccoons from climbing up trees by wrapping metal guards at least 18 inches wide around the trunk. Place the guards at least 3 feet above the ground.

Voles

Voles in the vegetable garden can cause significant feeding damage.

Voles are mouse-like with compact, heavy bodies and short legs. They grow 5 to 8 inches long. Voles work day and night, creating short, shallow burrows. Given snow cover, voles burrow in and through the snow to the surface. Especially under the cover of snow they damage fruit trees by eating their bark at or near ground level. Gnaw marks are about ⅛ inch wide and ⅜ inch long in irregular patches and at various angles. When voles gnaw off bark completely around the main stem of a plant the plant will die.

Control: Limit vole damage by exclusion and habitat modification. Eliminate tall weeds in which they hide, reduce or modify the use of mulch, and create weed-free strips around fruit trees, and voles will diminish in number. Clearing weeds and grass from around young trees also protect them, though not when there's snow. Use ¼-inch-mesh hardware cloth to make a 1-foot-tall cylinder that can encircle the lower trunk of trees.

Woodchucks

Buried woven wire fence excludes woodchucks.

Woodchucks live in underground burrows, from which they emerge in the early morning and late afternoon to feed. Primarily a problem in the North and Northeast, woodchucks prefer tender vegetables but occasionally gnaw on tree bark. These animals seldom invade gardens in large numbers. They do not tunnel to their food source but feed above ground. Woodchucks occasionally contract diseases that they may transmit to humans.

Control: The best way to eliminate damage is to fence out the woodchucks. Surround the area you wish to protect with a woven wire fence about 3 feet high. To prevent woodchucks from burrowing under the fence, bend the bottom 12 inches of the wire mesh outward before burying it a few inches deep in the soil. To prevent woodchucks from climbing over the top, leave the upper 18 inches of mesh unattached to the supporting stakes. Bend this upper portion outward. As the animal climbs the fence, the weight of its body will pull the upper portion down toward the ground. Traps may also be used. Before attempting to trap or kill woodchucks, contact your agricultural commissioner's office or Department of Fish and Game for proper regulations in your area. Always wear gloves and protective clothing when handling woodchucks because they may be diseased.

Resources

SELECTED UNIVERSITY WEB SITES

Arizona State University Master Gardener Manual
ag.arizona.edu/pubs/garden/mg/index.html

University of California Vegetable Research and Information Center
vric.ucdavis.edu/veginfo/homegarden.htm

Clemson University Home & Garden Information Center
hgic.clemson.edu/plants.htm#2

Colorado State University Cooperative Extension
www.ext.colostate.edu/mg/files/gardennotes/pub.html

Cornell University Vegetable Growing Guides
www.gardening.cornell.edu/homegardening/scene0391.html

University of Florida EDIS (Electronic Data Information Source)
edis.ifas.ufl.edu/TOPIC_Fruits_and_Vegetables

University of Illinois Extension Hort Corner
www.urbanext.uiuc.edu/hort/index.html

Ohio State University
ohioline.osu.edu/lines/hygs.html

Purdue University Consumer Horticulture Information
www.hort.purdue.edu/ext/garden_pubs.html

Texas A & M University Aggie Horticulture
aggie-horticulture.tamu.edu/home/home.html

Washington State University, Gardening in Western Washington
gardening.wsu.edu/index.htm

West Virginia Horticulture and Gardening
www.wvu.edu/~agexten/hortcult/index.html

VEGETABLES AND HERBS

Abundant Life Seeds
P.O. Box 157
Saginaw, OR 97472-0157
541/767-9606
www.abundantlifeseeds.com
Certified organic vegetable, herb, and flower seeds, garlic, and potato tubers. Organic fertilizers and pest controls.

Baker Creek Heirloom Seeds
2278 Baker Creek Rd.
Mansfield, MO 65704
417/924-8917
rareseeds.com
Non-treated, non-hybrid and non-GMO vegetable, herb, and flower seeds. Heirloom seeds from over 50 countries.

Bountiful Gardens
18001 Shafer Ranch Rd.
Willits, CA 95490
707/459-6410
www.bountifulgardens.org
Unusual vegetable varieties, cover crops, herbs, and grains.

The Chocolate Habañero
Sam Kaplin
P.O. Box 15091
Minneapolis, MN 55415
www.chocolatehabanero.com
Habañero peppers.

The Cook's Garden
P.O. Box C5030
Warminster, PA 18974
800/457-9703
www.cooksgarden.com
Culinary vegetables, herbs, and flowers. Salad mixes.

Dill's Atlantic Giant Pumpkin
Howard Dill Enterprises
RR#1 400 College Rd.
Windsor, Nova Scotia
Canada B0N 2T0
902/798-2728
www.howarddill.com
'Atlantic Giant' pumpkin and other pumpkin varieties.

Dixondale Farms
P.O. Box 129
Carrizo Springs, TX 78834-6129
877/367-1015
www.dixondalefarms.com
Sweet onion plants.

Fedco Seeds
P.O. Box 520
Waterville, ME 04903
207/873-7333
www.fedcoseeds.com
Untreated vegetable, herb, and flower seeds, seed potatoes, shallots, fruit trees, berries, cover crops, and organic fertilizers.

Filaree Farm
182 Conconully Hwy.
Okanogan, WA 98840
509/422-6940
www.filareefarm.com
Garlic.

Gurney Seed & Nursery Company
P.O. Box 4178
Greendale, IN 47025
513/354-1491
www.gurneys.com
Vegetable and flower seeds. Some berries, fruit trees, and supplies.

Harris Seeds
355 Paul Rd.
P.O. Box 24966
Rochester, NY 14624-0966
800/514-4441
gardeners.harrisseeds.com
Vegetable and flower seeds, plants, and products.

Heirloom Seeds
P.O. Box 245
W. Elizabeth, PA 15088-0245
412/384-0852
www.heirloomseeds.com
Heirloom vegetables and some products.

Henry Field's Seed & Nursery Co.
P.O. Box 397
Aurora, IN 47001-0397
513/354-1494
henryfields.com
Vegetable and flower seeds, some fruit trees, and berries.

Jersey Asparagus Farm
105 Porchtown Rd.
Pittsgrove, NJ 08318
856/358-2548
www.jerseyasparagus.com
Asparagus and strawberries.

Johnny's Selected Seeds
955 Benton Ave.
Winslow, ME 04901
877/564-6697
www.johnnyseeds.com
Vegetable, herb, and flower seeds, cover
crops, and seeds for sprouting. Northern
varieties. Some organic seeds.

J.W. Jung Seed Company
335 S. High St.
Randolph, WI 53956
800/297-3123
www.jungseed.com
Vegetable and flower seeds and products.

Kitazawa Seed Company
P.O. Box 13220
Oakland, CA 94661-3220
510/595-1188
www.kitazawaseed.com
Asian vegetables.

Native Seeds/SEARCH
526 N. Fourth Ave.
Tucson, AZ 85705
866/622-5561
www.nativeseeds.org
Southwestern Native American vegetable
varieties.

Natural Gardening Company
P.O. Box 750776
Petaluma CA 94975-0776
707/766-9303
www.naturalgardening.com
Certified organic vegetable seeds. Herb
and flower seeds and seedlings. Some
products.

Nichols Garden Nursery
1190 Old Salem Road NE
Albany, OR 97321-4580
800/422-3985
www.nicholsgardennursery.com
Vegetable and herb seeds and herb
plants.

Nourse Farms
41 River Rd.
South Deerfield, MA 01373
413/665-2658
www.noursefarms.com
Asparagus and small fruits.

Park Seed Company
1 Parkton Ave.
Greenwood, SC 29647
800/213-0076
www.parkseed.com
Vegetable, herb, and flower seeds.
Southern varieties.

Pinetree Garden Seeds
P.O. Box 300
New Gloucester, ME 04260
207/926-3400
www.superseeds.com
Vegetable, herb, and flower seeds. Small-
size packets. Some products.

R. H. Shumway's
334 W. Stroud St.
Randolph, WI 53956-1274
800/342-9461
www.rhshumway.com
Vegetable, herb, and flower seeds. Some
fruits, asparagus, and grass seed.

Richters Herbs
Goodwood, ON L0C 1A0
Canada
905/640-6677
www.richters.com
Herb seeds, plants, books, and dried
herbs.

Sandy Mush Herb Farm
316 Surrett Cove Rd.
Leicester, North Carolina, 28748
828/683-2014
www.sandymushherbs.com
Culinary and medicinal herb plants.

Seed Savers Heritage Farms
3094 North Winn Rd.
Decorah, IA 52101
563/382-5990
www.seedsavers.org
Associated with Seed Saver's Exchange.
Heirloom vegetable seeds.

Steele Plant Company
202 Collins St.
Gleason, TN 38229
731/648-5476
www.sweetpotatoplant.com
Sweet potato plants.

Southern Exposure Seed Exchange
P.O. Box 460
Mineral, VA 23117
540/894-9480
www.southernexposure.com
Heirloom vegetable, flower, and herb
varieties adapted to the South.

Stokes Seed Company
P.O. Box 548
Buffalo, NY 14240-0548
800/396-9238
www.stokeseeds.com
Vegetable, flower, and herb seeds.

Territorial Seed Company
P.O. Box 158
Cottage Grove, OR 97424-0061
800/626-0866
www.territorial-seed.com
Vegetable, flower, and herb seeds and
plants. Varieties for the Pacific
Northwest.

Thompson & Morgan Seedsmen, Inc.
220 Faraday Ave.
Jackson, NJ 08527
800/274-7333
seeds.thompson-morgan.com
English vegetable, flower, and herb seeds
and plants.

The Thyme Garden Herb Company
20546 Alsea Hwy.
Alsea, OR 97324
541/487-8671
www.thymegarden.com
Culinary and medicinal herb seeds and
plants.

Tomato Growers Supply Company
P.O. Box 60015
Fort Myers, FL 33906
888/478-7333
www.tomatogrowers.com
Tomato and pepper seeds.

Underwood Gardens
1414 Zimmerman Rd.
Woodstock, IL 60098
815/338-6279
www.underwoodgardens.com
Heirloom and unusual vegetable and
herb seeds.

Vermont Bean Seed Company
334 West Stroud St.
Randolph, WI 53956-1274
800/349-1071
www.vermontbean.com
Bean, flower, herb, other vegetable seeds,
and fruits.

Vesey Seeds
P.O. Box 9000
Calais, ME 04619-6102
902/368-7333
www.veseys.com
Vegetable and flower seeds adapted to
short growing season.

Victory Seed Company
P.O. Box 192
Molalla, OR 97038
503/829-3126
www.victoryseeds.com
Heirloom vegetable seeds.

W. Atlee Burpee & Co.
300 Park Ave.
Warminster, PA 18974
800/333-5808
www.burpee.com
Vegetable, herb, and flower seeds and plants.

Well-Sweep Herb Farm
205 Mount Bethel Rd.
Port Murray, NJ 07865
908/852-5390
www.wellsweep.com
Herbs and perennial flower plants.

Willhite Seed Company
P.O. Box 23
Poolville, TX 76487
800/828-1840
www.willhiteseed.com
Melons and other warm season vegetable seeds. Unusual Indian vegetable varieties.

Wood Prairie Farm
49 Kinney Rd.
Bridgewater, ME 04735
800/829-9765
www.woodprairie.com
Potatoes.

FRUITS AND BERRIES

Bay Laurel Nursery
2500 El Camino Real
Atascadero, CA 93422
805/466-3406
www.baylaurelnursery.com
Tree fruits for Southwest and Southern California.

Edible Landscaping
361 Spirit Ridge Ln.
Afton, VA 22920
800/524-4156
www.ediblelandscaping.com
Unusual fruits and citrus.

Four Winds Growers
P.O. Box 3538
Fremont, CA 94539-4725
510/656-2591
www.fourwindsgrowers.com
Citrus.

Grimo Nut Nursery
979 Lakeshore Rd
Niagara-on-the-Lake, ON
Canada LOS 1JO
905/934-6887
www.grimonut.com
Nut trees and some unusual fruits.

Hartman's Plant Company
P.O. Box 100
Lacota, MI 49063-0100
269/253-4281
www.hartmannsplantcompany.com
Blueberry plants and other small fruits.

Indiana Berry & Plant Company
5218 West 500 S.
Huntingburg, IN 47542
800/295-2226
www.indianaberry.com
Small fruits and asparagus.

Ison's Nursery & Vineyards
6855 Newnan Rd.
P.O. Box 190
Brooks, GA 30205
800/733-0324
www.isons.com
Grapes for the South.

Johnson Nursery, Inc.
1352 Big Creek Rd.
Ellijay, GA 30536
888/276-3187
www.johnsonnursery.com
Fruit trees, small fruits, and supplies.

Just Fruits & Exotics
30 St. Frances St.
Crawfordville FL 32327
850/926-5644
www.justfruitsandexotics.com
Tropical fruits and citrus.

Miller Nurseries
5060 West Lake Rd.
Canandaigua, NY 14424-8904
800/836-9630
www.millernurseries.com
Fruit trees, berries and supplies.

One Green World
28696 S. Cramer Rd.
Molalla, OR 97038
877/353-4028
www.onegreenworld.com
Unusual fruits, nuts, and berries with some supplies.

Raintree Nursery
391 Butts Rd.
Morton, WA 98356
360/496-6400
www.raintreenursery.com
Fruits, nuts, and berries for the Pacific Northwest.

St. Lawrence Nurseries
325 State Hwy. 345
Potsdam, NY 13676
315/265-6739
www.sln.potsdam.ny.us
Cold hardy fruit trees, berries, and shrub fruits.

Stark Brothers Nursery
P.O. Box 10
Louisiana, MO 63353-0010
800/325-4180
www.starkbros.com
Fruit trees and berries.

TyTy Nursery
4723 U.S. Hwy. 82 W.
P.O. Box 130
TyTy, GA. 31795
800/972-2101
www.tytyga.com
Fruit trees, berries, and nuts. Some unusual and tropical fruits.

Womack Nursery Co.
2551 Hwy. 6
DeLeon, TX 76444
254/893-6497
www.womacknursery.com
Fruit and nut trees.

GARDENING TOOLS & SUPPLIES

A.M. Leonard, Inc.
241 Fox Dr.
Piqua, Ohio 45356-0816
800/543-8955
www.amleo.com
Tools and supplies.

Arbico Organics
P.O. Box 8910
Tucson, AZ, 85738-0910
800/827-2847
www.arbico-organics.com
Beneficial insects and other organic gardening supplies.

Charley's Greenhouse & Garden Supply
17979 State Rte. 536
Mt. Vernon, WA 98273
800/322-4707
www.charleysgreenhouse.com
Greenhouses and greenhouse supplies.

Gardener's Supply Company
128 Intervale Rd.
Burlington, VT 05401
888/833-1412
www.gardeners.com
Home garden products.

Gardens Alive
5100 Schenley Place
Lawrenceburg, IN 47025
513/354-1482
www.gardensalive.com
Organic pest controls and fertilizers.

Harmony Farm Supply
3244 Hwy. 116 N.
Sebastopol, CA 95472
707/823-9125
www.harmonyfarm.com/
Irrigation equipment, fertilizers, and
pest controls.

Hydrofarm, Inc.
2249 S. McDowell Ext.
Petaluma, CA 94954
707/765-9990
www.hydrofarm.com
Hydroponic systems, lights and
products.

Kinsman Company
P.O. Box 428
Pipersville, PA 18947
800/733-4146
www.mailordercentral.com/
kinsmangarden
Gardening supplies and tools.

Lee Valley Tools, Ltd.
P.O. Box 1780
Ogdensburg, NY 13669-6780
800/871-8158
www.leevalley.com
Tools and supplies.

Peaceful Valley Farm & Garden Supply
P.O. Box 2209
Grass Valley, CA 95945
888/784-1722
www.groworganic.com
Organic fertilizers, pest controls, cover
crop seeds, and tools.

Planet Natural
1612 Gold Ave.
Bozeman, MT 59715
800/289-6656
www.planetnatural.com
Organic pest controls and supplies.

Walt Nicke Company
P.O. Box 433
Topsfield, MA 01983
978/887-3388
www.gardentalk.com
Gardening tools.

Worm's Way
7850 North State Rd. 37
Bloomington, IN 47404
800/274-9676
www.wormsway.com
Organic fertilizers, pest controls,
hydroponic supplies, indoor lights, and
other garden supplies.

Index

METRIC CONVERSIONS

U.S. UNITS TO METRIC EQUIVALENTS			METRIC EQUIVALENTS TO U.S. UNITS		
To convert from	Multiply by	To get	To convert from	Multiply by	To get
Inches	25.4	Millimeters	Millimeters	0.0394	Inches
Inches	2.54	Centimeters	Centimeters	0.3937	Inches
Feet	30.48	Centimeters	Centimeters	0.0328	Feet
Feet	0.3048	Meters	Meters	3.2808	Feet
Yards	0.9144	Meters	Meters	1.0936	Yards
Square inches	6.4516	Square centimeters	Square centimeters	0.1550	Square inches
Square feet	0.0929	Square meters	Square meters	10.764	Square feet
Square yards	0.8361	Square meters	Square meters	1.1960	Square yards
Acres	0.4047	Hectares	Hectares	2.4711	Acres
Cubic inches	16.387	Cubic centimeters	Cubic centimeters	0.0610	Cubic inches
Cubic feet	0.0283	Cubic meters	Cubic meters	35.315	Cubic feet
Cubic feet	28.316	Liters	Liters	0.0353	Cubic feet
Cubic yards	0.7646	Cubic meters	Cubic meters	1.308	Cubic yards
Cubic yards	764.55	Liters	Liters	0.0013	Cubic yards

To convert from degrees Fahrenheit (F) to degrees Celsius (C), first subtract 32, then multiply by ⁵/₉.

To convert from degrees Celsius (C) to degrees Fahrenheit (F), multiply by ⁹/₅, then add 32.

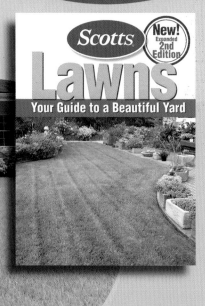